Wine Spectator's

Guide *to the* Best Wine Restaurants *in the* World

2004 Edition

Marvin R. Shanken
Editor and Publisher
Wine Spectator

www.winespectator.com

Printed in the United States

9 8 7 6 5 4 3 2 1
Digit on the right indicates the number of this printing
ISBN 0-7624-1769-2
Published by M. Shanken Communications, Inc.
387 Park Avenue South
New York, NY 10016
For subscriptions to *Wine Spectator*, please call:
(800)752-7799 in the U.S. and Canada, or write:
PO Box 37367
Boone, IA 50037-0367
Visit our website at: www.winespectator.com

Distributed by Running Press Book Publishers
125 South Twenty-second Street
Philadelphia, PA 19103-4399

Attention Restaurateurs!
If you are interested in learning more about *Wine Spectator*'s restaurant wine list award program or to apply,
please contact us by phone at (212)684-4224, ext. 781,
by fax at (212)481-0742,
or email at restaurantawards@mshanken.com.

Attention Diners!
If you would like to nominate a favorite restaurant for *Wine Spectator*'s restaurant wine list award program,
please contact us by phone at (212)684-4224, ext. 781,
by fax at (212) 481-0742,
or email at restaurantawards@mshanken.com

FRANCE

Alain Ducasse au Plaza Athénée *(since 1998)*
Au Crocodile *(since 1993)*
Georges Blanc *(since 1987)*
La Tour d'Argent *(since 1986)*
Le Cinq *(since 2003)*
Michel Rostang *(since 1993)*
Taillevent *(since 1984)*
Troisgros *(since 1996)*

GERMANY

Ente *(since 1985)*
Restaurant Jörg Müller *(since 1993)*

ITALY

Enoteca Pinchiorri *(since 1984)*
Guido Ristorante *(since 1996)*
Il Poeta Contadino *(since 1997)*

JAPAN

Enoteca Pinchiorri-Tokyo *(since 1994)*

MONACO

Le Louis XV–Alain Ducasse *(since 1995)*

SINGAPORE

Les Amis *(since 1996)*

SPAIN

Atrio *(since 2003)*

SWITZERLAND

Hotel Waldhaus am See *(since 1998)*
Landgasthof & Vinothek Farnsburg *(since 1992)*
Restaurant Riesbächli *(since 1990)*

WEST INDIES

Graycliff *(since 1988)*
Malliouhana Restaurant *(since 1999)*

Wine Spectator

2004 VINTAGE CHART

Vintage charts are, by necessity, general in nature. Vintage ratings listed here are averages for region and year. For current vintages and exceptional older years, you will find our score and drinkability rating. A score range indicates that most wines of the vintage were not yet released at press time.

100-Point Scale

95-100	Classic
90-94	Outstanding
85-89	Very Good
80-84	Good
70-79	Average
60-69	Below Average
50-59	Poor

WHITE WINE AND CHAMPAGNE

Vintage	Score	Drinkability
FRANCE/ALSACE		
2001	91	Drink/Hold
2000	93	Drink/Hold
1999	87	Drink/Hold
1998	90	Drink/Hold
1997	89	Drink/Hold
1996	92	Drink/Hold
1995	90	Drink/Hold
1994	91	Drink/Hold
1993	87	Drink
1990	93	Drink/Hold
1989	96	Drink/Hold
FRANCE/BURGUNDY WHITE		
2002	91-95	Not released
2001	89-90	Drink/Hold
2000	90	Drink/Hold
1999	88	Drink/Hold
1998	88	Drink/Hold
1997	88	Drink
1996	95	Drink/Hold
1995	93	Drink/Hold
1994	87	Drink
1992	89	Drink
1990	92	Drink
1989	92	Drink/Hold
1986	92	Drink
1985	94	Drink

Vintage	Score	Drinkability
FRANCE/CHAMPAGNE		
1996	90-94	Drink/Hold
1995	92	Drink/Hold
1993	87	Drink
1990	97	Drink/Hold
1989	90	Drink/Hold
1988	95	Drink/Hold
1985	96	Drink/Hold
1982	94	Drink
1979	91	Drink
FRANCE/SAUTERNES		
1997	92	Drink/Hold
1996	89	Drink/Hold
1990	97	Hold
1989	98	Hold
1988	93	Hold
1986	90	Hold
1983	95	Drink/Hold
GERMANY/RIESLING		
2001	98	Drink/Hold
2000	82	Drink/Hold
1999	90	Drink/Hold
1998	89	Drink/Hold
1997	88	Drink/Hold
1996	89	Drink/Hold
1995	88	Drink
1994	86	Drink/Hold
1993	89	Drink
1992	88	Drink
1991	85	Drink
1990	97	Drink/Hold
1989	92	Drink/Hold
1988	93	Drink

Vintage	Score	Drinkability
CALIFORNIA/CHARDONNAY		
2001	94	Drink/Hold
2000	88	Drink/Hold
1999	94	Drink/Hold
1998	85	Drink
1997	96	Drink/Hold
1996	97	Drink
1995	97	Drink
1994	95	Drink
1993	88	Drink
1992	93	Drink
1991	92	Drink
1990	92	Drink

RED WINE AND PORT

Vintage	Score	Drinkability
FRANCE/BORDEAUX RED		
2002	85-89	Not released
2001	86-91	Not released
2000	99	Hold
1999	83	Drink/Hold
1998	90	Drink/Hold
1996	87	Drink/Hold
1995	95	Hold
1994	85	Drink/Hold
1990	97	Hold
1989	98	Hold
1988	93	Drink/Hold
1986	95	Hold
1985	93	Drink/Hold
1982	95	Drink/Hold
1970	91	Drink/Hold
1961	99	Drink/Hold
FRANCE/BURGUNDY RED		
2002	90-94	Not released
2001	80-84	Not released
2000	83	Drink/Hold
1999	90	Drink/Hold
1998	89	Drink/Hold
1996	95	Drink/Hold
1995	88	Hold
1993	91	Drink/Hold
1991	86	Drink
1990	98	Drink/Hold
1989	93	Drink
1988	90	Drink/Hold
FRANCE/NORTHERN RHÔNE		
2001	85-89	Not Released
2000	88	Drink/Hold
1999	95	Drink/Hold
1998	89	Drink/Hold
1997	86	Drink/Hold
1996	90	Drink
1995	91	Drink/Hold
1994	88	Drink/Hold
1991	89	Drink/Hold
1990	97	Drink/Hold
1989	92	Drink/Hold
1988	90	Hold
FRANCE/SOUTHERN RHÔNE		
2001	85-89	Not Released
2000	93	Drink/Hold
1999	87	Drink/Hold
1998	95	Drink/Hold
1995	88	Drink/Hold
1994	86	Drink
1990	95	Drink/Hold
1989	96	Drink/Hold
1988	90	Drink/Hold
ITALY/BRUNELLO		
1997	99	Hold
1996	85	Drink/Hold
1995	91	Drink/Hold
1993	90	Drink/Hold
1991	84	Drink/Hold
1990	98	Drink/Hold
1988	94	Drink/Hold
1986	85	Drink/Hold
1985	94	Drink
ITALY/OTHER TUSCAN		
2001	88-92	Drink/Hold
2000	87	Drink/Hold
1999	92	Drink/Hold
1998	88	Drink/Hold
1997	99	Drink/Hold
1996	87	Drink/Hold
1995	85	Drink/Hold
1994	84	Drink/Hold
1990	98	Drink/Hold
1988	96	Drink/Hold
ITALY/PIEDMONT		
2000	100	Drink/Hold
1999	92	Drink/Hold
1998	93	Drink/Hold
1997	99	Hold
1996	98	Hold
1995	87	Drink/Hold
1993	87	Drink/Hold
1990	97	Hold
1989	97	Hold
1988	90	Drink/Hold
1985	94	Drink/Hold
1982	90	Drink/Hold

Vintage	Score	Drinkability
PORTUGAL/VINTAGE PORT		
2000	97	Hold
1997	96	Hold
1995	90	Hold
1994	99	Hold
1992	94	Hold
1991	93	Hold
1987	88	Drink/Hold
1985	93	Drink/Hold
1983	92	Hold
1980	87	Drink/Hold
1977	97	Hold
1970	95	Drink/Hold
1966	93	Drink/Hold
1963	98	Drink/Hold
CALIFORNIA/CABERNET		
2002	87-88	Not Released
2001	95-100	Not Released
2000	87	Drink/Hold
1999	96	Hold
1998	86	Drink/Hold
1997	98	Hold
1996	94	Drink/Hold
1995	94	Drink/Hold
1994	96	Hold
1993	90	Drink/Hold
1992	93	Drink/Hold
1991	94	Drink/Hold
1990	95	Drink
CALIFORNIA/MERLOT		
2001	89-93	Not released
2000	86	Drink/Hold
1999	90	Drink/Hold
1998	85	Drink
1997	89	Drink/Hold
1996	88	Drink/Hold
1995	87	Drink/Hold
1994	92	Drink/Hold
1992	89	Drink
1991	88	Drink/Hold
1990	89	Drink

Vintage	Score	Drinkability
CALIFORNIA/PINOT NOIR		
2001	94	Drink/Hold
2000	85	Drink
1999	88	Drink/Hold
1998	84	Drink
1997	88	Drink/Hold
1996	87	Drink
1995	92	Drink
1994	95	Drink
1992	92	Drink
1991	91	Drink
1990	92	Drink
CALIFORNIA/ZINFANDEL		
2001	90	Drink/Hold
2000	84	Drink
1999	89	Drink/Hold
1998	83	Drink
1997	90	Drink/Hold
1996	87	Drink/Hold
1995	95	Drink/Hold
1994	96	Drink/Hold
1992	93	Drink
1991	92	Drink
1990	93	Drink

UNITED STATES

ALABAMA

CAFÉ 615
615 Dauphin St., Mobile, AL 36602; (251) 432-8434 **Wine list** *California* **Wine prices** *Moderate* **Cuisine** *Contemporary American* **Menu prices** *$22–$32*

801 FRANKLIN
801 Franklin St., Huntsville, AL 35801; (256) 519-8019 **Wine list** *California* **Wine prices** *Moderate* **Cuisine** *American/continental* **Menu prices** *$18–$30*

THE FAIRHOPE INN & RESTAURANT
The Fairhope Inn, 63 S. Church St., Fairhope, AL 36532; (334) 928-6226 **Wine list** *California* **Wine prices** *Moderate* **Corkage** *$10* **Cuisine** *Contemporary French* **Menu prices** *$19–$28*

FLEMING'S PRIME STEAKHOUSE & WINE BAR
103 Summit Blvd., Birmingham, AL 35243; (205) 262-9463 **Wine list** *California* **Wine prices** *Moderate* **Corkage** *$15* **Cuisine** *Steak house* **Menu prices** *$17–$45*

FOX VALLEY
6745 Highway 17, Maylene, AL 35114; (205) 664-8341 **Wine list** *California* **Wine prices** Inexpensive **Corkage** *$12* **Cuisine** *Contemporary Southern* **Menu prices** *$15–$26*

G
1820 Fourth Ave. N., Birmingham, AL 35203; (205) 323-1820 **Wine list** *California* **Wine prices** *Moderate* **Corkage** *$20* **Cuisine** *Contemporary* **Menu prices** *$18–$27*

THE GLOBE
430 Main Ave., Northport, AL 35476; (205) 391-0949 **Wine list** *California* **Wine prices** *Moderate* **Cuisine** *International* **Menu prices** *$15–$27*

HOT & HOT FISH CLUB
2180 11th Court S., Birmingham, AL 35205; (205) 933-5474 **Wine list** *California, France* **Wine prices** *Moderate* **Corkage** *$15* **Cuisine** *Contemporary American* **Menu prices** *$19–$26*

LA JOLLA RESTAURANT 🍷
6854 E. Chase Parkway, Montgomery, AL 36117; (334) 356-2600 **Wine list** *California* **Wine prices** *Moderate* **Cuisine** *Contemporary* **Menu prices** *$16–$32*

195 MIZAN PLAZ 🍷
195 Vulcan Road, Birmingham, AL 35209; (205) 271-8228 **Wine list** *California, France* **Wine prices** *Moderate* **Cuisine** *Contemporary American* **Menu prices** *$12–$24*

RUTH'S CHRIS STEAK HOUSE 🍷
Embassy Suites, 2300 Woodcrest Place, Birmingham, AL 35209; (205) 879-9995 **Wine list** *California* **Wine prices** *Moderate* **Cuisine** *Steak house* **Menu prices** *$21–$63*

RUTH'S CHRIS STEAK HOUSE 🍷
2058 Airport Blvd., Mobile, AL 36606; (251) 476-0516 **Wine list** *California* **Wine prices** *Moderate* **Cuisine** *Steak house* **Menu prices** *$17–$30*

VINTAGE YEAR 🍷
405 Cloverdale Road, Montgomery, AL 36106; (334) 264-8463 **Wine list** *California* **Wine prices** Inexpensive **Cuisine** *Contemporary* **Menu prices** *$15–$30*

ALASKA

CORSAIR 🍷🍷
944 W. Fifth Ave., Anchorage, AK 99501; (907) 278-4502 **Wine list** *California, France* **Wine prices** *Moderate* **Cuisine** *Seafood* **Menu prices** *$21–$42*

THE CROW'S NEST 🍷🍷
The Hotel Captain Cook, 939 W. Fifth Ave., Anchorage, AK 99501; (907) 276-6000 **Wine list** *California, France* **Wine prices** *Expensive* **Corkage** *$20* **Cuisine** *Contemporary American* **Menu prices** *$26–$35*

DI SOPRA 🍷
429 W. Willoughby Ave., Juneau, AK 99801; (907) 586-3150 **Wine list** *California* **Wine prices** Inexpensive **Cuisine** *Italian* **Menu prices** *$16–$28*

THE FIDDLEHEAD 🍷
429 W. Willoughby Ave., Juneau, AK 99801; (907) 586-3150 **Wine list** *California* **Wine prices** *Moderate* **Cuisine** *Contemporary/Italian* **Menu prices** *$16–$25*

🍷🍷🍷 Grand Award 🍷🍷 Best of Award of Excellence 🍷 Award of Excellence

LAVELLE'S BISTRO
Marriott Springhill Suites, 575 First Ave., Fairbanks, AK 99701; (907) 450-0555 **Wine list** *California* **Wine prices** *Moderate* **Corkage** *$15* **Cuisine** *Contemporary American* **Menu prices** *$14–$35*

MARX BROS. CAFÉ
627 W. Third Ave., Anchorage, AK 99501; (907) 278-2133 **Wine list** *California, France* **Wine prices** *Moderate* **Corkage** *$20* **Cuisine** *American* **Menu prices** *$20–$35*

RISTORANTE ORSO
737 W. Fifth Ave., Anchorage, AK 99501; (907) 222-3232 **Wine list** *Italy, California* **Wine prices** Inexpensive **Corkage** *$10* **Cuisine** *Italian* **Menu prices** *$13–$37*

SACKS CAFÉ & RESTAURANT
328 G St., Anchorage, AK 99501; (907) 274-4022 **Wine list** *California* **Wine prices** *Moderate* **Corkage** *$15* **Cuisine** *Contemporary American* **Menu prices** *$19–$28*

SEVEN GLACIERS
Alyeska Prince Hotel, 1000 Arlberg Ave., Girdwood, AK 99587; (907) 754-2237 **Wine list** *California* **Wine prices** *Moderate* **Cuisine** *Steak house/seafood* **Menu prices** *$24–$42*

SOUTHSIDE BISTRO
1320 Huffman Park Drive, Anchorage, AK 99515; (907) 348-0088 **Wine list** *California* **Wine prices** Inexpensive **Corkage** *$20* **Cuisine** *American* **Menu prices** *$12–$24*

SULLIVAN'S STEAKHOUSE
320 W. Fifth Ave., Anchorage, AK 99501; (907) 258-2882 **Wine list** *California* **Wine prices** *Moderate* **Cuisine** *Steak house* **Menu prices** *$20–$55*

TALKEETNA ALASKAN LODGE
Milepost 12.5 Talkeetna Spur Road, Talkeetna, AK 99676; (907) 733-9500 **Wine list** *California* **Wine prices** Inexpensive **Corkage** *$15* **Cuisine** *American/continental* **Menu prices** *$16–$36*

ARIZONA

ANTHONY'S IN THE CATALINAS
6440 N. Campbell, Tucson, AZ 85718; (520) 299-1771 **Wine list** *California, Bordeaux* **Wine selections** *1,700* **Number of bottles** *25,000* **Wine prices** *Moderate* **Cuisine** *Continental* **Menu prices** *$20–$36* **Credit cards** *AX, MC, VS, DV*
Grand Award since 1993

THE ASYLUM
Jerome Grand Hotel, 200 Hill St., Jerome, AZ 86331; (928) 639-3197 **Wine list** *California* **Wine prices** *Moderate* **Cuisine** *Contemporary American* **Menu prices** *$18–$34*

BARCELONA
15440 Greenway-Hayden Loop, Scottsdale, AZ 85260; (480) 603-0367 **Wine list** *California* **Wine prices** *Moderate* **Cuisine** *Continental/Spanish/Mediterranean* **Menu prices** *$12–$32*

BARMOUCHE
3131 E. Camelback Road, Phoenix, AZ 85016; (602) 956-6900 **Wine list** *California* **Wine prices** *Moderate* **Cuisine** *American* **Menu prices** *$10–$25*

BISTRO ZIN
1865 E. River Road, Tucson, AZ 85718; (520) 299-7799 **Wine list** *California* **Wine prices** *Moderate* **Cuisine** *American/French* **Menu prices** *$13–$23*

BLOOM
8877 N. Scottsdale Road, Scottsdale, AZ 85253; (480) 922-5666 **Wine list** *California* **Wine prices** *Moderate* **Cuisine** *Contemporary American* **Menu prices** *$12–$24*

CACTUS FLOWER
Miraval Life In Balance Resort, 5000 E. Via Estancia Miraval, Catalina, AZ 85739; (520) 825-4000 **Wine list** *California* **Wine prices** *Expensive* **Cuisine** *Contemporary American* **Menu prices** *Prix fixe only; $50*

CAFÉ TERRA COTTA
3500 E. Sunrise Drive, Tucson, AZ 85718; (520) 577-8100 **Wine list** *California, France, Australia* **Wine prices** *Moderate* **Cuisine** *Contemporary Southwestern* **Menu prices** *$16–$24*

CHAPARRAL SUPPER CLUB
Marriott's Camelback Inn, 5402 E. Lincoln Drive, Scottsdale, AZ 85253; (480) 367-6169 **Wine list** *California* **Wine prices** *Moderate* **Corkage** *$15* **Cuisine** *American* **Menu prices** *$20–$38*

CHRISTOPHER'S FERMIER BRASSERIE & PAOLA'S WINE BAR 🍷
Biltmore Fashion Park, 2584 E. Camelback Road, Phoenix, AZ 85016; (602) 522-2344 **Wine list** *California, France* **Wine prices** *Moderate* **Cuisine** *French/American* **Menu prices** *$14–$28*

COTTAGE PLACE RESTAURANT 🍷
126 W. Cottage Ave., Flagstaff, AZ 86001; (928) 774-8431 **Wine list** *California, France* **Wine prices** *Moderate* **Cuisine** *Continental* **Menu prices** *$18–$26*

COWBOY CIAO 🍷🍷
7133 E. Stetson Drive, Scottsdale, AZ 85251; (480) WINE-111 **Wine list** *California, France, Australia* **Wine prices** Inexpensive **Cuisine** *Contemporary American* **Menu prices** *$18–$32*

DIFFERENT POINTE OF VIEW 🍷🍷
Pointe-Hilton at Tapatio Cliffs, 11111 N. Seventh St., Phoenix, AZ 85020; (602) 863-0912 **Wine list** *California, Bordeaux* **Wine prices** *Expensive* **Cuisine** *French/Italian/Mediterranean* **Menu prices** *$26–$40*

DURANT'S 🍷
2611 N. Central Ave., Phoenix, AZ 85004; (602) 264-5967 **Wine list** *California* **Wine prices** *Moderate* **Cuisine** *American* **Menu prices** *$15–$57*

EDDIE V'S EDGEWATER GRILLE 🍷
20715 N. Pima Road, Scottsdale, AZ 85255; (480) 538-8468 **Wine list** *California* **Wine prices** *Moderate* **Corkage** *$20* **Cuisine** *Seafood* **Menu prices** *$18–$29*

ELLE, A WINE COUNTRY RESTAURANT 🍷
3048 E. Broadway Blvd., Tucson, AZ 85716; (520) 327-0500 **Wine list** *California* **Wine prices** *Moderate* **Cuisine** *French/Italian* **Menu prices** *$12–$24*

FLEMING'S PRIME STEAKHOUSE & WINE BAR 🍷
905 N. 54th St., Chandler, AZ 85226; (480) 940-1900 **Wine list** *California* **Wine prices** *Moderate* **Cuisine** *Steak house* **Menu prices** *$18–$31*

FLEMING'S PRIME STEAKHOUSE & WINE BAR 🍷
20753 N. Pima Road, Scottsdale, AZ 85255; (480) 538-8000 **Wine list** *California* **Wine prices** *Moderate* **Cuisine** *Steak house* **Menu prices** *$18–$31*

FLEMING'S PRIME STEAKHOUSE & WINE BAR 🍷
Hilton Scottsdale Resort & Villas, 6333 N. Scottsdale Road, Scottsdale, AZ 85250; (480) 596-8265 **Wine list** *California* **Wine prices** *Moderate* **Cuisine** *Steak house* **Menu prices** *$18–$30*

FUEGO RESTAURANT BAR & GRILL 🍷
6958 E. Tanque Verde Road, Tucson, AZ 85715; (520) 886-1745 **Wine list** *California* **Wine prices** *Moderate* **Cuisine** *Southwestern* **Menu prices** *$13–$20*

THE GOLD ROOM 🍷
The Westward Look Resort, 245 E. Ina Road, Tucson, AZ 85704; (520) 297-1151 **Wine list** *California, France* **Wine prices** *Moderate* **Cuisine** *Continental* **Menu prices** *$20–$34*

GREGORY'S WORLD BISTRO 🍷
8120 N. Hayden Road, Scottsdale, AZ 85258; (480) 946-8700 **Wine list** *California* **Wine prices** *Moderate* **Cuisine** *Contemporary* **Menu prices** *$22–$32*

THE GRILL 🍷
The Fairmont Scottsdale Princess Resort, 7575 E. Princess Drive, Scottsdale, AZ 85255; (480) 585-4848 **Wine list** *California* **Wine prices** *Moderate* **Cuisine** *American* **Menu prices** *$19–$41*

THE GRILL AT HACIENDA DEL SOL 🍷🍷
5601 N. Hacienda del Sol Road, Tucson, AZ 85718; (520) 529-3500 **Wine list** *California, France* **Wine prices** *Moderate* **Cuisine** *American* **Menu prices** *$20–$38*

THE HEARTLINE CAFÉ 🍷
1610 W. Highway 89A, Sedona, AZ 86336; (928) 282-0785 **Wine list** *California* **Wine prices** *Moderate* **Cuisine** *Contemporary American* **Menu prices** *$14–$26*

JANOS 🍷🍷
The Westin La Paloma, 3770 E. Sunrise Drive, Tucson, AZ 85718; (520) 615-6100 **Wine list** *California, France, Australia* **Wine prices** *Moderate* **Cuisine** *Southwestern/French* **Menu prices** *$24–$42*

J BAR 🍷
The Westin La Paloma, 3770 E. Sunrise Drive, Tucson, AZ 85718; (520) 615-6100 **Wine list** *California, France* **Wine prices** *Moderate* **Cuisine** *Contemporary Latin/Caribbean* **Menu prices** *$13–$17*

KAZIMIERZ WORLD WINE BAR 🍷🍷
7137 E. Stetson Drive, Scottsdale, AZ 85251; (480) WINE-004 **Wine list** *France, California, Australia* **Wine prices** *Moderate* **Cuisine** *International* **Menu prices** *$10–$20*

KINCAID'S FISH, CHOP & STEAK HOUSE 🍷
2 S. Third St., Phoenix, AZ 85004; (602) 340-0000 **Wine list** *California* **Wine prices** *Moderate* **Cuisine** *Steak house* **Menu prices** *$15–$29*

KINGFISHER BAR AND GRILL 🍷
2564 E. Grant Road, Tucson, AZ 85716; (520) 323-7739 **Wine list** *California* **Wine prices** *Moderate* **Cuisine** *Seafood* **Menu prices** *$13–$19*

THE LATILLA RESTAURANT 🍷
The Boulders Resort & Golden Door Spa, 34631 N. Tom Darlington Drive, Carefree, AZ 85377; (480) 488-7316 **Wine list** *California, France* **Wine prices** *Expensive* **Cuisine** *Contemporary American* **Menu prices** *$28–$36*

L'AUBERGE DE SEDONA 🍷🍷
301 L'Auberge Lane, Sedona, AZ 86339; (928) 282-1667 **Wine list** *California, France* **Wine prices** *Expensive* **Cuisine** *French* **Menu prices** *$25–$40*

LON'S AT THE HERMOSA 🍷
5532 N. Palo Cristi Road, Paradise Valley, AZ 85253; (602) 955-7878 **Wine list** *California, France* **Wine prices** *Moderate* **Cuisine** *American* **Menu prices** *$20–$36*

MANCUSO'S AT THE BORGATA 🍷
6166 N. Scottsdale Road, Scottsdale, AZ 85253; (480) 948-9988 **Wine list** *California* **Wine prices** *Expensive* **Cuisine** *Italian/French* **Menu prices** *$16–$29*

MARQUESA 🍷
The Fairmont Scottsdale Princess Resort, 7575 E. Princess Drive, Scottsdale, AZ 85255; (480) 585-4848 **Wine list** *California* **Wine prices** *Expensive* **Cuisine** *Mediterranean* **Menu prices** *$38–$45*

MARY ELAINE'S 🍷🍷🍷
The Phoenician Resort, 6000 E. Camelback Road, Scottsdale, AZ 85251; (480) 423-2444 **Wine list** *France, California* **Wine selections** *2,200* **Number of bottles** *45,000* **Wine prices** *Moderate* **Cuisine** *French* **Menu prices** *$40–$45* **Credit cards** *AX, MC, VS, DV*
Grand Award since 2000

MASTRO'S STEAKHOUSE 🍷

8852 E. Pinnacle Peak Road, Scottsdale, AZ 85255; (480) 585-9500 **Wine list** *California* **Wine prices** *Moderate* **Cuisine** *Steak house* **Menu prices** *$20–$80*

MCMAHON'S PRIME STEAKHOUSE 🍷🍷

2959 N. Swan Road, Tucson, AZ 85712; (520) 327-7463 **Wine list** *California, Bordeaux, Burgundy, Italy* **Wine prices** *Moderate* **Cuisine** *Steak house* **Menu prices** *$19–$46*

THE MELTING POT 🍷

3626 E. Ray Road, Ahwatukee, AZ 85044; (480) 704-9206 **Wine list** *California* **Wine prices** *Moderate* **Cuisine** *Fondue* **Menu prices** *$18–$49*

THE MELTING POT 🍷

8320 N. Hayden Road, Scottsdale, AZ 85258; (480) 607-1799 **Wine list** *California* **Wine prices** *Moderate* **Cuisine** *Fondue* **Menu prices** *$15–$23*

MICHAEL'S AT THE CITADEL 🍷

8700 E. Pinnacle Peak Road, Scottsdale, AZ 85255; (480) 515-2575 **Wine list** *California* **Wine prices** *Moderate* **Cuisine** *Contemporary American* **Menu prices** *$18–$28*

MICHELANGELO 🍷

420 W. Magee Road, Tucson, AZ 85704; (520) 297-5772 **Wine list** *California, Italy* **Wine prices** *Moderate* **Cuisine** *Italian* **Menu prices** *$15–$20*

MORTON'S OF CHICAGO 🍷

2501 E. Camelback Road, Phoenix, AZ 85016; (602) 955-9577 **Wine list** *California* **Wine prices** *Expensive* **Cuisine** *Steak house* **Menu prices** *$20–$35*

MORTON'S OF CHICAGO 🍷

15233 Kierland Blvd., Scottsdale, AZ 85254; (480) 951-4440 **Wine list** *California* **Wine prices** *Expensive* **Cuisine** *Steak house* **Menu prices** *$22–$70*

MOSAIC 🍷

10600 E. Jomax Road, Scottsdale, AZ 85255; (480) 563-9600 **Wine list** *California, France* **Wine prices** *Moderate* **Cuisine** *Contemporary American* **Menu prices** *$22–$36*

OCEAN CLUB FISH HOUSE 🍷

15045 N. Kierland Blvd., Scottsdale, AZ 85254; (480) 443-8555 **Wine list** *California* **Wine prices** *Moderate* **Cuisine** *Seafood* **Menu prices** *$25–$75*

OVENS BISTRO & WINE BAR 🍷
St. Philips Plaza, 4280 N. Campbell Ave., Tucson, AZ 85718; (520) 577-9001 **Wine list** *California* **Wine prices** *Moderate* **Cuisine** *American* **Menu prices** *$8–$19*

PASTICHE MODERN EATERY 🍷
3025 N. Campbell Ave., Tucson, AZ 85719; (520) 325-3333 **Wine list** *California* **Wine prices** *Moderate* **Cuisine** *Contemporary American* **Menu prices** *$9–$24*

RED SKY CAFÉ 🍷
1661 N. Swan Road, Tucson, AZ 85712; (520) 326-5454 **Wine list** *California* **Wine prices** Inexpensive **Cuisine** *Californian/French* **Menu prices** *$11–$24*

THE REDSTONE CABIN 🍷
The Cowboy Club, 267 Van Deren Road, Sedona, AZ 86336; (928) 282-4200 **Wine list** *California* **Wine prices** *Moderate* **Cuisine** *Regional* **Menu prices** *$15–$50*

RENÉ AT TLAQUEPAQUE 🍷
336 Highway 179, Sedona, AZ 86336; (928) 282-9225 **Wine list** *California* **Wine prices** *Moderate* **Cuisine** *Continental* **Menu prices** *$19–$32*

RUTH'S CHRIS STEAK HOUSE 🍷
2201 E. Camelback Road, Phoenix, AZ 85016; (602) 957-9600 **Wine list** *California* **Wine prices** *Moderate* **Cuisine** *Steak house* **Menu prices** *$21–$34*

RUTH'S CHRIS STEAK HOUSE 🍷
7001 N. Scottsdale Road, Scottsdale, AZ 85253; (480) 991-5988 **Wine list** *California* **Wine prices** *Moderate* **Cuisine** *Steak house* **Menu prices** *$20–$30*

SEA SAW 🍷🍷
7133 E. Stetson Drive, Scottsdale, AZ 85251; (480) 481-WINE **Wine list** *California, France, Australia* **Wine prices** Inexpensive **Cuisine** *Contemporary* **Menu prices** *$10–$20*

STEAK & STICKS 🍷
Los Abrigados Resort & Spa, 160 Portal Lane, Sedona, AZ 86336; (928) 282-1777 **Wine list** *California* **Wine prices** *Moderate* **Cuisine** *Steak house* **Menu prices** *$14–$28*

SULLIVAN'S STEAKHOUSE 🍷
1785 E. River Road, Tucson, AZ 85718; (520) 299-4275 **Wine list** *California* **Wine prices** *Moderate* **Cuisine** *Steak house* **Menu prices** *$17–$29*

T. COOK'S 🍷

Royal Palms Hotel & Spa, 5200 E. Camelback Road, Phoenix, AZ 85018; (602) 808-0766 **Wine list** *California, France* **Wine prices** *Moderate* **Cuisine** *Mediterranean* **Menu prices** *$21–$31*

THE TACK ROOM 🍷

7300 E. Vactor Ranch Trail, Tucson, AZ 85715; (520) 722-2800 **Wine list** *California* **Wine prices** *Expensive* **Cuisine** *Southwestern* **Menu prices** *$26–$36*

TARBELL'S 🍷

3213 E. Camelback Road, Phoenix, AZ 85018; (602) 955-8100 **Wine list** *California, France* **Wine prices** *Moderate* **Cuisine** *American* **Menu prices** *$14–$30*

TOP OF THE ROCK RESTAURANT 🍷

Wyndham Buttes Resort, 2000 Westcourt Way, Tempe, AZ 85282; (602) 431-2370 **Wine list** *California* **Wine prices** *Moderate* **Cuisine** *Contemporary American* **Menu prices** *$24–$33*

VENETO TRATTORIA 🍷

6137 N. Scottsdale Road, Scottsdale, AZ 85250; (480) 948-9928 **Wine list** *Italy, California* **Wine prices** *Moderate* **Cuisine** *Northern Italian* **Menu prices** *$15–$22*

VENTANA ROOM 🍷🍷

Loews Ventana Canyon Resort, 7000 N. Resort Drive, Tucson, AZ 85750; (520) 299-2020 **Wine list** *California, France, Italy, Australia* **Wine prices** *Expensive* **Cuisine** *French* **Menu prices** *$28–$45*

VILLAGE TAVERN 🍷

8787 N. Scottsdale Road, Scottsdale, AZ 85253; (480) 951-6445 **Wine list** *California* **Wine prices** *Moderate* **Cuisine** *American* **Menu prices** *$10–$24*

VINCENT GUERITHAULT ON CAMELBACK 🍷🍷

3930 E. Camelback Road, Phoenix, AZ 85018; (602) 224-0225 **Wine list** *France, California* **Wine prices** *Moderate* **Cuisine** *French* **Menu prices** *$25–$35*

WINDOWS ON THE GREEN 🍷

The Phoenician Resort, 6000 E. Camelback Road, Scottsdale, AZ 85251; (480) 423-2530 **Wine list** *California* **Wine prices** *Expensive* **Cuisine** *Southwestern* **Menu prices** *$18–$32*

WRIGHT'S
Arizona Biltmore Resort & Spa, 2400 E. Missouri Ave., Phoenix, AZ 85016; (602) 954-2507 **Wine list** *California, France* **Wine prices** *Expensive* **Cuisine** *Contemporary American* **Menu prices** *$21–$29*

THE WRIGLEY MANSION CLUB
2501 E. Telawa Trail, Phoenix, AZ 85016; (602) 955-4079 **Wine list** *California* **Wine prices** *Moderate* **Cuisine** *Contemporary* **Menu prices** *$18–$32*

YAVAPAI RESTAURANT
Enchantment Resort, 525 Boynton Canyon Road, Sedona, AZ 86336; (520) 282-2900 **Wine list** *California* **Wine prices** *Moderate* **Cuisine** *Southwestern* **Menu prices** *$22–$38*

ARKANSAS

ANDERSON'S CAJUN'S WHARF
2400 Cantrell Road, Little Rock, AR 72202; (501) 375-5351 **Wine list** *California* **Wine prices** *Moderate* **Cuisine** *Steak house/seafood* **Menu prices** *$13–$43*

AUTUMN BREEZE RESTAURANT
Highway 23 S., Eureka Springs, AR 72632; (479) 253-7734 **Wine list** *California* **Wine prices** *Moderate* **Corkage** *$10* **Cuisine** *Continental* **Menu prices** *$10–$24*

CAPERS
14502 Cantrell Road, Little Rock, AR 72223; (501) 868-7600 **Wine list** *California* **Wine prices** *Moderate* **Cuisine** *Contemporary American* **Menu prices** *$9–$23*

CAPRICCIO
The Peabody Little Rock, 3 Statehouse Plaza, Little Rock, AR 72201; (501) 906-4000 **Wine list** *California* **Wine prices** *Moderate* **Cuisine** *Northern Italian* **Menu prices** *$16–$18*

FOLIE À DEUX
May Branch Square, 2909 Old Greenwood Road, Forth Smith, AR 72903; (479) 648-0041 **Wine list** *California* **Wine prices** *Moderate* **Cuisine** *American* **Menu prices** *$13–$26*

JAMES AT THE MILL
Inn at the Mill, 3906 Main St., Johnson, AR 72741; (501) 443-1400 **Wine list** *California* **Wine prices** *Moderate* **Cuisine** *American* **Menu prices** *$12–$25*

RIVER GRILLE 🍷
1003 McClain Road, Bentonville, AR 72712; (479) 271-4141 **Wine list** *California* **Wine prices** *Moderate* **Cuisine** *Steak house* **Menu prices** *$15–$38*

SONNY WILLIAMS' STEAK ROOM 🍷
500 President Clinton Ave., Little Rock, AR 72201; (501) 324-2999 **Wine list** *California* **Wine prices** *Moderate* **Corkage** *$10* **Cuisine** *Steak house* **Menu prices** *$19–$33*

CALIFORNIA

LOS ANGELES & VICINITY

A.O.C. 🍷
8022 W. Third St., Los Angeles, CA 90048; (323) 653-6359 **Wine list** *France, California* **Wine prices** *Moderate* **Corkage** *$25* **Cuisine** *French/Mediterranean* **Menu prices** *$18–$25*

AVENUE 🍷
301 N. Cañon Drive, Beverly Hills, CA 90210; (310) 275-2900 **Wine list** *California, France* **Wine prices** *Moderate* **Corkage** *$25* **Cuisine** *Contemporary American/French* **Menu prices** *$24–$39*

BASTIDE 🍷🍷
8475 Melrose Place, Los Angeles, CA 90069; (323) 651-5950 **Wine list** *Bordeaux, Burgundy, Rhône, Champagne* **Wine prices** *Expensive* **Cuisine** *French* **Menu prices** *Prix fixe only; $60–$100*

BROADWAY DELI 🍷
1457 Third St. Promenade, Santa Monica, CA 90401; (310) 451-0616 **Wine list** *California* **Wine prices** *Moderate* **Corkage** *$14* **Cuisine** *International* **Menu prices** *$12–$20*

CAFÉ PINOT 🍷
700 W. Fifth St., Los Angeles, CA 90071; (213) 239-6500 **Wine list** *California, France* **Wine prices** *Expensive* **Corkage** *No charge* **Cuisine** *Contemporary American* **Menu prices** *$20–$30*

CAPO 🍷
1810 Ocean Ave., Santa Monica, CA 90401; (310) 394-5550 **Wine list** *California, Italy, France* **Wine prices** *Moderate* **Cuisine** *Contemporary Italian* **Menu prices** *$18–$48*

CHAYA BRASSERIE 🍷
8741 Alden Drive, Los Angeles, CA 90048; (310) 859-8833 **Wine list** *California, France* **Wine prices** *Moderate* **Cuisine** *French/Italian/Japanese* **Menu prices** *$15–$28*

CHINOIS ON MAIN 🍷
2709 Main St., Santa Monica, CA 90405; (310) 392-9025 **Wine list** *California, France* **Wine prices** *Moderate* **Corkage** *$20* **Cuisine** *French/Chinese* **Menu prices** *$24–$33*

CIAO TRATTORIA 🍷
815 W. Seventh St., Los Angeles, CA 90017; (213) 624-2244 **Wine list** *Italy, California* **Wine prices** *Moderate* **Corkage** *$15* **Cuisine** *Italian* **Menu prices** *$12–$20*

CICADA RESTAURANT & LOUNGE 🍷
617 S. Olive St., Los Angeles, CA 90014; (213) 488-9488 **Wine list** *California, Italy* **Wine prices** *Moderate* **Corkage** *$20* **Cuisine** *Northern Italian* **Menu prices** *$18–$38*

CRUSTACEAN 🍷
9646 Little Santa Monica Blvd., Beverly Hills, CA 90210; (310) 205-8990 **Wine list** *California, France* **Wine prices** *Moderate* **Corkage** *$20* **Cuisine** *European/Asian* **Menu prices** *$19–$39*

DRAGO 🍷🍷
2628 Wilshire Blvd., Santa Monica, CA 90403; (310) 828-1585 **Wine list** *Italy* **Wine prices** *Moderate* **Corkage** *$20* **Cuisine** *Italian* **Menu prices** *$20–$32*

FABIOLUS CAFÉ 🍷
6270 Sunset Blvd., Hollywood, CA 90028; (323) 467-2882 **Wine list** *Italy* **Wine prices** *Moderate* **Corkage** *$8* **Cuisine** *Northern Italian* **Menu prices** *$9–$19*

FOUR OAKS RESTAURANT 🍷
2181 N. Beverly Glen Blvd., Los Angeles, CA 90077; (310) 470-2265 **Wine list** *California, France* **Wine prices** *Moderate* **Cuisine** *Contemporary French/American* **Menu prices** *$22–$30*

GREENBLATT'S 🍷
8017 Sunset Blvd., Hollywood, CA 90046; (323) 656-0606 **Wine list** *California, France* **Wine prices** *Moderate* **Cuisine** *American* **Menu prices** *$10–$16*

HOTEL BEL-AIR 🍷🍷
701 Stone Canyon Road, Los Angeles, CA 90077; (310) 472-1211 **Wine list** *California, France* **Wine prices** *Expensive* **Corkage** *$25* **Cuisine** *Californian/French* **Menu prices** *$26–$40*

I CUGINI 🍷
1501 Ocean Ave., Santa Monica, CA 90401; (310) 451-4595 **Wine list** *Italy, California* **Wine prices** *Moderate* **Cuisine** *Italian* **Menu prices** *$12–$29*

IL FORNAIO CUCINA ITALIANA 🍷
301 N. Beverly Drive, Beverly Hills, CA 90210; (310) 550-8330 **Wine list** *Italy, California* **Wine prices** *Moderate* **Corkage** *$10* **Cuisine** *Italian* **Menu prices** *$10–$25*

IL FORNAIO CUCINA ITALIANA 🍷
1551 Ocean Ave., Santa Monica, CA 90401; (310) 451-7800 **Wine list** *Italy, California* **Wine prices** *Moderate* **Corkage** *$10* **Cuisine** *Italian* **Menu prices** *$10–$25*

IL GRANO 🍷
11359 Santa Moncia Blvd., West Los Angeles, CA 90025; (310) 477-7886 **Wine list** *Italy, California* **Wine prices** *Moderate* **Corkage** *$15* **Cuisine** *Southern Italian* **Menu prices** *$16–$27*

JAMES' BEACH 🍷
60 N. Venice Blvd., Venice, CA 90291; (310) 823-5396 **Wine list** *California, France* **Wine prices** *Moderate* **Cuisine** *American* **Menu prices** *$11–$30*

JIRAFFE RESTAURANT 🍷
502 Santa Monica Blvd., Santa Monica, CA 90401; (310) 917-6671 **Wine list** *California* **Wine prices** *Moderate* **Corkage** *$20* **Cuisine** *Californian/French* **Menu prices** *$16–$28*

JOE'S RESTAURANT 🍷
1023 Abbot Kinney Blvd., Venice, CA 90291; (310) 399-5811 **Wine list** *California, France* **Wine prices** *Moderate* **Corkage** *$15* **Cuisine** *Californian/French* **Menu prices** *$20–$29*

JOSIE RESTAURANT 🍷
2424 Pico Blvd., Santa Monica, CA 90405; (310) 581-9888 **Wine list** *California* **Wine prices** *Moderate* **Corkage** *$20* **Cuisine** *American/French/Italian* **Menu prices** *$20–$31*

🍷🍷🍷 Grand Award 🍷🍷 Best of Award of Excellence 🍷 Award of Excellence

KNOLL'S BLACK FOREST INN 🍷
2454 Wilshire Blvd., Santa Monica, CA 90403; (310) 395-2212 **Wine list** *Germany, California* **Wine prices** Inexpensive **Corkage** *$15* **Cuisine** *German/continental* **Menu prices** *$17–$30*

LA CACHETTE 🍷
10506 Santa Monica Blvd., Los Angeles, CA 90025; (310) 470-4992 **Wine list** *France, California* **Wine prices** *Moderate* **Corkage** *$25* **Cuisine** *French* **Menu prices** *$20–$33*

LAWRY'S THE PRIME RIB 🍷
100 N. La Cienega Blvd., Beverly Hills, CA 90211; (310) 652-2827 **Wine list** *California* **Wine prices** *Moderate* **Cuisine** *Steak house* **Menu prices** *$24–$39*

LINQ RESTAURANT & LOUNGE 🍷
8338 W. Third St., Los Angeles, CA 90048; (323) 655-4555 **Wine list** *California, Bordeaux* **Wine prices** *Moderate* **Corkage** *$15* **Cuisine** *International* **Menu prices** *$15–$28*

LOCANDA DEL LAGO 🍷
231 Arizona Ave., Santa Monica, CA 90401; (310) 451-3525 **Wine list** *Italy, California* **Wine prices** *Moderate* **Corkage** *$10* **Cuisine** *Northern Italian* **Menu prices** *$18–$32*

L'ORANGERIE 🍷🍷
903 N. La Cienega Blvd., Los Angeles, CA 90069; (310) 652-9770 **Wine list** *France, California* **Wine prices** *Expensive* **Cuisine** *Contemporary French* **Menu prices** *$30–$42*

LUCQUES 🍷
8474 Melrose Ave., Los Angeles, CA 90069; (323) 655-6277 **Wine list** *California, France* **Wine prices** *Moderate* **Corkage** *$16* **Cuisine** *French/Mediterranean* **Menu prices** *$18–$30*

MÉLISSE 🍷🍷
1104 Wilshire Blvd., Santa Monica, CA 90401; (310) 395-0881 **Wine list** *France, California* **Wine prices** *Moderate* **Corkage** *$30* **Cuisine** *Contemporary American/French* **Menu prices** *$32–$60*

MICHAEL'S 🍷🍷
1147 Third St., Santa Monica, CA 90403; (310) 451-0843 **Wine list** *France, California* **Wine prices** *Moderate* **Corkage** *$20* **Cuisine** *Contemporary American* **Menu prices** *$27–$39*

CALIFORNIA

MORELS FRENCH STEAKHOUSE & BISTRO 🍷
189 Grove Drive, Los Angeles, CA 90036; (323) 965-9595 **Wine list** *California, France* **Wine prices** *Moderate* **Corkage** *$15* **Cuisine** *French* **Menu prices** *$18–$30*

MORTON'S OF CHICAGO 🍷
735 S. Figueroa St., Los Angeles, CA 90017; (213) 553-4566 **Wine list** *California* **Wine prices** *Expensive* **Corkage** *$15* **Cuisine** *Steak house* **Menu prices** *$23–$75*

MORTON'S OF CHICAGO 🍷
435 S. La Cienega Blvd., Los Angeles, CA 90048; (310) 246-1501 **Wine list** *California* **Wine prices** *Expensive* **Corkage** *$15* **Cuisine** *Steak house* **Menu prices** *$27–$36*

NAPA VALLEY GRILLE 🍷
1100 Glendon Ave., Los Angeles, CA 90024; (310) 824-3322 **Wine list** *California* **Wine prices** *Moderate* **Corkage** *$15* **Cuisine** *Californian* **Menu prices** *$17–$28*

NICK & STEF'S STEAKHOUSE 🍷
330 S. Hope St., Los Angeles, CA 90071; (213) 680-0330 **Wine list** *California* **Wine prices** *Expensive* **Cuisine** *Steak house* **Menu prices** *$45–$65*

OCEAN AVENUE SEAFOOD 🍷
1401 Ocean Ave., Santa Monica, CA 90401; (310) 394-5669 **Wine list** *California* **Wine prices** *Moderate* **Corkage** *$15* **Cuisine** *Seafood* **Menu prices** *$16–$36*

THE PALM 🍷
1100 S. Flower St., Los Angeles, CA 90015; (213) 763-4600 **Wine list** *California* **Wine prices** *Moderate* **Corkage** *$20* **Cuisine** *Steak house* **Menu prices** *$17–$38*

THE PALM 🍷
9001 Santa Monica Blvd., Los Angeles, CA 90069; (310) 550-8811 **Wine list** *California* **Wine prices** *Moderate* **Corkage** *$30* **Cuisine** *Steak house* **Menu prices** *$40–$60*

PATINA RESTAURANT 🍷🍷🍷
5955 Melrose Ave., Los Angeles, CA 90038; (323) 467-1108 **Wine list** *Bordeaux, California, Burgundy* **Wine selections** *1,600* **Number of bottles** *14,000* **Wine prices** *Moderate* **Corkage** *$20* **Cuisine** *French/Californian* **Menu prices** *$29–$35* **Credit cards** *AX, MC, VS, DV*
Grand Award since 1994

PIZZICOTTO 🍷
11758 San Vicente Blvd., Brentwood, CA 90049; (310) 442-7188 **Wine list** *Italy, California* **Wine prices** *Moderate* **Corkage** *$8* **Cuisine** *Italian* **Menu prices** *$10–$16*

THE POLO LOUNGE 🍷
The Beverly Hills Hotel & Bungalows, 9641 Sunset Blvd., Beverly Hills, CA 90210; (310) 276-2251 **Wine list** *France, California* **Wine prices** *Moderate* **Corkage** *$50* **Cuisine** *Continental/Asian* **Menu prices** *$36–$38*

PRIMITIVO WINE BISTRO 🍷
1025 Abbot Kinney Blvd., Venice, CA 90291; (310) 396-5353 **Wine list** *California* **Wine prices** *Moderate* **Corkage** *$10* **Cuisine** *Tapas* **Menu prices** *$5–$16*

PRIZZI'S PIAZZA 🍷
5923 Franklin Ave., Los Angeles, CA 90028; (323) 467-0168 **Wine list** *California, Italy* **Wine prices** *Moderate* **Cuisine** *Italian* **Menu prices** *$12–$28*

RÖCKENWAGNER 🍷
2435 Main St., Santa Monica, CA 90405; (310) 399-6504 **Wine list** *California, Germany, Austria* **Wine prices** *Moderate* **Corkage** *$20* **Cuisine** *Californian/French* **Menu prices** *$21–$27*

RUTH'S CHRIS STEAK HOUSE 🍷
224 S. Beverly Drive, Beverly Hills, CA 90212; (310) 859-8744 **Wine list** *California* **Wine prices** *Moderate* **Corkage** *$20* **Cuisine** *Steak house* **Menu prices** *$24–$58*

SPAGO BEVERLY HILLS 🍷🍷
176 N. Cañon Drive, Beverly Hills, CA 90210; (310) 385-0880 **Wine list** *California, France* **Wine prices** *Moderate* **Corkage** *$20* **Cuisine** *Californian* **Menu prices** *$28–$38*

SPRAZZO CUCINA ITALIANA 🍷
1389 Westwood Blvd., Los Angeles, CA 90024; (310) 479-3337 **Wine list** *California, Italy* **Wine prices** *Moderate* **Corkage** *$10* **Cuisine** *Italian* **Menu prices** *$10–$24*

TANINO RISTORANTE 🍷
1043 Westwood Blvd., Westwood Village, Los Angeles, CA 90024; (310) 208-0444 **Wine list** *Italy, California* **Wine prices** *Moderate* **Corkage** *$12* **Cuisine** *Italian* **Menu prices** *$22–$30*

TESORO TRATTORIA 🍷
300 S. Grand Ave. No. 9, Plaza Level, Los Angeles, CA 90071; (213) 680-0000 **Wine list** *Italy, California* **Wine prices** *Moderate* **Corkage** *$15* **Cuisine** *Italian* **Menu prices** *$13–$26*

TOSCANA 🍷
11633 San Vicente Blvd., Los Angeles, CA 90049; (310) 820-2448 **Wine list** *Italy, California* **Wine prices** *Moderate* **Corkage** *$20* **Cuisine** *Northern Italian* **Menu prices** *$12–$32*

VALENTINO 🍷🍷🍷
3115 Pico Blvd., Santa Monica, CA 90405; (310) 829-4313 **Wine list** *Italy, France, California* **Wine selections** *3,200* **Number of bottles** *200,000* **Wine prices** *Moderate* **Cuisine** *Italian* **Menu prices** *$25–$30* **Credit cards** *AX, MC, VS*
Grand Award since 1981

WATER GRILL 🍷🍷
544 S. Grand Ave., Los Angeles, CA 90071; (213) 891-0900 **Wine list** *California, France* **Wine prices** *Moderate* **Corkage** *$20* **Cuisine** *French/seafood* **Menu prices** *$25–$58*

ZAX RESTAURANT 🍷
11604 San Vicente Blvd., Brentwood, CA 90049; (310) 571-3800 **Wine list** *California* **Wine prices** *Moderate* **Corkage** *$15* **Cuisine** *Contemporary American* **Menu prices** *$18–$27*

ZUCCA 🍷🍷
801 S. Figueroa St., Los Angeles, CA 90017; (213) 614-7800 **Wine list** *Italy, California* **Wine prices** *Moderate* **Corkage** *$12* **Cuisine** *Italian* **Menu prices** *$17–$26*

CALIFORNIA

SAN FRANCISCO

ABSINTHE BRASSERIE & BAR 🍷🍷
398 Hayes St., San Francisco, CA 94102; (415) 551-1590 **Wine list** *France, California, Germany* **Wine prices** *Moderate* **Corkage** *$15* **Cuisine** *Mediterranean* **Menu prices** *$18–$28*

ANA MANDARA 🍷
891 Beach St., San Francisco, CA 94109; (415) 771-6800 **Wine list** *California* **Wine prices** *Moderate* **Corkage** *$15* **Cuisine** *Contemporary Vietnamese* **Menu prices** *$15–$29*

ANDALU 🍷
3198 16th St., San Francisco, CA 94103; (415) 621-2211
Wine list *California, France* **Wine prices** *Moderate* **Corkage** *$15* **Cuisine** *Tapas* **Menu prices** *$6–$18*

A. SABELLA'S RESTAURANT 🍷
2766 Taylor St. Third Floor, San Francisco, CA 94133; (415) 771-6775 **Wine list** *California* **Wine prices** Inexpensive **Corkage** *$15* **Cuisine** *Californian* **Menu prices** *$10–$50*

ASIA SF 🍷
201 Ninth St., San Francisco, CA 94103; (415) 255-ASIA
Wine list *California* **Wine prices** Inexpensive **Corkage** *$15* **Cuisine** *Californian/Asian* **Menu prices** *$9–$20*

AZIE 🍷
826 Folsom St., San Francisco, CA 94107; (415) 538-0918
Wine list *France, California* **Wine prices** *Moderate* **Corkage** *$15* **Cuisine** *French/Asian* **Menu prices** *$17–$26*

BACAR 🍷🍷
448 Brannan St., San Francisco, CA 94107; (415) 904-4100 **Wine list** *California, Burgundy, Oregon, Austria, Italy* **Wine prices** *Expensive* **Corkage** *$25* **Cuisine** *American/French/Italian* **Menu prices** *$18–$30*

BEAUCOUP 🍷
1001 California St., San Francisco, CA 94108; (415) 409-8500 **Wine list** *France* **Wine prices** *Moderate* **Corkage** *$20* **Cuisine** *French* **Menu prices** *$14–$28*

THE BIG FOUR 🍷
Huntington Hotel, 1075 California St., San Francisco, CA 94108; (415) 771-1140 **Wine list** *California* **Wine prices** *Expensive* **Corkage** *$24* **Cuisine** *Contemporary American* **Menu prices** *$20–$30*

BOULEVARD 🍷🍷
1 Mission St., San Francisco, CA 94105; (415) 543-6084
Wine list *California, France, Italy* **Wine prices** *Expensive* **Corkage** *$25* **Cuisine** *Contemporary American* **Menu prices** *$19–$32*

THE BUBBLE LOUNGE 🍷
714 Montgomery St., San Francisco, CA 94111; (415) 434-4204 **Wine list** *Champagne* **Wine prices** *Moderate* **Corkage** *$25* **Cuisine** *Californian* **Menu prices** *$8–$45*

THE CARNELIAN ROOM 🍷🍷🍷

555 California St., San Francisco, CA 94104; (415) 433-7500 **Wine list** *Bordeaux, Burgundy, California, Port* **Wine selections** *1,825* **Number of bottles** *45,000* **Wine prices** *Expensive* **Cuisine** *American/continental* **Menu prices** *$19–$39* **Credit cards** *AX, MC, VS, DV*
Grand Award since 1982

THE COSMOPOLITAN 🍷

121 Spear St., San Francisco, CA 94105; (415) 543-4001 **Wine list** *California* **Wine prices** *Moderate* **Corkage** *$15* **Cuisine** *Contemporary American* **Menu prices** *$16–$23*

COZMO'S GRILL 🍷

2001 Chestnut St., San Francisco, CA 94123; (415) 351-0175 **Wine list** *California* **Wine prices** *Moderate* **Corkage** *$15* **Cuisine** *Californian* **Menu prices** *$15–$22*

CRUSTACEAN 🍷

1475 Polk St., San Francisco, CA 94109; (415) 776-CRAB **Wine list** *California, France* **Wine prices** *Moderate* **Cuisine** *European/Vietnamese/Asian* **Menu prices** *$10–$37*

THE DINING ROOM 🍷🍷

The Ritz-Carlton San Francisco, 600 Stockton St., San Francisco, CA 94108; (415) 773-6198 **Wine list** *California, Burgundy, Bordeaux, Champagne* **Wine prices** *Expensive* **Corkage** *$25* **Cuisine** *Contemporary French* **Menu prices** *Prix fixe only; $73–$80*

ELISABETH DANIEL 🍷

550 Washington St., San Francisco, CA 94111; (415) 397-6129 **Wine list** *California, France* **Wine prices** *Expensive* **Corkage** *$30* **Cuisine** *Contemporary American* **Menu prices** *Prix fixe only; $70–$95*

FARALLON 🍷

450 Post St., San Francisco, CA 94102; (415) 956-6969 **Wine list** *California* **Wine prices** *Moderate* **Corkage** *$25* **Cuisine** *Californian* **Menu prices** *$25–$35*

FIFTH FLOOR 🍷🍷🍷

Hotel Palomar, 12 Fourth St., San Francisco, CA 94103; (415) 348-1555 **Wine list** *Burgundy, California, Rhône, Germany* **Wine selections** *1,400* **Number of bottles** *10,000* **Wine prices** *Expensive* **Corkage** *$30* **Cuisine** *Contemporary French* **Menu prices** *$28–$45* **Credit cards** *AX, MC, VS, DV*
Grand Award since 2001

FIRST CRUSH RESTAURANT 🍷
101 Cyril Magnin St., San Francisco, CA 94102; (415) 982-7874 **Wine list** *California* **Wine prices** *Moderate* **Corkage** *$15* **Cuisine** *Californian* **Menu prices** *$11–$22*

FLEUR DE LYS 🍷🍷
777 Sutter St., San Francisco, CA 94109; (415) 673-7779 **Wine list** *California, France* **Wine prices** *Expensive* **Cuisine** *Contemporary French* **Menu prices** *$28–$36*

FOURNOU'S OVENS 🍷🍷
Renaissance Stanford Court, 905 California St., San Francisco, CA 94108; (415) 989-1910 **Wine list** *California* **Wine prices** *Moderate* **Corkage** *$25* **Cuisine** *Californian/Mediterranean* **Menu prices** *$19–$33*

FRASCATI 🍷
1901 Hyde St., San Francisco, CA 94109; (415) 928-1406 **Wine list** *California, France* **Wine prices** *Moderate* **Cuisine** *Californian/Mediterranean* **Menu prices** *$16–$23*

GREENS 🍷
Fort Mason, Building A, San Francisco, CA 94123; (415) 771-6222 **Wine list** *California, France* **Wine prices** *Moderate* **Corkage** *$15* **Cuisine** *Vegetarian* **Menu prices** *$14–$19*

HAYES STREET GRILL 🍷
320 Hayes St., San Francisco, CA 94102; (415) 863-5545 **Wine list** *California* **Wine prices** Inexpensive **Corkage** *$15* **Cuisine** *Seafood* **Menu prices** *$16–$22*

INCANTO 🍷
1550 Church St., San Francisco, CA 94131; (415) 641-4500 **Wine list** *Italy, California* **Wine prices** *Moderate* **Corkage** *$20* **Cuisine** *Californian/Italian* **Menu prices** *$12–$24*

INDIGO 🍷🍷
687 McAllister St., San Francisco, CA 94102; (415) 673-9353 **Wine list** *California* **Wine prices** *Expensive* **Corkage** *$15* **Cuisine** *Contemporary American* **Menu prices** *$14–$19*

JARDINIÈRE RESTAURANT 🍷🍷
300 Grove St., San Francisco, CA 94102; (415) 861-5555 **Wine list** *France, California* **Wine prices** *Moderate* **Corkage** *$25* **Cuisine** *Californian/French* **Menu prices** *$22–$37*

JULIUS' CASTLE RESTAURANT 🍷🍷
1541 Montgomery St., San Francisco, CA 94133; (415) 392-2222 **Wine list** *California, Bordeaux* **Wine prices** *Expensive* **Corkage** *$20* **Cuisine** *Contemporary European* **Menu prices** *$18–$36*

LA FOLIE 🍷
2316 Polk St., San Francisco, CA 94109; (415) 776-5577 **Wine list** *France, California* **Wine prices** *Moderate* **Corkage** *$35* **Cuisine** *French* **Menu prices** *$30–$45*

LE COLONIAL 🍷
20 Cosmo Place, San Francisco, CA 94109; (415) 931-3600 **Wine list** *California* **Wine prices** *Moderate* **Corkage** *$15* **Cuisine** *Vietnamese* **Menu prices** *$18–$33*

MASA'S 🍷🍷
Hotel Vintage Court, 648 Bush St., San Francisco, CA 94108; (415) 989-7154 **Wine list** *France, Germany, California* **Wine prices** *Expensive* **Corkage** *$30* **Cuisine** *Contemporary French* **Menu prices** *Prix fixe only; $65–$109*

THE MATTERHORN SWISS RESTAURANT 🍷
2323 Van Ness Ave., San Francisco, CA 94109; (415) 885-6116 **Wine list** *Switzerland, California* **Wine prices** *Moderate* **Corkage** *$20* **Cuisine** *Swiss* **Menu prices** *$14–$23*

MCCORMICK & KULETO'S 🍷
900 N. Point St., San Francisco, CA 94109; (415) 929-1730 **Wine list** *California* **Wine prices** Inexpensive **Corkage** *$15* **Cuisine** *Seafood* **Menu prices** *$19–$29*

MOOSE'S 🍷
1652 Stockton St., San Francisco, CA 94133; (415) 989-7800 **Wine list** *California, France* **Wine prices** *Moderate* **Corkage** *$15* **Cuisine** *Contemporary American* **Menu prices** *$18–$29*

MORTON'S OF CHICAGO 🍷
400 Post St., San Francisco, CA 94102; (415) 986-5830 **Wine list** *California* **Wine prices** *Expensive* **Corkage** *$15* **Cuisine** *Steak house* **Menu prices** *$20–$36*

NOB HILL RESTAURANT 🍷
InterContinental Mark Hopkins, 1 Nob Hill, 999 California St., San Francisco, CA 94108; (415) 616-6944 **Wine list** *California* **Wine prices** *Expensive* **Corkage** *$25* **Cuisine** *Californian* **Menu prices** *$24–$35*

ONE MARKET RESTAURANT
1 Market St., San Francisco, CA 94105; (415) 777-5577 **Wine list** *California* **Wine prices** *Moderate* **Cuisine** *Contemporary American* **Menu prices** *$19–$30*

PALIO D'ASTI
640 Sacramento St., San Francisco, CA 94111; (415) 395-9800 **Wine list** *California, Italy* **Wine prices** *Moderate* **Corkage** *$15* **Cuisine** *Italian* **Menu prices** *$16–$25*

PLUMPJACK CAFÉ
3127 Fillmore St., San Francisco, CA 94123; (415) 563-4755 **Wine list** *California, France* **Wine prices** Inexpensive **Corkage** *$15* **Cuisine** *Californian* **Menu prices** *$15–$30*

POSTRIO
545 Post St., San Francisco, CA 94102; (415) 776-7825 **Wine list** *California, France, Italy* **Wine prices** *Moderate* **Cuisine** *Californian/Asian/Mediterranean* **Menu prices** *$27–$36*

RESTAURANT GARY DANKO
800 N. Point St., San Francisco, CA 94109; (415) 749-2060 **Wine list** *Bordeaux, Burgundy, Rhône, California* **Wine selections** *1,450* **Number of bottles** *10,000* **Wine prices** *Expensive* **Corkage** *$25* **Cuisine** *French/Californian* **Menu prices** *$55–$74* **Credit cards** *AX, MC, VS, DV*
Grand Award since 2001

RESTAURANT LULU
816 Folsom St., San Francisco, CA 94107; (415) 495-5775 **Wine list** *California* **Wine prices** *Moderate* **Corkage** *$15* **Cuisine** *Southern French* **Menu prices** *$14–$25*

ROSE PISTOLA
532 Columbus Ave., San Francisco, CA 94133; (415) 399-0499 **Wine list** *Italy, California* **Wine prices** *Moderate* **Corkage** *$15* **Cuisine** *Northern Italian* **Menu prices** *$15–$29*

ROY'S OF SAN FRANCISCO
101 Second St., San Francisco, CA 94105; (415) 777-0277 **Wine list** *California* **Wine prices** *Moderate* **Corkage** *$15* **Cuisine** *Contemporary/Hawaiian* **Menu prices** *$16–$28*

CALIFORNIA

RUBICON 🍷🍷🍷
558 Sacramento St., San Francisco, CA 94111; (415) 434-4100 **Wine list** *California, Burgundy, Rhône, Port* **Wine selections** *1,800* **Number of bottles** *20,000* **Wine prices** *Moderate* **Corkage** *$20* **Cuisine** *French/Californian* **Menu prices** *$22–$33* **Credit cards** *AX, MC, VS, DV*
Grand Award since 1998

RUTH'S CHRIS STEAK HOUSE 🍷
1601 Van Ness Ave., San Francisco, CA 94109; (415) 673-0557 **Wine list** *California* **Wine prices** *Moderate* **Corkage** *$15* **Cuisine** *Steak house* **Menu prices** *$19–$35*

SCALA'S BISTRO 🍷
Sir Francis Drake, 432 Powell St., San Francisco, CA 94102; (415) 395-8555 **Wine list** *California, Italy* **Wine prices** *Moderate* **Cuisine** *Italian/French* **Menu prices** *$12–$22*

SHANGHAI 1930 🍷
133 Steuart St., San Francisco, CA 94105; (415) 896-5600 **Wine list** *California, France* **Wine prices** *Moderate* **Corkage** *$20* **Cuisine** *Chinese* **Menu prices** *$12–$32*

THE VERANDA RESTAURANT 🍷
Renaissance Parc 55, 55 Cyril Magnin St., San Francisco, CA 94102; (415) 392-8000 **Wine list** *California* **Wine prices** *Moderate* **Corkage** *$15* **Cuisine** *Californian* **Menu prices** *$12–$28*

XYZ 🍷
W San Francisco, 181 Third St., San Francisco, CA 94103; (415) 817-7836 **Wine list** *California, France* **Wine prices** *Moderate* **Corkage** *$15* **Cuisine** *Californian* **Menu prices** *$18–$34*

YABBIES COASTAL KITCHEN 🍷
2237 Polk St., San Francisco, CA 94109; (415) 474-4088 **Wine list** *California* **Wine prices** *Moderate* **Cuisine** *Seafood* **Menu prices** *$13–$18*

CALIFORNIA

OTHER CITIES

THE ADMIRAL RISTY 🍷
31250 Palos Verdes Drive, Rancho Palos Verdes, CA 90275; (310) 377-0050 **Wine list** *California* **Wine prices** *Inexpensive* **Corkage** *$10* **Cuisine** *Californian* **Menu prices** *$17–$31*

THE AHWAHNEE DINING ROOM
The Ahwahnee Hotel, Yosemite, CA 95389; (209) 372-1488
Wine list *California* **Wine prices** *Moderate* **Corkage** *$20*
Cuisine *American* **Menu prices** *$22–$28*

ALBION RIVER INN
3790 N. Highway 1, Albion, CA 95410; (707) 937-1919
Wine list *California* **Wine prices** *Moderate* **Cuisine**
Coastal/Pacific Rim **Menu prices** *$17–$33*

ALFIERE
Sheraton San Diego, 1590 Harbor Island Drive, San Diego, CA 92101; (619) 692-2778 **Wine list** *Italy, California* **Wine prices** *Moderate* **Corkage** *$10* **Cuisine** *Italian/Mediterranean* **Menu prices** *$15–$37*

ALLORO
1215 Spring St., Paso Robles, CA 93446; (805) 238-9091
Wine list *California, Italy* **Wine prices** Inexpensive **Corkage**
$10 **Cuisine** *Italian* **Menu prices** *$11–$19*

ANAHEIM WHITE HOUSE
887 S. Anaheim Blvd., Anaheim, CA 92805; (714) 772-1381 **Wine list** *California, France, Italy* **Wine prices** *Moderate* **Corkage** *$15* **Cuisine** *Northern Italian* **Menu prices** *$19–$38*

ANTON & MICHEL RESTAURANT
Mission Street between Ocean and Seventh, Carmel, CA 93921; (831) 624-2406 **Wine list** *California, Bordeaux* **Wine prices** *Moderate* **Corkage** *$20* **Cuisine** *Continental* **Menu prices** *$19–$33*

APPLEWOOD INN & RESTAURANT
13555 Highway 116, Guerneville, CA 95446; (707) 869-9093 **Wine list** *California* **Wine prices** *Moderate* **Corkage** *$20* **Cuisine** *Californian/Provençal* **Menu prices** *$19–$28*

A.P. STUMPS
163 W. Santa Clara, San Jose, CA 95113; (408) 292-9928
Wine list *California, France* **Wine prices** *Moderate* **Corkage**
$18 **Cuisine** *Contemporary American* **Menu prices** *$18–$34*

AQUARELLA
8990 University Center Lane, San Diego, CA 92122; (858) 546-8797 **Wine list** *California, Argentina, Chile* **Wine prices** Inexpensive **Corkage** *$20* **Cuisine** *Mexican* **Menu prices** *$13–$27*

ARROYO CHOP HOUSE 🍷
536 S. Arroyo Parkway, Pasadena, CA 91105; (626) 577-7463 **Wine list** *California* **Wine prices** *Moderate* **Cuisine** *Steak house* **Menu prices** *$19–$36*

ARTERRA 🍷
San Diego Marriott Del Mar, 11966 El Camino Real, San Diego, CA 92130; (858) 369-6032 **Wine list** *California, Washington* **Wine prices** *Moderate* **Corkage** *$15* **Cuisine** *American* **Menu prices** *$19–$30*

A.R. VALENTIEN 🍷
The Lodge at Torrey Pines, 11480 N. Torrey Pines Road, La Jolla, CA 92037; (858) 777-6635 **Wine list** *California* **Wine prices** Inexpensive **Corkage** *$25* **Cuisine** *Californian* **Menu prices** *$23–$38*

AUBERGE DU SOLEIL RESTAURANT 🍷🍷
180 Rutherford Hill Road, Rutherford, CA 94573; (707) 963-1211 **Wine list** *California, France* **Wine prices** *Moderate* **Corkage** *$30* **Cuisine** *French/Mediterranean* **Menu prices** *$29–$37*

AZZURA POINT 🍷
Loews Coronado Bay Resort, 4000 Coronado Bay Road, Coronado, CA 92118; (619) 424-4000 **Wine list** *California* **Wine prices** *Moderate* **Cuisine** *Californian* **Menu prices** *$21–$32*

BALBOA 🍷
The Grafton Hotel, 8462 W. Sunset Blvd., West Hollywood, CA 90069; (323) 650-8383 **Wine list** *California* **Wine prices** *Expensive* **Corkage** *$20* **Cuisine** *Steak house* **Menu prices** *$18–$39*

BAYSIDE RESTAURANT 🍷
900 Bayside Drive, Newport Beach, CA 92660; (949) 721-1222 **Wine list** *California* **Wine prices** *Moderate* **Corkage** *$15* **Cuisine** *Contemporary American* **Menu prices** *$20–$30*

BELLA VISTA RESTAURANT 🍷🍷
13451 Skyline Blvd., Woodside, CA 94062; (650) 851-1229 **Wine list** *California* **Wine prices** *Moderate* **Corkage** *$20* **Cuisine** *Continental* **Menu prices** *$16–$32*

THE BENBOW INN 🍷
445 Lake Benbow Drive, Garberville, CA 95542; (707) 923-2124 **Wine list** *California* **Wine prices** *Moderate* **Corkage** *$12* **Cuisine** *Contemporary American* **Menu prices** *$17–$30*

BERNARD'O 🍷
12457 Rancho Bernardo Road, San Diego, CA 92128; (858) 487-7171 **Wine list** *California, France* **Wine prices** Inexpensive **Corkage** *$20* **Cuisine** *French/Californian* **Menu prices** *$15–$27*

BERTRAND AT MISTER A'S 🍷
2550 Fifth Ave., San Diego, CA 92103; (619) 239-1377 **Wine list** *California, Bordeaux* **Wine prices** *Expensive* **Corkage** *$30* **Cuisine** *Mediterranean/continental* **Menu prices** *$26–$39*

BIBA 🍷
2801 Capitol Ave., Sacramento, CA 95816; (916) 455-BIBA **Wine list** *California, Italy* **Wine prices** *Moderate* **Corkage** *$15* **Cuisine** *Italian* **Menu prices** *$20–$30*

BILLY'S AT THE BEACH 🍷
2751 W. Coast Highway, Newport Beach, CA 92663; (949) 722-1100 **Wine list** *California* **Wine prices** *Moderate* **Corkage** *$20* **Cuisine** *Seafood* **Menu prices** *$19–$30*

BISTANGO 🍷
19100 Von Karman Ave., Irvine, CA 92612; (949) 752-5222 **Wine list** *California, Bordeaux* **Wine prices** *Moderate* **Cuisine** *Contemporary American* **Menu prices** *$17–$30*

BISTRO 45 🍷🍷
45 S. Mentor Ave., Pasadena, CA 91106; (626) 795-BISTRO **Wine list** *California, Bordeaux* **Wine prices** *Moderate* **Corkage** *$15* **Cuisine** *Californian/French* **Menu prices** *$19–$29*

BISTRO LAURENT 🍷
1202 Pine St., Paso Robles, CA 93446; (805) 226-8191 **Wine list** *California, France* **Wine prices** *Moderate* **Cuisine** *French* **Menu prices** *$15–$23*

BISTRO LE CRILLON 🍷
2523 Eastbluff Drive, Newport Beach, CA 92660; (949) 640-8181 **Wine list** *France* **Wine prices** *Moderate* **Corkage** *$15* **Cuisine** *French* **Menu prices** *$17–$28*

BLACKHAWK GRILLE 🍷
3540 Blackhawk Plaza Circle, Danville, CA 94506; (925) 736-4295 **Wine list** *California* **Wine prices** Inexpensive **Corkage** *$15* **Cuisine** *Californian* **Menu prices** *$15–$36*

BLUE
998 Monterey St., San Luis Obispo, CA 93401; (805) 783-1135 **Wine list** *California* **Wine prices** Inexpensive **Corkage** *$12* **Cuisine** *Contemporary* **Menu prices** *$8–$26*

BLUE MOON
The Spindrift Hotel, 654 Cannery Row, Monterey, CA 93940; (831) 375-4155 **Wine list** *California* **Wine prices** Inexpensive **Corkage** *$12* **Cuisine** *Pacific Rim* **Menu prices** *$17–$28*

BLUE POINT COASTAL CUISINE
565 Fifth Ave., San Diego, CA 92101; (619) 233-6623 **Wine list** *California* **Wine prices** *Moderate* **Corkage** *$15* **Cuisine** *Seafood* **Menu prices** *$20–$40*

BOTTLE INN RISTORANTE
26 22nd St., Hermosa Beach, CA 90254; (310) 376-9595 **Wine list** *California* **Wine prices** *Moderate* **Corkage** *$18* **Cuisine** *Italian* **Menu prices** *$12–$22*

BOUCHON SANTA BARBARA
9 W. Victoria St., Santa Barbara, CA 93101; (805) 730-1160 **Wine list** *California* **Wine prices** *Moderate* **Corkage** *$21* **Cuisine** *Californian* **Menu prices** *Prix fixe only; $25–$35*

THE BRAMBLES DINNER HOUSE
4005 Burton Drive, Cambria, CA 93428; (805) 927-4716 **Wine list** *California* **Wine prices** *Moderate* **Corkage** *$15* **Cuisine** *Continental* **Menu prices** *$13–$26*

BRIDGES
44 Church St., Danville, CA 94526; (925) 820-7200 **Wine list** *California* **Wine prices** *Moderate* **Corkage** *$15* **Cuisine** *French* **Menu prices** *$18–$36*

BRIGITTE'S
1325 State St., Santa Barbara, CA 93101; (805) 966-9676 **Wine list** *California, France* **Wine prices** Inexpensive **Corkage** *$15* **Cuisine** *Californian* **Menu prices** *$9–$20*

BRIX RESTAURANT
7377 St. Helena Highway, Napa, CA 94558; (707) 944-2749 **Wine list** *California* **Wine prices** *Moderate* **Corkage** *$15* **Cuisine** *Californian* **Menu prices** *$17–$30*

THE BUNGALOW 🍷
2441 E. Coast Highway, Corona Del Mar, CA 92625; (949) 673-6585 **Wine list** *California* **Wine prices** *Moderate* **Corkage** *$20* **Cuisine** *American* **Menu prices** *$21–$35*

BUONA TAVOLA 🍷
1037 Monterey St., San Luis Obispo, CA 93401; (805) 545-8000 **Wine list** *California, Italy* **Wine prices** Inexpensive **Corkage** *$12* **Cuisine** *Northern Italian* **Menu prices** *$9–$25*

BUTTERFIELD 🍷
La Casa del Zorro, 3845 Yaqui Pass Road, Borrego Springs, CA 92004; (760) 767-5323 **Wine list** *California* **Wine prices** *Moderate* **Corkage** *$25* **Cuisine** *American/continental* **Menu prices** *$25–$35*

CAFÉ DEL REY 🍷
4451 Admiralty Way, Marina del Rey, CA 90292; (310) 823-6395 **Wine list** *California* **Wine prices** *Moderate* **Corkage** *$20* **Cuisine** *Californian/Pacific Rim* **Menu prices** *$17–$32*

CAFÉ ESIN 🍷
2416 San Ramon Valley Blvd., San Ramon, CA 94583; (925) 314-0974 **Wine list** *California* **Wine prices** Inexpensive **Corkage** *$12* **Cuisine** *American* **Menu prices** *$15–$20*

CAFÉ FIORE 🍷
1169 Ski Run Blvd., South Lake Tahoe, CA 96151; (530) 541-2908 **Wine list** *California* **Wine prices** *Moderate* **Corkage** *$15* **Cuisine** *Italian* **Menu prices** *$13–$30*

CAFÉ MARCELLA 🍷🍷
368 Village Lane, Los Gatos, CA 95030; (408) 354-8006 **Wine list** *France, California, Italy* **Wine prices** *Moderate* **Corkage** *$20* **Cuisine** *French/Italian/Mediterranean* **Menu prices** *$14–$35*

CAFÉ MED 🍷
4809 Stockdale Highway, Bakersfield, CA 93309; (661) 834-4433 **Wine list** *California* **Wine prices** *Moderate* **Cuisine** *Mediterranean/Californian* **Menu prices** *$11–$40*

CAFÉ PACIFICA 🍷
2414 San Diego Ave., San Diego, CA 92110; (619) 291-6666 **Wine list** *California* **Wine prices** *Moderate* **Corkage** *$12* **Cuisine** *Seafood* **Menu prices** *$15–$28*

CAFÉ PIERRE 🍷🍷

317 Manhattan Beach Blvd., Manhattan Beach, CA 90266; (310) 545-5252 **Wine list** *California, France* **Wine prices** *Moderate* **Corkage** *$15* **Cuisine** *Californian/French* **Menu prices** *$12–$28*

CAFÉ ROMA 🍷

1020 Railroad Ave., San Luis Obispo, CA 93401; (805) 541-6800 **Wine list** *California, Italy* **Wine prices** Inexpensive **Corkage** *$12* **Cuisine** *Italian* **Menu prices** *$9–$22*

THE CALIFORNIA MARKET 🍷

Highlands Inn–Park Hyatt Carmel, 120 Highlands Drive, Carmel, CA 93923; (831) 622-5450 **Wine list** *California* **Wine prices** *Moderate* **Cuisine** *Californian* **Menu prices** *$13–$21*

CAMPS AT GREENHORN CREEK 🍷

The Cottages at Greenhorn Creek, 696 McCauley Ranch Road, Angels Camp, CA 95222; (209) 736-8181 **Wine list** *California* **Wine prices** *Moderate* **Corkage** *$10* **Cuisine** *Californian* **Menu prices** *$18–$30*

THE CAPRICE 🍷

2000 Paradise Drive, Tiburon, CA 94920; (415) 435-3400 **Wine list** *California* **Wine prices** *Moderate* **Corkage** *$18* **Cuisine** *European/Californian* **Menu prices** *$20–$30*

CARMEL CHOP HOUSE 🍷

Fifth & San Carlos Streets, Carmel, CA 93921; (831) 625-1199 **Wine list** *California* **Wine prices** *Moderate* **Corkage** *$15* **Cuisine** *Steak house* **Menu prices** *$19–$40*

CARNEROS RESTAURANT 🍷

The Lodge at Sonoma, 1325 Broadway, Sonoma, CA 95476; (707) 931-2042 **Wine list** *California* **Wine prices** *Moderate* **Corkage** *$10* **Cuisine** *Californian* **Menu prices** *$18–$32*

CASABLANCA RESTAURANT 🍷

Casablanca Inn, 101 Main St., Santa Cruz, CA 95060; (831) 426-9063 **Wine list** *California* **Wine prices** *Moderate* **Cuisine** *Californian/continental* **Menu prices** *$17–$31*

CASANOVA RESTAURANT 🍷🍷🍷
Fifth Street between Mission and San Carlos, Carmel, CA 93921; (831) 625-0501 **Wine list** *France, Italy* **Wine selections** *1,700* **Number of bottles** *25,000* **Wine prices** *Moderate* **Corkage** *$30* **Cuisine** *Italian/French* **Menu prices** *$25–$43* **Credit cards** *AX, MC, VS, DV*
Grand Award since 1990

THE CAT & THE CUSTARD CUP 🍷
800 E. Whittier Blvd., La Habra, CA 90631; (562) 694-3812 **Wine list** *California* **Wine prices** *Moderate* **Corkage** *$10* **Cuisine** *Contemporary American* **Menu prices** *$18–$28*

CELADON 🍷
500 Main St., Napa, CA 94559; (707) 254-9690 **Wine list** *California* **Wine prices** Inexpensive **Corkage** *$15* **Cuisine** *International* **Menu prices** *$14–$24*

THE CELLAR 🍷🍷🍷
305 N. Harbor Blvd., Fullerton, CA 92832; (714) 525-5682 **Wine list** *California, Bordeaux, Burgundy* **Wine selections** *1,475* **Number of bottles** *16,150* **Wine prices** *Moderate* **Cuisine** *French* **Menu prices** *$18–$30* **Credit cards** *AX, MC, VS, DV*
Grand Award since 1992

CENTRAL PARK BISTRO 🍷
181 E. Fourth Ave., San Mateo, CA 94401; (650) 558-8401 **Wine list** *California* **Wine prices** *Moderate* **Corkage** *$10* **Cuisine** *Mediterranean* **Menu prices** *$12–$19*

CETRELLA 🍷
845 Main St., Half Moon Bay, CA 94019; (650) 726-4090 **Wine list** *California, France* **Wine prices** *Moderate* **Corkage** *$15* **Cuisine** *Mediterranean* **Menu prices** *$17–$28*

CHEZ MELANGE 🍷
1716 Pacific Coast Highway, Redondo Beach, CA 90277; (310) 540-1222 **Wine list** *California* **Wine prices** *Moderate* **Corkage** *$10* **Cuisine** *Californian* **Menu prices** *$9–$27*

CHRISTAKIS 🍷
13011 Newport Ave., Tustin, CA 92680; (714) 731-1179 **Wine list** *California* **Wine prices** *Moderate* **Corkage** *$15* **Cuisine** *Greek/Mediterranean* **Menu prices** *$12–$31*

CHRISTOPHE'S FRENCH RESTAURANT 🍷
2304 E. Bidwell St., Folsom, CA 95630; (916) 983-4883
Wine list *California, France* **Wine prices** *Moderate* **Corkage** *$20* **Cuisine** *French* **Menu prices** *$21–$37*

CHRISTY HILL 🍷
115 Grove St., Tahoe City, CA 96145; (530) 583-8551
Wine list *California* **Wine prices** *Moderate* **Corkage** *$15* **Cuisine** *Californian/French* **Menu prices** *$20–$40*

CHRISTY'S 🍷
3937 E. Broadway, Long Beach, CA 90803; (562) 433-7133
Wine list *California* **Wine prices** *Moderate* **Corkage** *$15* **Cuisine** *Southern Italian* **Menu prices** *$12–$28*

CHUCK'S STEAK HOUSE OF HAWAII 🍷
3888 State St., Santa Barbara, CA 93105; (805) 687-4417
Wine list *California* **Wine prices** Inexpensive **Cuisine** *Steak house* **Menu prices** *$9–$30*

CICCIOTTI'S TRATTORIA ITALIANA 🍷
1933 San Elijo Ave., Encinitas, CA 92007; (760) 634-2335
Wine list *Italy, California* **Wine prices** *Moderate* **Corkage** *$10* **Cuisine** *Italian* **Menu prices** *$7–$23*

CIELO 🍷
Ventana Inn & Spa, Highway 1, Big Sur, CA 93920; (831) 667-2331 **Wine list** *California* **Wine prices** *Moderate* **Corkage** *$20* **Cuisine** *Californian/Mediterranean* **Menu prices** *$25–$34*

CITRONE RESTAURANT 🍷
328 Orange St., Redlands, CA 92373; (909) 793-6635
Wine list *California* **Wine prices** *Moderate* **Corkage** *$20* **Cuisine** *Californian* **Menu prices** *$11–$28*

CITRONELLE 🍷
Santa Barbara Inn, 901 E. Cabrillo Blvd., Santa Barbara, CA 93103; (805) 963-0111 **Wine list** *California, France* **Wine prices** *Moderate* **Corkage** *$20* **Cuisine** *Californian/French* **Menu prices** *$20–$32*

CITY HOTEL 🍷
Columbia City Hotel, Main Street, Columbia State Park, Columbia, CA 95310; (800) 532-1479 **Wine list** *California* **Wine prices** *Moderate* **Corkage** *$12* **Cuisine** *Californian/French* **Menu prices** *$17–$25*

CITY TREASURE RESTAURANT
1730 L St., Sacramento, CA 95814; (916) 447-7380 **Wine list** *California* **Wine prices** *Moderate* **Corkage** *$10* **Cuisine** *Californian* **Menu prices** *$15–$29*

CLAES'
Hotel Laguna, 425 S. Coast Highway, Laguna Beach, CA 92651; (949) 376-WAVE **Wine list** *California* **Wine prices** *Moderate* **Corkage** *$15* **Cuisine** *Seafood* **Menu prices** *$24–$35*

COLE'S CHOP HOUSE
1122 Main St., Napa, CA 94559; (707) 224-6328 **Wine list** *California* **Wine prices** *Moderate* **Corkage** *$15* **Cuisine** *Steak house* **Menu prices** *$15–$38*

CUISTOT
73-111 El Paseo, Palm Desert, CA 92260; (760) 340-1000 **Wine list** *California* **Wine prices** *Moderate* **Corkage** *$25* **Cuisine** *French* **Menu prices** *$24–$39*

CUVEE, WINE COUNTRY CUISINE
5656 La Jolla Blvd., La Jolla, CA 92037; (858) 551-4090 **Wine list** *California* **Wine prices** *Moderate* **Corkage** *$10* **Cuisine** *Californian* **Menu prices** *$13–$19*

DAKOTA GRILL & SPIRITS
901 Fifth Ave., San Diego, CA 92101; (619) 234-5554 **Wine list** *California* **Wine prices** *Moderate* **Cuisine** *American/regional* **Menu prices** *$13–$26*

DELIUS RESTAURANT
3550 Long Beach Blvd., Long Beach, CA 90807; (562) 426-0694 **Wine list** *California* **Wine prices** Inexpensive **Corkage** *$15* **Cuisine** *International* **Menu prices** *Prix fixe only; $43*

DEPOT HOTEL CUCINA RUSTICA
241 First St. W., Sonoma, CA 95476; (707) 938-2980 **Wine list** *California, Italy* **Wine prices** Inexpensive **Corkage** *$10* **Cuisine** *Northern Italian* **Menu prices** *$8–$20*

DEREK'S BISTRO
181 E. Glenarm St., Pasadena, CA 91105; (626) 799-5252 **Wine list** *California, France* **Wine prices** *Moderate* **Corkage** *$15* **Cuisine** *Contemporary Californian* **Menu prices** *$18–$29*

CALIFORNIA

DESERT SAGE 🍷
78-085 Avenida La Fonda, La Quinta, CA 92253; (760) 564-8744 **Wine list** *California* **Wine prices** *Moderate* **Corkage** *$20* **Cuisine** *Contemporary American* **Menu prices** *$22–$39*

DEWZ 🍷
1101 I St., Modesto, CA 95354; (209) 549-1101 **Wine list** *California, France* **Wine prices** Inexpensive **Cuisine** *Californian* **Menu prices** *$15–$25*

THE DINING ROOM 🍷🍷
The Ritz-Carlton Laguna Niguel, 1 Ritz-Carlton Drive, Dana Point, CA 92629; (949) 240-2000 **Wine list** *California, France* **Wine prices** *Expensive* **Corkage** *$50* **Cuisine** *French/Mediterranean* **Menu prices** *$35–$42*

THE DINING ROOM 🍷
The Ritz-Carlton Marina Del Rey, 4375 Admiralty Way, Marina Del Rey, CA 90292; (310) 823-1700 **Wine list** *California, France* **Wine prices** *Expensive* **Corkage** *$25* **Cuisine** *International* **Menu prices** *$24–$45*

THE DINING ROOM AT THE INN 🍷
The Inn at Rancho Santa Fe, 5951 Linea del Cielo, Rancho Santa Fe, CA 92067; (800) 843-4661 **Wine list** *California* **Wine prices** *Moderate* **Corkage** *$15* **Cuisine** *Californian* **Menu prices** *$17–$26*

DOMAINE CHANDON 🍷
1 California Drive, Yountville, CA 94599; (707) 944-2892 **Wine list** *California* **Wine prices** *Moderate* **Cuisine** *French/Californian* **Menu prices** *$24–$38*

DOMENICO'S ON THE WHARF 🍷🍷
50 Fisherman's Wharf, Monterey, CA 93940; (831) 372-3655 **Wine list** *California, France* **Wine prices** *Moderate* **Corkage** *$12* **Cuisine** *Italian* **Menu prices** *$18–$40*

DONOVAN'S STEAK & CHOP HOUSE 🍷🍷
4340 La Jolla Village Drive, La Jolla, CA 92122; (858) 450-6666 **Wine list** *California, France, Italy* **Wine prices** *Moderate* **Corkage** *$20* **Cuisine** *Steak house* **Menu prices** *$24–$46*

DOUG ARANGO'S 🍷
8826 Melrose Ave., West Hollywood, CA 90069; (310) 378-DOUG **Wine list** *California, France* **Wine prices** *Moderate* **Corkage** *$15* **Cuisine** *International/Italian* **Menu prices** *$12–$36*

🍷🍷🍷 Grand Award 🍷🍷 Best of Award of Excellence 🍷 Award of Excellence

DRY CREEK KITCHEN 🍷🍷
Hotel Healdsburg, 317 Healdsburg Ave., Healdsburg, CA 95448; (707) 431-0330 **Wine list** *California* **Wine prices** *Moderate* **Corkage** *$15* **Cuisine** *Contemporary American* **Menu prices** *$18–$29*

DUANE'S PRIME STEAKS & SEAFOOD 🍷
Mission Inn, 3649 Mission Inn Ave., Riverside, CA 92501; (909) 341-6767 **Wine list** *California* **Wine prices** *Moderate* **Corkage** *$15* **Cuisine** *Steak house* **Menu prices** *$20–$50*

THE DUCK CLUB 🍷
Lafayette Park Hotel & Spa, 3287 Mount Diablo Blvd., Lafayette, CA 94549; (925) 283-7108 **Wine list** *California* **Wine prices** *Moderate* **Corkage** *$12* **Cuisine** *American/French/Thai* **Menu prices** *$18–$28*

EL BIZCOCHO 🍷🍷
Rancho Bernardo Inn, 17550 Bernardo Oaks Drive, San Diego, CA 92128; (858) 675-8550 **Wine list** *California, Bordeaux, Burgundy, Italy, Australia* **Wine prices** *Expensive* **Corkage** *$25* **Cuisine** *French* **Menu prices** *$19–$38*

ELBOW ROOM 🍷
Fig Garden Village, 731 W. San Jose Ave., Fresno, CA 93704; (559) 227-1234 **Wine list** *California* **Wine prices** *Moderate* **Corkage** *$12* **Cuisine** *American* **Menu prices** *$12–$27*

EL PASEO RESTAURANT 🍷🍷🍷
7 El Paseo, Mill Valley, CA 94941; (415) 388-0741 **Wine list** *Bordeaux, Burgundy, California* **Wine selections** *1,600* **Number of bottles** *42,000* **Wine prices** *Moderate* **Corkage** *$20* **Cuisine** *French/Californian* **Menu prices** *$16–$30* **Credit cards** *AX, MC, VS, DV*
Grand Award since 1987

EMILE'S 🍷
545 S. Second St., San Jose, CA 95112; (408) 289-1960 **Wine list** *California* **Wine prices** *Moderate* **Corkage** *$20* **Cuisine** *Contemporary European* **Menu prices** *$25–$32*

ENOTRIA CAFÉ & WINE BAR 🍷
1431 Del Paso Blvd., Sacramento, CA 95815; (916) 922-6792 **Wine list** *California, France* **Wine prices** *Moderate* **Corkage** *$12* **Cuisine** *Californian/Mediterranean* **Menu prices** *$13–$25*

ERNA'S ELDERBERRY HOUSE 🍷🍷
The Estate by the Elderberries, 48688 Victoria Lane, Oakhurst, CA 93644; (559) 683-6800 **Wine list** *California, Burgundy, Austria* **Wine prices** Inexpensive **Corkage** *$30* **Cuisine** *European/Californian* **Menu prices** *Prix fixe only; $68–$82*

FANDANGO 🍷🍷
223 17th St., Pacific Grove, CA 93950; (831) 372-3456 **Wine list** *Bordeaux, California, Burgundy, Italy* **Wine prices** *Moderate* **Corkage** *$18* **Cuisine** *European* **Menu prices** *$13–$24*

THE FIREHOUSE 🍷🍷
1112 Second St., Sacramento, CA 95814; (916) 442-4772 **Wine list** *California* **Wine prices** *Moderate* **Corkage** *$20* **Cuisine** *Californian* **Menu prices** *$19–$54*

FIRENZE TRATTORIA 🍷
162 S. Rancho Santa Fe Road, Encinitas, CA 92024; (760) 944-9000 **Wine list** *California, Italy* **Wine prices** Inexpensive **Corkage** *$15* **Cuisine** *Italian* **Menu prices** *$11–$29*

FIVE CROWNS 🍷🍷
3801 E. Coast Highway, Corona Del Mar, CA 92625; (949) 760-0331 **Wine list** *California* **Wine prices** *Moderate* **Corkage** *$15* **Cuisine** *Californian/continental* **Menu prices** *$18–$34*

555 EAST 🍷🍷
555 E. Ocean Blvd., Long Beach, CA 90802; (562) 437-0626 **Wine list** *California, France, Australia* **Wine prices** *Moderate* **Corkage** *$15* **Cuisine** *Steak house* **Menu prices** *$20–$30*

5' RESTAURANT 🍷🍷
328 Glenneyre St., Laguna Beach, CA 92651; (949) 497-4955 **Wine list** *California, Burgundy, Bordeaux* **Wine prices** *Moderate* **Corkage** *$15* **Cuisine** *Chinese/French/Californian* **Menu prices** *$18–$36*

FLEMING'S PRIME STEAKHOUSE & WINE BAR 🍷
2301 Rosecrans Ave., El Segundo, CA 90245; (310) 643-6911 **Wine list** *California* **Wine prices** *Moderate* **Corkage** *$20* **Cuisine** *Steak house* **Menu prices** *$18–$33*

FLEMING'S PRIME STEAKHOUSE & WINE BAR 🍷
455 Newport Center Drive, Newport Beach, CA 92660; (949) 720-9633 **Wine list** *California* **Wine prices** *Moderate* **Corkage** *$20* **Cuisine** *Steak house* **Menu prices** *$17–$48*

FLEMING'S PRIME STEAKHOUSE & WINE BAR 🍷
71800 Highway 111, Rancho Mirage, CA 92270; (760) 776-6685 **Wine list** *California* **Wine prices** *Moderate* **Cuisine** *Steak house* **Menu prices** *$17–$30*

FLEMING'S PRIME STEAKHOUSE & WINE BAR 🍷
8970 University Center Lane, San Diego, CA 92122; (858) 535-0078 **Wine list** *California* **Wine prices** *Moderate* **Corkage** *$20* **Cuisine** *Steak house* **Menu prices** *$18–$31*

THE FRENCH LAUNDRY 🍷🍷
6640 Washington St., Yountville, CA 94599; (707) 944-2380 **Wine list** *California, Burgundy* **Wine prices** *Expensive* **Cuisine** *American/French* **Menu prices** *Prix fixe only; $115–$135*

FRENCH 75 BISTRO & CHAMPAGNE BAR 🍷
1464 S. Coast Highway, Laguna Beach, CA 92651; (949) 494-8444 **Wine list** *France, California* **Wine prices** *Moderate* **Corkage** *$15* **Cuisine** *French* **Menu prices** *$18–$34*

FRESH CREAM RESTAURANT 🍷
99 Pacific St., Monterey, CA 93940; (831) 375-9798 **Wine list** *California* **Wine prices** *Moderate* **Corkage** *$20* **Cuisine** *French/Californian* **Menu prices** *$23–$35*

FRESH SEAFOOD RESTAURANT & BAR 🍷
1044 Wall St., La Jolla, CA 92037; (858) 551-7575 **Wine list** *California* **Wine prices** *Moderate* **Corkage** *$20* **Cuisine** *Seafood* **Menu prices** *$14–$29*

GALLEY RESTAURANT 🍷
899 Embarcadero, Morro Bay, CA 93442; (805) 772-2806 **Wine list** *California* **Wine prices** Inexpensive **Corkage** *$10* **Cuisine** *Seafood* **Menu prices** *$10–$34*

GEORGE'S AT THE COVE 🍷
1250 Prospect St., La Jolla, CA 92037; (858) 454-4244 **Wine list** *California* **Wine prices** *Moderate* **Corkage** *$25* **Cuisine** *Californian* **Menu prices** *$25–$35*

THE GIRL & THE FIG 🍷
110 W. Spain St., Sonoma, CA 95476; (707) 938-3634 **Wine list** *California* **Wine prices** Inexpensive **Corkage** *$12* **Cuisine** *French* **Menu prices** *$15–$23*

THE GLEN ELLEN INN RESTAURANT 🍷
13670 Arnold Drive, Glen Ellen, CA 95442; (707) 996-6409 **Wine list** *California* **Wine prices** *Moderate* **Corkage** *$13* **Cuisine** *Californian* **Menu prices** *$11–$25*

GLISSANDI 🍷
Resort at Squaw Creek, 400 Squaw Creek Road, Olympic Valley, CA 96146; (530) 583-6300 **Wine list** *California, France* **Wine prices** *Moderate* **Corkage** *$20* **Cuisine** *Contemporary Californian* **Menu prices** *$28–$36*

THE GOLDEN TRUFFLE 🍷
1767 Newport Blvd., Costa Mesa, CA 92627; (949) 645-9858 **Wine list** *California* **Wine prices** *Moderate* **Corkage** *$15* **Cuisine** *French/Caribbean* **Menu prices** *$14–$32*

GRAHAM'S AT SQUAW VALLEY 🍷🍷
1650 Squaw Valley Road, Olympic Valley, CA 96146; (530) 581-0454 **Wine list** *California, France* **Wine prices** *Moderate* **Corkage** *$25* **Cuisine** *Southern European* **Menu prices** *$20–$28*

GRASING'S 🍷
Sixth and Mission Streets, Carmel, CA 93921; (831) 624-6562 **Wine list** *California* **Wine prices** *Moderate* **Corkage** *$15* **Cuisine** *Contemporary Californian* **Menu prices** *$17–$29*

GREAT OAK STEAKHOUSE 🍷
Pechanga Resort & Casino, 45000 Pechanga Parkway, Temecula, CA 92592; (909) 719-8507 **Wine list** *California, France* **Wine prices** *Moderate* **Corkage** *$20* **Cuisine** *Steak house* **Menu prices** *$18–$38*

GREYSTONE THE STEAKHOUSE 🍷
658 Fifth Ave., San Diego, CA 92101; (619) 232-0225 **Wine list** *California, France, Italy* **Wine prices** *Moderate* **Cuisine** *Steak house* **Menu prices** *$18–$36*

HAP'S ORIGINAL 🍷
122 W. Neal St., Pleasanton, CA 94566; (925) 600-9200 **Wine list** *California* **Wine prices** *Moderate* **Cuisine** *Steak house* **Menu prices** *$23–$75*

THE HARBOR HOUSE INN 🍷
The Harbor House Inn, 5600 S. Highway 1, Elk, CA 95432; (707) 877-3203 **Wine list** *California* **Wine prices** *Inexpensive* **Corkage** *$15* **Cuisine** *Californian* **Menu prices** *Prix fixe only; $45*

🍷🍷🍷 Grand Award 🍷🍷 Best of Award of Excellence 🍷 Award of Excellence

THE HARBOR RESTAURANT 🍷
210 Stearns Wharf, Santa Barbara, CA 93101; (805) 963-3311 **Wine list** *California* **Wine prices** *Moderate* **Cuisine** *Continental* **Menu prices** *$22–$27*

THE HOBBIT 🍷🍷
2932 E. Chapman Ave., Orange, CA 92869; (714) 997-1972 **Wine list** *California, France, Germany* **Wine prices** *Moderate* **Corkage** *$25* **Cuisine** *French/continental* **Menu prices** *Prix fixe only; $65*

HORSESHOE BAR GRILL 🍷
3645 Taylor Road, Loomis, CA 95650; (916) 652-2222 **Wine list** *California* **Wine prices** *Moderate* **Corkage** *$15* **Cuisine** *American/French* **Menu prices** *$15–$36*

HUMPHREY'S BY THE BAY 🍷
Humphrey's Half Moon Inn & Suites, 2241 Shelter Island Drive, San Diego, CA 92106; (619) 224-3411 **Wine list** *California* **Wine prices** *Moderate* **Corkage** *$10* **Cuisine** *Contemporary* **Menu prices** *$17–$36*

IL DAVIDE 🍷
901 A St., San Rafael, CA 94901; (415) 454-8080 **Wine list** *California* **Wine prices** *Moderate* **Cuisine** *Tuscan* **Menu prices** *$11–$23*

IL FORNAIO CUCINA ITALIANA 🍷
1333 First St., Coronado, CA 92118; (619) 437-4911 **Wine list** *Italy, California* **Wine prices** *Moderate* **Corkage** *$15* **Cuisine** *Italian* **Menu prices** *$12–$25*

IL FORNAIO CUCINA ITALIANA 🍷
223 Corte Madera Town Center, Corte Madera, CA 94925; (415) 927-4400 **Wine list** *California, Italy* **Wine prices** *Moderate* **Corkage** *$10* **Cuisine** *Italian* **Menu prices** *$10–$25*

IL FORNAIO CUCINA ITALIANA 🍷
1555 Camino Del Mar, Del Mar, CA 92014; (858) 755-8876 **Wine list** *Italy, California* **Wine prices** *Moderate* **Corkage** *$12* **Cuisine** *Italian* **Menu prices** *$10–$25*

IL FORNAIO CUCINA ITALIANA 🍷
18051 Von Karman Ave., Irvine, CA 92612; (949) 261-1444 **Wine list** *Italy, California* **Wine prices** *Moderate* **Corkage** *$16* **Cuisine** *Italian* **Menu prices** *$15–$25*

IL FORNAIO CUCINA ITALIANA
1800 Rosecrans Ave., Manhattan Beach, CA 90266; (310) 725-9555 **Wine list** *California* **Wine prices** *Moderate* **Cuisine** *Italian* **Menu prices** *$9–$22*

IL FORNAIO CUCINA ITALIANA
1. W. Colorado Blvd., Pasadena, CA 91103; (626) 683-9797 **Wine list** *California, Italy* **Wine prices** *Moderate* **Corkage** *$10* **Cuisine** *Italian* **Menu prices** *$8–$20*

IL FORNAIO CUCINA ITALIANA
1179 Galleria Blvd., Roseville, CA 95678; (916) 788-1200 **Wine list** *California, Italy* **Wine prices** *Moderate* **Cuisine** *Italian* **Menu prices** *$10–$25*

IL FORNAIO CUCINA ITALIANA
400 Capitol Mall, Sacramento, CA 95814; (916) 446-4100 **Wine list** *California* **Wine prices** *Moderate* **Cuisine** *Italian* **Menu prices** *$15–$25*

JELLYFISH RESTAURANT
Sheraton Petaluma Hotel, 745 Baywood Drive, Petaluma, CA 94954; (707) 283-2900 **Wine list** *California* **Wine prices** *Moderate* **Corkage** *$12* **Cuisine** *Pan-Asian* **Menu prices** *$18–$26*

J.M. ROSEN'S WATERFRONT GRILL
54 E. Washington St., Petaluma, CA 94952; (707) 773-3200 **Wine list** *California* **Wine prices** Inexpensive **Cuisine** *Contemporary American* **Menu prices** *$15–$30*

JOE GREENSLEEVES
220 N. Orange St., Redlands, CA 92374; (909) 792-6969 **Wine list** *California* **Wine prices** *Moderate* **Cuisine** *Steak house* **Menu prices** *$18–$30*

JOHANNES
196 S. Indian Canyon, Palm Springs, CA 92262; (760) 778-0017 **Wine list** *California* **Wine prices** *Moderate* **Corkage** *$10* **Cuisine** *Contemporary* **Menu prices** *$17–$34*

JOHN ASH & CO.
Vintners Inn, 4330 Barnes Road, Santa Rosa, CA 95403; (707) 527-7687 **Wine list** *California, France* **Wine prices** *Moderate* **Corkage** *$20* **Cuisine** *American* **Menu prices** *$18–$30*

Grand Award   Best of Award of Excellence   Award of Excellence

JORDAN'S AT THE CLAREMONT
Claremont Resort, Ashby & Domingo Aves., Oakland, CA 94623; (510) 549-8510 **Wine list** *California* **Wine prices** *Moderate* **Corkage** *$15* **Cuisine** *Californian/Pacific Rim* **Menu prices** *$20–$30*

J. TAYLOR'S
L'Auberge Del Mar, 1540 Camino Del Mar, Del Mar, CA 92014; (858) 793-6460 **Wine list** *California* **Wine prices** Inexpensive **Corkage** *$15* **Cuisine** *Californian* **Menu prices** *$16–$32*

KELLY'S RESTAURANT
5716 E. Second St., Naples Island, CA 90803; (562) 433-4983 **Wine list** *California* **Wine prices** *Moderate* **Corkage** *$15* **Cuisine** *Steak house* **Menu prices** *$19–$70*

KEMO SABE
3958 Fifth Ave., San Diego, CA 92103; (619) 220-6802 **Wine list** *California* **Wine prices** *Moderate* **Corkage** *$10* **Cuisine** *Asian/regional* **Menu prices** *$13–$26*

KIRBY'S CREEKSIDE RESTAURANT & BAR
101 Broad St., Nevada City, CA 95959; (530) 265-3445 **Wine list** *California, Oregon* **Wine prices** *Moderate* **Corkage** *$14* **Cuisine** *American/European* **Menu prices** *$16–$27*

THE KITCHEN
2225 Hurley Way, Sacramento, CA 95825; (916) 568-7171 **Wine list** *California* **Wine prices** *Moderate* **Corkage** *$18* **Cuisine** *Contemporary* **Menu prices** *Prix fixe only; $115*

KULETO'S ITALIAN RESTAURANT
Hotel Los Gatos, 210 E. Main St., Los Gatos, CA 95030; (408) 354-8290 **Wine list** *California, Italy* **Wine prices** *Moderate* **Corkage** *$15* **Cuisine** *Californian/Italian* **Menu prices** *$16–$28*

KULETO'S TRATTORIA
1095 Rollins Road, Burlingame, CA 94010; (650) 342-4922 **Wine list** *California, Italy* **Wine prices** *Moderate* **Corkage** *$12* **Cuisine** *Northern Italian* **Menu prices** *$11–$22*

LA MARINA
Four Seasons Resort Santa Barbara, 1260 Channel Drive, Santa Barbara, CA 93108; (805) 565-8238 **Wine list** *California* **Wine prices** *Expensive* **Corkage** *$20* **Cuisine** *Californian* **Menu prices** *$19–$36*

LA QUINTA GRILL 🍷
78-045 Calle Cadiz, La Quinta, CA 92253; (760) 564-4443 **Wine list** *California* **Wine prices** Inexpensive **Cuisine** *Californian* **Menu prices** *$13–$29*

THE LARK CREEK INN 🍷
234 Magnolia Ave., Larkspur, CA 94939; (415) 924-7766 **Wine list** *California* **Wine prices** *Moderate* **Cuisine** *Contemporary American* **Menu prices** *$16–$31*

LASALETTE 🍷
18625 Sonoma Highway 12, Sonoma, CA 95476; (707) 938-1927 **Wine list** *California, Portugal* **Wine prices** Inexpensive **Cuisine** *Portuguese* **Menu prices** *$16–$20*

LA TOQUE 🍷
Rancho Caymus Inn, 1140 Rutherford Road, Rutherford, CA 94573; (707) 963-9770 **Wine list** *California, France* **Wine prices** *Moderate* **Corkage** *$18* **Cuisine** *French* **Menu prices** *Prix fixe only; $92*

LA TRAVIATA RESTAURANT 🍷
301 Cedar Ave., Long Beach, CA 90802; (562) 432-8022 **Wine list** *California* **Wine prices** *Moderate* **Corkage** *$15* **Cuisine** *Italian* **Menu prices** *$14–$29*

LAUREL RESTAURANT & BAR 🍷🍷
505 Laurel St., San Diego, CA 92101; (619) 239-2222 **Wine list** *California, France* **Wine prices** *Moderate* **Corkage** *$25* **Cuisine** *Mediterranean* **Menu prices** *$21–$32*

LAVANDA 🍷
185 University Ave., Palo Alto, CA 94301; (650) 321-3514 **Wine list** *California, France, Italy* **Wine prices** *Moderate* **Corkage** *$15* **Cuisine** *Mediterranean* **Menu prices** *$13–$29*

LA VIE EN ROSE RESTAURANT 🍷
240 S. State College Blvd., Brea, CA 92821; (714) 529-8333 **Wine list** *California, France* **Wine prices** *Moderate* **Corkage** *$15* **Cuisine** *Provençal* **Menu prices** *Prix fixe only; $35–$48*

LE CAFÉ 🍷
32037 Agoura Road, Westlake Village, CA 91361; (818) 889-9105 **Wine list** *California* **Wine prices** *Moderate* **Cuisine** *American/Mediterranean* **Menu prices** *$12–$26*

🍷🍷🍷 Grand Award 🍷🍷 Best of Award of Excellence 🍷 Award of Excellence

LE CHÊNE RESTAURANT
12625 Sierra Highway, Sleepy Valley, CA 91390; (661) 251-4315 **Wine list** *California, France* **Wine prices** *Moderate* **Cuisine** *French* **Menu prices** *$14–$25*

LEFT BANK
507 Magnolia Ave., Larkspur, CA 94939; (415) 927-3331 **Wine list** *France, California* **Wine prices** *Moderate* **Corkage** *$10* **Cuisine** *French* **Menu prices** *$11–$22*

LEFT BANK
635 Santa Cruz Ave., Menlo Park, CA 94025; (650) 473-6543 **Wine list** *California, France* **Wine prices** *Moderate* **Corkage** *$10* **Cuisine** *French* **Menu prices** *$11–$22*

LEFT BANK
60 Crescent Drive, Pleasant Hill, CA 94523; (925) 288-1222 **Wine list** *France, California* **Wine prices** *Moderate* **Corkage** *$10* **Cuisine** *French* **Menu prices** *$11–$22*

LEGACY RESTAURANT
1701 S. Catalina Ave., Redondo Beach, CA 90277; (310) 375-8006 **Wine list** *California, France* **Wine prices** *Moderate* **Corkage** *$10* **Cuisine** *Northern Italian* **Menu prices** *$10–$28*

LE PAON
45-640 Highway 74, Palm Desert, CA 92260; (760) 568-3651 **Wine list** *California* **Wine prices** *Expensive* **Cuisine** *French/continental* **Menu prices** *$18–$40*

LE PAPILLON RESTAURANT
410 Saratoga Ave., San Jose, CA 95129; (408) 296-3730 **Wine list** *California, Burgundy, Bordeaux* **Wine prices** *Moderate* **Corkage** *$20* **Cuisine** *Contemporary French* **Menu prices** *$25–$48*

LE PETIT PIER
7238 North Lake Blvd., Tahoe Vista, CA 96148; (530) 546-4464 **Wine list** *California, France* **Wine prices** *Moderate* **Corkage** *$20* **Cuisine** *French* **Menu prices** *$17–$30*

L'ESCALE RESTAURANT
Coronado Island Marriott Resort, 2000 Second St., Coronado, CA 92118; (619) 522-3150 **Wine list** *California* **Wine prices** *Moderate* **Cuisine** *Californian* **Menu prices** *$14–$27*

LEWMARNELS RESTAURANT

Best Western Station House Inn, 901 Park Ave., South Lake Tahoe, CA 96150; (530) 542-1072 **Wine list** *California* **Wine prices** *Moderate* **Corkage** *$15* **Cuisine** *American/continental* **Menu prices** *$18–$39*

L'OPERA RISTORANTE

101 Pine Ave., Long Beach, CA 90802; (562) 491-0066 **Wine list** *Italy, California* **Wine prices** *Moderate* **Corkage** *$15* **Cuisine** *Italian* **Menu prices** *$17–$25*

LG'S PRIME STEAKHOUSE

78525 Highway 111, La Quinta, CA 92253; (760) 771-9911 **Wine list** *California* **Wine prices** *Moderate* **Corkage** *$20* **Cuisine** *Steak house* **Menu prices** *$20–$64*

LG'S PRIME STEAKHOUSE

74225 Highway 111, Palm Desert, CA 92260; (760) 779-9799 **Wine list** *California* **Wine prices** *Expensive* **Corkage** *$20* **Cuisine** *Steak house* **Menu prices** *$20–$68*

LG'S PRIME STEAKHOUSE

255 S. Palm Canyon Drive, Palm Springs, CA 92262; (760) 416-1779 **Wine list** *California* **Wine prices** *Expensive* **Corkage** *$20* **Cuisine** *Steak house* **Menu prices** *$24–$68*

LOS GATOS BREWING CO.

130-G N. Santa Cruz Ave., Los Gatos, CA 95030; (408) 395-9929 **Wine list** *California* **Wine prices** *Moderate* **Corkage** *$18* **Cuisine** *Californian* **Menu prices** *$12–$28*

LOU & MICKEY'S AT THE GASLAMP

224 Fifth Ave., San Diego, CA 92101; (619) 237-4900 **Wine list** *California, France* **Wine prices** *Moderate* **Corkage** *$10* **Cuisine** *Steak house* **Menu prices** *$19–$29*

LUCKY'S

1279 Coast Village Road, Montecito, CA 93108; (805) 565-7540 **Wine list** *France, California* **Wine prices** *Moderate* **Corkage** *$15* **Cuisine** *Steak house* **Menu prices** *$12–$56*

MADRONA MANOR

Madrona Manor Country Inn, 1001 Westside Road, Healdsburg, CA 95448; (707) 433-4231 **Wine list** *California* **Wine prices** *Moderate* **Corkage** *$15* **Cuisine** *Californian/French* **Menu prices** *Prix fixe only; $17–$29*

MAGIC LAMP INN
8189 Foothill Blvd., Rancho Cucamonga, CA 91730; (909) 981-8659 **Wine list** *California* **Wine prices** *Moderate* **Corkage** *$10* **Cuisine** *American* **Menu prices** *$18–$37*

MARCHÉ
898 Santa Cruz Ave., Menlo Park, CA 94025; (650) 324-9092 **Wine list** *Burgundy, California* **Wine prices** *Moderate* **Corkage** *$25* **Cuisine** *French* **Menu prices** *$24–$36*

MARCHÉ AUX FLEURS
23 Ross Common, Ross, CA 94957; (415) 925-9200 **Wine list** *California* **Wine prices** *Moderate* **Corkage** *$15* **Cuisine** *Provençal/Californian* **Menu prices** *$16–$24*

THE MARINE ROOM
La Jolla Beach & Tennis Club, 2000 Spindrift Drive, La Jolla, CA 92037; (858) 459-7222 **Wine list** *California* **Wine prices** *Moderate* **Corkage** *$20* **Cuisine** *International* **Menu prices** *$24–$34*

MARINUS RESTAURANT
Bernardus Lodge, 415 Carmel Valley Road, Carmel Valley, CA 93924; (831) 658-3500 **Wine list** *California, Burgundy, Bordeaux, Champagne* **Wine selections** *1,765* **Number of bottles** *34,000* **Wine prices** *Moderate* **Corkage** *$30* **Cuisine** *Californian/French* **Menu prices** *$24–$38* **Credit cards** *AX, MC, VS*
Grand Award since 2001

MARIO'S PLACE
3646 Mission Inn Ave., Riverside, CA 92501; (909) 684-7755 **Wine list** *California, Italy* **Wine prices** *Moderate* **Corkage** *$10* **Cuisine** *Northern Italian* **Menu prices** *$13–$29*

MARKET CITY CAFFÉ
164 E. Palm Ave., Burbank, CA 91502; (818) 840-7036 **Wine list** *California, Italy* **Wine prices** *Moderate* **Cuisine** *Italian* **Menu prices** *$15–$20*

MARTINI HOUSE
1245 Spring St., St. Helena, CA 94574; (707) 963-2233 **Wine list** *California, France, Italy* **Wine prices** *Moderate* **Corkage** *$20* **Cuisine** *Californian* **Menu prices** *$19–$32*

MASSIMO RISTORANTE ITALIANO
69-820 Highway 111, Rancho Mirage, CA 92270; (760) 321-6835 **Wine list** *California, Italy* **Wine prices** *Moderate* **Cuisine** *Italian* **Menu prices** *$15–$35*

MAX RESTAURANT 🍷
13355 Ventura Blvd., Sherman Oaks, CA 91423; (818) 784-2915 **Wine list** *California* **Wine prices** *Moderate* **Corkage** *$12* **Cuisine** *Californian/Asian* **Menu prices** *$16–$24*

MERITAGE RESTAURANT & BAR 🍷
897 S. Coast Highway 101, Encinitas, CA 92024; (760) 634-3350 **Wine list** *California* **Wine prices** *Moderate* **Cuisine** *Contemporary American* **Menu prices** *$14–$26*

MICHI 🍷
903 Manhattan Ave., Manhattan Beach, CA 90266; (310) 376-0613 **Wine list** *California* **Wine prices** Inexpensive **Corkage** *$10* **Cuisine** *Pacific Rim/French/Italian* **Menu prices** *$10–$28*

MILLE FLEURS 🍷
6009 Paseo Delicias, Rancho Santa Fe, CA 92067; (858) 756-3085 **Wine list** *California, France* **Wine prices** *Expensive* **Corkage** *$30* **Cuisine** *Californian/French* **Menu prices** *$28–$39*

MI PIACE 🍷
801 N. San Fernando Road, Burbank, CA 91501; (818) 843-1111 **Wine list** *Italy, California* **Wine prices** *Moderate* **Cuisine** *Northern Italian* **Menu prices** *$8–$18*

MI PIACE 🍷
4799 Commons Way, Calabasas, CA 91302; (818) 591-8822 **Wine list** *California, Italy* **Wine prices** *Moderate* **Corkage** *$8* **Cuisine** *Italian* **Menu prices** *$12–$28*

MI PIACE 🍷
25 E. Colorado Blvd., Pasadena, CA 91105; (626) 795-3131 **Wine list** *California, Italy* **Wine prices** *Moderate* **Corkage** *$8* **Cuisine** *Italian* **Menu prices** *$11–$25*

MIRÓ 🍷🍷
Bacara Resort & Spa, 8301 Hollister Ave., Santa Barbara, CA 93117; (805) 968-0100 **Wine list** *California, France, Italy* **Wine prices** *Expensive* **Cuisine** *French/Californian* **Menu prices** *$25–$38*

MISTRAL 🍷
370-6 Bridge Parkway, Redwood Shores, CA 94065; (650) 802-9222 **Wine list** *California* **Wine prices** *Moderate* **Corkage** *$15* **Cuisine** *International* **Menu prices** *$14–$25*

MISTRAL 🍷
13422 Ventura Blvd., Sherman Oaks, CA 91423; (818) 981-6650 **Wine list** *California* **Wine prices** *Moderate* **Corkage** *$10* **Cuisine** *French* **Menu prices** *$18–$35*

MIXX RESTAURANT & BAR 🍷
135 Fourth St., Santa Rosa, CA 95401; (707) 573-1344 **Wine list** *California* **Wine prices** *Moderate* **Corkage** *$15* **Cuisine** *Regional* **Menu prices** *$13–$27*

MONTRIO 🍷
414 Calle Principal, Monterey, CA 93940; (831) 648-8880 **Wine list** *California* **Wine prices** Inexpensive **Corkage** *$12* **Cuisine** *American/European* **Menu prices** *$14–$32*

MORTON'S OF CHICAGO 🍷
3400 W. Olive Ave., Burbank, CA 91505; (818) 238-0424 **Wine list** *California* **Wine prices** *Expensive* **Corkage** *$15* **Cuisine** *Steak house* **Menu prices** *$25–$45*

MORTON'S OF CHICAGO 🍷
74-880 Country Club Drive, Palm Desert, CA 92260; (760) 340-6865 **Wine list** *California* **Wine prices** *Expensive* **Corkage** *$15* **Cuisine** *Steak house* **Menu prices** *$30–$35*

MORTON'S OF CHICAGO 🍷
521 L St., Sacramento, CA 95814; (916) 442-5091 **Wine list** *California* **Wine prices** *Expensive* **Corkage** *$15* **Cuisine** *Steak house* **Menu prices** *$22–$72*

MORTON'S OF CHICAGO 🍷
The Harbor Club, 285 J. St., San Diego, CA 92101; (619) 696-3369 **Wine list** *California* **Wine prices** *Expensive* **Corkage** *$15* **Cuisine** *Steak house* **Menu prices** *$24–$36*

MORTON'S OF CHICAGO 🍷
1641 W. Sunflower Ave., Santa Ana, CA 92704; (714) 444-4834 **Wine list** *California* **Wine prices** *Expensive* **Corkage** *$15* **Cuisine** *Steak house* **Menu prices** *$20–$64*

MR. STOX 🍷🍷🍷
1105 E. Katella Ave., Anaheim, CA 92805; (714) 634-2994 **Wine list** *Bordeaux, California* **Wine selections** *900* **Number of bottles** *24,000* **Wine prices** *Moderate* **Corkage** *$15* **Cuisine** *Contemporary American* **Menu prices** *$19–$34* **Credit cards** *AX, MC, VS, DV*
Grand Award since 1983

NAPA 29 🍷

280 Teller St., Corona, CA 92879; (909) 273-0529 **Wine list** *California* **Wine prices** *Moderate* **Corkage** *$20* **Cuisine** *Regional* **Menu prices** *$18–$38*

NAPA ROSE RESTAURANT 🍷🍷

Disney's Grand Californian Hotel, 1600 S. Disneyland Drive, Anaheim, CA 92802; (714) 300-7170 **Wine list** *California* **Wine prices** *Expensive* **Corkage** *$17* **Cuisine** *Contemporary Californian* **Menu prices** *$18–$30*

NAPA VALLEY GRILLE 🍷🍷

6795 Washington St., Yountville, CA 94599; (707) 944-8686 **Wine list** *California* **Wine prices** *Moderate* **Corkage** *$15* **Cuisine** *Californian* **Menu prices** *$13–$24*

NAVIO 🍷🍷

The Ritz-Carlton Half Moon Bay, 1 Miramontes Point Road, Half Moon Bay, CA 94019; (650) 712-7000 **Wine list** *California, France* **Wine prices** *Expensive* **Corkage** *$25* **Cuisine** *Californian* **Menu prices** *$22–$32*

NEPENTHE 🍷

Highway 1, Big Sur, CA 93920; (831) 667-2345 **Wine list** *California* **Wine prices** *Moderate* **Corkage** *$15* **Cuisine** *Californian* **Menu prices** *$12–$35*

NEPHELES 🍷

1169 Ski Run Blvd., South Lake Tahoe, CA 96150; (530) 544-8130 **Wine list** *California* **Wine prices** *Moderate* **Corkage** *$15* **Cuisine** *Californian* **Menu prices** *$18–$26*

NICO'S 🍷

5760 E. Second St., Long Beach, CA 90803; (562) 434-4479 **Wine list** *California* **Wine prices** *Moderate* **Corkage** *$15* **Cuisine** *American* **Menu prices** *$22–$44*

NIEBAUM-COPPOLA PALO ALTO 🍷

473 University Ave., Palo Alto, CA 94301; (650) 752-0350 **Wine list** *California* **Wine prices** Inexpensive **Corkage** *$15* **Cuisine** *Southern Italian* **Menu prices** *$10–$29*

OLD BATH HOUSE RESTAURANT 🍷

620 Ocean View Blvd., Pacific Grove, CA 93950; (831) 375-5195 **Wine list** *California* **Wine prices** *Moderate* **Corkage** *$20* **Cuisine** *Contemporary American* **Menu prices** *$25–$50*

OLIO E LIMONE RISTORANTE 🍷
11 W. Victoria St., Santa Barbara, CA 93101; (805) 899-2699 **Wine list** *Italy, California* **Wine prices** *Moderate* **Corkage** *$15* **Cuisine** *Italian* **Menu prices** *$17–$34*

OLIVETO 🍷
5655 College Ave., Oakland, CA 94618; (510) 547-5356 **Wine list** *Italy* **Wine prices** *Expensive* **Corkage** *$18* **Cuisine** *Italian* **Menu prices** *$14–$28*

OMRI & BONI RESTAURANT 🍷
47474 Washington St., La Quinta, CA 92253; (760) 777-1315 **Wine list** *California* **Wine prices** *Moderate* **Corkage** *$20* **Cuisine** *Mediterranean* **Menu prices** *$24–$38*

OSTERIA PANEVINO 🍷
722 Fifth Ave., San Diego, CA 92101; (619) 595-7959 **Wine list** *Italy, California* **Wine prices** *Moderate* **Corkage** *$15* **Cuisine** *Italian* **Menu prices** *$15–$30*

OYSTERS 🍷🍷
2515 E. Coast Highway, Corona Del Mar, CA 92625; (949) 675-7411 **Wine list** *California* **Wine prices** *Moderate* **Corkage** *$15* **Cuisine** *Pacific Rim* **Menu prices** *$12–$30*

PACIFIC FISH COMPANY RESTAURANT & BAR 🍷
Embassy Suites San Diego Bay, 601 Pacific Highway, San Diego, CA 92101; (619) 232-0274 **Wine list** *California* **Wine prices** *Moderate* **Corkage** *$10* **Cuisine** *Seafood* **Menu prices** *$15–$35*

PACIFIC'S EDGE 🍷🍷🍷
Highlands Inn–Park Hyatt Carmel, 120 Highlands Drive, Carmel, CA 93923; (831) 622-5445 **Wine list** *California, Bordeaux, Burgundy, Champagne* **Wine selections** *1,700* **Number of bottles** *32,000* **Wine prices** *Expensive* **Cuisine** *Contemporary Californian* **Menu prices** *$48–$64* **Credit cards** *AX, MC, VS, DV*
Grand Award since 1991

PACIFICA DEL MAR 🍷
1555 Camino Del Mar, Del Mar, CA 92014; (858) 792-0476 **Wine list** *California* **Wine prices** *Moderate* **Corkage** *$15* **Cuisine** *Californian* **Menu prices** *$17–$30*

PACIFICA IN THE DESERT 🍷
73505 El Paseo, Palm Desert, CA 92260; (760) 674-8666 **Wine list** *California* **Wine prices** *Moderate* **Corkage** *$15* **Cuisine** *Seafood* **Menu prices** *$18–$28*

PAJARO STREET GRILL 🍷
435 Pajaro St., Salinas, CA 93901; (831) 754-3738 **Wine list** *California* **Wine prices** *Moderate* **Corkage** *$7* **Cuisine** *Californian* **Menu prices** *$10–$22*

PAMPLEMOUSSE GRILLE 🍷🍷
514 Via De La Valle, Solana Beach, CA 92075; (858) 792-9090 **Wine list** *California, Bordeaux, Burgundy* **Wine prices** *Moderate* **Corkage** *$20* **Cuisine** *French/continental* **Menu prices** *$22–$34*

PANGAEA 🍷
250 Main St., Point Arena, CA 95468; (707) 882-3001 **Wine list** *California* **Wine prices** *Moderate* **Corkage** *$13* **Cuisine** *Californian/French* **Menu prices** *$18–$27*

PAOLO'S 🍷🍷
333 W. San Carlos St., San Jose, CA 95110; (408) 294-2558 **Wine list** *Italy, France, California* **Wine prices** *Moderate* **Corkage** *$15* **Cuisine** *Contemporary Italian* **Menu prices** *$15–$32*

PARCEL 104 🍷
Santa Clara Marriott, 2700 Mission College Blvd., Santa Clara, CA 95054; (408) 970-6104 **Wine list** *California* **Wine prices** *Moderate* **Corkage** *$20* **Cuisine** *Contemporary American* **Menu prices** *$16–$32*

PARKWAY GRILL 🍷
510 S. Arroyo Parkway, Pasadena, CA 91105; (626) 795-1001 **Wine list** *California* **Wine prices** *Moderate* **Cuisine** *American* **Menu prices** *$15–$32*

PASSIONFISH 🍷
701 Lighthouse Ave., Pacific Grove, CA 93950; (831) 655-3311 **Wine list** *California* **Wine prices** Inexpensive **Corkage** *$20* **Cuisine** *Californian* **Menu prices** *$13–$21*

PATRICK DAVID'S RESTAURANT & BAR 🍷
416 Sycamore Valley Road W., Danville, CA 94526; (925) 838-7611 **Wine list** *California, France* **Wine prices** *Moderate* **Corkage** *$15* **Cuisine** *Californian/Asian* **Menu prices** *$23–$29*

PEARL ALLEY BISTRO 🍷
110 Pearl Alley, Santa Cruz, CA 95060; (831) 429-8070 **Wine list** *Italy, California* **Wine prices** *Moderate* **Corkage** *$10* **Cuisine** *Contemporary European* **Menu prices** *$15–$25*

PÈPPOLI
The Inn at Spanish Bay, 2700 17 Mile Drive, Pebble Beach, CA 93953; (831) 647-7433 **Wine list** *California, Bordeaux, Italy* **Wine prices** *Expensive* **Corkage** *$20* **Cuisine** *Tuscan* **Menu prices** *$18–$29*

PIACERE
727 Laurel St., San Carlos, CA 94070; (650) 592-3536 **Wine list** *California, Italy* **Wine prices** *Moderate* **Cuisine** *Italian* **Menu prices** *$14–$26*

PINOT BISTRO
12969 Ventura Blvd., Studio City, CA 91604; (818) 990-0500 **Wine list** *California, France* **Wine prices** *Moderate* **Corkage** *No charge* **Cuisine** *French/Californian* **Menu prices** *$16–$24*

PINOT BLANC
641 Main St., St. Helena, CA 94574; (707) 963-6191 **Wine list** *California* **Wine prices** *Moderate* **Corkage** *No charge* **Cuisine** *Californian/French* **Menu prices** *$15–$26*

PINOT PROVENCE
Westin South Coast Plaza, 686 Anton Blvd., Costa Mesa, CA 92626; (714) 444-5900 **Wine list** *Burgundy, California, Bordeaux* **Wine prices** *Expensive* **Corkage** *No charge* **Cuisine** *French/Mediterranean* **Menu prices** *$18–$36*

PIZZAIOLI
3920 Grand Ave., Unit A, Chino, CA 91710; (909) 590-5454 **Wine list** *California, Italy* **Wine prices** *Moderate* **Corkage** *$10* **Cuisine** *Italian* **Menu prices** *$12–$32*

THE PLUMED HORSE
14555 Big Basin Way, Saratoga, CA 95070; (408) 867-4711 **Wine list** *California, Burgundy* **Wine selections** *750* **Number of bottles** *19,800* **Wine prices** *Moderate* **Corkage** *$25* **Cuisine** *French/Californian* **Menu prices** *$20–$34* **Credit cards** *AX, MC, VS, DV*
Grand Award since 1987

PLUMPJACK CAFÉ
Squaw Valley Inn, 1920 Squaw Valley Road, Olympic Valley, CA 96146; (530) 583-1576 **Wine list** *California* **Wine prices** *Moderate* **Corkage** *$14* **Cuisine** *Mediterranean/American* **Menu prices** *$20–$28*

PRIMA 🍷🍷
1522 N. Main St., Walnut Creek, CA 94596; (925) 935-7780 **Wine list** *California, France, Italy, Germany* **Wine prices** *Moderate* **Cuisine** *Italian* **Menu prices** *$16–$25*

PRIME 10 STEAKHOUSE 🍷
Polo Plaza, 3702 Via de la Valle, Del Mar, CA 92014; (858) 523-0007 **Wine list** *California* **Wine prices** *Moderate* **Corkage** *$20* **Cuisine** *Steak house* **Menu prices** *$16–$52*

PRIME CHOP HOUSE 🍷
74-040 Highway 111, Palm Desert, CA 92260; (760) 779-9888 **Wine list** *California* **Wine prices** *Moderate* **Corkage** *$15* **Cuisine** *Steak house* **Menu prices** *$19–$39*

PRIME CHOP HOUSE 🍷
262 S. Palm Canyon, Palm Springs, CA 92262; (760) 320-4500 **Wine list** *California* **Wine prices** *Moderate* **Corkage** *$15* **Cuisine** *Steak house* **Menu prices** *$19–$49*

PRINCE OF WALES 🍷
Hotel del Coronado, 1500 Orange Ave., Coronado, CA 92118; (619) 522-8490 **Wine list** *Bordeaux* **Wine prices** *Expensive* **Cuisine** *Continental* **Menu prices** *$22–$33*

THE QUIET WOMAN 🍷
3224 E. Pacific Coast Highway, Corona Del Mar, CA 92625; (949) 640-7440 **Wine list** *California* **Wine prices** *Moderate* **Cuisine** *American* **Menu prices** *$20–$28*

RAINWATER'S 🍷🍷
1202 Kettner Blvd., San Diego, CA 92101; (619) 233-5757 **Wine list** *California, Bordeaux, Port* **Wine prices** *Moderate* **Corkage** *$15* **Cuisine** *American* **Menu prices** *$23–$43*

THE RANCH HOUSE RESTAURANT 🍷🍷
South Lomita, Ojai, CA 92869; (805) 646-2360 **Wine list** *California* **Wine prices** *Moderate* **Corkage** *$17* **Cuisine** *Continental* **Menu prices** *$20–$32*

RANCHO VALENCIA RESTAURANT 🍷
Rancho Valencia Resort, 5921 Valencia Circle, Rancho Santa Fe, CA 92067; (619) 756-3645 **Wine list** *California, France* **Wine prices** *Moderate* **Corkage** *$25* **Cuisine** *Californian/Asian* **Menu prices** *$27–$36*

THE RATTLESNAKE 🍷
Trump 29 Casino & Hotel, 46-200 Harrison Place, Coachella, CA 92236; (760) 775-2880 **Wine list** *California* **Wine prices** *Moderate* **Corkage** *$15* **Cuisine** *Contemporary American* **Menu prices** *$19–$34*

REDWOOD FOREST RESTAURANT 🍷
121 W. Third St., Chico, CA 95928; (530) 343-4315 **Wine list** *California* **Wine prices** Inexpensive **Corkage** *$5* **Cuisine** *Californian* **Menu prices** *$11–$18*

RENDEZVOUS INN & RESTAURANT 🍷
647 N. Main St., Fort Bragg, CA 95437; (800) 491-8142 **Wine list** *California* **Wine prices** Inexpensive **Corkage** *$13* **Cuisine** *French/Californian* **Menu prices** *$16–$25*

RESTAURANT 301 AT THE HOTEL CARTER 🍷🍷🍷
Carter House Inns, 301 L St., Eureka, CA 95501; (707) 445-1390 **Wine list** *California, Bordeaux, Burgundy, Oregon, Port, Germany* **Wine selections** *3,880* **Number of bottles** *32,000* **Wine prices** *Moderate* **Corkage** *$25* **Cuisine** *Californian/French* **Menu prices** *$18–$26* **Credit cards** *AX, MC, VS, DV*
Grand Award since 1998

THE RESTAURANT AT MEADOWOOD 🍷
Meadowood Napa Valley, 900 Meadowood Lane, St. Helena, CA 94574; (800) 458-8080 **Wine list** *California* **Wine prices** *Moderate* **Corkage** *$15* **Cuisine** *Californian* **Menu prices** *$29–$36*

THE RESTAURANT AT STEVENSWOOD 🍷
Stevenswood Lodge, 8211 N. Highway 1, Little River, CA 95456; (800) 421-2810 **Wine list** *California* **Wine prices** *Moderate* **Corkage** *$20* **Cuisine** *Continental* **Menu prices** *$25–$38*

RESTAURANT NINE-TEN 🍷
The Grande Colonial Hotel, 910 Prospect St., La Jolla, CA 92037; (858) 964-5400 **Wine list** *California* **Wine prices** *Moderate* **Corkage** *$20* **Cuisine** *Californian* **Menu prices** *$16–$34*

RIO GRILL 🍷
101 Crossroads Blvd., Carmel, CA 93923; (831) 625-5436 **Wine list** *California* **Wine prices** *Moderate* **Cuisine** *Southwestern* **Menu prices** *$10–$28*

RISTORANTE MAMMA GINA 🍷
73-705 El Paseo, Palm Desert, CA 92260; (760) 568-9898 **Wine list** *California, Italy* **Wine prices** *Expensive* **Corkage** *$20* **Cuisine** *Tuscan* **Menu prices** *$15–$32*

RISTORANTE RUMARI 🍷
1826 S. Coast Highway, Laguna Beach, CA 92651; (949) 494-0400 **Wine list** *Italy, California* **Wine prices** *Moderate* **Corkage** *$15* **Cuisine** *Italian* **Menu prices** *$12–$38*

RISTORANTE TUSCANY 🍷
Desert Springs Marriott, 74855 Country Club Drive, Palm Desert, CA 92260; (760) 341-2211 **Wine list** *California, Italy* **Wine prices** *Moderate* **Corkage** *$20* **Cuisine** *Northern Italian* **Menu prices** *$24–$33*

THE RITZ RESTAURANT 🍷
880 Newport Center Drive, Newport Beach, CA 92660; (949) 720-1800 **Wine list** *California* **Wine prices** *Moderate* **Corkage** *$25* **Cuisine** *Continental* **Menu prices** *$23–$38*

RIVER'S END RESTAURANT & INN 🍷
11048 Highway 1, Jenner, CA 95450; (707) 865-2484 **Wine list** *California* **Wine prices** *Moderate* **Corkage** *$12* **Cuisine** *Continental* **Menu prices** *$19–$29*

ROPPONGI 🍷
875 Prospect St., La Jolla, CA 92037; (858) 551-5252 **Wine list** *California* **Wine prices** *Moderate* **Corkage** *$20* **Cuisine** *Asian* **Menu prices** *$18–$29*

ROXANNE'S 🍷
320 Magnolia Ave., Larkspur, CA 94939; (415) 924-5004 **Wine list** *France* **Wine prices** *Moderate* **Corkage** *$20* **Cuisine** *Contemporary* **Menu prices** *$20–$29*

ROY'S LA JOLLA 🍷
Costa Verde Center, 8670 Genesee Ave., San Diego, CA 92122; (858) 455-1616 **Wine list** *California* **Wine prices** *Moderate* **Cuisine** *Contemporary/Hawaiian* **Menu prices** *$15–$29*

ROY'S OF NEWPORT BEACH 🍷
453 Newport Center Drive, Newport Beach, CA 92660; (949) 640-7697 **Wine list** *California* **Wine prices** *Moderate* **Corkage** *$15* **Cuisine** *Contemporary/Hawaiian* **Menu prices** *$22–$35*

RUTH'S CHRIS STEAK HOUSE
11582 El Camino Real, Del Mar, CA 92130; (858) 755-1454 **Wine list** *California* **Wine prices** *Moderate* **Corkage** *$15* **Cuisine** *Steak house* **Menu prices** *$19–$33*

RUTH'S CHRIS STEAK HOUSE
2961-A Michelson Drive, Irvine, CA 92612; (949) 252-8848 **Wine list** *California* **Wine prices** *Moderate* **Corkage** *$15* **Cuisine** *Steak house* **Menu prices** *$19–$35*

RUTH'S CHRIS STEAK HOUSE
74-740 Highway 111, Palm Desert, CA 92260; (760) 779-1998 **Wine list** *California* **Wine prices** *Moderate* **Corkage** *$15* **Cuisine** *Steak house* **Menu prices** *$23–$69*

RUTH'S CHRIS STEAK HOUSE
1355 N. Harbor Drive, San Diego, CA 92101; (619) 233-1422 **Wine list** *California* **Wine prices** *Moderate* **Corkage** *$15* **Cuisine** *Steak house* **Menu prices** *$20–$35*

SADDLE PEAK LODGE
419 Cold Canyon Road, Calabasas, CA 91302; (818) 222-3888 **Wine list** *California* **Wine prices** *Expensive* **Corkage** *$15* **Cuisine** *American* **Menu prices** *$26–$42*

SADDLES STEAKHOUSE AT MACARTHUR PLACE
MacArthur Place Inn & Spa, 29 E. MacArthur St., Sonoma, CA 95476; (800) 722-1866 **Wine list** *California* **Wine prices** *Moderate* **Corkage** *$18* **Cuisine** *Steak house* **Menu prices** *$14–$48*

SALT CREEK GRILLE
32802 Pacific Coast Highway, Dana Point, CA 92629; (949) 661-7799 **Wine list** *California* **Wine prices** *Moderate* **Cuisine** *American* **Menu prices** *$10–$33*

SANTÉ
The Fairmont Sonoma Mission Inn, 100 Boyes Blvd., Boyes Hot Springs, CA 95416; (800) 862-4945 **Wine list** *California* **Wine prices** *Moderate* **Cuisine** *Californian* **Menu prices** *$23–$29*

SANTE RISTORANTE
7811 Herschel Ave., La Jolla, CA 92037; (858) 454-1315 **Wine list** *Italy* **Wine prices** *Expensive* **Cuisine** *Northern Italian* **Menu prices** *$11–$32*

SANTI RESTAURANT 🍷

21047 Geyserville Ave., Geyserville, CA 95441; (707) 857-1790 **Wine list** *California* **Wine prices** Inexpensive **Corkage** *$15* **Cuisine** *Northern Italian* **Menu prices** *$16–$25*

THE SARDINE FACTORY 🍷🍷🍷

701 Wave St., Monterey, CA 93940; (831) 373-3775 **Wine list** *California, Burgundy, Bordeaux* **Wine selections** *1,250* **Number of bottles** *25,000* **Wine prices** *Moderate* **Corkage** *$15* **Cuisine** *Seafood* **Menu prices** *$17–$26* **Credit cards** *AX, MC, VS, DV*

Grand Award since 1982

SAVANNAH STEAK & CHOP HOUSE 🍷

32441 Golden Lantern, Laguna Niguel, CA 92677; (949) 493-7107 **Wine list** *California* **Wine prices** *Moderate* **Corkage** *$12* **Cuisine** *Steak house* **Menu prices** *$11–$32*

SBICCA 🍷

215 15th St., Del Mar, CA 92014; (858) 481-1001 **Wine list** *California* **Wine prices** *Moderate* **Corkage** *$12* **Cuisine** *Contemporary American* **Menu prices** *$14–$24*

SCOTCH & SIRLOIN 🍷

1510 Anchors Way, Ventura, CA 93001; (805) 644-5566 **Wine list** *California* **Wine prices** Inexpensive **Corkage** *$10* **Cuisine** *Steak house* **Menu prices** *$14–$27*

SCOTT'S AMERICAN GRILL 🍷

27321 La Paz Road, Laguna Niguel, CA 92677; (949) 389-0055 **Wine list** *California* **Wine prices** *Moderate* **Cuisine** *American* **Menu prices** *$17–$32*

SCOTT'S SEAFOOD GRILL & BAR 🍷

3300 Bristol St., Costa Mesa, CA 92626; (714) 979-2400 **Wine list** *California* **Wine prices** *Moderate* **Corkage** *$15* **Cuisine** *American* **Menu prices** *$18–$32*

SEAGRILLE 🍷

Desert Springs AJW Marriott Resort & Spa, 74-855 Country Club Drive, Palm Desert, CA 92260; (760) 341-1725 **Wine list** *California* **Wine prices** *Expensive* **Corkage** *$20* **Cuisine** *Regional* **Menu prices** *$19–$39*

SHADOWBROOK RESTAURANT 🍷

1750 Wharf Road, Capitola-by-the-Sea, CA 95010; (831) 475-1511 **Wine list** *California* **Wine prices** *Moderate* **Corkage** *$15* **Cuisine** *Californian/continental* **Menu prices** *$13–$26*

SICILIAN CAFÉ 🍷
1020 Main St., Chico, CA 95928; (530) 345-2233 **Wine list** *California, Italy* **Wine prices** Inexpensive **Cuisine** *Californian/Italian* **Menu prices** *$9–$24*

SIERRA MAR 🍷🍷🍷
Post Ranch Inn, Highway 1, Big Sur, CA 93920; (831) 667-2800 **Wine list** *California, France* **Wine selections** *3,950* **Number of bottles** *24,200* **Wine prices** *Expensive* **Corkage** *$25* **Cuisine** *Californian* **Menu prices** *$33–$38* **Credit cards** *AX, MC, VS*
Grand Award since 1993

SKY ROOM 🍷🍷
La Valencia Hotel, 1132 Prospect St., La Jolla, CA 92037; (858) 454-0771 **Wine list** *California, France* **Wine prices** *Expensive* **Corkage** *$25* **Cuisine** *French/continental* **Menu prices** *$35–$50*

THE SKY ROOM 🍷
40 S. Locust Ave., Long Beach, CA 90802; (562) 983-2703 **Wine list** *France, California* **Wine prices** *Expensive* **Corkage** *$15* **Cuisine** *Contemporary American/French* **Menu prices** *$21–$38*

SMITTY'S GRILL 🍷
110 S. Lake Ave., Pasadena, CA 91101; (626) 792-9999 **Wine list** *California* **Wine prices** *Moderate* **Cuisine** *American* **Menu prices** *$9–$26*

SOLANO GRILL & BAR 🍷🍷
1133 Solano Ave., Albany, CA 94706; (510) 525-8686 **Wine list** *California, Bordeaux* **Wine prices** *Moderate* **Corkage** *$10* **Cuisine** *Californian/Asian* **Menu prices** *$13–$20*

SPAGHETTINI ITALIAN GRILL 🍷
3005 Old Ranch Parkway, Seal Beach, CA 90740; (562) 596-2199 **Wine list** *California* **Wine prices** *Moderate* **Corkage** *$12* **Cuisine** *Northern Italian* **Menu prices** *$22–$34*

SPAGO PALO ALTO 🍷
265 Lytton Ave., Palo Alto, CA 94301; (650) 833-1000 **Wine list** *California, France* **Wine prices** *Moderate* **Corkage** *$16* **Cuisine** *American* **Menu prices** *$14–$35*

ST. JAMES AT THE VINEYARD
265 S. Palm Canyon Drive, Palm Springs, CA 92262; (760) 320-8041 **Wine list** *California* **Wine prices** *Moderate* **Corkage** *$12* **Cuisine** *International* **Menu prices** *$18–$38*

STAR OF THE SEA
1360 N. Harbor Drive, San Diego, CA 92101; (619) 232-7408 **Wine list** *California* **Wine prices** Inexpensive **Cuisine** *Seafood* **Menu prices** *$18–$36*

STEAMER'S THE GRILLHOUSE
104 University Ave., Los Gatos, CA 95030; (408) 395-2722 **Wine list** *California* **Wine prices** *Moderate* **Corkage** *$12* **Cuisine** *Seafood* **Menu prices** *$17–$24*

SULLIVAN'S STEAKHOUSE
73505 El Paseo, Palm Desert, CA 92260; (760) 341-3560 **Wine list** *California* **Wine prices** *Moderate* **Corkage** *$20* **Cuisine** *Steak house* **Menu prices** *$17–$29*

SUNDANCE THE STEAKHOUSE
1921 El Camino Real, Palo Alto, CA 94306; (650) 321-6798 **Wine list** *California, France* **Wine prices** *Moderate* **Cuisine** *Steak house* **Menu prices** *$18–$40*

SUZANNE'S CUISINE
502 W. Ojai Ave., Ojai, CA 93023; (805) 640-1961 **Wine list** *California* **Wine prices** *Moderate* **Corkage** *$15* **Cuisine** *Contemporary* **Menu prices** *$19–$32*

THE SYCAMORE INN
8318 Foothill Blvd., Rancho Cucamonga, CA 91730; (909) 982-1104 **Wine list** *California* **Wine prices** *Moderate* **Cuisine** *Steak house* **Menu prices** *$16–$30*

SYRAH RESTAURANT
205 Fifth St., Santa Rosa, CA 95401; (707) 568-4002 **Wine list** *California, France, Australia* **Wine prices** Inexpensive **Corkage** *$15* **Cuisine** *Californian/French* **Menu prices** *$16–$24*

TAPENADE
7612 Fay Ave., La Jolla, CA 92037; (858) 551-7500 **Wine list** *California, France* **Wine prices** *Moderate* **Corkage** *$20* **Cuisine** *Provençal* **Menu prices** *$20–$26*

TAPS FISH HOUSE & BREWERY
101 E. Imperial Highway, Brea, CA 92821; (714) 257-0101 **Wine list** *California* **Wine prices** *Moderate* **Cuisine** *American* **Menu prices** *$15–$33*

TARPY'S ROADHOUSE
Highway 68 at Canyon Del Rey, Monterey, CA 93940; (831) 647-1444 **Wine list** *California* **Wine prices** *Moderate* **Corkage** *$12* **Cuisine** *American* **Menu prices** *$12–$30*

TERRA RESTAURANT & BAR
1270 Cleveland Ave., San Diego, CA 92103; (619) 293-7088 **Wine list** *California* **Wine prices** Inexpensive **Corkage** *$15* **Cuisine** *American* **Menu prices** *$14–$25*

THEO'S
3101 N. Main St., Soquel, CA 95073; (831) 462-3657 **Wine list** *California* **Wine prices** *Moderate* **Corkage** *$15* **Cuisine** *Californian* **Menu prices** *$18–$30*

TOP OF THE COVE
1216 Prospect St., La Jolla, CA 92037; (858) 454-7779 **Wine list** *California, France, Italy* **Wine prices** *Moderate* **Corkage** *$25* **Cuisine** *American* **Menu prices** *$24–$38*

TOP OF THE MARKET
750 N. Harbor Drive, San Diego, CA 92101; (619) 234-4TOP **Wine list** *California* **Wine prices** *Moderate* **Corkage** *$10* **Cuisine** *Californian/seafood* **Menu prices** *$15–$65*

TRATTORIA ACQUA
1298 Prospect St., La Jolla, CA 92037; (858) 454-0709 **Wine list** *Italy, California* **Wine prices** *Moderate* **Corkage** *$20* **Cuisine** *Northern Italian* **Menu prices** *$10–$28*

TUSCANY IL RISTORANTE
968 S. Westlake Blvd., Westlake Village, CA 91361; (805) 495-2768 **Wine list** *Italy, California, Bordeaux* **Wine prices** *Moderate* **Corkage** *$15* **Cuisine** *Northern Italian* **Menu prices** *$16–$28*

TUTTI MANGIA ITALIAN GRILL
102 Harvard Ave., Claremont, CA 91711; (909) 625-4669 **Wine list** *California, Italy* **Wine prices** *Moderate* **Corkage** *$12* **Cuisine** *Italian* **Menu prices** *$15–$25*

UNCLE YU'S
2005 Crow Canyon Place, San Ramon, CA 94583; (925) 275-1818 **Wine list** *California, France* **Wine prices** *Moderate* **Corkage** *$15* **Cuisine** *Chinese* **Menu prices** *$8–$24*

VIBRATO GRILL & JAZZ
2930 Beverly Glen Circle, Bel Air, CA 90077; (310) 474-9400 **Wine list** *California* **Wine prices** *Expensive* **Cuisine** *Steak house* **Menu prices** *$19–$36*

VIC STEWART'S, FAMOUS FOR STEAKS 🍷
850 South Broadway, Walnut Creek, CA 94596; (925) 943-5666 **Wine list** *California* **Wine prices** *Moderate* **Corkage** *$15* **Cuisine** *Steak house* **Menu prices** *$16–$32*

THE VICTORIAN RESTAURANT 🍷
Mendocino Hotel & Garden Suites, 45080 Main St., Mendocino, CA 95460; (707) 937-0511 **Wine list** *California* **Wine prices** *Moderate* **Corkage** *$13* **Cuisine** *Continental* **Menu prices** *$19–$32*

VICTORIAN ROOM 🍷
The Groveland Hotel at Yosemite National Park, 18767 Main St., Groveland, CA 95321; (209) 962-4000 **Wine list** *California* **Wine prices** *Moderate* **Corkage** *$15* **Cuisine** *Californian* **Menu prices** *$16–$22*

VIGILUCCI'S SEAFOOD & STEAKHOUSE 🍷
3878 Carlsbad Blvd., Carlsbad, CA 92008; (760) 434-2580 **Wine list** *Italy, California* **Wine prices** *Moderate* **Corkage** *$20* **Cuisine** *Steak house* **Menu prices** *$15–$35*

VIGILUCCI'S TRATTORIA 🍷
505 S. Coast Highway 101, Encinitas, CA 92024; (760) 942-7332 **Wine list** *Italy, California* **Wine prices** *Moderate* **Corkage** *$10* **Cuisine** *Italian* **Menu prices** *$10–$30*

VILLA CREEK 🍷
1144 Pine St., Paso Robles, CA 93446; (805) 238-3000 **Wine list** *California* **Wine prices** Inexpensive **Cuisine** *Californian* **Menu prices** *$10–$25*

VILLA NOVA 🍷🍷
3131 W. Coast Highway, Newport Beach, CA 92663; (949) 642-7880 **Wine list** *California, Bordeaux, Italy* **Wine prices** *Moderate* **Cuisine** *Italian* **Menu prices** *$10–$28*

THE VILLAGE PUB 🍷🍷
2967 Woodside Road, Woodside, CA 94062; (650) 851-9888 **Wine list** *California, France, Spain, Germany* **Wine prices** *Expensive* **Corkage** *$25* **Cuisine** *Contemporary American* **Menu prices** *$11–$34*

VINTAGE PRESS RESTAURANTE 🍷🍷
216 N. Willis St., Visalia, CA 93291; (559) 733-3033 **Wine list** *California, France, Italy* **Wine prices** *Moderate* **Cuisine** *Continental/European* **Menu prices** *$15–$35*

THE VINTAGE ROOM 🍷

Fess Parker's Wine Country Inn & Spa, 2860 Grand Ave., Los Olivos, CA 93441; (805) 688-7788 **Wine list** *California* **Wine prices** Inexpensive **Corkage** *$15* **Cuisine** *Californian* **Menu prices** *$18–$32*

VIOGNIER 🍷🍷

222 E. Fourth Ave., San Mateo, CA 94401; (650) 685-3727 **Wine list** *Burgundy, California, Italy, Bordeaux* **Wine prices** *Moderate* **Corkage** *$20* **Cuisine** *Californian/French* **Menu prices** *$17–$39*

VIVACE RISTORANTE 🍷

1910 Ralston Ave., Belmont, CA 94002; (650) 637-0611 **Wine list** *California, Italy* **Wine prices** *Moderate* **Corkage** *$15* **Cuisine** *Italian* **Menu prices** *$18–$22*

WALT'S WHARF 🍷

201 Main St., Seal Beach, CA 90740; (562) 598-4433 **Wine list** *California* **Wine prices** Inexpensive **Corkage** *$10* **Cuisine** *Seafood* **Menu prices** *$10–$30*

WAPPO BAR BISTRO 🍷

1226-B Washington St., Calistoga, CA 94515; (707) 942-4712 **Wine list** *California* **Wine prices** Inexpensive **Corkage** *$10* **Cuisine** *International* **Menu prices** *$12–$18*

WENTE VINEYARDS RESTAURANT 🍷🍷

5050 Arroyo Road, Livermore, CA 94550; (925) 456-2450 **Wine list** *California* **Wine prices** *Moderate* **Corkage** *$15* **Cuisine** *American* **Menu prices** *$20–$36*

WHALING STATION PRIME STEAKS & SEAFOOD 🍷

763 Wave St., Monterey, CA 93940; (831) 373-3778 **Wine list** *California, Bordeaux* **Wine prices** *Moderate* **Corkage** *$12* **Cuisine** *Steak house/seafood* **Menu prices** *$16–$30*

WICKETS BAR & BISTRO 🍷

Bernardus Lodge, 415 Carmel Valley Road, Carmel Valley, CA 93924; (831) 658-3500 **Wine list** *California, Burgundy, Bordeaux, Champagne* **Wine prices** *Moderate* **Corkage** *$20* **Cuisine** *French* **Menu prices** *$12–$19*

WINE CASK 🍷🍷🍷

813 Anacapa St., Santa Barbara, CA 93101; (805) 966-9463 **Wine list** *California, Burgundy, Bordeaux* **Wine selections** *2,000* **Number of bottles** *35,000* **Wine prices** *Moderate* **Corkage** *$25* **Cuisine** *Californian* **Menu prices** *$19–$28* **Credit cards** *AX, MC, VS*
Grand Award since 1994

THE WINESELLAR & BRASSERIE 🍷🍷🍷

9550 Waples St., San Diego, CA 92121; (858) 450-9576
Wine list *California, Bordeaux* **Wine selections** *2,680* **Number of bottles** *21,170* **Wine prices** *Moderate* **Cuisine** *Contemporary French* **Menu prices** *$18–$35* **Credit cards** *AX, MC, VS, DV*
Grand Award since 1989

WOLFDALE'S 🍷

640 N. Lake Blvd., Tahoe City, CA 96145; (530) 583-5700
Wine list *California* **Wine prices** *Moderate* **Corkage** *$20*
Cuisine *American* **Menu prices** *$18–$26*

ZAZU 🍷

3535 Guerneville Road, Santa Rosa, CA 95401; (707) 523-4814 **Wine list** *California* **Wine prices** *Moderate* **Corkage** *$15* **Cuisine** *Contemporary* **Menu prices** *$16–$24*

ZIBIBBO 🍷

430 Kipling St., Palo Alto, CA 94301; (650) 328-6722
Wine list *California* **Wine prices** *Moderate* **Corkage** *$15*
Cuisine *Mediterranean* **Menu prices** *$12–$25*

ZIN RESTAURANT & WINE BAR 🍷

344 Center St., Healdsburg, CA 95448; (707) 473-0946
Wine list *California* **Wine prices** *Moderate* **Corkage** *$15*
Cuisine *American* **Menu prices** *$13–$26*

COLORADO

ADEGA 🍷🍷

1700 Wynkoop St., Denver, CO 80202; (303) 534-2222
Wine list *France, California, Italy, Austria, Germany* **Wine prices** *Moderate* **Cuisine** *Contemporary American* **Menu prices** *$18–$30*

AJAX TAVERN 🍷

685 E. Durant Ave., Aspen, CO 81611; (970) 920-9333
Wine list *California* **Wine prices** *Moderate* **Cuisine** *Northern Italian* **Menu prices** *$18–$32*

ALLRED'S 🍷

Gondola Station, St. Sophia, Telluride, CO 81435; (970) 728-7474 **Wine list** *California, France, Germany* **Wine prices** *Moderate* **Cuisine** *American* **Menu prices** *$21–$36*

ALPENGLOW STUBE 🍷
Keystone Resort, Keystone, CO 80435; (970) 496-4FUN **Wine list** *California, France* **Wine prices** *Expensive* **Cuisine** *Regional* **Menu prices** *Prix fixe only; $85–$95*

ANTARES RESTAURANT 🍷
57 1/2 Eighth St., Steamboat Springs, CO 80477; (970) 879-9939 **Wine list** *California* **Wine prices** *Moderate* **Cuisine** *Contemporary* **Menu prices** *$16–$32*

ANTICA ROMA 🍷
1308 Pearl St., Boulder, CO 80302; (303) 442-0378 **Wine list** *Italy* **Wine prices** *Moderate* **Cuisine** *Italian* **Menu prices** *$12–$23*

BAROLO GRILL 🍷🍷
3030 E. Sixth Ave., Denver, CO 80206; (303) 393-1040 **Wine list** *Italy* **Wine prices** *Moderate* **Cuisine** *Northern Italian* **Menu prices** *$20–$34*

BEANO'S CABIN 🍷
Beaver Creek Resort, Beaver Creek, CO 81620; (970) 949-9090 **Wine list** *California, France* **Wine prices** *Expensive* **Cuisine** *Contemporary American* **Menu prices** *Prix fixe only; $89*

BLOOM 🍷
1 W. Flatiron Circle The Village at Flatiron Crossing, Broomfield, CO 80021; (720) 887-2800 **Wine list** *California* **Wine prices** *Moderate* **Cuisine** *Contemporary American* **Menu prices** *$12–$22*

THE BLUE STAR 🍷🍷
1645 S. Tejon, Colorado Springs, CO 80906; (719) 632-1086 **Wine list** *California, France* **Wine prices** *Moderate* **Cuisine** *American* **Menu prices** *$8–$28*

BLUEPOINT GRILL & NOIR BAR 🍷
123 S. Oak St., Telluride, CO 81435; (970) 728-8862 **Wine list** *California, France* **Wine prices** *Moderate* **Cuisine** *Contemporary American* **Menu prices** *$12–$25*

BON TON RESTAURANT 🍷
St. Elmo Hotel, 426 Main St., Ouray, CO 81427; (970) 325-4951 **Wine list** *California* **Wine prices** *Moderate* **Cuisine** *Contemporary American* **Menu prices** *$10–$28*

BOULDER CORK 🍷
3295 30th St., Boulder, CO 80301; (303) 443-9505 **Wine list** *California, France* **Wine prices** *Moderate* **Cuisine** *American* **Menu prices** *$14–$28*

BRAVO! RISTORANTE 🍷
Adams Mark Hotel Denver, 1550 Court Place, Denver, CO 80202; (303) 626-2581 **Wine list** *Italy* **Wine prices** *Moderate* **Cuisine** *Italian* **Menu prices** *$12–$30*

THE BRISTOL AT ARROWHEAD 🍷
676 Sawatch Drive, Edwards, CO 81632; (970) 926-2111 **Wine list** *California* **Wine prices** *Moderate* **Cuisine** *American* **Menu prices** *$18–$34*

BROOK'S STEAK HOUSE & CELLAR 🍷🍷
6538 S. Yosemite Circle, Greenwood VIllage, CO 80111; (303) 770-1177 **Wine list** *California, France, Italy* **Wine prices** *Expensive* **Cuisine** *Steak house* **Menu prices** *$22–$60*

THE CABIN 🍷
Steamboat Grand Resort Hotel & Conference Center, 2300 Mount Werner Circle, Steamboat Springs, CO 80487; (970) 871-5550 **Wine list** *California, France* **Wine prices** *Moderate* **Cuisine** *Steak house* **Menu prices** *$17–$36*

CAFÉ ALPINE 🍷
106 E. Adams Ave., Breckenridge, CO 80424; (970) 453-8218 **Wine list** *California* **Wine prices** Inexpensive **Cuisine** *American* **Menu prices** *$16–$29*

CALIFORNIA CAFÉ BAR & GRILL 🍷
8505 Park Meadows Center Drive, Littleton, CO 80124; (303) 649-1111 **Wine list** *California* **Wine prices** *Moderate* **Cuisine** *American* **Menu prices** *$16–$30*

CAMPAGNA 🍷
435 W. Pacific Ave., Telluride, CO 81435; (970) 728-6190 **Wine list** *Italy* **Wine prices** *Moderate* **Cuisine** *Tuscan* **Menu prices** *$16–$35*

THE CENTURY ROOM 🍷
Hotel Jerome, 330 E. Main St., Aspen, CO 81611; (970) 920-1000 **Wine list** *California, France* **Wine prices** *Expensive* **Cuisine** *American* **Menu prices** *$26–$35*

CHARLES COURT 🍷🍷
The Broadmoor, 1 Lake Ave., Colorado Springs, CO 80906; (719) 577-5774 **Wine list** *California, Bordeaux* **Wine prices** *Expensive* **Cuisine** *Regional* **Menu prices** *$17–$42*

CHEFS' 🍷

936 North Ave., Grand Junction, CO 81501; (970) 243-9673 **Wine list** *California* **Wine prices** Inexpensive **Cuisine** *International* **Menu prices** *$13–$28*

CHEZ GRAND-MÈRE 🍷

3 Depot Place, Durango, CO 81301; (970) 247-7979 **Wine list** *France, California* **Wine prices** *Moderate* **Cuisine** *French* **Menu prices** *Prix fixe only; $55*

CIAÓ VINO 🍷

126 W. Mountain Ave., Fort Collins, CO 80524; (970) 484-8466 **Wine list** *Italy, California* **Wine prices** *Moderate* **Cuisine** *Continental* **Menu prices** *$5–$9*

THE CLIFF HOUSE DINING ROOM 🍷

The Cliff House at Pikes Peak, 306 Cañon Ave., Manitou Springs, CO 80829; (719) 685-3000 **Wine list** *California, France* **Wine prices** *Moderate* **Cuisine** *Contemporary American* **Menu prices** *$24–$36*

THE COSMOPOLITAN RESTAURANT 🍷

Hotel Columbia, 300 W. San Juan Ave., Telluride, CO 81435; (970) 728-1292 **Wine list** *California* **Wine prices** *Moderate* **Cuisine** *American* **Menu prices** *$18–$28*

CUCINA COLORE 🍷

3041 E. Third Ave., Denver, CO 80206; (303) 393-6917 **Wine list** *Italy* **Wine prices** *Moderate* **Cuisine** *Contemporary Italian* **Menu prices** *$17–$24*

DEL FRISCO'S DOUBLE EAGLE STEAK HOUSE 🍷🍷

8100 E. Orchard Road, Greenwood Village, CO 80111; (303) 796-0100 **Wine list** *California, France* **Wine prices** *Expensive* **Cuisine** *Steak house* **Menu prices** *$18–$35*

DIAMOND CABARET & STEAKHOUSE 🍷

1222 Glenarm Place, Denver, CO 80204; (303) 571-4242 **Wine list** *California, Bordeaux* **Wine prices** *Expensive* **Cuisine** *Steak house* **Menu prices** *$23–$54*

EXCELSIOR CAFÉ 🍷

200 W. Colorado Ave., Telluride, CO 81435; (970) 728-4250 **Wine list** *California, Italy* **Wine prices** Inexpensive **Cuisine** *Italian* **Menu prices** *$15–$25*

1515 RESTAURANT 🍷

1515 Market St., Denver, CO 80202; (303) 571-0011 **Wine list** *California* **Wine prices** *Moderate* **Cuisine** *American* **Menu prices** *$14–$33*

FLAGSTAFF HOUSE RESTAURANT 🍷🍷🍷
1138 Flagstaff Road, Boulder, CO 80302; (303) 442-4640 **Wine list** *Burgundy, Bordeaux, California* **Wine selections** *2,655* **Number of bottles** *20,000* **Wine prices** *Moderate* **Cuisine** *American/French* **Menu prices** *$25–$40* **Credit cards** *AX, MC, VS, DV*
Grand Award since 1983

FLATZ 🍷
Renaissance Suites Hotel, 500 Flatiron Blvd., Broomfield, CO 80021; (303) 465-0153 **Wine list** *California* **Wine prices** *Moderate* **Cuisine** *American* **Menu prices** *$9–$25*

FOURTH STORY RESTAURANT & BAR 🍷
2955 E. First Ave., Denver, CO 80206; (303) 322-1824 **Wine list** *California* **Wine prices** *Moderate* **Cuisine** *Contemporary American* **Menu prices** *$12–$24*

GAME CREEK 🍷
600 Lionshead Circle, Vail, CO 81658; (970) 479-4275 **Wine list** *California, France* **Wine prices** *Expensive* **Cuisine** *Regional* **Menu prices** *Prix fixe only; $89*

GIOVANNI'S RISTORANTE & TRATTORIA 🍷
127 11th St., Steamboat Springs, CO 80487; (970) 879-4141 **Wine list** *Italy* **Wine prices** *Moderate* **Cuisine** *Northern Italian* **Menu prices** *$15–$28*

GREAT NORTHERN TAVERN 🍷
91 River Run Road, Keystone, CO 80435; (970) 262-2202 **Wine list** *California* **Wine prices** *Moderate* **Cuisine** *Regional* **Menu prices** *$14–$28*

THE GREENBRIAR INN 🍷🍷
8735 N. Foothills Highway, Boulder, CO 80302; (303) 440-7979 **Wine list** *California, France, Australia, Italy, Germany* **Wine prices** *Moderate* **Cuisine** *American* **Menu prices** *$18–$36*

GROUSE MOUNTAIN GRILL 🍷
Beaver Creek Resort, 141 Scott Hill Road, Avon, CO 81620; (970) 949-0600 **Wine list** *California* **Wine prices** *Moderate* **Cuisine** *American* **Menu prices** *$25–$39*

HARMONS 🍷🍷
300 S. Townsend Ave., Telluride, CO 81435; (970) 728-3773 **Wine list** *California, France, Australia* **Wine prices** *Moderate* **Cuisine** *Contemporary American* **Menu prices** *$21–$32*

THE HEARTHSTONE RESTAURANT
130 S. Ridge St., Breckenridge, CO 80424; (970) 453-1148 **Wine list** *California* **Wine prices** Inexpensive **Cuisine** *American* **Menu prices** *$14–$29*

JAKE & TELLY'S GREEK CUISINE
2616 W. Colorado Ave., Colorado Springs, CO 80904; (719) 633-0406 **Wine list** *Greece, California* **Wine prices** Inexpensive **Cuisine** *Greek/Mediterranean* **Menu prices** *$11–$19*

JAY'S BISTRO
135 W. Oak St., Fort Collins, CO 80524; (970) 482-1876 **Wine list** *California* **Wine prices** *Moderate* **Cuisine** *American* **Menu prices** *$14–$32*

JUNIPER RESTAURANT
97 Main St., Edwards, CO 81632; (970) 926-7001 **Wine list** *California* **Wine prices** *Moderate* **Cuisine** *Contemporary American* **Menu prices** *$20–$26*

KEN & SUE'S
636 Main Ave., Durango, CO 81301; (970) 385-1810 **Wine list** *California* **Wine prices** *Moderate* **Cuisine** *Contemporary American* **Menu prices** *$7–$20*

THE KEYSTONE RANCH RESTAURANT
1239 Ranch Road, Keystone, CO 80435; (970) 496-4161 **Wine list** *California, France* **Wine prices** *Moderate* **Cuisine** *Continental* **Menu prices** *Prix fixe only; $68–$72*

L'APOGEE
911 Lincoln Ave., Steamboat Springs, CO 80477; (970) 879-1919 **Wine list** *California, Burgundy* **Wine prices** *Moderate* **Cuisine** *Contemporary* **Menu prices** *$9–$32*

LA PETITE MAISON
1015 W. Colorado Ave., Colorado Springs, CO 80904; (719) 632-4887 **Wine list** *France, California* **Wine prices** *Moderate* **Cuisine** *Contemporary American* **Menu prices** *$9–$29*

LA TOUR RESTAURANT
122 E. Meadow Drive, Vail, CO 81657; (970) 476-4403 **Wine list** *France, California* **Wine prices** *Expensive* **Cuisine** *Contemporary French* **Menu prices** *$25–$36*

LARKSPUR 🍷
Golden Peak Lodge, 458 Vail Valley Drive, Vail, CO 81657; (970) 479-8050 **Wine list** *California* **Wine prices** *Moderate* **Cuisine** *American* **Menu prices** *$22–$32*

LAUDISIO 🍷
2785 Iris Ave., Boulder, CO 80304; (303) 442-1300 **Wine list** *Italy* **Wine prices** *Moderate* **Cuisine** *Italian* **Menu prices** *$12–$27*

LE BOSQUET 🍷
Sixth and Belleview, Majestic Plaza, Crested Butte, CO 81224; (970) 349-5808 **Wine list** *France, California* **Wine prices** *Inexpensive* **Cuisine** *French* **Menu prices** *$15–$30*

LUDWIG'S 🍷
Sonnenalp Resort of Vail, 20 Vail Road, Vail, CO 81657; (970) 479-5429 **Wine list** *California, France* **Wine prices** *Moderate* **Cuisine** *Contemporary* **Menu prices** *$22–$40*

MAMBO ITALIANO 🍷
521 Lincoln Ave., Steamboat Springs, CO 80477; (970) 870-0500 **Wine list** *Italy* **Wine prices** *Moderate* **Cuisine** *Italian* **Menu prices** *$10–$17*

MEL'S RESTAURANT & BAR 🍷
235 Fillmore St., Denver, CO 80206; (303) 333-3979 **Wine list** *France, California* **Wine prices** *Moderate* **Cuisine** *Contemporary American* **Menu prices** *$14–$25*

MIRABELLE RESTAURANT AT BEAVER CREEK 🍷
55 Village Road, Avon, CO 81620; (970) 949-7728 **Wine list** *California, France* **Wine prices** *Moderate* **Cuisine** *French/Belgian* **Menu prices** *$19–$35*

MONTAGNA 🍷🍷🍷
The Little Nell, 675 E. Durant Ave., Aspen, CO 81611; (970) 920-4600 **Wine list** *Bordeaux, Burgundy, California, Italy, Germany* **Wine selections** *1,200* **Number of bottles** *15,000* **Wine prices** *Expensive* **Cuisine** *Contemporary American* **Menu prices** *$23–$39*
Credit cards *AX, MC, VS, DV*
Grand Award since 1997

MONTAUK SEAFOOD GRILL 🍷
549 E. Lionshead Circle, Vail, CO 81657; (970) 476-2601 **Wine list** *California* **Wine prices** *Moderate* **Cuisine** *Seafood* **Menu prices** *$18–$38*

🍷🍷🍷 Grand Award 🍷🍷 Best of Award of Excellence 🍷 Award of Excellence

MORTON'S OF CHICAGO
1710 Wynkoop, Denver, CO 80202; (303) 825-3353 **Wine list** *California* **Wine prices** *Expensive* **Cuisine** *Steak house* **Menu prices** *$25–$36*

MORTON'S OF CHICAGO
8480 E. Belleview Ave., Englewood, CO 80111; (303) 409-1177 **Wine list** *California* **Wine prices** *Expensive* **Cuisine** *Steak house* **Menu prices** *$30–$35*

NICO'S CATACOMBS
115 S. College Ave., Fort Collins, CO 80524; (970) 484-6029 **Wine list** *California, France, Germany* **Wine prices** *Expensive* **Cuisine** *Continental* **Menu prices** *$18–$35*

OLIVES ASPEN
315 E. Dean St., Aspen, CO 81611; (970) 920-7356 **Wine list** *California* **Wine prices** *Moderate* **Cuisine** *Mediterranean* **Menu prices** *$17–$32*

PALACE ARMS
The Brown Palace Hotel, 321 17th St., Denver, CO 80202; (303) 297-3111 **Wine list** *California, France* **Wine prices** *Moderate* **Cuisine** *Contemporary* **Menu prices** *$29–$42*

THE PALM
The Westin Hotel, 1672 Lawrence St., Denver, CO 80202; (303) 825-7256 **Wine list** *California* **Wine prices** *Moderate* **Cuisine** *Steak house* **Menu prices** *$15–$35*

THE PENROSE ROOM
The Broadmoor, 1 Lake Ave., Colorado Springs, CO 80901; (719) 577-5733 **Wine list** *California* **Wine prices** *Moderate* **Cuisine** *Contemporary French* **Menu prices** *$23–$42*

PIÑONS
105 S. Mill St., Aspen, CO 81611; (970) 920-2021 **Wine list** *California, France* **Wine prices** *Moderate* **Cuisine** *American* **Menu prices** *$22–$36*

PULCINELLA RISTORANTE
2100 W. Drake Road, Fort Collins, CO 80526; (970) 221-1444 **Wine list** *Italy, California* **Wine prices** *Moderate* **Cuisine** *Italian* **Menu prices** *$18–$35*

REMINGTON'S
The Ritz-Carlton Bachelor Gulch, 0130 Daybreak Ridge, Avon, CO 81620; (970) 748-6200 **Wine list** *California* **Wine prices** *Expensive* **Cuisine** *Regional* **Menu prices** *$24–$36*

RENAISSANCE RESTAURANT 🍷🍷
304 E. Hopkins Ave., Aspen, CO 81611; (970) 925-2402 **Wine list** *California, Burgundy, Bordeaux* **Wine prices** *Expensive* **Cuisine** *Contemporary French* **Menu prices** *$28–$38*

RESTAURANT KEVIN TAYLOR 🍷🍷
Hotel Teatro, 1106 14th St., Denver, CO 80202; (303) 820-2600 **Wine list** *California, France* **Wine prices** *Moderate* **Cuisine** *Contemporary American/French* **Menu prices** *$20–$35*

RESTAURANT PICASSO 🍷
The Lodge at Cordillera, 2205 Cordillera Way, Edwards, CO 81632; (800) 548-2721 **Wine list** *California* **Wine prices** *Expensive* **Cuisine** *European* **Menu prices** *$12–$29*

RESTAURANT SIX89 🍷
689 Main St., Carbondale, CO 81623; (970) 963-6890 **Wine list** *California, Australia, France* **Wine prices** *Moderate* **Cuisine** *Contemporary* **Menu prices** *$17–$24*

ROY'S OF CHERRY CREEK 🍷
3000 E. First Ave., Denver, CO 80206; (303) 333-9300 **Wine list** *California* **Wine prices** *Moderate* **Cuisine** *Seafood* **Menu prices** *$15–$28*

RUSTICO RISTORANTE 🍷🍷
114 E. Colorado Ave., Telluride, CO 81435; (970) 728-4046 **Wine list** *Piedmont, Tuscany* **Wine prices** *Expensive* **Cuisine** *Italian* **Menu prices** *$23–$36*

RUTH'S CHRIS STEAK HOUSE 🍷
1445 Market St., Denver, CO 80202; (303) 446-2233 **Wine list** *California, France* **Wine prices** *Moderate* **Cuisine** *Steak house* **Menu prices** *$21–$70*

SALT CREEK RESTAURANT & SALOON 🍷
110 E. Lincoln Ave., Breckenridge, CO 80424; (970) 453-4949 **Wine list** *California* **Wine prices** *Moderate* **Cuisine** *American* **Menu prices** *$14–$26*

SEASONS ROTISSERIE-GRILL 🍷
764 Main Ave., Durango, CO 81301; (970) 382-9790 **Wine list** *California* **Wine prices** *Moderate* **Cuisine** *Contemporary American* **Menu prices** *$15–$30*

SOLERA
5410 E. Colfax Ave., Denver, CO 80220; (303) 388-8429 **Wine list** *California, Bordeaux, Burgundy, Piedmont* **Wine prices** *Moderate* **Cuisine** *Contemporary American* **Menu prices** *$16–$33*

SPLENDIDO AT THE CHATEAU
17 Chateau Lane, Beaver Creek, CO 81620; (970) 845-8808 **Wine list** *California, France* **Wine prices** *Expensive* **Cuisine** *American/Mediterranean* **Menu prices** *$27–$45*

SULLIVAN'S STEAKHOUSE
1745 Wazee St., Denver, CO 80202; (303) 295-2664 **Wine list** *California* **Wine prices** *Expensive* **Cuisine** *Steak house* **Menu prices** *$17–$29*

SWEET BASIL
193 E. Gore Creek Drive, Vail, CO 81657; (970) 476-0125 **Wine list** *California, France* **Wine prices** *Moderate* **Cuisine** *American/Mediterranean/Asian* **Menu prices** *$22–$36*

TANTE LOUISE
4900 E. Colfax Ave., Denver, CO 80220; (303) 355-4488 **Wine list** *France, California* **Wine prices** *Moderate* **Cuisine** *Contemporary French* **Menu prices** *$21–$35*

TERRA BISTRO
Vail Mountain Lodge & Spa, 352 E. Meadow Drive, Vail, CO 81657; (970) 476-6836 **Wine list** *California* **Wine prices** *Moderate* **Cuisine** *International* **Menu prices** *$18–$36*

TOSCANINI
41 Avondale Lane, Avon, CO 81620; (970) 845-5590 **Wine list** *Italy* **Wine prices** *Moderate* **Cuisine** *Italian* **Menu prices** *$16–$35*

TRAMONTI
Charter Hotel Beaver Creek, 120 Offerson Road, Avon, CO 81620; (970) 949-5552 **Wine list** *Italy, California* **Wine prices** *Moderate* **Cuisine** *Northern Italian* **Menu prices** *$19–$36*

TRIOS ENOTECA
1730 Wynkoop St., Denver, CO 80302; (303) 293-2887 **Wine list** *California, France* **Wine prices** *Moderate* **Cuisine** *Contemporary American* **Menu prices** *$8–$15*

TRIOS GRILLE & WINE BAR
1155 Canyon Blvd., Boulder, CO 80302; (303) 442-8400 **Wine list** *California, France* **Wine prices** *Moderate* **Cuisine** *Contemporary American* **Menu prices** *$17–$32*

TUNDRA RESTAURANT
Beaumont Hotel, 505 Main St., Ouray, CO 81427; (970) 325-7040 **Wine list** *California, France* **Wine prices** *Moderate* **Cuisine** *Continental* **Menu prices** *$17–$34*

THE TYROLEAN
400 E. Meadow Drive, Vail, CO 81657; (970) 476-2204 **Wine list** *Austria, France California* **Wine prices** *Moderate* **Cuisine** *Contemporary European* **Menu prices** *$18–$36*

VILLAGE TAVERN
The Village at Flatiron Crossing, 1 W. Flatiron Circle, Broomfield, CO 80021; (720) 887-6900 **Wine list** *California, Australia* **Wine prices** *Moderate* **Cuisine** *American* **Menu prices** *$10–$24*

VISTA
48 E. Beaver Creek Blvd., Avon, CO 81620; (970) 949-3366 **Wine list** *California* **Wine prices** Inexpensive **Cuisine** *Contemporary American* **Menu prices** *$13–$22*

VUE
Park Hyatt Beaver Creek, 50 W. Thomas Place, Avon, CO 81620; (970) 949-1234 **Wine list** *California* **Wine prices** *Moderate* **Cuisine** *French* **Menu prices** *$28–$45*

THE WILDFLOWER
The Lodge at Vail, 174 E. Gore Creek Drive, Vail, CO 81657; (970) 476-5011 **Wine list** *California, France, Italy* **Wine prices** *Moderate* **Cuisine** *American* **Menu prices** *$23–$45*

THE WINERY RESTAURANT
642 Main St., Grand Junction, CO 81501; (970) 242-4100 **Wine list** *California* **Wine prices** *Moderate* **Corkage** *$15* **Cuisine** *Steak house* **Menu prices** *$11–$65*

ZINO RISTORANTE
Riverwalk Center, Edwards, CO 81632; (970) 926-0444 **Wine list** *California, Italy* **Wine prices** *Moderate* **Cuisine** *Italian* **Menu prices** *$14–$29*

CONNECTICUT

ANN HOWARD'S APRICOTS
1593 Farmington Ave., Farmington, CT 06032; (860) 673-5405 **Wine list** *California* **Wine prices** *Moderate* **Cuisine** *Contemporary American* **Menu prices** *$19–$28*

THE BEE & THISTLE INN
100 Lyme St., Old Lyme, CT 06371; (860) 434-1667 **Wine list** *California, France* **Wine prices** *Moderate* **Corkage** *$10* **Cuisine** *Contemporary American* **Menu prices** *$21–$30*

BENNETT'S STEAK & FISH
24-26 Spring St., Stamford, CT 06901; (203) 978-7995 **Wine list** *California, France* **Wine prices** *Expensive* **Cuisine** *Steak house* **Menu prices** *$18–$37*

BENTARA
76 Orange St., New Haven, CT 06510; (203) 562-2511 **Wine list** *California, Bordeaux, Italy* **Wine prices** *Moderate* **Corkage** *$10* **Cuisine** *Malaysian* **Menu prices** *$10–$28*

BERNARD'S INN AT RIDGEFIELD
20 West Lane, Ridgefield, CT 06877; (203) 438-8282 **Wine list** *Burgundy, California, Bordeaux* **Wine prices** *Moderate* **Corkage** *$35* **Cuisine** *Contemporary French* **Menu prices** *$21–$34*

CAFÉ ROUTIER
1353 Boston Post Road, Westbrook, CT 06498; (860) 399-8700 **Wine list** *California, France* **Wine prices** *Moderate* **Corkage** *$10* **Cuisine** *French/American* **Menu prices** *$16–$21*

CARMEN ANTHONY FISH HOUSE
51 E. Main St., Avon, CT 06001; (860) 677-7788 **Wine list** *California* **Wine prices** *Moderate* **Cuisine** *Italian/seafood* **Menu prices** *$16–$40*

CARMEN ANTHONY FISH HOUSE
1770 Berlin Turnpike, Wethersfield, CT 06109; (860) 529-7557 **Wine list** *California* **Wine prices** *Moderate* **Cuisine** *Italian/seafood* **Menu prices** *$18–$40*

CARMEN ANTHONY FISH HOUSE
757 Main St. S., Woodbury, CT 06798; (203) 266-0011 **Wine list** *California* **Wine prices** *Moderate* **Cuisine** *Italian/seafood* **Menu prices** *$19–$28*

CARMEN ANTHONY STEAKHOUSE 🍷
496 Chase Ave., Waterbury, CT 06704; (203) 757-3040
Wine list *California* **Wine prices** *Moderate* **Cuisine** *Steak house* **Menu prices** *$17–$40*

CAROL PECK'S GOOD NEWS CAFÉ 🍷
694 Main St. S., Woodbury, CT 06798; (203) 266-GOOD
Wine list *California* **Wine prices** *Moderate* **Cuisine** *Contemporary American* **Menu prices** *$16–$28*

CAVEY'S RESTAURANT 🍷🍷
45 E. Center St., Manchester, CT 06040; (860) 643-2751
Wine list *France, California* **Wine prices** *Moderate* **Cuisine** *Contemporary French* **Menu prices** *$27–$35*

CIAO! CAFÉ & WINE BAR 🍷
2B Ives St., Danbury, CT 06810; (203) 791-0404 **Wine list** *California* **Wine prices** *Inexpensive* **Cuisine** *Contemporary Italian* **Menu prices** *$11–$20*

COBB'S MILL INN 🍷
12 Old Mill Road, Weston, CT 06883; (203) 227-7221
Wine list *California, France* **Wine prices** *Moderate* **Cuisine** *American* **Menu prices** *$16–$33*

DA PIETRO'S 🍷
36 Riverside Ave., Westport, CT 06880; (203) 454-1213
Wine list *Italy, California* **Wine prices** *Expensive* **Cuisine** *Northern Italian/Southern French* **Menu prices** *$16–$32*

ELM STREET OYSTER HOUSE 🍷
11 W. Elm St., Greenwich, CT 06830; (203) 629-5795
Wine list *California* **Wine prices** *Moderate* **Cuisine** *Seafood* **Menu prices** *$18–$35*

FIFE 'N DRUM RESTAURANT & INN 🍷🍷
53 N. Main St., Route 7, Kent, CT 06757; (860) 927-3509
Wine list *California, France, Italy, Germany* **Wine prices** *Moderate* **Cuisine** *Continental* **Menu prices** *$14–$31*

THE HARVEST 🍷
37 Putnam Road, Pomfret, CT 06258; (860) 928-0008
Wine list *France, California* **Wine prices** *Moderate* **Cuisine** *International* **Menu prices** *$13–$30*

HARVEST 🍷
834 Federal Road, Brookfield, CT 06804; (203) 740-7601
Wine list *California, France* **Wine prices** *Inexpensive* **Corkage** *$10* **Cuisine** *Contemporary American* **Menu prices** *$17–$29*

🍷🍷🍷 Grand Award 🍷🍷 Best of Award of Excellence 🍷 Award of Excellence

IL FALCO RISTORANTE
59 Broad St., Stamford, CT 06901; (203) 327-0002 **Wine list** *Italy, California, France* **Wine prices** *Moderate* **Cuisine** *Italian* **Menu prices** *$16–$29*

THE INN AT NEWTOWN
19 Main St., Newtown, CT 06470; (203) 270-1876 **Wine list** *California, France* **Wine prices** Inexpensive **Corkage** *$10* **Cuisine** *Contemporary American* **Menu prices** *$15–$28*

JOHN'S CAFÉ
693 Main St. S., Woodbury, CT 06798; (203) 263-0188 **Wine list** *California* **Wine prices** *Moderate* **Cuisine** *Contemporary American* **Menu prices** *$16–$26*

KENSINGTON'S
The Spa at Norwich Inn, 607 W. Thames St., Norwich, CT 06360; (860) 886-2401 **Wine list** *California* **Wine prices** *Moderate* **Cuisine** *Contemporary* **Menu prices** *$19–$35*

LA COLLINE VERTE
75 Hillside Road, Fairfield, CT 06430; (203) 256-9242 **Wine list** *France* **Wine prices** *Moderate* **Corkage** *$25* **Cuisine** *French* **Menu prices** *$20–$29*

LITTLE KITCHEN RESTAURANT
423 Post Road E., Westport, CT 06680; (203) 454-5540 **Wine list** *California* **Wine prices** *Moderate* **Corkage** *$15* **Cuisine** *Pan-Asian* **Menu prices** *$15–$28*

MATCH
98 Washington St., South Norwalk, CT 06854; (203) 852-1088 **Wine list** *California* **Wine prices** *Moderate* **Corkage** *$15* **Cuisine** *Contemporary American* **Menu prices** *$19–$30*

METRO BIS
7B Simsbury Shops, 928 Hopmeadow St., Simsbury, CT 06070; (860) 651-1908 **Wine list** *California, France* **Wine prices** *Moderate* **Corkage** *$20* **Cuisine** *American* **Menu prices** *$19–$25*

MICHAEL JORDAN'S STEAK HOUSE
Mohegan Sun Casino, 1 Mohegan Sun Blvd., Uncasville, CT 06382; (860) 862-8600 **Wine list** *California* **Wine prices** *Expensive* **Corkage** *$25* **Cuisine** *Steak house* **Menu prices** *$17–$52*

MORTON'S OF CHICAGO 🍷

30 State House Square, Hartford, CT 06103; (860) 724-0044 **Wine list** *California* **Wine prices** *Expensive* **Cuisine** *Steak house* **Menu prices** *$19–$33*

MORTON'S OF CHICAGO 🍷

377 N. State St., Stamford, CT 06901; (203) 324-3939 **Wine list** *California* **Wine prices** *Expensive* **Cuisine** *Steak house* **Menu prices** *$19–$32*

OLD LYME INN 🍷

85 Lyme St., Old Lyme, CT 06371; (800) 434-2600 **Wine list** *California* **Wine prices** *Moderate* **Cuisine** *American* **Menu prices** *$12–$38*

PACI RESTAURANT 🍷

96 Station St., Southport, CT 06890; (203) 259-9600 **Wine list** *Italy* **Wine prices** *Expensive* **Cuisine** *Italian* **Menu prices** *$21–$38*

PASTIS 🍷

201 Ann St., Hartford, CT 06103; (860) 278-8852 **Wine list** *France* **Wine prices** *Moderate* **Corkage** *$20* **Cuisine** *French* **Menu prices** *$17–$25*

PEPPERCORN'S GRILL 🍷

357 Main St., Hartford, CT 06106; (860) 547-1714 **Wine list** *California, Italy* **Wine prices** *Moderate* **Cuisine** *Contemporary Italian* **Menu prices** *$16–$24*

PICCOLO ARANCIO 🍷

The Farmington Inn, 819 Farmington Ave., Farmington, CT 06032; (860) 674-1224 **Wine list** *Italy* **Wine prices** *Moderate* **Cuisine** *Italian* **Menu prices** *$16–$24*

POLO GRILLE & WINE BAR 🍷🍷

7 Elm St., New Haven, CT 06510; (203) 787-9000 **Wine list** *California, Italy, Bordeaux* **Wine prices** *Moderate* **Cuisine** *Steak house* **Menu prices** *$14–$22*

RAFFAELLO'S RESTAURANT 🍷🍷

2987 Whitney Ave., Hamden, CT 06518; (203) 230-0228 **Wine list** *Italy, California, France* **Wine prices** *Moderate* **Cuisine** *Italian* **Menu prices** *$14–$26*

REBECCA'S 🍷

265 Glenville Road, Greenwich, CT 06831; (203) 532-9270 **Wine list** *California, France* **Wine prices** *Expensive* **Cuisine** *Contemporary American* **Menu prices** *$27–$75*

THE REDDING ROADHOUSE
406 Redding Road, Redding, CT 06896; (203) 938-3388
Wine list *California* **Wine prices** *Moderate* **Corkage** *$20*
Cuisine *American* **Menu prices** *$16–$29*

RESTAURANT JEAN-LOUIS
61 Lewis St., Greenwich, CT 06830; (203) 622-8450 **Wine list** *France, California* **Wine prices** *Expensive* **Cuisine** *French*
Menu prices *$27–$39*

RIVER CAT GRILL
148 Rowayton Ave., Rowayton, CT 06853; (203) 854-0860
Wine list *California, France* **Wine prices** *Moderate* **Corkage** *$10* **Cuisine** *Contemporary American* **Menu prices** *$10–$30*

TAIPAN
376 Post Road E., Westport, CT 06880; (203) 227-7400
Wine list *California* **Wine prices** *Moderate* **Corkage** *$15*
Cuisine *Pan-Asian* **Menu prices** *$15–$28*

TELLURIDE
245 Bedford St., Stamford, CT 06901; (203) 357-7679
Wine list *California* **Wine prices** *Moderate* **Corkage** *$10*
Cuisine *Contemporary* **Menu prices** *$17–$50*

THOMAS HENKELMANN
Homestead Inn, 420 Field Point Road, Greenwich, CT 06830; (203) 869-7500 **Wine list** *California, Bordeaux, Burgundy* **Wine prices** *Expensive* **Cuisine** *Contemporary French* **Menu prices** *$32–$42*

THE THREE BEARS RESTAURANT
333 Wilton Road, Westport, CT 06880; (203) 227-7219
Wine list *California, Bordeaux* **Wine prices** Inexpensive
Corkage *$15* **Cuisine** *Contemporary American* **Menu prices** *$18–$27*

TRE SCALINI
100 Wooster St., New Haven, CT 06511; (203) 777-3373
Wine list *Italy, California* **Wine prices** *Moderate* **Cuisine** *Italian* **Menu prices** *$13–$20*

TUSCAN OVEN TRATTORIA
544 Main Ave., Norwalk, CT 06851; (203) 846-4600 **Wine list** *Italy* **Wine prices** *Moderate* **Cuisine** *Italian* **Menu prices** *$16–$29*

UNION LEAGUE CAFÉ 🍷
1032 Chapel St., New Haven, CT 06510; (203) 562-4299 **Wine list** *France* **Wine prices** *Moderate* **Cuisine** *French* **Menu prices** *$20–$26*

VALBELLA 🍷🍷
1309 E. Putnam Ave., Riverside, CT 06878; (203) 637-1155 **Wine list** *California, Italy, France* **Wine prices** *Expensive* **Cuisine** *Northern Italian* **Menu prices** *$27–$34*

WEST MAIN 🍷
8 Holley St., Lakeville, CT 06039; (860) 435-1450 **Wine list** *California* **Wine prices** *Moderate* **Corkage** *$20* **Cuisine** *Contemporary* **Menu prices** *$9–$27*

WEST STREET GRILL 🍷
43 West St., Litchfield, CT 06759; (860) 567-3885 **Wine list** *California* **Wine prices** *Moderate* **Corkage** *$20* **Cuisine** *Contemporary* **Menu prices** *$19–$34*

DELAWARE

BLUE MOON 🍷
35 Baltimore Ave., Rehoboth Beach, DE 19971; (302) 227-6515 **Wine list** *California* **Wine prices** *Moderate* **Cuisine** *American/international* **Menu prices** *$18–$32*

BRANDYWINE ROOM 🍷
Hotel Dupont, 11th & Market Streets, Wilmington, DE 19801; (302) 594-3251 **Wine list** *California, France* **Wine prices** *Expensive* **Cuisine** *American/continental* **Menu prices** *$21–$31*

CELSIUS 🍷
50 Wilmington Ave., Rehoboth Beach, DE 19971; (302) 227-5767 **Wine list** *California, France* **Wine prices** *Moderate* **Cuisine** *French/Mediterranean* **Menu prices** *$16–$29*

CHEZ LA MER 🍷
210 Second St., Rehoboth Beach, DE 19971; (302) 227-6494 **Wine list** *California, France* **Wine prices** *Moderate* **Corkage** *$10* **Cuisine** *Regional* **Menu prices** *$17–$32*

COLUMBUS INN 🍷
2216 Pennsylvania Ave., Wilmington, DE 19806; (302) 571-1492 **Wine list** *California, France* **Wine prices** *Moderate* **Cuisine** *American* **Menu prices** *$17–$27*

🍷🍷🍷 Grand Award 🍷🍷 Best of Award of Excellence 🍷 Award of Excellence

DEEP BLUE
111 W. 11th St., Wilmington, DE 19801; (302) 777-2040 **Wine list** *California* **Wine prices** *Moderate* **Cuisine** *Seafood* **Menu prices** *$14–$26*

GREEN ROOM
Hotel Dupont, 11th & Market Streets, Wilmington, DE 19801; (302) 594-3154 **Wine list** *California, France* **Wine prices** *Expensive* **Cuisine** *Contemporary French* **Menu prices** *$25–$37*

HARRY'S SAVOY GRILL
2020 Naamans Road, Wilmington, DE 19810; (302) 475-3000 **Wine list** *California, France* **Wine prices** *Moderate* **Cuisine** *Steak house* **Menu prices** *$18–$29*

KRAZY KAT'S
Inn at Montchanin Village, Route 100 and Kirk Road, Montchanin, DE 19710; (302) 888-4200 **Wine list** *California, France* **Wine prices** *Moderate* **Cuisine** *Contemporary American* **Menu prices** *$20–$30*

MORO RESTAURANT
1307 N. Scott St., Wilmington, DE 19806; (302) 777-1800 **Wine list** *California* **Wine prices** *Moderate* **Cuisine** *Contemporary American* **Menu prices** *$22–$27*

RESTAURANT 821
821 N. Market St., Wilmington, DE 19801; (302) 652-8821 **Wine list** *California* **Wine prices** *Expensive* **Cuisine** *Mediterranean* **Menu prices** *$20–$32*

SULLIVAN'S STEAKHOUSE
5525 Concord Pike, Wilmington, DE 19803; (302) 479-7970 **Wine list** *California* **Wine prices** *Moderate* **Cuisine** *Steak house* **Menu prices** *$17–$29*

TOSCANA KITCHEN & BAR
1412 N. DuPont St., Wilmington, DE 19806; (302) 654-8001 **Wine list** *Italy* **Wine prices** Inexpensive **Cuisine** *Italian* **Menu prices** *$12–$24*

VALLE CUCINA ITALIANA
4752 Limestone Road, Wilmington, DE 19808; (302) 998-9999 **Wine list** *California, Italy* **Wine prices** *Moderate* **Cuisine** *Italian* **Menu prices** *$12–$43*

DISTRICT OF COLUMBIA

ARDEO RESTAURANT
3311 Connecticut Ave. N.W., Washington, DC 20008; (202) 244-6750 **Wine list** *California* **Wine prices** Inexpensive **Corkage** *$15* **Cuisine** *Contemporary American* **Menu prices** *$13–$23*

BISTRO BIS
The Hotel George, 15 E St. N.W., Washington, DC 20001; (202) 661-2700 **Wine list** *France, California* **Wine prices** *Moderate* **Corkage** *$15* **Cuisine** *Contemporary* **Menu prices** *$19–$29*

BISTRO FRANÇAIS
3124-28 M St., Washington, DC 20007; (202) 338-3830 **Wine list** *France* **Wine prices** *Moderate* **Cuisine** *French* **Menu prices** *$14–$19*

BLACKIE'S
1217 22nd St. N.W., Washington, DC 20037; (202) 333-1100 **Wine list** *California, France* **Wine prices** *Moderate* **Cuisine** *American* **Menu prices** *$26–$38*

CAFÉ ATLANTICO
405 Eighth St. N.W., Washington, DC 20004; (202) 393-0812 **Wine list** *Chile, Argentina* **Wine prices** *Moderate* **Cuisine** *Contemporary Latin* **Menu prices** *$17–$25*

THE CAPITAL GRILLE
601 Pennsylvania Ave. N.W., Washington, DC 20004; (202) 737-6200 **Wine list** *California* **Wine prices** *Expensive* **Cuisine** *Steak house* **Menu prices** *$17–$30*

THE CAUCUS ROOM
401 Ninth St. N.W., Washington, DC 20004; (202) 393-1300 **Wine list** *California, France* **Wine prices** *Expensive* **Corkage** *$15* **Cuisine** *Continental* **Menu prices** *$24–$36*

CLYDE'S
3236 M St. N.W., Washington, DC 20007; (202) 333-9180 **Wine list** *California* **Wine prices** *Moderate* **Cuisine** *American* **Menu prices** *$11–$24*

CORDUROY
1201 K St. N.W., Washington, DC 20005; (202) 589-0699 **Wine list** *California, France* **Wine prices** *Moderate* **Corkage** *$15* **Cuisine** *American* **Menu prices** *$18–$27*

Grand Award Best of Award of Excellence Award of Excellence

DC COAST
The Tower Building, 1401 K St., N.W., Washington, DC 20005; (202) 216-5988 **Wine list** *California* **Wine prices** *Moderate* **Corkage** *$20* **Cuisine** *Contemporary American* **Menu prices** *$19–$29*

EQUINOX
818 Connecticut Ave. N.W., Washington, DC 20006; (202) 331-8118 **Wine list** *California* **Wine prices** *Moderate* **Cuisine** *Contemporary American* **Menu prices** *$25–$31*

FIREFLY
Hotel Madera, 1310 New Hampshire Ave. N.W., Washington, DC 20036; (202) 861-1310 **Wine list** *California* **Wine prices** *Moderate* **Corkage** *$15* **Cuisine** *Contemporary American* **Menu prices** *$14–$23*

GALILEO DA ROBERTO DONNA
1110 21st St. N.W., Washington, DC 20036; (202) 293-7191 **Wine list** *Piedmont, Tuscany, California, France* **Wine selections** *1,150* **Number of bottles** *32,100* **Wine prices** *Moderate* **Corkage** *$15* **Cuisine** *Italian* **Menu prices** *$20–$30* **Credit cards** *AX, MC, VS*
Grand Award since 1997

JALEO
480 Seventh St. N.W., Washington, DC 20004; (202) 628-7949 **Wine list** *Spain* **Wine prices** *Moderate* **Corkage** *$1* **Cuisine** *Spanish* **Menu prices** *$12–$15*

LEGAL SEA FOODS
2020 K St. N.W., Washington, DC 20006; (202) 496-1111 **Wine list** *California* **Wine prices** *Inexpensive* **Cuisine** *Seafood* **Menu prices** *$11–$62*

LEGAL SEA FOODS
704-708 Seventh St., Washington, DC 20001; (202) 347-0007 **Wine list** *California* **Wine prices** *Inexpensive* **Cuisine** *Seafood* **Menu prices** *$11–$28*

MELROSE
Park Hyatt Hotel, 1201 24th St. N.W., Washington, DC 20037; (202) 419-6755 **Wine list** *California, France* **Wine prices** *Moderate* **Cuisine** *American* **Menu prices** *$27–$34*

MENDOCINO GRILLE & WINE BAR
2917 M St. N.W., Washington, DC 20007; (202) 333-2912 **Wine list** *California* **Wine prices** *Moderate* **Corkage** *$20* **Cuisine** *Californian* **Menu prices** *$17–$32*

MORRISON-CLARK RESTAURANT
Massachusetts Avenue and 11th Street N.W., Washington, DC 20001; (202) 898-1200 **Wine list** *California* **Wine prices** *Moderate* **Cuisine** *International* **Menu prices** *$19–$28*

MORTON'S OF CHICAGO
1050 Connecticut Ave. N.W., Washington, DC 20036; (202) 955-5997 **Wine list** *California* **Wine prices** *Expensive* **Cuisine** *Steak house* **Menu prices** *$20–$35*

MORTON'S OF CHICAGO
3251 Prospect St. N.W., Washington, DC 20007; (202) 342-6258 **Wine list** *California* **Wine prices** *Expensive* **Corkage** *$15* **Cuisine** *Steak house* **Menu prices** *$22–$35*

NICK & STEF'S STEAKHOUSE
601 F St. N.W., Washington, DC 20004; (202) 661-5040 **Wine list** *California, France* **Wine prices** *Expensive* **Corkage** *$20* **Cuisine** *Steak house* **Menu prices** *$20–$30*

THE OCCIDENTAL
1475 Pennsylvania Ave. N.W., Washington, DC 20004; (202) 783-1475 **Wine list** *California* **Wine prices** Inexpensive **Corkage** *$18* **Cuisine** *American* **Menu prices** *$20–$34*

THE OCEANAIRE SEAFOOD ROOM
1201 F St. N.W., Washington, DC 20004; (202) 347-2277 **Wine list** *California* **Wine prices** *Moderate* **Corkage** *$20* **Cuisine** *Seafood* **Menu prices** *$20–$68*

OLD EBBITT GRILL
675 15th St. N.W., Washington, DC 20005; (202) 347-4801 **Wine list** *California* **Wine prices** *Moderate* **Cuisine** *American* **Menu prices** *$12–$25*

OLIVES DC
World Center Building, 1600 K St. N.W., Washington, DC 20005; (202) 452-1866 **Wine list** *California, France, Italy* **Wine prices** *Moderate* **Corkage** *$25* **Cuisine** *Mediterranean* **Menu prices** *$17–$32*

ORTANIQUE
730 11th St. N.W., Washington, DC 20004; (202) 393-0975 **Wine list** *California* **Wine prices** *Moderate* **Corkage** *$20* **Cuisine** *Contemporary* **Menu prices** *$20–$35*

THE OVAL ROOM
Lafayette Square, 800 Connecticut Ave. N.W., Washington, DC 20006; (202) 463-8700 **Wine list** *California* **Wine prices** *Moderate* **Corkage** *$15* **Cuisine** *Contemporary American* **Menu prices** *$18–$26*

THE PALM
1225 19th St. N.W., Washington, DC 20036; (202) 293-9091 **Wine list** *California* **Wine prices** *Expensive* **Corkage** *$15* **Cuisine** *Steak house* **Menu prices** *$16–$58*

THE PRIME RIB
2020 K St. N.W., Washington, DC 20006; (202) 466-8811 **Wine list** *California* **Wine prices** *Moderate* **Cuisine** *Steak house* **Menu prices** *$18–$39*

RED SAGE
605 14th St. N.W., Washington, DC 20005; (202) 638-4444 **Wine list** *California, France* **Wine prices** *Moderate* **Cuisine** *Contemporary American* **Menu prices** *$19–$37*

RUTH'S CHRIS STEAK HOUSE
1801 Connecticut Ave. N.W., Washington, DC 20009; (202) 797-0033 **Wine list** *California* **Wine prices** *Moderate* **Corkage** *$15* **Cuisine** *Steak house* **Menu prices** *$18–$58*

RUTH'S CHRIS STEAK HOUSE
724 Ninth St., Washington, DC 20001; (202) 393-4488 **Wine list** *California* **Wine prices** *Moderate* **Corkage** *$15* **Cuisine** *Steak house* **Menu prices** *$23–$55*

SAM & HARRY'S
1200 19th St. N.W., Washington, DC 20036; (202) 296-4333 **Wine list** *California, France* **Wine prices** *Moderate* **Corkage** *$15* **Cuisine** *American* **Menu prices** *$18–$56*

SESTO SENSO
1214 18th St. N.W., Washington, DC 20036; (202) 785-9525 **Wine list** *Italy, California* **Wine prices** *Moderate* **Corkage** *$15* **Cuisine** *Italian* **Menu prices** *$14–$22*

701 PENNSYLVANIA AVE.
701 Pennsylvania Ave. N.W., Washington, DC 20004; (202) 393-0701 **Wine list** *California* **Wine prices** *Moderate* **Corkage** *$15* **Cuisine** *American* **Menu prices** *$16–$25*

1789 RESTAURANT
1226 36th St. N.W., Washington, DC 20007; (202) 965-1789 **Wine list** *California, France* **Wine prices** *Moderate* **Cuisine** *American* **Menu prices** *$18–$38*

SMITH & WOLLENSKY
1112 19th St. N.W., Washington, DC 20036; (202) 466-1100 **Wine list** *California* **Wine prices** *Moderate* **Cuisine** *Steak house* **Menu prices** *$19–$29*

THE TABARD INN
1739 N St. N.W., Washington, DC 20036; (202) 785-1277 **Wine list** *France* **Wine prices** Inexpensive **Corkage** *$15* **Cuisine** *Contemporary American* **Menu prices** *$18–$26*

TENPENH
1001 Pennsylvania Ave. N.W., Washington, DC 20004; (202) 393-4500 **Wine list** *California, Australia* **Wine prices** *Moderate* **Corkage** *$20* **Cuisine** *Contemporary American/ Asian* **Menu prices** *$13–$28*

VIA PACIFICA
Grand Hyatt Washington, 1000 H St. N.W., Washington, DC 20001; (202) 637-4735 **Wine list** *California* **Wine prices** *Moderate* **Corkage** *$15* **Cuisine** *Contemporary* **Menu prices** *$18–$28*

VIDALIA
1990 M St. N.W., Washington, DC 20036; (202) 659-1990 **Wine list** *California, France* **Wine prices** *Moderate* **Corkage** *$15* **Cuisine** *American* **Menu prices** *$20–$35*

ZOLA
1319 F St. N.W., Washington, DC 20004; (202) 654-0999 **Wine list** *California, France* **Wine prices** *Moderate* **Corkage** *$15* **Cuisine** *American* **Menu prices** *$15–$30*

FLORIDA

THE ADDISON
2 E. Camino Real, Boca Raton, FL 33432; (561) 395-9335 **Wine list** *California, France* **Wine prices** *Moderate* **Corkage** *$20* **Cuisine** *American/continental* **Menu prices** *$22–$38*

ALFANO'S RESTAURANT
1702 Clearwater Largo Road, Clearwater, FL 33756; (727) 584-2125 **Wine list** *California, Italy* **Wine prices** *Moderate* **Cuisine** *Italian* **Menu prices** *$13–$26*

ANDRE'S STEAKHOUSE
2800 N. Tamiami Trail, Naples, FL 34103; (941) 263-5851 **Wine list** *California* **Wine prices** *Moderate* **Cuisine** *Steak house* **Menu prices** *$14–$31*

Grand Award · Best of Award of Excellence · Award of Excellence

ARMANI'S
Grand Hyatt Tampa Bay, 6200 Courtney Campbell Causeway, Tampa, FL 33607; (813) 207-6800 **Wine list** *California* **Wine prices** *Moderate* **Cuisine** *Northern Italian* **Menu prices** *$18–$30*

ARTURO'S RESTAURANT
6750 N. Federal Highway, Boca Raton, FL 33487; (561) 997-7373 **Wine list** *California, Italy, Bordeaux* **Wine prices** *Moderate* **Corkage** *$25* **Cuisine** *Northern Italian* **Menu prices** *$16–$35*

ASHLEY STREET GRILLE
Radisson River Walk Hotel, 200 N. Ashley St., Tampa, FL 33602; (813) 226-4400 **Wine list** *California* **Wine prices** Inexpensive **Cuisine** *Contemporary American* **Menu prices** *$15–$28*

AU PARADIS
11412 Tamiami Trail E., Naples, FL 34113; (941) 775-7667 **Wine list** *California* **Wine prices** Inexpensive **Cuisine** *French/Floridian* **Menu prices** *$18–$30*

AURA
290 E. Atlantic Ave., Delray Beach, FL 33444; (561) 243-2686 **Wine list** *California* **Wine prices** *Moderate* **Corkage** *$10* **Cuisine** *American* **Menu prices** *$17–$34*

AZUL
Mandarin Oriental Hotel Miami, 500 Brickell Key Drive, Miami, FL 33131; (305) 913-8254 **Wine list** *California, France* **Wine prices** *Expensive* **Corkage** *$45* **Cuisine** *French/Mediterranean* **Menu prices** *$26–$38*

BARNACLE BILL'S SEAFOOD ON MAIN
1526 Main St., Sarasota, FL 34236; (941) 365-6800 **Wine list** *California* **Wine prices** Inexpensive **Corkage** *$10* **Cuisine** *Seafood* **Menu prices** *$10–$24*

BEACH BISTRO
6600 Gulf Drive, Holmes Beach, FL 34217; (941) 778-6444 **Wine list** *California* **Wine prices** *Moderate* **Cuisine** *Floridian/Mediterranean* **Menu prices** *$18–$42*

THE BEACH WALK CAFÉ
Inn at Crystal Beach, 2996 Highway 98 E., Destin, FL 32541; (850) 650-7100 **Wine list** *California* **Wine prices** *Moderate* **Corkage** *$15* **Cuisine** *French/Asian* **Menu prices** *$23–$59*

BERN'S STEAK HOUSE 🍷🍷🍷
1208 S. Howard Ave., Tampa, FL 33606; (813) 251-2421 **Wine list** *California, France* **Wine selections** *2,500* **Number of bottles** *400,000* **Wine prices** *Moderate* **Cuisine** *Steak house* **Menu prices** *$18–$48* **Credit cards** *AX, MC, VS, DV*
Grand Award since 1981

BIJOU CAFÉ 🍷
1287 First St., Sarasota, FL 34236; (941) 366-8111 **Wine list** *California, France* **Wine prices** *Moderate* **Corkage** *$15* **Cuisine** *Continental* **Menu prices** *$15–$30*

BLEU PROVENCE 🍷
1234 Eighth St. S., Naples, FL 34102; (239) 261-8239 **Wine list** *France, California* **Wine prices** *Moderate* **Cuisine** *French* **Menu prices** *$17–$34*

BLUE HEAVEN 🍷
729 Thomas St., Key West, FL 33040; (305) 296-8666 **Wine list** *California* **Wine prices** *Moderate* **Corkage** *$6* **Cuisine** *American* **Menu prices** *$15–$44*

BOB HEILMAN'S BEACHCOMBER RESTAURANT 🍷🍷
447 Mandalay Ave., Clearwater Beach, FL 33767; (727) 442-4144 **Wine list** *California, Burgundy* **Wine prices** *Moderate* **Cuisine** *American/continental* **Menu prices** *$10–$23*

BOGERT'S CHOP HOUSE 🍷
5990 Winkler Road, Fort Myers, FL 33919; (239) 590-6772 **Wine list** *California* **Wine prices** *Moderate* **Corkage** *$10* **Cuisine** *Steak house* **Menu prices** *$17–$35*

BOHEME BISTRO 🍷
1118 E. Atlantic Ave., Delray Beach, FL 33483; (561) 278-4899 **Wine list** *California, France, Italy* **Wine prices** *Moderate* **Cuisine** *International* **Menu prices** *$16–$26*

BRASSERIE LAS OLAS 🍷
333 E. Las Olas Blvd., Fort Lauderdale, FL 33301; (954) 779-7374 **Wine list** *California* **Wine prices** Inexpensive **Corkage** *$10* **Cuisine** *Contemporary* **Menu prices** *$12–$25*

BRETT'S WATERWAY CAFÉ 🍷
Fernandina Harbour Marina, 1 S. Front St., Amelia Island, FL 32035; (904) 261-2660 **Wine list** *California* **Wine prices** *Moderate* **Cuisine** *Continental* **Menu prices** *$15–$27*

BUD & ALLEY'S RESTAURANT 🍷

2236 E. Coast Highway 30-A, Santa Rosa Beach, FL 32459; (850) 231-5900 **Wine list** *California, France* **Wine prices** *Moderate* **Corkage** *$12* **Cuisine** *Mediterranean/Basque/Floridian* **Menu prices** *$18–$29*

CABANA NUEVO LATINO 🍷

118 Clematis St., West Palm Beach, FL 33401; (561) 833-4773 **Wine list** *California* **Wine prices** *Moderate* **Corkage** *$10* **Cuisine** *Contemporary Latin* **Menu prices** *$12–$35*

CAFÉ BACI 🍷

4001 S. Tamiami Trail, Sarasota, FL 34231; (941) 921-4848 **Wine list** *Italy, California* **Wine prices** *Moderate* **Cuisine** *Italian* **Menu prices** *$10–$23*

CAFÉ CABERNET 🍷🍷

1019 N. Monroe St., Tallahassee, FL 32303; (850) 224-1175 **Wine list** *California, France, Italy* **Wine prices** *Moderate* **Cuisine** *Contemporary* **Menu prices** *$18–$30*

CAFÉ CHARDONNAY 🍷🍷

4533 PGA Blvd., Palm Beach Gardens, FL 33418; (561) 627-2662 **Wine list** *California, France* **Wine prices** *Moderate* **Cuisine** *American* **Menu prices** *$22–$34*

CAFÉ L'EUROPE 🍷🍷

331 S. County Road, Palm Beach, FL 33480; (561) 655-4020 **Wine list** *California, Italy, France* **Wine prices** *Moderate* **Corkage** *$50* **Cuisine** *International* **Menu prices** *$27–$39*

CAFÉ L'EUROPE 🍷

431 Saint Armand's Circle, Sarasota, FL 34236; (941) 388-4415 **Wine list** *California, France* **Wine prices** *Moderate* **Corkage** *$10* **Cuisine** *Continental/contemporary European* **Menu prices** *$19–$37*

CAFÉ SEVILLE 🍷

2768 E. Oakland Park Blvd., Fort Lauderdale, FL 33306; (954) 565-1148 **Wine list** *Spain, California* **Wine prices** *Moderate* **Cuisine** *Mediterranean/Spanish* **Menu prices** *$13–$25*

CAFÉ THIRTY-A 🍷

3899 E. Scenic Highway 30-A, Seagrove Beach, FL 32459; (850) 231-2166 **Wine list** *California* **Wine prices** *Moderate* **Corkage** *$15* **Cuisine** *Contemporary* **Menu prices** *$12–$30*

FLORIDA

CAFFÉ LUNA ROSA 🍷
34 S. Ocean Blvd., Delray Beach, FL 33483; (561) 274-9404 **Wine list** *Italy* **Wine prices** Inexpensive **Corkage** *$20* **Cuisine** *Floridian/Mediterranean* **Menu prices** *$13–$36*

CALIFORNIA CAFÉ BAR & GRILL 🍷
2301 S.E. 17th St. Causeway, Fort Lauderdale, FL 33316; (954) 728-3500 **Wine list** *California* **Wine prices** *Moderate* **Cuisine** *Californian/Floridian* **Menu prices** *$15–$33*

CALIFORNIA GRILL 🍷
Contemporary Resort at Disney World, 4600 N. World Drive, Lake Buena Vista, FL 32830; (407) 939-3463 **Wine list** *California* **Wine prices** *Moderate* **Cuisine** *Californian* **Menu prices** *$17–$29*

THE CAPITAL GRILLE 🍷
444 Brickell Ave., Miami, FL 33131; (305) 374-4500 **Wine list** *California, Bordeaux* **Wine prices** *Moderate* **Cuisine** *Steak house* **Menu prices** *$18–$33*

CAPT. ANDERSON'S 🍷
5551 N. Lagoon Drive, Panama City Beach, FL 32408; (850) 234-2225 **Wine list** *California, Bordeaux* **Wine prices** *Moderate* **Cuisine** *Steak house/seafood* **Menu prices** *$11–$35*

CARMINE'S OCEAN GRILL 🍷
2460 PGA Blvd., Palm Beach Gardens, FL 33410; (561) 624-1141 **Wine list** *California* **Wine prices** *Moderate* **Corkage** *$10* **Cuisine** *Seafood/sushi* **Menu prices** *$15–$25*

CASA D'ANGELO 🍷
1201 N. Federal Highway, Fort Lauderdale, FL 33304; (954) 564-1234 **Wine list** *Italy, California* **Wine prices** *Moderate* **Corkage** *$35* **Cuisine** *Italian* **Menu prices** *$14–$34*

CASA JUANCHO 🍷🍷
2436 S.W. Eighth St., Miami, FL 33135; (305) 642-2452 **Wine list** *Spain, California* **Wine prices** *Moderate* **Cuisine** *Spanish* **Menu prices** *$14–$34*

THE CAVE 🍷
11-B W. Granada Blvd., Ormond Beach, FL 32174; (386) 671-2008 **Wine list** *California* **Wine prices** Inexpensive **Cuisine** *Contemporary* **Menu prices** *Prix fixe only; $60–$65*

CHARDONNAY 🍷
2331 Tamiami Trail N., Naples, FL 34103; (239) 261-1744 **Wine list** *France, California* **Wine prices** *Moderate* **Cuisine** *French* **Menu prices** *$19–$32*

🍷🍷🍷 Grand Award 🍷🍷 Best of Award of Excellence 🍷 Award of Excellence

CHARLEY'S STEAK HOUSE
8255 International Drive, Orlando, FL 32819; (407) 363-0228 **Wine list** *California* **Wine prices** *Moderate* **Cuisine** *Steak house* **Menu prices** *$20–$35*

CHEF ALLEN'S
19088 N.E. 29th Ave., Aventura, FL 33180; (305) 935-2900 **Wine list** *California* **Wine prices** *Expensive* **Corkage** *$25* **Cuisine** *International* **Menu prices** *$27–$45*

CHINA GRILL
404 Washington Ave., Miami Beach, FL 33139; (305) 534-2211 **Wine list** *California* **Wine prices** Inexpensive **Cuisine** *International* **Menu prices** *$25–$60*

CHOP'S CITY GRILL
8200 Health Park Center, Bonita Springs, FL 34135; (941) 992-4677 **Wine list** *California* **Wine prices** *Moderate* **Corkage** *$10* **Cuisine** *Steak house* **Menu prices** *$14–$34*

CHOP'S CITY GRILL
837 Fifth Ave. S., Naples, FL 34102; (941) 262-4677 **Wine list** *California* **Wine prices** *Moderate* **Corkage** *$10* **Cuisine** *Steak house* **Menu prices** *$15–$35*

CÍTRICOS RESTAURANT
Disney's Grand Floridian Resort & Spa, 4401 Grand Floridian Way, Lake Buena Vista, FL 32830; (407) WDW-DINE **Wine list** *California, France* **Wine prices** *Moderate* **Corkage** *$15* **Cuisine** *Contemporary American* **Menu prices** *$22–$33*

CITY CELLAR WINE BAR & GRILL
CityPlace, 700 S. Rosemary Ave., West Palm Beach, FL 33401; (561) 366-0071 **Wine list** *California, France, Italy* **Wine prices** *Moderate* **Corkage** *$10* **Cuisine** *Mediterranean* **Menu prices** *$14–$28*

CITY OYSTER
213 E. Atlantic Ave., Delray Beach, FL 33444; (561) 272-0220 **Wine list** *California* **Wine prices** *Moderate* **Corkage** *$7* **Cuisine** *Seafood* **Menu prices** *$16–$28*

THE CLUB AT EDGEWATER
Edgewater Beach Hotel, 1901 Gulf Shore Blvd. N., Naples, FL 34102; (941) 403-2190 **Wine list** *California* **Wine prices** *Moderate* **Cuisine** *Continental/Caribbean* **Menu prices** *$22–$42*

THE COLONY RESTAURANTS 🍷
The Colony Beach & Tennis Resort, 1620 Gulf of Mexico Drive, Longboat Key, FL 34228; (941) 383-5558 **Wine list** *California, France* **Wine prices** *Moderate* **Corkage** *$20* **Cuisine** *American* **Menu prices** *$19–$38*

COLUMBIA RESTAURANT 🍷
2117 E. Seventh Ave., Tampa, FL 33605; (813) 248-4961 **Wine list** *Spain* **Wine prices** *Moderate* **Corkage** *$10* **Cuisine** *Spanish* **Menu prices** *$13–$28*

CONTINENTAL FLAMBÉ 🍷
936 E. New Haven Ave., Melbourne, FL 32901; (321) 768-2445 **Wine list** *California, France* **Wine prices** *Moderate* **Corkage** *$20* **Cuisine** *Continental* **Menu prices** *$17–$27*

THE COPPER GRILL 🍷
11225 Highway 98 W., Destin, FL 32550; (850) 654-6900 **Wine list** *California* **Wine prices** *Moderate* **Corkage** *$18* **Cuisine** *Steak house* **Menu prices** *$19–$45*

COSIMO'S BRICK OVEN 🍷
201 Southgate Plaza, Sarasota, FL 34239; (941) 363-0211 **Wine list** *California, Italy* **Wine prices** *Moderate* **Cuisine** *Italian/American* **Menu prices** *$11–$24*

CRIBB & GREENBAUM'S NEW YORK PRIME 🍷
2350 N.W. Executive Center Drive, Boca Raton, FL 33431; (561) 998-3881 **Wine list** *California, Bordeaux* **Wine prices** *Moderate* **Cuisine** *Steak house* **Menu prices** *$34–$68*

CRIOLLA'S 🍷🍷
170 E. Scenic Highway 30-A, Grayton Beach, FL 32459; (850) 267-1267 **Wine list** *California, France, Italy* **Wine prices** *Moderate* **Corkage** *$10* **Cuisine** *Caribbean/creole* **Menu prices** *$19–$31*

THE CROW'S NEST 🍷
1968 Tarpon Center Drive, Venice, FL 34285; (941) 484-9551 **Wine list** *California, France* **Wine prices** *Moderate* **Corkage** *$15* **Cuisine** *Seafood* **Menu prices** *$12–$25*

CUCINA D'ANGELO 🍷
5050 Town Center Circle, Boca Raton, FL 33486; (561) 750-2344 **Wine list** *Italy, California* **Wine prices** *Moderate* **Corkage** *$20* **Cuisine** *Northern Italian* **Menu prices** *$14–$32*

CUVÉE BEACH CELLAR & WINE BAR RESTAURANT
36120 Emerald Coast Parkway, Destin, FL 32541; (850) 650-8900 **Wine list** *California, Oregon, Washington* **Wine prices** *Moderate* **Corkage** *$12* **Cuisine** *Regional/Californian* **Menu prices** *$16–$28*

DANIELA'S RISTORANTE
2441 N.W. 43rd St., Gainesville, FL 32606; (352) 377-0996 **Wine list** *California, Italy* **Wine prices** *Moderate* **Cuisine** *Contemporary Italian* **Menu prices** *$18–$28*

DARREL & OLIVER'S CAFÉ MAXX
2601 E. Atlantic Blvd., Pompano Beach, FL 33062; (954) 782-0606 **Wine list** *California* **Wine prices** *Expensive* **Corkage** *$15* **Cuisine** *Floridian/New World* **Menu prices** *$20–$40*

DESTIN CHOPS
320 Highway 98-E, Destin, FL 32541; (850) 654-4944 **Wine list** *California* **Wine prices** *Moderate* **Cuisine** *Steak house* **Menu prices** *$14–$48*

THE DINING ROOM
The Ritz-Carlton Naples, 280 Vanderbilt Beach Road, Naples, FL 34108; (941) 598-6644 **Wine list** *France, California, Italy, Germany* **Wine prices** *Moderate* **Cuisine** *French* **Menu prices** *Prix fixe only; $68–$80*

DOMENIC'S CAPRI ITALIAN RESTAURANT
411 Mandalay Ave., Clearwater Beach, FL 33767; (727) 441-1111 **Wine list** *California, Italy* **Wine prices** *Moderate* **Cuisine** *Italian* **Menu prices** *$11–$28*

DONATELLO
232 N. Dale Mabry Highway, Tampa, FL 33609; (813) 875-6660 **Wine list** *Italy, California, France* **Wine prices** *Moderate* **Cuisine** *Northern Italian* **Menu prices** *$19–$30*

DUX
The Peabody Orlando, 9801 International Drive, Orlando, FL 32819; (407) 345-4570 **Wine list** *California* **Wine prices** *Moderate* **Cuisine** *Contemporary* **Menu prices** *$18–$54*

ELEPHANT WALK RESTAURANT
Sandestin Resort, 9300 Highway 98 W., Destin, FL 32550; (850) 267-4800 **Wine list** *California* **Wine prices** *Moderate* **Corkage** *$25* **Cuisine** *International* **Menu prices** *$18–$41*

ELLIE'S 🍷

41 Royal Palm Pointe, Vero Beach, FL 32960; (772) 778-2600 **Wine list** *California* **Wine prices** *Moderate* **Corkage** *$15* **Cuisine** *Regional/French* **Menu prices** *$20–$30*

EMERIL'S RESTAURANT ORLANDO 🍷🍷

6000 Universal Blvd. No. 702, Orlando, FL 32819; (407) 224-2424 **Wine list** *California, France, Australia* **Wine prices** *Moderate* **Cuisine** *Contemporary New Orleans* **Menu prices** *$20–$38*

EUPHEMIA HAYE 🍷

5540 Gulf of Mexico Drive, Longboat Key, FL 34228; (941) 383-3633 **Wine list** *California, France* **Wine prices** *Expensive* **Corkage** *$10* **Cuisine** *International* **Menu prices** *$17–$37*

FETISHES FINE DINING 🍷

6690 Gulf Blvd., St. Pete Beach, FL 33706; (727) 363-3700 **Wine list** *California* **Wine prices** *Moderate* **Cuisine** *Contemporary American* **Menu prices** *$18–$36*

THE FISH HOUSE 🍷

600 Barracks St., Pensacola, FL 32501; (850) 470-0003 **Wine list** *California* **Wine prices** *Moderate* **Cuisine** *Seafood* **Menu prices** *$15–$22*

FISH OUT OF WATER 🍷

34 Goldenrod Circle, Seagrove Beach, FL 32459; (850) 534-5050 **Wine list** *California* **Wine prices** *Expensive* **Corkage** *$20* **Cuisine** *Regional* **Menu prices** *$24–$34*

FISHBONES 🍷

6707 Sand Lake Road, Orlando, FL 32819; (407) 352-0135 **Wine list** *California* **Wine prices** *Moderate* **Corkage** *$15* **Cuisine** *Steak house/seafood* **Menu prices** *$13–$36*

FLAGLER GRILL 🍷

47 S.W. Flagler Ave., Stuart, FL 34994; (561) 221-9517 **Wine list** *California* **Wine prices** *Moderate* **Cuisine** *American* **Menu prices** *$17–$28*

FLEMING'S PRIME STEAKHOUSE & WINE BAR 🍷

4322 W. Boy Scout Blvd., Tampa, FL 33607; (813) 874-9463 **Wine list** *California* **Wine prices** *Moderate* **Cuisine** *Steak house* **Menu prices** *$18–$27*

FLYING FISH CAFÉ
Walt Disney World Boardwalk Resort, 1300 Epcot Resorts Blvd., Lake Buena Vista, FL 32830; (407) 939-2FLY **Wine list** *California, Champagne* **Wine prices** *Moderate* **Corkage** *$15* **Cuisine** *Seafood* **Menu prices** *$18–$45*

THE FORGE
432 41st St., Miami Beach, FL 33140; (305) 538-8533 **Wine list** *Bordeaux, California* **Wine prices** *Moderate* **Cuisine** *Steak house* **Menu prices** *$22–$60*

FORLINI'S RISTORANTE & BAR
435 Mandalay Ave., Clearwater Beach, FL 33767; (727) 445-1155 **Wine list** *California, Italy, France* **Wine prices** *Moderate* **Cuisine** *Italian* **Menu prices** *$11–$28*

FRED'S
1924 S. Osprey Ave., Sarasota, FL 34239; (941) 364-5811 **Wine list** *France, California, Italy, Spain* **Wine prices** *Moderate* **Corkage** *$15* **Cuisine** *American* **Menu prices** *$13–$28*

THE FRENCH BAKERY CAFÉ
1023 Kane Concourse, Bay Harbor Island, FL 33154; (305) 868-5212 **Wine list** *California, France* **Wine prices** Inexpensive **Corkage** *$10* **Cuisine** *Contemporary French* **Menu prices** *$10–$20*

FULTON'S CRAB HOUSE
1670 Lake Buena Vista Drive, Lake Buena Vista, FL 32830; (407) 934-2628 **Wine list** *California* **Wine prices** *Moderate* **Cuisine** *Seafood* **Menu prices** *$17–$45*

GIGI'S TAVERN, OYSTER BAR & CAFÉ
Mizner Park, 346 Plaza Real, Boca Raton, FL 33432; (561) 368-4488 **Wine list** *California* **Wine prices** Inexpensive **Cuisine** *French/seafood* **Menu prices** *$14–$30*

GIOVANNI'S
1161 Beach Blvd., Jacksonville Beach, FL 32250; (904) 249-7787 **Wine list** *California, Italy* **Wine prices** *Moderate* **Cuisine** *Continental/Italian* **Menu prices** *$16–$36*

GRAZIANO'S RESTAURANTE Y ASADOR 
9227 Bird Road, Miami, FL 33165; (305) 225-0008 **Wine list** *Argentina, Italy, France, California* **Wine prices** *Moderate* **Corkage** *$10* **Cuisine** *Argentinean* **Menu prices** *$14–$29*

FLORIDA

GREEN STREET CAFÉ 🍷
3110 Commodore Plaza, Coconut Grove, FL 33133; (305) 444-0244 **Wine list** *California, France* **Wine prices** *Moderate* **Cuisine** *Italian/French* **Menu prices** *$11–$20*

THE GRILL 🍷🍷
The Ritz-Carlton Amelia Island, 4750 Amelia Island Parkway, Amelia Island, FL 32034; (904) 277-1100 **Wine list** *France, California* **Wine prices** *Expensive* **Corkage** *$20* **Cuisine** *International* **Menu prices** *Prix fixe only; $65–$125*

THE GRILL 🍷🍷
The Ritz-Carlton Naples, 280 Vanderbilt Beach Road, Naples, FL 34108; (941) 598-3300 **Wine list** *France, California, Italy, Germany* **Wine prices** *Expensive* **Cuisine** *Steak house* **Menu prices** *$35–$41*

THE GRILL 🍷
The Ritz-Carlton Palm Beach, 100 S. Ocean Blvd., Manalapan, FL 33462; (561) 533-6000 **Wine list** *California, France* **Wine prices** *Expensive* **Corkage** *$20* **Cuisine** *American/European* **Menu prices** *$22–$52*

HARRY'S CONTINENTAL KITCHENS 🍷
525 Saint Jude's Drive, Longboat Key, FL 34228; (941) 383-0777 **Wine list** *California* **Wine prices** *Moderate* **Cuisine** *Continental/seafood* **Menu prices** *$19–$32*

HENRY'S 🍷
16850 Jog Road, Delray Beach, FL 33446; (561) 638-1949 **Wine list** *California* **Wine prices** *Moderate* **Corkage** *$12* **Cuisine** *American* **Menu prices** *$15–$26*

HI-LIFE CAFÉ 🍷
3000 N. Federal Highway, Fort Lauderdale, FL 33306; (954) 563-1395 **Wine list** *California* **Wine prices** *Moderate* **Corkage** *$10* **Cuisine** *Contemporary American* **Menu prices** *$15–$25*

HOBO'S FISH JOINT 🍷
10317 Royal Palm Blvd., Coral Springs, FL 33065; (954) 346-5484 **Wine list** *California* **Wine prices** *Moderate* **Cuisine** *Seafood* **Menu prices** *$20–$35*

HOLLYWOOD PRIME 🍷
The Westin Diplomat Resort & Spa, 3555 S. Ocean Drive, Hollywood, FL 33019; (954) 602-6000 **Wine list** *California, France* **Wine prices** *Expensive* **Cuisine** *Steak house* **Menu prices** *$27–$78*

🍷🍷🍷 Grand Award 🍷🍷 Best of Award of Excellence 🍷 Award of Excellence

IAN'S TROPICAL GRILL
927 N. U.S. 1, Fort Pierce, FL 34950; (772) 595-5950 **Wine list** *California* **Wine prices** *Moderate* **Corkage** *$15* **Cuisine** *Floridian/French* **Menu prices** *$14–$26*

IL TERRAZZO
Tampa Marriott Waterside, 700 S. Florida Ave., Tampa, FL 33602; (813) 204-6343 **Wine list** *Italy* **Wine prices** *Moderate* **Corkage** *$20* **Cuisine** *Northern Italian* **Menu prices** *$21–$39*

ISLAND WAY GRILL
20 Island Way, Clearwater Beach, FL 33767; (727) 461-6617 **Wine list** *California, France* **Wine prices** *Moderate* **Corkage** *$15* **Cuisine** *Pacific Rim* **Menu prices** *$11–$36*

JACKSON'S
400 S. Palafox St., Pensacola, FL 32501; (850) 469-9898 **Wine list** *France, California* **Wine prices** *Moderate* **Corkage** *$20* **Cuisine** *Regional* **Menu prices** *$24–$54*

JACKSON'S BISTRO
601 S. Harbor Island Blvd., Tampa, FL 33602; (813) 277-0112 **Wine list** *California* **Wine prices** *Moderate* **Corkage** *$10* **Cuisine** *International* **Menu prices** *$15–$30*

JACKSON'S STEAKHOUSE
450 E. Las Olas Blvd., Fort Lauderdale, FL 33301; (954) 522-4450 **Wine list** *California* **Wine prices** *Moderate* **Cuisine** *Steak house* **Menu prices** *$16–$39*

JAKE'S BAR & GRILL
6901 S.W. 57th Ave., Coral Gables, FL 33143; (305) 662-8632 **Wine list** *California* **Wine prices** *Moderate* **Corkage** *$5* **Cuisine** *American* **Menu prices** *$15–$24*

JIKO
Disney's Animal Kingdom Lodge, 2901 Osecola Parkway, Bay Lake, FL 32830; (407) WDW-DINE **Wine list** *South Africa* **Wine prices** *Moderate* **Corkage** *$20* **Cuisine** *African* **Menu prices** *$18–$29*

JOHANNES
47 E. Palmetto Park Road, Boca Raton, FL 33432; (561) 394-0007 **Wine list** *France, California* **Wine prices** *Moderate* **Cuisine** *Contemporary* **Menu prices** *Prix fixe only; $79*

JONATHAN'S
6777 Manatee Ave. W., Bradenton, FL 34209; (941) 761-1177 **Wine list** *California* **Wine prices** *Moderate* **Corkage** *$25* **Cuisine** *American* **Menu prices** *$18–$35*

JUBILEE RESTAURANT
400 Quietwater Beach Road, Pensacola Beach, FL 32561; (850) 934-3108 **Wine list** *California* **Wine prices** *Moderate* **Cuisine** *International* **Menu prices** *$21–$33*

KELLY'S FOR JUST ABOUT . . . ANYTHING!
319 Main St., Dunedin, FL 34698; (727) 736-5284 **Wine list** *California* **Wine prices** Inexpensive **Corkage** *$10* **Cuisine** *Contemporary American* **Menu prices** *$12–$20*

L'ESCALIER AT THE FLORENTINE ROOM
The Breakers, 1 S. County Road, Palm Beach, FL 33480; (561) 659-8480 **Wine list** *France, California* **Wine selections** *1,200* **Number of bottles** *22,000* **Wine prices** *Moderate* **Cuisine** *Contemporary French* **Menu prices** *Prix fixe only; $70* **Credit cards** *AX, MC, VS, DV*
Grand Award since 1981

LA PARISIENNE
60 Hypolita St., St. Augustine, FL 32084; (904) 829-0055 **Wine list** *California* **Wine prices** *Moderate* **Cuisine** *Contemporary French* **Menu prices** *$18–$28*

LAFITE
Registry Resort, 475 Seagate Drive, Naples, FL 34103; (941) 597-3232 **Wine list** *California* **Wine prices** *Expensive* **Corkage** *$32* **Cuisine** *American* **Menu prices** *$28–$50*

LATITUDES CAFÉ
Sunset Key Resort, 245 Front St., Key West, FL 33040; (305) 292-5394 **Wine list** *California* **Wine prices** *Moderate* **Corkage** *$15* **Cuisine** *Regional* **Menu prices** *$28–$38*

LE COQ AU VIN
4800 S. Orange Ave., Orlando, FL 32806; (407) 851-6980 **Wine list** *France, Washington, Oregon* **Wine prices** *Moderate* **Corkage** *$15* **Cuisine** *French* **Menu prices** *$15–$27*

LEGAL SEA FOODS
Boca Raton Towne Center, 6000 W. Glades Road, Boca Raton, FL 33431; (561) 447-2112 **Wine list** *California* **Wine prices** Inexpensive **Cuisine** *Seafood* **Menu prices** *$11–$48*

Grand Award · Best of Award of Excellence · Award of Excellence

LEGAL SEA FOODS

The Oasis at Sawgrass Mills, 2602 Sawgrass Mills Circle, Sunrise, FL 33323; (954) 846-9011 **Wine list** *California* **Wine prices** Inexpensive **Cuisine** *Seafood* **Menu prices** *$11–$48*

LEGAL SEA FOODS

City Place Mall, 550 S. Rosemary Ave., West Palm Beach, FL 33401; (561) 838-9000 **Wine list** *California* **Wine prices** Inexpensive **Cuisine** *Seafood* **Menu prices** *$11–$48*

LEMONIA

The Ritz-Carlton Golf Resort Naples, 2600 Tiburon Drive, Naples, FL 34109; (239) 254-3373 **Wine list** *California, Italy, France* **Wine prices** *Expensive* **Cuisine** *Tuscan* **Menu prices** *$23–$32*

LEMONT

515 N. Flagler Drive, 20th floor, West Palm Beach, FL 33401; (561) 820-2442 **Wine list** *California, France* **Wine prices** *Expensive* **Corkage** *$10* **Cuisine** *Continental* **Menu prices** *$27–$39*

LUCCA

Boca Raton Resort & Club, 501 E. Camino Real, Boca Raton, FL 33432; (561) 447-5822 **Wine list** *Italy, California* **Wine prices** *Moderate* **Corkage** *$25* **Cuisine** *Northern Italian* **Menu prices** *$22–$45*

MAISON & JARDIN RESTAURANT

430 S. Wymore Road, Altamonte Springs, FL 32714; (407) 862-4410 **Wine list** *California, Bordeaux, Burgundy* **Wine selections** *1,500* **Number of bottles** *16,000* **Wine prices** *Moderate* **Cuisine** *Contemporary* **Menu prices** *$22–$35* **Credit cards** *AX, MC, VS, DV*

Grand Award since 1995

MANCINI'S

1017 E. Las Olas Blvd., Fort Lauderdale, FL 33301; (954) 764-5510 **Wine list** *Italy* **Wine prices** *Moderate* **Corkage** *$15* **Cuisine** *Italian* **Menu prices** *$18–$36*

MANGIA MANGIA

900 Southard St., Key West, FL 33040; (305) 294-2469 **Wine list** *Bordeaux, California, Italy* **Wine prices** *Moderate* **Corkage** *$10* **Cuisine** *Italian* **Menu prices** *$10–$17*

MARCELLO'S LA SIRENA 🍷🍷
6316 S. Dixie Highway, West Palm Beach, FL 33405; (561) 585-3128 **Wine list** *Italy, California, France* **Wine prices** *Moderate* **Cuisine** *Italian* **Menu prices** *$14–$36*

MARINA CAFÉ 🍷
404 E. Highway 98, Destin, FL 32541; (850) 837-7960 **Wine list** *California, France* **Wine prices** *Moderate* **Cuisine** *Mediterranean/creole/Pan-Asian* **Menu prices** *$15–$29*

MARIO'S TUSCAN GRILL 🍷
1450 N. Federal Highway, Boca Raton, FL 33432; (561) 362-7407 **Wine list** *Italy* **Wine prices** *Moderate* **Cuisine** *Italian* **Menu prices** *$16–$38*

THE MARITANA GRILLE 🍷
The Don Cesar Beach Resort & Spa, 3400 Gulf Blvd., St. Pete Beach, FL 33706; (727) 360-1882 **Wine list** *California, France* **Wine prices** *Moderate* **Cuisine** *American/International* **Menu prices** *$28–$33*

MARK'S LAS OLAS 🍷
1032 E. Las Olas Blvd., Fort Lauderdale, FL 33301; (954) 463-1000 **Wine list** *California* **Wine prices** *Moderate* **Corkage** *$16* **Cuisine** *Contemporary* **Menu prices** *$24–$38*

MARK'S SOUTH BEACH 🍷
Hotel Nash, 1120 Collins Ave., Miami Beach, FL 33139; (305) 604-9050 **Wine list** *California* **Wine prices** *Moderate* **Corkage** *$15* **Cuisine** *Mediterranean/Floridian* **Menu prices** *$25–$42*

THE MARLIN GRILL 🍷
9100 Baytowne Wharf Blvd., Sandestin, FL 32550; (850) 351-1990 **Wine list** *California* **Wine prices** Inexpensive **Cuisine** *Continental* **Menu prices** *$19–$38*

MATTHEW'S RESTAURANT 🍷
2107 Hendricks Ave., Jacksonville, FL 32207; (904) 396-9922 **Wine list** *California* **Wine prices** *Moderate* **Corkage** *$15* **Cuisine** *Continental* **Menu prices** *$18–$36*

MAX & EDDIE'S CUCINA 🍷
2441 Beach Court, Singer Island, FL 33404; (561) 842-5200 **Wine list** *California, Italy* **Wine prices** *Moderate* **Cuisine** *Italian* **Menu prices** *$16–$26*

MAX'S GRILLE 🍷
404 Plaza Real, Boca Raton, FL 33432; (561) 368-0080
Wine list *California* **Wine prices** *Expensive* **Corkage** *$20*
Cuisine *American* **Menu prices** *$9–$29*

MCGUIRE'S IRISH PUB 🍷
600 E. Gregory St., Pensacola, FL 32501; (850) 433-6789
Wine list *California* **Wine prices** Inexpensive **Cuisine** *Steak house* **Menu prices** *$16–$27*

THE MELTING POT 🍷
5455 N. Federal Highway, Boca Raton, FL 33487; (561) 997-7472 **Wine list** *California, Bordeaux* **Wine prices** *Moderate* **Corkage** *$15* **Cuisine** *Fondue* **Menu prices** *$15–$29*

THE MELTING POT 🍷
25822 U.S. Highway 19 N., Clearwater, FL 34623; (727) 797-4426 **Wine list** *California* **Wine prices** *Moderate* **Cuisine** *Fondue* **Menu prices** *$17–$29*

THE MELTING POT 🍷
2221 Fourth St. N., St. Petersburg, FL 33704; (727) 895-6358 **Wine list** *California* **Wine prices** *Moderate* **Cuisine** *Fondue* **Menu prices** *$17–$29*

THE MELTING POT 🍷
13164 N. Dale Mabry Highway, Tampa, FL 33618; (813) 962-6936 **Wine list** *California* **Wine prices** *Moderate* **Cuisine** *Fondue* **Menu prices** *$17–$29*

MICHAEL'S ON EAST 🍷
1212 East Ave. S., Sarasota, FL 34239; (941) 366-0007
Wine list *California, France* **Wine prices** *Moderate* **Corkage** *$10* **Cuisine** *Contemporary American* **Menu prices** *$17–$32*

MILDRED'S BIG CITY FOOD 🍷
3445 W. University Ave., Gainesville, FL 32607; (352) 371-1711 **Wine list** *California* **Wine prices** Inexpensive **Cuisine** *Regional* **Menu prices** *$14–$21*

MONTE'S 🍷🍷
1517 S. Ocean Drive, Vero Beach, FL 32963; (561) 231-6612 **Wine list** *Italy, California* **Wine prices** *Moderate* **Cuisine** *Italian* **Menu prices** *$10–$40*

MOONFISH RESTAURANT 🍷
7525 W. Sand Lake Road, Orlando, FL 32819; (407) 363-7262 **Wine list** *California* **Wine prices** *Moderate* **Corkage** *$15* **Cuisine** *Seafood* **Menu prices** *$14–$30*

MORTON'S OF CHICAGO
5050 Town Center Circle, Boca Raton, FL 33486; (561) 392-7724 **Wine list** *California* **Wine prices** *Expensive* **Corkage** *$15* **Cuisine** *Steak house* **Menu prices** *$22–$35*

MORTON'S OF CHICAGO
1510 Riverplace Blvd., Jacksonville, FL 32207; (904) 399-3933 **Wine list** *California* **Wine prices** *Expensive* **Corkage** *$15* **Cuisine** *Steak house* **Menu prices** *$20–$35*

MORTON'S OF CHICAGO
1200 Brickell Ave., Miami, FL 33131; (305) 400-9990 **Wine list** *California* **Wine prices** *Expensive* **Corkage** *$15* **Cuisine** *Steak house* **Menu prices** *$19–$33*

MORTON'S OF CHICAGO
17399 Biscayne Blvd., North Miami Beach, FL 33160; (305) 945-3131 **Wine list** *California* **Wine prices** *Expensive* **Corkage** *$15* **Cuisine** *Steak house* **Menu prices** *$20–$35*

MORTON'S OF CHICAGO
The Market Place, 7600 Dr. Phillips Blvd., Orlando, FL 32819; (407) 248-3485 **Wine list** *California* **Wine prices** *Expensive* **Cuisine** *Steak house* **Menu prices** *$20–$35*

MORTON'S OF CHICAGO
777 S. Flagler Drive, West Palm Beach, FL 33401; (561) 835-9664 **Wine list** *California* **Wine prices** *Expensive* **Cuisine** *Steak house* **Menu prices** *$20–$34*

MUNROE'S RESTAURANT & JAZZ TAVERN
1296 First St., Sarasota, FL 34236; (941) 316-0609 **Wine list** *California* **Wine prices** *Moderate* **Corkage** *$15* **Cuisine** *American* **Menu prices** *$16–$45*

95 CORDOVA & COBALT LOUNGE
Casa Monica Hotel, 95 Cordova St., St. Augustine, FL 32084; (904) 810-6810 **Wine list** *California* **Wine prices** *Moderate* **Cuisine** *International* **Menu prices** *$16–$39*

NORMAN'S
21 Almeria Ave., Coral Gables, FL 33134; (305) 446-6767 **Wine list** *France, California* **Wine prices** *Expensive* **Corkage** *$28* **Cuisine** *International* **Menu prices** *$29–$44*

NORWOOD'S RESTAURANT
400 Second Ave., New Smyrna Beach, FL 32169; (386) 428-4621 **Wine list** *California, France, Italy* **Wine prices** Inexpensive **Cuisine** *Steak house/seafood* **Menu prices** *$8–$25*

Grand Award | Best of Award of Excellence | Award of Excellence

OCEAN GRILL
1050 Sexton Plaza, Vero Beach, FL 32963; (561) 231-5409
Wine list *California* **Wine prices** Inexpensive **Corkage** *$10*
Cuisine *American* **Menu prices** *$14–$30*

OLD HICKORY STEAKHOUSE
Gaylord Palms Resort & Conference Center, 6000 W. Osceola Parkway, Kissimmee, FL 34746; (407) 586-1600 **Wine list** *California* **Wine prices** *Moderate* **Cuisine** *Steak house* **Menu prices** *$24–$45*

ORTANIQUE
278 Miracle Mile, Coral Gables, FL 33134; (305) 446-7710
Wine list *California* **Wine prices** *Moderate* **Corkage** *$15*
Cuisine *Caribbean/Latin* **Menu prices** *$16–$32*

OYSTERCATCHER'S
Grand Hyatt Tampa Bay, 6200 Courtney Campbell Causeway, Tampa, FL 33607; (813) 207-6815 **Wine list** *California* **Wine prices** *Moderate* **Cuisine** *Seafood* **Menu prices** *$19–$29*

THE PALM
9650 E. Bay Harbor Drive, Bay Harbor Island, FL 33154; (305) 868-7256 **Wine list** *California, France* **Wine prices** *Expensive* **Corkage** *$25* **Cuisine** *Steak house* **Menu prices** *$17–$126*

THE PALM
4425 Ponce de Leon Blvd., Coral Gables, FL 33146; (786) 552-7256 **Wine list** *California* **Wine prices** *Moderate* **Corkage** *$20* **Cuisine** *Steak house* **Menu prices** *$16–$100*

THE PALM
Hard Rock Hotel, 5800 Universal Blvd., Orlando, FL 32819; (407) 503-7256 **Wine list** *California, Italy* **Wine prices** *Expensive* **Corkage** *$15* **Cuisine** *Steak house* **Menu prices** *$15–$60*

THE PALM
205 Westshore Plaza Drive, Tampa, FL 33609; (813) 849-7256 **Wine list** *California* **Wine prices** *Moderate* **Corkage** *$20* **Cuisine** *Steak house* **Menu prices** *$17–$60*

PANDORA'S STEAK HOUSE
1120-B Santa Rosa Blvd., Fort Walton Beach, FL 32548; (850) 244-8669 **Wine list** *California* **Wine prices** *Moderate* **Corkage** *$10* **Cuisine** *Steak house* **Menu prices** *$14–$25*

FLORIDA

PAZZO! 🍷
853 Fifth Ave. S., Naples, FL 34102; (941) 434-8494 **Wine list** *California, Italy* **Wine prices** *Moderate* **Corkage** *$10* **Cuisine** *Italian* **Menu prices** *$14–$25*

PELICAN 🍷
Pelican Hotel, 826 Ocean Drive, Miami Beach, FL 33139; (305) 673-3373 **Wine list** *California, Italy* **Wine prices** *Moderate* **Cuisine** *Italian/American* **Menu prices** *$15–$29*

PETE'S OF BOCA RATON 🍷
7940 Glades Road, Boca Raton, FL 33434; (561) 487-1600 **Wine list** *California* **Wine prices** *Moderate* **Corkage** *$15* **Cuisine** *Contemporary American* **Menu prices** *$20–$39*

PISCES BY CAFÉ DES ARTISTES 🍷
1007 Simonton St., Key West, FL 33040; (305) 294-7100 **Wine list** *France, California* **Wine prices** *Moderate* **Cuisine** *American* **Menu prices** *$25–$42*

POM'S THAI BISTRO 🍷
1974 San Marco Blvd., Jacksonville, FL 32207; (904) 338-0269 **Wine list** *California* **Wine prices** *Moderate* **Corkage** *$15* **Cuisine** *Thai* **Menu prices** *$14–$34*

PONTE VEDRA INN & CLUB 🍷
200 Ponte Vedra Blvd., Ponte Vedra Beach, FL 32082; (904) 285-1111 **Wine list** *France, California* **Wine prices** *Moderate* **Cuisine** *Continental* **Menu prices** *$25–$35*

THE PORTOBELLO YACHT CLUB 🍷
Pleasure Island, 1650 Buena Vista Drive, Lake Buena Vista, FL 32830; (407) 934-8888 **Wine list** *Italy, California* **Wine prices** *Moderate* **Cuisine** *Italian* **Menu prices** *$14–$34*

PRIMAVERA RESTAURANT 🍷
Primavera Plaza, 830 E. Oakland Park Blvd., Fort Lauderdale, FL 33334; (954) 564-6363 **Wine list** *Italy* **Wine prices** *Moderate* **Corkage** *$15* **Cuisine** *Italian* **Menu prices** *$13–$60*

PROFUSION 🍷
2223 N. Westshore Blvd., Tampa, FL 33607; (813) 353-8400 **Wine list** *France, California* **Wine prices** *Moderate* **Cuisine** *Steak house/sushi* **Menu prices** *$14–$27*

RAINTREE RESTAURANT 🍷
102 San Marco Ave., St. Augustine, FL 32084; (904) 824-7211 **Wine list** *California* **Wine prices** *Moderate* **Cuisine** *Continental* **Menu prices** *$18–$25*

🍷🍷🍷 Grand Award 🍷🍷 Best of Award of Excellence 🍷 Award of Excellence

FLORIDA

THE RESTAURANT
Four Seasons Resort Palm Beach, 2800 S. Ocean Blvd., Palm Beach, FL 33480; (561) 533-3750 **Wine list** *California, France* **Wine prices** *Expensive* **Corkage** *$35* **Cuisine** *Regional* **Menu prices** *$30–$42*

RESTAURANT MEDURE
818 N. A1A, Ponte Vedra Beach, FL 32082; (904) 543-3797 **Wine list** *California* **Wine prices** *Moderate* **Corkage** *$15* **Cuisine** *Contemporary* **Menu prices** *$14–$27*

THE RIVER HOUSE RESTAURANT
2373 PGA Blvd., Palm Beach Gardens, FL 33410; (407) 694-1188 **Wine list** *California* **Wine prices** *Moderate* **Corkage** *$20* **Cuisine** *American* **Menu prices** *$13–$40*

ROESSLER'S
2033 Vamo Way, Sarasota, FL 34238; (941) 966-5688 **Wine list** *California, France* **Wine prices** *Moderate* **Corkage** *$15* **Cuisine** *Continental* **Menu prices** *$18–$34*

RONNIE'S STEAKHOUSE
7500 International Drive, Orlando, FL 32819; (407) 313-3000 **Wine list** *California* **Wine prices** *Expensive* **Cuisine** *Steak house* **Menu prices** *$15–$28*

ROY'S TAMPA
4342 Boy Scout Blvd., Tampa, FL 33607; (813) 873-7697 **Wine list** *California* **Wine prices** *Moderate* **Cuisine** *Contemporary/Hawaiian* **Menu prices** *$18–$28*

RUSTY PELICAN
2425 Rocky Point Drive, Tampa, FL 33607; (813) 281-1943 **Wine list** *California* **Wine prices** *Moderate* **Corkage** *$10* **Cuisine** *American* **Menu prices** *$19–$33*

RUTH'S CHRIS STEAK HOUSE
225 N.E. Mizner Blvd., Boca Raton, FL 33432; (561) 392-6746 **Wine list** *California* **Wine prices** *Moderate* **Corkage** *$15* **Cuisine** *Steak house* **Menu prices** *$18–$33*

RUTH'S CHRIS STEAK HOUSE
2320 Salzedo St., Coral Gables, FL 33134; (305) 461-8360 **Wine list** *California* **Wine prices** *Moderate* **Corkage** *$15* **Cuisine** *Steak house* **Menu prices** *$25–$60*

RUTH'S CHRIS STEAK HOUSE
2525 N. Federal Highway, Fort Lauderdale, FL 33305; (954) 565-2338 **Wine list** *California* **Wine prices** *Moderate* **Cuisine** *Steak house* **Menu prices** *$18–$32*

RUTH'S CHRIS STEAK HOUSE 🍷
661 U.S. Highway 1, North Palm Beach, FL 33408; (561) 863-0660 **Wine list** *California* **Wine prices** *Moderate* **Corkage** *$15* **Cuisine** *Steak house* **Menu prices** *$20–$45*

RUTH'S CHRIS STEAK HOUSE 🍷
814 A1A N., Ponte Vedra Beach, FL 32082; (904) 285-0014 **Wine list** *California* **Wine prices** *Moderate* **Corkage** *$20* **Cuisine** *Steak house* **Menu prices** *$16–$35*

RUTH'S CHRIS STEAK HOUSE 🍷
6700 S. Tamiami Trail, Sarasota, FL 34231; (941) 924-9442 **Wine list** *California* **Wine prices** *Moderate* **Corkage** *$15* **Cuisine** *Steak house* **Menu prices** *$18–$65*

RUTH'S CHRIS STEAK HOUSE 🍷
1700 N. Westshore Blvd., Tampa, FL 33607; (813) 282-1118 **Wine list** *California* **Wine prices** *Moderate* **Corkage** *$18* **Cuisine** *Steak house* **Menu prices** *$18–$55*

RUTH'S CHRIS STEAK HOUSE 🍷
610 N. Orlando Ave., Winter Park, FL 32789; (407) 622-2444 **Wine list** *California* **Wine prices** *Moderate* **Cuisine** *Steak house* **Menu prices** *$18–$31*

RUTHERFORDS 465 RESTAURANT 🍷
465 Regatta Bay Blvd., Destin, FL 32541; (850) 337-8888 **Wine list** *California* **Wine prices** *Expensive* **Corkage** *$8* **Cuisine** *French/regional* **Menu prices** *$21–$40*

SALT ROCK GRILL 🍷
19325 Gulf Blvd., Indian Shores, FL 33785; (727) 593-7625 **Wine list** *California* **Wine prices** *Moderate* **Corkage** *$15* **Cuisine** *Steak house/seafood* **Menu prices** *$10–$35*

SANDS POINTE 🍷
The Resort at Longboat Key, 301 Gulf of Mexico Drive, Longboat Key, FL 34228; (941) 387-1626 **Wine list** *California* **Wine prices** *Expensive* **Cuisine** *Seafood* **Menu prices** *$17–$36*

THE SANIBEL STEAK HOUSE 🍷
24041 S. Tamiami Trail, Bonita Springs, FL 34134; (941) 390-0400 **Wine list** *California* **Wine prices** *Moderate* **Cuisine** *Steak house* **Menu prices** *$20–$30*

SEAGAR'S RESTAURANT

Sandestin Hilton, 4000 Sandestin Blvd. S., Destin, FL 32550; (850) 622-1500 **Wine list** *California* **Wine prices** *Moderate* **Corkage** *$25* **Cuisine** *Steak house/seafood* **Menu prices** *$19–$43*

SEASONS 52

770 Sandlake Road, Orlando, FL 32819; (407) 354-5212 **Wine list** *California* **Wine prices** *Moderate* **Cuisine** *Contemporary* **Menu prices** *$10–$20*

SHULA'S ON THE BEACH

Wyndham Beach Resort, 1435 Simonton St., Key West, FL 33040; (305) 296-6144 **Wine list** *California* **Wine prices** *Moderate* **Cuisine** *Steak house* **Menu prices** *$21–$35*

SHULA'S STEAK HOUSE

Walt Disney World Dolphin Hotel, 1500 Epcot Resorts Blvd., Lake Buena Vista, FL 32830; (407) 934-1362 **Wine list** *California* **Wine prices** *Moderate* **Cuisine** *Steak house* **Menu prices** *$21–$33*

SIDEBERN'S

2208 W. Morrison Ave., Tampa, FL 33606; (813) 258-CAFE **Wine list** *California, France* **Wine prices** *Moderate* **Corkage** *$20* **Cuisine** *Contemporary American* **Menu prices** *$18–$32*

SIX TABLES

4267 Henderson Blvd., Tampa, FL 33629; (813) 207-0527 **Wine list** *California* **Wine prices** *Moderate* **Corkage** *$25* **Cuisine** *Continental* **Menu prices** *Prix fixe only; $60–$100*

SMITH & WOLLENSKY

South Pointe Park, 1 Washington Ave., Miami Beach, FL 33139; (305) 673-2800 **Wine list** *Bordeaux, California* **Wine prices** *Expensive* **Cuisine** *Steak house* **Menu prices** *$19–$39*

SNAPPERS SEAFOOD & PASTA

398 N. Congress Ave., Boynton Beach, FL 33426; (561) 375-8600 **Wine list** *California* **Wine prices** *Moderate* **Corkage** *$8* **Cuisine** *Seafood* **Menu prices** *$15–$25*

SOLEIL ET LUNA

747 Highway 98 E., Destin, FL 32541; (850) 650-0332 **Wine list** *California* **Wine prices** Inexpensive **Cuisine** *Regional* **Menu prices** *$10–$20*

ST. TROPEZ AL FRESCO BISTRO 🍷
2075 Indian River Blvd., Vero Beach, FL 32960; (561) 778-9565 **Wine list** *France, California* **Wine prices** *Moderate* **Corkage** *$15* **Cuisine** *French/Italian* **Menu prices** *$16–$37*

STEVE'S CAFÉ AMERICAIN 🍷
12 W. University Ave., Gainesville, FL 32601; (352) 377-9337 **Wine list** *California* **Wine prices** Inexpensive **Corkage** *$5* **Cuisine** *American* **Menu prices** *$16–$26*

THE SUMMERHOUSE 🍷
6101 Midnight Pass Road, Sarasota, FL 34242; (941) 349-1100 **Wine list** *California* **Wine prices** *Moderate* **Cuisine** *Continental* **Menu prices** *$19–$36*

SUNFISH GRILL 🍷
2771 E. Atlantic Blvd., Pompano Beach, FL 33062; (954) 788-2434 **Wine list** *California* **Wine prices** *Moderate* **Corkage** *$25* **Cuisine** *Seafood* **Menu prices** *$21–$34*

SYRAH RESTAURANT 🍷
475 Bayfront Place, Naples, FL 34102; (941) 417-9724 **Wine list** *California* **Wine prices** *Moderate* **Cuisine** *International* **Menu prices** *$18–$34*

TANGOS 🍷
3001 Ocean Drive, Vero Beach, FL 32963; (772) 231-1550 **Wine list** *California, Italy* **Wine prices** *Moderate* **Corkage** *$15* **Cuisine** *Seafood* **Menu prices** *$21–$30*

TANTRA RESTAURANT & LOUNGE 🍷
1445 Pennsylvania Ave., Miami Beach, FL 33139; (305) 672-4765 **Wine list** *California, France, Italy* **Wine prices** *Expensive* **Cuisine** *International* **Menu prices** *$28–$48*

THE TASTING ROOM AT JD FORD 🍷🍷
1925 S. Osprey Ave., Sarasota, FL 34239; (941) 364-5811 **Wine list** *France, California, Italy, Spain* **Wine prices** *Moderate* **Corkage** *$15* **Cuisine** *American* **Menu prices** *$10–$28*

THE TEMPTATION RESTAURANT 🍷
350 Park Ave., Boca Grande, FL 33921; (941) 964-2610 **Wine list** *California* **Wine prices** Inexpensive **Cuisine** *Floridian* **Menu prices** *$15–$26*

30° BLUE 🍷
3900 Marriott Drive, Panama City, FL 32411; (850) 236-1115 **Wine list** *California* **Wine prices** *Moderate* **Corkage** *$16* **Cuisine** *American* **Menu prices** *$16–$27*

3030 OCEAN
3030 Holiday Drive, Fort Lauderdale, FL 33316; (954) 765-3030 **Wine list** *California* **Wine prices** *Moderate* **Corkage** *$9* **Cuisine** *American* **Menu prices** *$21–$35*

32 EAST
32 E. Atlantic Ave., Delray Beach, FL 33444; (561) 276-7868 **Wine list** *California* **Wine prices** *Moderate* **Cuisine** *Contemporary American* **Menu prices** *$18–$33*

THE TIDES
3103 Cardinal Drive, Vero Beach, FL 32963; (561) 234-3966 **Wine list** *California* **Wine prices** *Moderate* **Cuisine** *Floridian* **Menu prices** *$16–$27*

TIO PEPE RESTAURANTE
2930 Gulf to Bay Blvd., Clearwater, FL 33759; (727) 799-3082 **Wine list** *Spain, France, California* **Wine prices** *Moderate* **Cuisine** *Mediterranean/continental/Latin American* **Menu prices** *$10–$30*

TREVINI RISTORANTE
150 Worth Ave., Palm Beach, FL 33480; (561) 833-3883 **Wine list** *Italy, California* **Wine prices** *Moderate* **Corkage** *$18* **Cuisine** *Italian* **Menu prices** *$24–$30*

THE VERANDA
Turnberry Isle Resort & Club, 19999 W. Country Club Drive, Aventura, FL 33180; (305) 932-6200 **Wine list** *Bordeaux, California, Burgundy* **Wine prices** *Moderate* **Corkage** *$20* **Cuisine** *Contemporary* **Menu prices** *$25–$40*

VESUVIO RESTAURANT
2715 E. Atlantic Blvd., Pompano Beach, FL 33062; (954) 941-1594 **Wine list** *Italy, California* **Wine prices** *Moderate* **Corkage** *$12* **Cuisine** *Southern Italian* **Menu prices** *$15–$30*

VICTORIA & ALBERT'S
Disney's Grand Floridian Resort & Spa, 4401 Grand Floridian Way, Lake Buena Vista, FL 32830; (407) 939-7707 **Wine list** *California, France, Italy* **Wine prices** *Expensive* **Corkage** *$25* **Cuisine** *American* **Menu prices** *Prix fixe only; $85–$115*

VILLAGE CAFÉ
14970 Captiva Drive, Captiva Island, FL 33924; (239) 472-1956 **Wine list** *California, France* **Wine prices** *Expensive* **Corkage** *$25* **Cuisine** *American/French* **Menu prices** *$18–$38*

(VIN'TIJ) WINE BOUTIQUE & BISTRO 🍷
10859 W. Emerald Coast Parkway, Destin, FL 32550; (850) 650-9820 **Wine list** *California* **Wine prices** Inexpensive **Cuisine** *Regional* **Menu prices** *$12–$24*

VITO'S CHOP HOUSE 🍷
8633 International Drive, Orlando, FL 32819; (407) 354-2467 **Wine list** *California, Italy* **Wine prices** *Moderate* **Cuisine** *Steak house* **Menu prices** *$13–$30*

THE WINE CELLAR 🍷
1314 Prudential Drive, Jacksonville, FL 32207; (904) 398-8989 **Wine list** *California* **Wine prices** *Moderate* **Corkage** *$10* **Cuisine** *Continental* **Menu prices** *$14–$29*

WISH 🍷
The Hotel, 801 Collins Ave., Miami Beach, FL 33139; (305) 674-9474 **Wine list** *California, Spain* **Wine prices** *Moderate* **Cuisine** *Contemporary American* **Menu prices** *$23–$32*

YABBA ISLAND GRILL 🍷
711 Fifth Ave. S., Naples, FL 34102; (239) 262-5787 **Wine list** *California* **Wine prices** Inexpensive **Corkage** *$10* **Cuisine** *Seafood* **Menu prices** *$10–$24*

YACHTSMAN STEAKHOUSE 🍷
Disney's Yacht Club Resort, 1700 Epcot Resorts Blvd., Lake Buena Vista, FL 32830; (407) 939-3463 **Wine list** *California* **Wine prices** *Expensive* **Corkage** *$15* **Cuisine** *Steak house* **Menu prices** *$19–$50*

ZOË'S 🍷🍷
720 Fifth Ave. S., Naples, FL 34102; (239) 403-0083 **Wine list** *California, Italy, Bordeaux, Australia* **Wine prices** *Expensive* **Corkage** *$20* **Cuisine** *American* **Menu prices** *$15–$39*

GEORGIA

THE ABBEY 🍷🍷
163 Ponce de Leon Ave. N.E., Atlanta, GA 30308; (404) 876-8532 **Wine list** *Bordeaux, California* **Wine prices** *Expensive* **Cuisine** *Contemporary* **Menu prices** *$22–$38*

ANTHONY'S 🍷
3109 Piedmont Road N.E., Atlanta, GA 30305; (404) 262-7379 **Wine list** *California, France* **Wine prices** *Expensive* **Cuisine** *Contemporary American/regional* **Menu prices** *$18–$52*

ANTICA POSTA 🍷
519 E. Paces Ferry Road N.E., Atlanta, GA 30305; (404) 262-7112 **Wine list** *Italy, California* **Wine prices** *Moderate* **Corkage** *$10* **Cuisine** *Italian* **Menu prices** *$14–$25*

ASPENS SIGNATURE STEAKS 🍷
2942 Shallowford Road, Marietta, GA 30066; (678) 236-1400 **Wine list** *California* **Wine prices** Inexpensive **Corkage** *$15* **Cuisine** *Steak house* **Menu prices** *$15–$26*

ATLANTA FISH MARKET 🍷
265 Pharr Road, Atlanta, GA 30305; (404) 262-3165 **Wine list** *California* **Wine prices** *Moderate* **Corkage** *$10* **Cuisine** *Seafood* **Menu prices** *$16–$32*

ATLANTA GRILL 🍷
The Ritz-Carlton Atlanta, 181 Peachtree St. N.E., Atlanta, GA 30303; (404) 659-0400 **Wine list** *California* **Wine prices** *Expensive* **Cuisine** *Regional* **Menu prices** *$23–$38*

BENTLEY'S STEAKHOUSE 🍷
Atlanta Airport Marriott, 4711 Best Road, College Park, GA 30337; (404) 766-7900 **Wine list** *California* **Wine prices** *Moderate* **Cuisine** *Steak house* **Menu prices** *$18–$33*

BERT'S 🍷
442 Cherry St., Macon, GA 31201; (478) 742-9100 **Wine list** *California* **Wine prices** Inexpensive **Cuisine** *Contemporary Southern* **Menu prices** *$16–$20*

BLUEPOINTE 🍷
3455 Peachtree Road, Atlanta, GA 30326; (404) 237-9070 **Wine list** *California, France* **Wine prices** *Moderate* **Corkage** *$15* **Cuisine** *Asian* **Menu prices** *$17–$32*

BONE'S 🍷🍷
3130 Piedmont Road, Atlanta, GA 30305; (404) 237-2663 **Wine list** *California, France* **Wine prices** *Expensive* **Corkage** *$5* **Cuisine** *Steak house* **Menu prices** *$22–$50*

CANOE 🍷
4199 Paces Ferry Road N.W., Atlanta, GA 30339; (770) 43-CANOE **Wine list** *California* **Wine prices** *Moderate* **Cuisine** *Contemporary American* **Menu prices** *$17–$22*

THE CAPITAL GRILLE 🍷
255 E. Paces Ferry Road, Atlanta, GA 30305; (404) 262-1162 **Wine list** *California* **Wine prices** *Expensive* **Cuisine** *Steak house* **Menu prices** *$17–$34*

CHOPS 🍷
70 W. Paces Ferry Road, Atlanta, GA 30305; (404) 262-2675 **Wine list** *California, France* **Wine prices** *Moderate* **Corkage** *$15* **Cuisine** *Steak house* **Menu prices** *$18–$38*

CITY GRILL 🍷
50 Hurt Plaza, Atlanta, GA 30303; (404) 524-2489 **Wine list** *California* **Wine prices** *Moderate* **Cuisine** *American* **Menu prices** *$14–$32*

COMMUNE 🍷
1198 Howell Mill Road, Atlanta, GA 30318; (404) 609-5000 **Wine list** *California, France* **Wine prices** *Moderate* **Corkage** *$15* **Cuisine** *American* **Menu prices** *$16–$22*

DAILEY'S RESTAURANT & BAR 🍷
17 International Blvd., Atlanta, GA 30303; (404) 681-3303 **Wine list** *California* **Wine prices** *Moderate* **Cuisine** *American/continental* **Menu prices** *$18–$30*

DANTE'S DOWN THE HATCH 🍷
3380 Peachtree Road N.E., Atlanta, GA 30326; (404) 266-1600 **Wine list** *California* **Wine prices** *Moderate* **Cuisine** *Swiss* **Menu prices** *$14–$28*

DI PAOLO 🍷
8560 Holcomb Bridge Road, Alpharetta, GA 30022; (770) 587-1051 **Wine list** *Italy* **Wine prices** *Moderate* **Cuisine** *Contemporary Italian* **Menu prices** *$13–$22*

DICK & HARRY'S 🍷
1570 Holcomb Bridge Road, Roswell, GA 30076; (770) 641-8757 **Wine list** *California* **Wine prices** *Moderate* **Cuisine** *Contemporary American* **Menu prices** *$15–$30*

THE DINING ROOM 🍷🍷
The Ritz-Carlton Buckhead, 3434 Peachtree Road N.E., Atlanta, GA 30326; (404) 240-7035 **Wine list** *Bordeaux, California* **Wine prices** *Expensive* **Corkage** *$35* **Cuisine** *French/Japanese* **Menu prices** *Prix fixe only; $72–$85*

DISH 🍷
870 N. Highland Ave., Atlanta, GA 30306; (404) 897-DINE **Wine list** *California* **Wine prices** *Inexpensive* **Corkage** *$10* **Cuisine** *American* **Menu prices** *$15–$25*

EAST-WEST BISTRO 🍷
351 E. Broad St., Athens, GA 30601; (706) 546-4240
Wine list *California* **Wine prices** Inexpensive **Cuisine** *Northern Italian* **Menu prices** *$13–$22*

ENO 🍷
800 Peachtree St., Atlanta, GA 30308; (404) 685-3191
Wine list *California, Italy* **Wine prices** *Moderate* **Corkage** *$25* **Cuisine** *European/Mediterranean* **Menu prices** *$17–$26*

FOGO DE CHÃO 🍷
3101 Piedmont Road, Atlanta, GA 30305; (404) 266-9988
Wine list *California, Argentina, Chile* **Wine prices** *Expensive* **Cuisine** *Brazilian* **Menu prices** *Prix fixe only; $42*

THE FOOD STUDIO 🍷
887 W. Marietta St., Studio K102, Atlanta, GA 30318; (404) 815-6677 **Wine list** *California* **Wine prices** *Moderate* **Cuisine** *American* **Menu prices** *$16–$29*

G.W. JANOUSEK'S 🍷
5450 Peachtree Parkway Plaza, Norcross, GA 30092; (770) 449-8585 **Wine list** *California* **Wine prices** Inexpensive **Corkage** *$10* **Cuisine** *American/continental* **Menu prices** *$10–$21*

GOLDFISH 🍷
4400 Ashford Dunwoody Road, Atlanta, GA 30346; (770) 671-0100 **Wine list** *California* **Wine prices** *Moderate* **Cuisine** *Seafood* **Menu prices** *$16–$32*

HALYARDS 🍷
600 Sea Island Road, St. Simons Island, GA 31522; (912) 638-9100 **Wine list** *California* **Wine prices** Inexpensive **Corkage** *$12* **Cuisine** *Contemporary American* **Menu prices** *$18–$31*

IL PASTICCIO 🍷
2 E. Broughton St., Savannah, GA 31401; (912) 231-8888
Wine list *Italy, California* **Wine prices** *Moderate* **Cuisine** *Italian* **Menu prices** *$16–$32*

JOËL 🍷🍷
3290 Northside Parkway, Atlanta, GA 30327; (404) 233-3500 **Wine list** *France, California, Italy* **Wine prices** *Moderate* **Corkage** *$25* **Cuisine** *French/Mediterranean/Asian* **Menu prices** *$20–$36*

GEORGIA

KILLER CREEK CHOPHOUSE 🍷
1700 Mansell Road, Alpharetta, GA 30004; (770) 649-0064 **Wine list** *California, France* **Wine prices** *Moderate* **Corkage** *$10* **Cuisine** *Steak house* **Menu prices** *$16–$32*

KYMA 🍷
3085 Piedmont Road, Atlanta, GA 30305; (404) 262-0702 **Wine list** *Greece* **Wine prices** *Moderate* **Corkage** *$15* **Cuisine** *Greek* **Menu prices** *$17–$32*

LA MAISON ON TELFAIR 🍷
404 Telfair St., Augusta, GA 30901; (706) 722-4805 **Wine list** *California, France* **Wine prices** *Moderate* **Corkage** *$10* **Cuisine** *French/continental* **Menu prices** *$16–$45*

LA TAVOLA TRATTORIA 🍷
992 Virginia Ave. N.E., Atlanta, GA 30306; (404) 873-5430 **Wine list** *California, Italy* **Wine prices** *Moderate* **Corkage** *$10* **Cuisine** *Southern Italian* **Menu prices** *$12–$24*

LAST RESORT GRILL 🍷
174/184 W. Clayton St., Athens, GA 30601; (706) 549-0810 **Wine list** *California* **Wine prices** *Moderate* **Cuisine** *Regional* **Menu prices** *$8–$14*

LITTLE GARDENS 🍷
3571 Lawrenceville Highway, Lawrenceville, GA 30044; (770) 923-3434 **Wine list** *California* **Wine prices** Inexpensive **Cuisine** *American/continental* **Menu prices** *$14–$26*

THE MAIN DINING ROOM 🍷🍷
The Cloister, 100 Hudson Place, Sea Island, GA 31561; (800) SEA-ISLAND **Wine list** *Bordeaux, California, Port* **Wine prices** *Moderate* **Cuisine** *Regional* **Menu prices** *$25–$35*

MCKENDRICK'S STEAK HOUSE 🍷
4505 Ashford Dunwoody Road, Atlanta, GA 30346; (770) 512-8888 **Wine list** *Bordeaux, California* **Wine prices** *Expensive* **Corkage** *$10* **Cuisine** *Steak house* **Menu prices** *$25–$75*

MORTON'S OF CHICAGO 🍷
303 Peachtree St. N.E., Atlanta, GA 30308; (404) 577-4366 **Wine list** *California* **Wine prices** *Expensive* **Cuisine** *Steak house* **Menu prices** *$23–$65*

MORTON'S OF CHICAGO
3379 Peachtree Road N.E., Atlanta, GA 30326; (404) 816-6535 **Wine list** *California* **Wine prices** *Expensive* **Cuisine** *Steak house* **Menu prices** *$20–$34*

MURPHY'S
997 Virginia Ave., Atlanta, GA 30306; (404) 872-0904 **Wine list** *France, California* **Wine prices** *Moderate* **Corkage** *$10* **Cuisine** *Contemporary American* **Menu prices** *$9–$18*

NAVA
Buckhead Plaza, 3060 Peachtree Road, Atlanta, GA 30305; (404) 240-1984 **Wine list** *California* **Wine prices** *Moderate* **Corkage** *$10* **Cuisine** *Southwestern* **Menu prices** *$16–$29*

NAZZARO'S
196 Retreat Village, St. Simons Island, GA 31522; (912) 634-6161 **Wine list** *California, Italy* **Wine prices** *Moderate* **Corkage** *$10* **Cuisine** *Italian* **Menu prices** *$12–$25*

NIKOLAI'S ROOF RESTAURANT
Atlanta Hilton, 255 Courtland St., Atlanta, GA 30303; (404) 221-6362 **Wine list** *France, California* **Wine prices** *Moderate* **Cuisine** *French/continental* **Menu prices** *Prix fixe only; $49–$84*

THE OLDE PINK HOUSE
23 Abercorn St., Savannah, GA 31401; (912) 232-4286 **Wine list** *California* **Wine prices** *Moderate* **Cuisine** *Regional* **Menu prices** *$15–$25*

THE PALM
Swiss Hotel, 3391 Peachtree Road N.E., Atlanta, GA 30326; (404) 814-1955 **Wine list** *California* **Wine prices** *Expensive* **Corkage** *$20* **Cuisine** *Steak house* **Menu prices** *$16–$60*

PANO'S & PAUL'S RESTAURANT
1232 W. Paces Ferry Road N.W., Atlanta, GA 30327; (404) 261-3662 **Wine list** *California* **Wine prices** *Moderate* **Corkage** *$15* **Cuisine** *Continental* **Menu prices** *$19–$38*

THE PORTERHOUSE GRILL
459 E. Broad St., Athens, GA 30601; (706) 369-0990 **Wine list** *California* **Wine prices** *Moderate* **Corkage** *$10* **Cuisine** *Steak house* **Menu prices** *$16–$29*

PORTOFINO
3199 Paces Ferry Place, Atlanta, GA 30305; (404) 231-1136 **Wine list** *California, Italy* **Wine prices** *Moderate* **Cuisine** *Italian/American* **Menu prices** *$12–$20*

PRICCI 🍷
500 Pharr Road, Atlanta, GA 30305; (404) 237-2941 **Wine list** *Italy* **Wine prices** *Moderate* **Corkage** *$15* **Cuisine** *Italian* **Menu prices** *$14–$27*

RAINWATER RESTAURANT 🍷
11655 Haynes Bridge Road, Alpharetta, GA 30004; (770) 777-0033 **Wine list** *California* **Wine prices** Inexpensive **Corkage** *$10* **Cuisine** *Contemporary American* **Menu prices** *$18–$25*

RAY'S ON THE RIVER 🍷
6700 Powers Ferry Road, Atlanta, GA 30339; (770) 995-1187 **Wine list** *California* **Wine prices** *Moderate* **Corkage** *$15* **Cuisine** *Seafood* **Menu prices** *$15–$35*

THE RIVER ROOM RESTAURANT & TAVERN 🍷
4403 Northside Parkway, Atlanta, GA 30327; (404) 233-5455 **Wine list** *California, France* **Wine prices** Inexpensive **Corkage** *$15* **Cuisine** *Contemporary American* **Menu prices** *$17–$30*

RUTH'S CHRIS STEAK HOUSE 🍷
Atlanta Plaza, 950 E. Paces Ferry Road, Atlanta, GA 30326; (404) 365-0660 **Wine list** *California* **Wine prices** *Moderate* **Cuisine** *Steak house* **Menu prices** *$17–$45*

RUTH'S CHRIS STEAK HOUSE 🍷
Embassy Suites Centennial Park, 267 Marietta St., Atlanta, GA 30313; (404) 223-6500 **Wine list** *California* **Wine prices** *Moderate* **Cuisine** *Steak house* **Menu prices** *$17–$30*

RUTH'S CHRIS STEAK HOUSE 🍷
5788 Roswell Road N.W., Atlanta, GA 30328; (404) 255-0035 **Wine list** *California* **Wine prices** *Moderate* **Cuisine** *Steak house* **Menu prices** *$18–$58*

SAPPHIRE GRILL 🍷
110 W. Saint Julian St., Savannah, GA 31401; (912) 443-9962 **Wine list** *California* **Wine prices** *Moderate* **Corkage** *$15* **Cuisine** *Regional* **Menu prices** *$19–$37*

SEEGER'S RESTAURANT 🍷🍷
111 W. Paces Ferry Road, Atlanta, GA 30305; (404) 846-9779 **Wine list** *France, California, Germany* **Wine prices** *Moderate* **Corkage** *$40* **Cuisine** *Contemporary* **Menu prices** *Prix fixe only; $48–$85*

SIA'S
10305 Medlock Bridge Road, Duluth, GA 30097; (770) 497-9727 **Wine list** *California* **Wine prices** *Moderate* **Corkage** *$25* **Cuisine** *American* **Menu prices** *$17–$29*

SOUTH CITY KITCHEN
1144 Crescent Ave., Atlanta, GA 30309; (404) 873-7358 **Wine list** *California* **Wine prices** *Moderate* **Cuisine** *Contemporary Southern* **Menu prices** *$14–$24*

TIBURON GRILLE
1190-B N. Highland Ave., Atlanta, GA 30306; (404) 892-2393 **Wine list** *California* **Wine prices** *Moderate* **Corkage** *$12* **Cuisine** *Contemporary* **Menu prices** *$13–$27*

TONI'S CASA NAPOLI
2486 Mount Vernon Road, Atlanta, GA 30338; (770) 394-9359 **Wine list** *Italy, California* **Wine prices** *Moderate* **Corkage** *$20* **Cuisine** *Italian* **Menu prices** *$15–$30*

VAN GOGH'S RESTAURANT & BAR
70 W. Crossville Road, Roswell, GA 30075; (770) 993-1156 **Wine list** *California, France* **Wine prices** *Moderate* **Cuisine** *American* **Menu prices** *$18–$33*

VENI VIDI VICI
41 14th St., Atlanta, GA 30309; (404) 875-8424 **Wine list** *Italy* **Wine prices** *Moderate* **Corkage** *$10* **Cuisine** *Italian* **Menu prices** *$12–$27*

VILLAGE TAVERN
11555 Rainwater Drive, Alpharetta, GA 30004; (770) 777-6490 **Wine list** *California* **Wine prices** Inexpensive **Cuisine** *American* **Menu prices** *$10–$24*

VINNY'S ON WINDWARD
5355 Windward Parkway, Alpharetta, GA 30004; (770) 772-4644 **Wine list** *Italy* **Wine prices** *Moderate* **Corkage** *$25* **Cuisine** *American/Italian* **Menu prices** *$14–$27*

VINOCITY
36 13th St., Atlanta, GA 30309; (404) 870-8886 **Wine list** *California* **Wine prices** *Moderate* **Corkage** *$15* **Cuisine** *Contemporary American* **Menu prices** *$17–$30*

WATERSHED
406 W. Ponce de Leon Ave., Decatur, GA 30030; (404) 378-4900 **Wine list** *California* **Wine prices** *Moderate* **Corkage** *$15* **Cuisine** *Contemporary American* **Menu prices** *$9–$25*

WOODFIRE GRILL 🍷
1782 Cheshire Bridge Road, Atlanta, GA 30324; (404) 347-9055 **Wine list** *California, France* **Wine prices** *Moderate* **Corkage** *$10* **Cuisine** *Californian* **Menu prices** *$14–$32*

HAWAII

AARON'S 🍷
The Ala Moano Hotel, 410 Atkinson Drive, Honolulu, Oahu, HI 96814; (808) 955-4466 **Wine list** *California* **Wine prices** *Moderate* **Corkage** *$25* **Cuisine** *American/continental* **Menu prices** *$20–$44*

BALI BY THE SEA 🍷
Hilton Hawaiian Village, 2005 Kalia Road, Honolulu, Oahu, HI 96815; (808) 941-2254 **Wine list** *France* **Wine prices** *Expensive* **Cuisine** *Pacific Rim* **Menu prices** *$26–$34*

CASTAWAY CAFÉ 🍷
Maui Kaanapali Villa Resort, 45 Kai Ala Drive, Kaanapali Beach, Lahaina, Maui, HI 96761; (808) 661-9091 **Wine list** *California* **Wine prices** Inexpensive **Cuisine** *Hawaiian* **Menu prices** *$15–$23*

THE CLUB GRILLE 🍷
Hualalai Resort, 100 Ka'upulehu Drive, Ka'upulehu-Kona, HI 96745; (808) 325-8525 **Wine list** *California* **Wine prices** *Moderate* **Cuisine** *Pacific Rim* **Menu prices** *$13–$38*

DAVID PAUL'S LAHAINA GRILL 🍷
127 Lahainaluna Road, Lahaina, Maui, HI 96761; (808) 667-5117 **Wine list** *California* **Wine prices** *Expensive* **Cuisine** *Contemporary American* **Menu prices** *$29–$49*

GERARD'S 🍷
The Plantation Inn, 174 Lahainaluna Road, Lahaina, Maui, HI 96761; (808) 661-8939 **Wine list** *France, California* **Wine prices** *Moderate* **Cuisine** *French* **Menu prices** *$27–$39*

THE GRILL 🍷
The Fairmont Orchid, 1 N. Kaniku Drive, Kohala Coast, Hawaii, HI 96743; (808) 885-2000 **Wine list** *California, France* **Wine prices** *Expensive* **Corkage** *$35* **Cuisine** *Contemporary American* **Menu prices** *$28–$50*

HY'S STEAK HOUSE
2440 Kuhio Ave., Honolulu, Oahu, HI 96815; (808) 922-5555 **Wine list** *California* **Wine prices** *Expensive* **Corkage** *$25* **Cuisine** *Steak house* **Menu prices** *$18–$59*

I'O
505 Front St., Lahaina, Maui, HI 96761; (808) 661-8422 **Wine list** *California* **Wine prices** *Expensive* **Cuisine** *Pacific Rim* **Menu prices** *$23–$32*

LA MER
Halekulani Hotel, 2199 Kalia Road, Honolulu, Oahu, HI 96815; (808) 923-2311 **Wine list** *California, France* **Wine prices** *Expensive* **Corkage** *$25* **Cuisine** *Contemporary French* **Menu prices** *$35–$46*

LONGHI'S LAHAINA
888 Front St., Lahaina, Maui, HI 96761; (808) 667-2288 **Wine list** *California, France* **Wine prices** *Expensive* **Cuisine** *Continental* **Menu prices** *$15–$30*

LONGHI'S WAILEA
3750 Wailea Alanui Drive, Wailea, Maui, HI 96753; (808) 891-8883 **Wine list** *California, Italy* **Wine prices** *Moderate* **Cuisine** *Italian/Mediterranean* **Menu prices** *$16–$30*

MAMA'S FISH HOUSE
799 Poho Place, Kuau, Maui, HI 96779; (808) 579-8488 **Wine list** *California* **Wine prices** *Moderate* **Cuisine** *Seafood* **Menu prices** *$29–$58*

MERRIMAN'S RESTAURANT
Opelo Plaza, 65-1227 Opelo Road, Kamuela, HI 96743; (808) 885-6822 **Wine list** *California* **Wine prices** *Moderate* **Corkage** *$15* **Cuisine** *Hawaiian* **Menu prices** *$19–$32*

MORTON'S OF CHICAGO
1450 Ala Moana Blvd., Honolulu, Oahu, HI 96814; (808) 949-1300 **Wine list** *California* **Wine prices** *Expensive* **Corkage** *$15* **Cuisine** *Steak house* **Menu prices** *$22–$65*

NICK'S FISHMARKET
The Kea Lani Hotel & Resort, 4100 Wailea Alanui, Wailea, Maui, HI 96753; (808) 879-7224 **Wine list** *California, Bordeaux* **Wine prices** *Moderate* **Corkage** *$25* **Cuisine** *Seafood* **Menu prices** *$25–$49*

PACIFIC'O 🍷
505 Front St., Lahaina, Maui, HI 96761; (808) 667-4341 **Wine list** *California* **Wine prices** *Moderate* **Cuisine** *Pacific Rim* **Menu prices** *$22–$38*

PADOVANI'S RESTAURANT & WINE BAR 🍷
Doubletree Alana Hotel, 1956 Ala Moana Blvd., Honolulu, Oahu, HI 96815; (808) 946-3456 **Wine list** *California, France* **Wine prices** *Expensive* **Corkage** *$30* **Cuisine** *Mediterranean/Hawaiian* **Menu prices** *$28–$44*

RUTH'S CHRIS STEAK HOUSE 🍷
3750 Wailea Alanui Drive, Wailea, Maui, HI 96753; (808) 874-8880 **Wine list** *California* **Wine prices** *Expensive* **Cuisine** *Steak house* **Menu prices** *$20–$72*

SANSEI SEAFOOD RESTAURANT & SUSHI BAR 🍷
115 Bay Drive, Kapalua, Maui, HI 96761; (808) 669-6286 **Wine list** *California* **Wine prices** *Moderate* **Cuisine** *Asian/Pacific Rim* **Menu prices** *$18–$35*

SARENTO'S 🍷
Ilkilai Hotel, 1777 Ala Moana Blvd., Honolulu, Oahu, HI 96815; (808) 955-5559 **Wine list** *California, Bordeaux* **Wine prices** *Moderate* **Corkage** *$25* **Cuisine** *Italian/Mediterranean* **Menu prices** *$17–$42*

SARENTO'S ON THE BEACH 🍷
2980 S. Kihei Road, Kihei, Maui, HI 96753; (808) 875-7555 **Wine list** *Italy, Bordeaux* **Wine prices** *Expensive* **Corkage** *$25* **Cuisine** *Italian* **Menu prices** *$22–$40*

SPAGO MAUI 🍷
Four Seasons Resort Maui at Wailea, 3900 Wailea Alanui, Wailea, Maui, HI 96753; (808) 879-2999 **Wine list** *California, France* **Wine prices** *Moderate* **Cuisine** *American* **Menu prices** *$18–$35*

3660 ON THE RISE 🍷
3660 Waialae Ave., Honolulu, Oahu, HI 96816; (808) 737-1177 **Wine list** *California* **Wine prices** *Moderate* **Corkage** *$15* **Cuisine** *Pacific Rim* **Menu prices** *$18–$32*

THE WATERFRONT RESTAURANT 🍷
50 Hauoli St., Maalaea, Maui, HI 96793; (808) 244-9028 **Wine list** *California, France* **Wine prices** *Moderate* **Cuisine** *Continental/seafood* **Menu prices** *$20–$50*

IDAHO

BARDENAY RESTAURANT & DISTILLERY
610 Grove, Boise, ID 83702; (208) 426-0538 **Wine list** *California* **Wine prices** Inexpensive **Cuisine** *American/Asian* **Menu prices** *$8–$17*

BEVERLY'S
The Coeur d'Alene Resort, On the Lake, Coeur d'Alene, ID 83814; (800) 688-4142 **Wine list** *California, Oregon, Washington* **Wine prices** *Moderate* **Corkage** *$20* **Cuisine** *Pacific Northwestern/international* **Menu prices** *$20–$34*

BITTERCREEK & THE RED FEATHER LOUNGE
246 N. Eighth St., Boise, ID 83702; (208) 345-1813 **Wine list** *California, Washington* **Wine prices** Inexpensive **Corkage** *$10* **Cuisine** *Regional* **Menu prices** *$7–$16*

CHANDLER'S
Trail Creek Village, 200 S. Main St., Ketchum, ID 83340; (208) 726-1776 **Wine list** *California, France* **Wine prices** *Moderate* **Cuisine** *American* **Menu prices** *$16–$35*

THE CONTINENTAL BISTRO
140 S. Main St., Pocatello, ID 83204; (208) 233-4433 **Wine list** *California* **Wine prices** *Moderate* **Corkage** *$10* **Cuisine** *Contemporary American* **Menu prices** *$13–$22*

COTTONWOOD GRILLE
913 W. River St., Boise, ID 83702; (208) 333-9800 **Wine list** *California, Italy* **Wine prices** Inexpensive **Corkage** *$15* **Cuisine** *Contemporary American* **Menu prices** *$14–$29*

EVERGREEN BISTRO
171 First Ave., Ketchum, ID 83340; (208) 726-3888 **Wine list** *California, Washington, France* **Wine prices** *Moderate* **Cuisine** *American/French* **Menu prices** *$18–$34*

THE LODGE DINING ROOM
Sun Valley Resort, 1 Sun Valley Road, Sun Valley, ID 83353; (208) 622-4111 **Wine list** *California, France* **Wine prices** *Moderate* **Corkage** *$20* **Cuisine** *French/American* **Menu prices** *$18–$66*

THE LODGE ON HIDDEN LAKES
151 Clubhouse Way, Sandpoint, ID 83864; (208) 263-1642 **Wine list** *California* **Wine prices** *Moderate* **Corkage** *$10* **Cuisine** *Italian/Pacific Northwestern* **Menu prices** *$16–$35*

MORTIMER'S RESTAURANT

110 S. Fifth St., Boise, ID 83702; (208) 338-6550 **Wine list** *California* **Wine prices** *Moderate* **Corkage** *$7* **Cuisine** *Contemporary American* **Menu prices** *$18–$25*

ROCK CREEK

200 Addison Ave. W., Twin Falls, ID 83301; (208) 734-4154 **Wine list** *California* **Wine prices** Inexpensive **Cuisine** *Steak house* **Menu prices** *$10–$39*

SCHWEITZER'S CHIMNEY ROCK GRILL

Schweitzer Mountain Resort, 10000 Schweitzer Mountain Road, Sandpoint, ID 83864; (208) 255-3071 **Wine list** *Washington, California* **Wine prices** Inexpensive **Corkage** *$8* **Cuisine** *Regional* **Menu prices** *$15–$28*

ILLINOIS

CHICAGO

AMBRIA

2300 N. Lincoln Park W., Chicago, IL 60614; (773) 472-5959 **Wine list** *France, Calfornia, Spain* **Wine prices** *Expensive* **Cuisine** *French* **Menu prices** *$28–$35*

ARUN'S RESTAURANT

4156 N. Kedzie Ave., Chicago, IL 60618; (773) 539-1909 **Wine list** *France, Austria* **Wine prices** *Expensive* **Cuisine** *Thai* **Menu prices** *Prix fixe only; $85*

BIN 36

Marina City, 339 N. Dearborn St., Chicago, IL 60610; (312) 755-9463 **Wine list** *California, France* **Wine prices** *Moderate* **Corkage** *$15* **Cuisine** *American* **Menu prices** *$16–$25*

BISTRO 110

110 E. Pearson St., Chicago, IL 60611; (312) 266-3110 **Wine list** *California, France* **Wine prices** *Moderate* **Corkage** *$20* **Cuisine** *French* **Menu prices** *$16–$32*

CALITERRA

Wyndham Hotel, 633 N. Saint Clair St., Chicago, IL 60611; (312) 274-4444 **Wine list** *California, France, Italy, Germany* **Wine prices** *Moderate* **Cuisine** *Californian/Tuscan* **Menu prices** *$15–$35*

Grand Award Best of Award of Excellence Award of Excellence

THE CAPITAL GRILLE 🍷
633 N. Saint Clair St., Chicago, IL 60611; (312) 337-9400 **Wine list** *California, Bordeaux* **Wine prices** *Moderate* **Cuisine** *Steak house* **Menu prices** *$16–$32*

CHARLIE TROTTER'S 🍷🍷🍷
816 W. Armitage Ave., Chicago, IL 60614; (773) 248-6228 **Wine list** *Bordeaux, Burgundy, California, Rhône, Germany, Austria* **Wine selections** *1,750* **Number of bottles** *26,500* **Wine prices** *Expensive* **Cuisine** *Contemporary American* **Menu prices** *Prix fixe only; $100–$175* **Credit cards** *AX, MC, VS, DV*
Grand Award since 1993

CHICAGO CHOP HOUSE 🍷
60 W. Ontario St., Chicago, IL 60610; (800) 229-2356 **Wine list** *California, France* **Wine prices** *Moderate* **Corkage** *$20* **Cuisine** *Steak house* **Menu prices** *$18–$39*

CITÉ 🍷
Lake Point Tower, 505 N. Lake Shore Drive, Chicago, IL 60611; (312) 644-4050 **Wine list** *California, France* **Wine prices** *Expensive* **Corkage** *$20* **Cuisine** *Contemporary American/French* **Menu prices** *$24–$35*

CYRANO'S BISTROT & WINE BAR 🍷
546 N. Wells St., Chicago, IL 60610; (312) 467-0546 **Wine list** *France* **Wine prices** *Moderate* **Cuisine** *French* **Menu prices** *$12–$24*

THE DINING ROOM 🍷🍷🍷
The Ritz-Carlton Chicago, 160 E. Pearson St., Chicago, IL 60611; (312) 266-1000 **Wine list** *Bordeaux, California* **Wine selections** *700* **Number of bottles** *20,000* **Wine prices** *Moderate* **Corkage** *$25* **Cuisine** *Contemporary French* **Menu prices** *$30–$40* **Credit cards** *AX, MC, VS, DV*
Grand Award since 1982

ERAWAN ROYAL THAI CUISINE 🍷
729 N. Clark St., Chicago, IL 60611; (312) 642-6888 **Wine list** *France, California, Austria, Germany* **Wine prices** *Moderate* **Corkage** *$50* **Cuisine** *Thai* **Menu prices** *$18–$38*

ERWIN, AN AMERICAN CAFÉ & BAR 🍷
2925 N. Halsted St., Chicago, IL 60657; (773) 528-7200 **Wine list** *California, France* **Wine prices** *Moderate* **Corkage** *$20* **Cuisine** *Contemporary American* **Menu prices** *$12–$25*

EVEREST 🍷🍷
440 S. LaSalle St., 40th Floor, Chicago, IL 60605; (312) 663-8920 **Wine list** *Alsace, Bordeaux* **Wine prices** *Moderate* **Cuisine** *French* **Menu prices** *$30–$46*

FOGO DE CHÃO 🍷
661 N. LaSalle St., Chicago, IL 60610; (312) 932-9330 **Wine list** *California* **Wine prices** *Moderate* **Corkage** *$20* **Cuisine** *Brazilian* **Menu prices** *Prix fixe only; $44*

FORTUNATO 🍷
2005 W. Division St., Chicago, IL 60622; (773) 645-7200 **Wine list** *Italy* **Wine prices** *Moderate* **Cuisine** *Italian* **Menu prices** *$16–$22*

FRONTERA GRILL/TOPOLOBAMPO 🍷
445 N. Clark St., Chicago, IL 60610; (312) 661-1434 **Wine list** *California* **Wine prices** *Expensive* **Cuisine** *Mexican* **Menu prices** *$17–$29*

GREAT STREET RESTAURANT & BAR 🍷
Renaissance Chicago, 1 W. Wacker Drive, Chicago, IL 60601; (312) 795-3333 **Wine list** *California* **Wine prices** *Moderate* **Cuisine** *American* **Menu prices** *$12–$30*

HARRY CARAY'S 🍷
33 W. Kinzie St., Chicago, IL 60610; (312) 828-0966 **Wine list** *California, Italy* **Wine prices** *Moderate* **Cuisine** *Steak house* **Menu prices** *$12–$60*

ITALIAN VILLAGE RESTAURANT 🍷🍷🍷
71 W. Monroe St., Chicago, IL 60603; (312) 332-7005 **Wine list** *California, Italy, Bordeaux* **Wine selections** *1,000* **Number of bottles** *45,000* **Wine prices** *Moderate* **Corkage** *$25* **Cuisine** *Italian* **Menu prices** *$10–$25* **Credit cards** *AX, MC, VS, DV*
Grand Award since 1984

JILLY'S ITALIAN STEAK JOYNT 🍷
1009 N. Rush St., Chicago, IL 60611; (312) 664-2100 **Wine list** *California* **Wine prices** *Moderate* **Cuisine** *Steak house* **Menu prices** *$13–$85*

JOE'S SEAFOOD, PRIME STEAK & STONE CRAB 🍷
60 E. Grand Ave., Chicago, IL 60611; (312) 379-5637 **Wine list** *California* **Wine prices** *Moderate* **Cuisine** *Steak house* **Menu prices** *$16–$39*

🍷🍷🍷 Grand Award 🍷🍷 Best of Award of Excellence 🍷 Award of Excellence

KINZIE CHOPHOUSE 🍷
400 N. Wells St., Chicago, IL 60610; (312) 822-0191 **Wine list** *California* **Wine prices** Inexpensive **Cuisine** *Steak house* **Menu prices** *$11–$40*

LA CANTINA ENOTECA 🍷🍷
71 W. Monroe St., Chicago, IL 60603; (312) 332-7005 **Wine list** *California, Italy, Bordeaux* **Wine prices** *Moderate* **Corkage** *$25* **Cuisine** *Italian/seafood* **Menu prices** *$15–$25*

LA SARDINE 🍷
111 N. Carpenter St., Chicago, IL 60607; (312) 421-2800 **Wine list** *France* **Wine prices** *Moderate* **Cuisine** *French* **Menu prices** *$13–$19*

LAWRY'S THE PRIME RIB 🍷
100 E. Ontario St., Chicago, IL 60611; (312) 787-5000 **Wine list** *California* **Wine prices** *Expensive* **Corkage** *$10* **Cuisine** *Steak house* **Menu prices** *$24–$39*

MERITAGE CAFÉ & WINE BAR 🍷
2118 N. Damen Ave., Chicago, IL 60647; (773) 235-6434 **Wine list** *California* **Wine prices** *Moderate* **Cuisine** *Pacific Northwestern/Asian* **Menu prices** *$18–$29*

MIKE DITKA'S - CHICAGO 🍷
Tremont Hotel, 100 E. Chestnut St., Chicago, IL 60611; (312) 587-8989 **Wine list** *California* **Wine prices** *Expensive* **Corkage** *$15* **Cuisine** *American* **Menu prices** *$14–$36*

MK 🍷
868 N. Franklin St., Chicago, IL 60610; (312) 482-9179 **Wine list** *California, France* **Wine prices** *Moderate* **Corkage** *$25* **Cuisine** *Contemporary American* **Menu prices** *$16–$32*

MORTON'S OF CHICAGO 🍷
1050 N. State St., Chicago, IL 60610; (312) 266-4820 **Wine list** *California* **Wine prices** *Expensive* **Cuisine** *Steak house* **Menu prices** *$20–$35*

N9NE 🍷
440 W. Randolph St., Chicago, IL 60606; (312) 575-9900 **Wine list** *California, France* **Wine prices** *Moderate* **Cuisine** *Steak house* **Menu prices** *$17–$35*

NAPA VALLEY GRILLE 🍷
626 N. State St., Chicago, IL 60610; (312) 587-1166 **Wine list** *California* **Wine prices** *Moderate* **Corkage** *$10* **Cuisine** *Californian* **Menu prices** *$14–$25*

NOMI 🍷🍷
Park Hyatt Chicago, 800 N. Michigan Ave., Chicago, IL 60611; (312) 239-4030 **Wine list** *Burgundy, California, Italy, Germany, Austria* **Wine prices** *Moderate* **Cuisine** *Contemporary French* **Menu prices** *$25–$37*

NORTH POND 🍷
2610 N. Cannon Drive, Chicago, IL 60614; (773) 477-5845 **Wine list** *California* **Wine prices** *Moderate* **Cuisine** *Contemporary American* **Menu prices** *$24–$30*

ODYSSEY CRUISES 🍷
Navy Pier, 600 E. Grand Ave., Chicago, IL 60611; (888) 957-2322 **Wine list** *California* **Wine prices** *Moderate* **Cuisine** *American* **Menu prices** *Prix fixe only; $80–$97*

ONE SIXTYBLUE 🍷
160 N. Loomis St., Chicago, IL 60607; (312) 850-0303 **Wine list** *California, France* **Wine prices** *Moderate* **Corkage** *$25* **Cuisine** *Contemporary American* **Menu prices** *$19–$29*

THE OUTPOST 🍷
3438 N. Clark St., Chicago, IL 60657; (773) 244-1166 **Wine list** *California* **Wine prices** Inexpensive **Corkage** *$10* **Cuisine** *International* **Menu prices** *$12–$24*

THE PALM 🍷
323 E. Wacker Drive, Chicago, IL 60601; (312) 616-1000 **Wine list** *California* **Wine prices** *Expensive* **Corkage** *$25* **Cuisine** *Steak house* **Menu prices** *$15–$60*

PANE CALDO 🍷
72 E. Walton St., Chicago, IL 60611; (312) 649-0055 **Wine list** *Italy, Champagne* **Wine prices** *Moderate* **Corkage** *$50* **Cuisine** *Contemporary Italian* **Menu prices** *$22–$42*

RHAPSODY 🍷
65 E. Adams St., Chicago, IL 60603; (312) 786-9911 **Wine list** *France, California* **Wine prices** *Moderate* **Corkage** *$20* **Cuisine** *Contemporary American* **Menu prices** *$19–$31*

RUTH'S CHRIS STEAK HOUSE 🍷
431 N. Dearborn St., Chicago, IL 60610; (312) 321-2725 **Wine list** *California* **Wine prices** *Moderate* **Corkage** *$20* **Cuisine** *Steak house* **Menu prices** *$15–$35*

SALPICÓN 🍷🍷
1252 N. Wells St., Chicago, IL 60610; (312) 988-7811 **Wine list** *California, Spain, Austria, Italy* **Wine prices** *Moderate* **Cuisine** *Contemporary Mexican* **Menu prices** *$16–$27*

🍷🍷🍷 Grand Award 🍷🍷 Best of Award of Excellence 🍷 Award of Excellence

CAFÉ LUCCI
609 Milwaukee Ave., Glenview, IL 60025; (847) 729-2268
Wine list *California, Italy* **Wine prices** *Moderate* **Corkage** *$10*
Cuisine *Italian* **Menu prices** *$12–$34*

CARLOS' RESTAURANT
429 Temple Ave., Highland Park, IL 60035; (847) 432-0770
Wine list *California, Burgundy, Bordeaux* **Wine selections** *2,300* **Number of bottles** *21,000* **Wine prices** *Expensive*
Corkage *$20* **Cuisine** *Contemporary French* **Menu prices** *$32–$39* **Credit cards** *AX, MC, VS, DV*
Grand Award since 1990

CHEF'S STATION
915 Davis St., Evanston, IL 60201; (847) 570-9821 **Wine list** *California* **Wine prices** *Moderate* **Corkage** *$12* **Cuisine** *Contemporary American* **Menu prices** *$14–$24*

CHICAGO PRIME STEAKHOUSE
1370 Bank Drive, Schaumburg, IL 60173; (847) 969-9900
Wine list *California* **Wine prices** *Moderate* **Corkage** *$25*
Cuisine *Steak house* **Menu prices** *$18–$65*

THE CLUBHOUSE
298 Oakbrook Center, Oakbrook, IL 60523; (630) 472-0600
Wine list *California* **Wine prices** *Moderate* **Corkage** *$20*
Cuisine *American* **Menu prices** *$9–$29*

COURTRIGHT'S RESTAURANT
8989 Archer Ave., Willow Springs, IL 60480; (708) 839-8000 **Wine list** *California, Bordeaux* **Wine prices** *Moderate*
Corkage *$15* **Cuisine** *American* **Menu prices** *$25–$32*

DEER PATH INN
Deer Path Inn, 255 E. Illinois Road, Lake Forest, IL 60045; (847) 234-2280 **Wine list** *California, France* **Wine prices** *Moderate* **Corkage** *$20* **Cuisine** *Continental* **Menu prices** *$24–$35*

ECLECTIC RESTAURANT
117 North Ave., Barrington, IL 60010; (847) 277-7300
Wine list *California, France* **Wine prices** *Moderate* **Corkage** *$15* **Cuisine** *International* **Menu prices** *$17–$25*

FAIRBANKS STEAKHOUSE
49 W. Galena Blvd., Aurora, IL 60506; (630) 801-7333
Wine list *California, France* **Wine prices** *Moderate* **Cuisine** *Steak house* **Menu prices** *$12–$60*

FRIED GREEN TOMATOES 🍷
1301 Irish Hollow Road, Galena, IL 61036; (815) 777-3938
Wine list *California* **Wine prices** *Moderate* **Corkage** *$10*
Cuisine *Italian* **Menu prices** *$13–$27*

GABRIEL'S 🍷🍷
310 Greenbay Road, Highwood, IL 60040; (847) 433-0031
Wine list *California, France, Italy* **Wine prices** *Moderate*
Cuisine *French/Italian* **Menu prices** *$25–$35*

GRILL ON FULTON 🍷
456 Fulton St., Peoria, IL 61602; (309) 674-6870 **Wine list** *California* **Wine prices** *Moderate* **Cuisine** *American* **Menu prices** *$16–$22*

HARRY CARAY'S 🍷
10233 W. Higgins Road, Rosemont, IL 60018; (847) 699-1200 **Wine list** *California, Italy* **Wine prices** *Moderate*
Cuisine *Steak house* **Menu prices** *$11–$32*

INDIGO 🍷
3013 Lindbergh Blvd., Springfield, IL 62704; (217) 726-3487
Wine list *California* **Wine prices** *Moderate* **Cuisine** *Contemporary American* **Menu prices** *$16–$39*

JACKY'S BISTRO 🍷
2545 Prairie Ave., Evanston, IL 60201; (847) 733-0899
Wine list *California, France* **Wine prices** *Moderate* **Corkage** *$25* **Cuisine** *French/American* **Menu prices** *$14–$23*

LE TITI DE PARIS 🍷🍷
1015 W. Dundee Road, Arlington Heights, IL 60004; (847) 506-0222 **Wine list** *California, Bordeaux, Burgundy* **Wine prices** *Expensive* **Cuisine** *French* **Menu prices** *$28–$30*

LOVELLS OF LAKE FOREST 🍷
915 S. Waukegan Road, Lake Forest, IL 60045; (847) 234-8013 **Wine list** *California* **Wine prices** *Expensive* **Corkage** *$15* **Cuisine** *American* **Menu prices** *$22–$50*

MORTON'S OF CHICAGO 🍷
9525 W. Bryn Mawr Ave., Rosemont, IL 60018; (847) 678-5155 **Wine list** *California* **Wine prices** *Expensive* **Cuisine** *Steak house* **Menu prices** *$20–$34*

MORTON'S OF CHICAGO 🍷
1470 McConnor Parkway, Schaumburg, IL 60173; (847) 413-8771 **Wine list** *California* **Wine prices** *Expensive*
Cuisine *Steak house* **Menu prices** *$20–$34*

🍷🍷🍷 Grand Award 🍷🍷 Best of Award of Excellence 🍷 Award of Excellence

MORTON'S OF CHICAGO
1 Westbrook Corporate Center, 22nd and Wolf Road, Westchester, IL 60153; (708) 562-7000 **Wine list** *California* **Wine prices** *Expensive* **Cuisine** *Steak house* **Menu prices** *$20–$34*

ONE 20 OCEAN PLACE
120 N. Hale St., Wheaton, IL 60187; (630) 690-2100 **Wine list** *California, France* **Wine prices** *Moderate* **Cuisine** *Seafood* **Menu prices** *$17–$50*

PHILANDER'S
Carleton of Oak Park, 1120 Pleasant St., Oak Park, IL 60302; (708) 848-4250 **Wine list** *California* **Wine prices** *Moderate* **Corkage** *$15* **Cuisine** *American/continental* **Menu prices** *$16–$44*

PORT EDWARD RESTAURANT
20 W. Algonquin Road, Algonquin, IL 60102; (847) 658-5441 **Wine list** *California, France* **Wine prices** Inexpensive **Corkage** *$15* **Cuisine** *Seafood* **Menu prices** *$15–$70*

REMY'S STEAKHOUSE
620 S. First St., Springfield, IL 62704; (217) 744-3333 **Wine list** *California* **Wine prices** *Moderate* **Cuisine** *Steak house* **Menu prices** *$17–$35*

RUTH'S CHRIS STEAK HOUSE
933 Skokie Blvd., Northbrook, IL 60062; (847) 498-6889 **Wine list** *California* **Wine prices** *Moderate* **Corkage** *$20* **Cuisine** *Steak house* **Menu prices** *$16–$34*

1776
397 Virginia St., Route 14, Crystal Lake, IL 60014; (815) 356-1776 **Wine list** *California* **Wine prices** *Moderate* **Cuisine** *Contemporary American* **Menu prices** *$10–$23*

THE STAINED GLASS
1735 Benson Ave., Evanston, IL 60201; (847) 864-8600 **Wine list** *California, Italy, France* **Wine prices** *Moderate* **Cuisine** *American* **Menu prices** *$16–$28*

SULLIVAN'S STEAKHOUSE
244 S. Main St., Naperville, IL 60540; (630) 305-0230 **Wine list** *California* **Wine prices** *Moderate* **Cuisine** *Steak house* **Menu prices** *$17–$29*

TOM'S PLACE 🍷

17107 N. U.S. Highway 51, De Soto, IL 62924; (618) 867-3033 **Wine list** *California, France* **Wine prices** *Moderate* **Corkage** *$10* **Cuisine** *Contemporary* **Menu prices** *$17–$45*

VA PENSIERO 🍷

Margarita European Inn, 1566 Oak Ave., Evanston, IL 60201; (847) 475-7779 **Wine list** *Italy* **Wine prices** *Moderate* **Cuisine** *Italian* **Menu prices** *$23–$27*

INDIANA

THE CARRIAGE HOUSE DINING ROOM 🍷🍷

24460 Adams Road, South Bend, IN 46628; (574) 272-9220 **Wine list** *California, France* **Wine prices** *Expensive* **Cuisine** *Continental/classic French* **Menu prices** *$20–$35*

CIRCLE CITY BAR & GRILLE 🍷

Indianapolis Marriott Downtown, 350 W. Maryland St., Indianapolis, IN 46225; (317) 405-6100 **Wine list** *California* **Wine prices** *Moderate* **Cuisine** *Regional* **Menu prices** *$13–$28*

DUNAWAY'S PALAZZO OSSIGENO 🍷🍷

351 S. East St., Indianapolis, IN 46204; (317) 638-7663 **Wine list** *California, Italy, France* **Wine prices** *Moderate* **Cuisine** *Mediterranean* **Menu prices** *$17–$39*

EDDIE MERLOT'S 🍷

1502 Illinois Road S., Fort Wayne, IN 46804; (260) 459-2222 **Wine list** *California* **Wine prices** *Moderate* **Cuisine** *Steak house* **Menu prices** *$20–$36*

HESTON BAR 🍷

2003 E. 1000 N., LaPorte, IN 46350; (219) 778-2938 **Wine list** *California, France* **Wine prices** *Moderate* **Cuisine** *American* **Menu prices** *$15–$42*

JACK BINION'S STEAK HOUSE 🍷

Horseshoe Casino Hammond, 777 Casino Center Drive, Hammond, IN 46320; (219) 473-6028 **Wine list** *California* **Wine prices** *Moderate* **Cuisine** *Steak house* **Menu prices** *$15–$39*

JOSEPH DECUIS 🍷

191 N. Main St., Roanoke, IN 46783; (260) 672-1715 **Wine list** *California, France, Italy* **Wine prices** *Moderate* **Cuisine** *Contemporary American* **Menu prices** *$22–$35*

MAJESTIC RESTAURANT

47 S. Pennsylvania Ave., Indianapolis, IN 46204; (317) 636-5418 **Wine list** *California* **Wine prices** *Moderate* **Cuisine** *American* **Menu prices** *$14–$39*

THE MARKER RESTAURANT

Adams Mark Hotel Indianapolis Airport, 2544 Executive Drive, Indianapolis, IN 46241; (317) 381-6146 **Wine list** *California* **Wine prices** *Moderate* **Corkage** *$10* **Cuisine** *American/French* **Menu prices** *$16–$37*

MORTON'S OF CHICAGO

41 E. Washington St., Indianapolis, IN 46204; (317) 229-4700 **Wine list** *California* **Wine prices** *Expensive* **Cuisine** *Steak house* **Menu prices** *$24–$34*

OPUS 24

6328 W. Jefferson Blvd., Fort Wayne, IN 46804; (260) 459-2459 **Wine list** *California* **Wine prices** *Moderate* **Cuisine** *American/Italian* **Menu prices** *$24–$34*

PEPPERCORNS & CINNAMON STICKS

105 S. Main St., Monticello, IN 47960; (574) 583-5700 **Wine list** *California* **Wine prices** *Moderate* **Cuisine** *Contemporary American* **Menu prices** *$18–$28*

PETERSON'S

7690 E. 96th St., Fishers, IN 46038; (317) 598-8863 **Wine list** *California* **Wine prices** *Moderate* **Corkage** *$25* **Cuisine** *American* **Menu prices** *$23–$36*

RUTH'S CHRIS STEAK HOUSE

45 S. Illinois St., Indianapolis, IN 46204; (317) 633-1313 **Wine list** *California* **Wine prices** *Moderate* **Cuisine** *Steak house* **Menu prices** *$18–$34*

RUTH'S CHRIS STEAK HOUSE

9445 Threel Road, Indianapolis, IN 46240; (317) 844-1155 **Wine list** *California* **Wine prices** *Moderate* **Cuisine** *Steak house* **Menu prices** *$18–$34*

ST. ELMO STEAK HOUSE

127 S. Illinois St., Indianapolis, IN 46225; (317) 635-0636 **Wine list** *California, Bordeaux* **Wine prices** *Moderate* **Cuisine** *Steak house* **Menu prices** *$23–$38*

SCHOLARS INN GOURMET CAFÉ & WINE BAR 🍷
Scholars Inn Bed & Breakfast, 717 N. College Ave., Bloomington, IN 47404; (812) 323-1531 **Wine list** *California* **Wine prices** *Moderate* **Cuisine** *Contemporary American* **Menu prices** *$12–$28*

SHULA'S STEAK HOUSE 🍷
The Westin Indianapolis, 50 S. Capitol Ave., Indianapolis, IN 46204; (317) 231-3900 **Wine list** *California* **Wine prices** *Moderate* **Cuisine** *Steak house* **Menu prices** *$29–$50*

SMITH'S ROW FOOD & SPIRITS 🍷
418 Fourth St., Columbus, IN 47201; (812) 373-9382 **Wine list** *California* **Wine prices** Inexpensive **Cuisine** *Continental* **Menu prices** *$9–$23*

SOMETHING DIFFERENT 🍷
4939 E. 82nd St., Indianapolis, IN 46250; (317) 570-7700 **Wine list** *California* **Wine prices** *Moderate* **Cuisine** *American* **Menu prices** *$20–$35*

SULLIVAN'S STEAKHOUSE 🍷
3316 E. 86th St., Indianapolis, IN 46240; (317) 580-1280 **Wine list** *California* **Wine prices** *Moderate* **Cuisine** *Steak house* **Menu prices** *$18–$29*

IOWA

BISTRO ON FIRST 🍷
401 First St. S.E., Cedar Rapids, IA 52401; (319) 862-2062 **Wine list** *California* **Wine prices** Inexpensive **Corkage** *$15* **Cuisine** *Contemporary American* **Menu prices** *$16–$25*

DAVID'S MILWAUKEE DINER 🍷
Hotel Pattee, 1112 Willis Ave., Perry, IA 50220; (515) 465-3511 **Wine list** *California* **Wine prices** *Moderate* **Corkage** *$10* **Cuisine** *American* **Menu prices** *$13–$32*

801 STEAK & CHOP HOUSE 🍷
801 Grand Ave., Des Moines, IA 50309; (515) 288-6000 **Wine list** *California* **Wine prices** *Expensive* **Corkage** *$15* **Cuisine** *Steak house* **Menu prices** *$20–$40*

FORTY-THREE RESTAURANT & BAR 🍷
Hotel Fort Des Moines, 1000 Walnut St., Des Moines, IA 50309; (515) 362-5224 **Wine list** *California* **Wine prices** *Moderate* **Corkage** *$10* **Cuisine** *Californian* **Menu prices** *$16–$36*

LINN STREET CAFÉ
121 N. Linn St., Iowa City, IA 52245; (319) 337-7370 **Wine list** *California, Australia* **Wine prices** *Moderate* **Corkage** *$15* **Cuisine** *Contemporary American* **Menu prices** *$16–$24*

MONTAGE
222 Main St., Cedar Falls, IA 50613; (319) 268-7222 **Wine list** *California* **Wine prices** Inexpensive **Cuisine** *International* **Menu prices** *$11–$22*

RED CROW GRILLE
2504 53rd Ave., Bettendorf, IA 52722; (563) 332-2370 **Wine list** *California* **Wine prices** *Moderate* **Corkage** *$10* **Cuisine** *Contemporary* **Menu prices** *$17–$35*

SAGE, THE RESTAURANT
6587 University Ave., Des Moines, IA 50311; (515) 255-7722 **Wine list** *California* **Wine prices** *Moderate* **Corkage** *$10* **Cuisine** *Contemporary American* **Menu prices** *$16–$26*

SPLASH SEAFOOD BAR & GRILL
303 Locust St., Des Moines, IA 50309; (515) 244-5686 **Wine list** *California* **Wine prices** *Moderate* **Cuisine** *Seafood* **Menu prices** *$14–$50*

TROSTEL'S GREENBRIAR RESTAURANT & BAR
5810 Merle Hay Road, Johnston, IA 50131; (515) 253-0124 **Wine list** *California* **Wine prices** *Moderate* **Corkage** *$15* **Cuisine** *American* **Menu prices** *$12–$28*

KANSAS

40 SARDINES
11942 Roe Ave., Overland Park, KS 66209; (913) 451-1040 **Wine list** *California* **Wine prices** *Moderate* **Corkage** *$20* **Cuisine** *Continental* **Menu prices** *$17–$26*

KIELTYKA'S STONEWALL INN
10240 Pflumm Road, Lenexa, KS 66215; (913) 492-3066 **Wine list** *California* **Wine prices** *Moderate* **Cuisine** *American/Polish* **Menu prices** *$12–$30*

SOUTHWINDS BAR & GRILL
Hyatt Regency Wichita, 400 W. Waterman St., Wichita, KS 67202; (316) 293-1234 **Wine list** *California* **Wine prices** *Moderate* **Cuisine** *Southwestern* **Menu prices** *$16–$30*

KENTUCKY

AVALON
1314 Bardstown Road, Louisville, KY 40204; (502) 454-5336 **Wine list** *California* **Wine prices** Inexpensive **Cuisine** *Contemporary American* **Menu prices** *$14–$24*

AZALEA
3612 Brownsboro Road, Louisville, KY 40207; (502) 895-5493 **Wine list** *California* **Wine prices** Inexpensive **Corkage** *$15* **Cuisine** *Contemporary American* **Menu prices** *$10–$23*

BRISTOL BAR & GRILLE
300 N. Hurstbourne Parkway, Louisville, KY 40222; (502) 426-0627 **Wine list** *California* **Wine prices** Inexpensive **Cuisine** *Regional* **Menu prices** *$6–$20*

CLUB GROTTO
2116 Bardstown Road, Louisville, KY 40205; (502) 459-5275 **Wine list** *California, France* **Wine prices** Inexpensive **Cuisine** *American* **Menu prices** *$14–$35*

DUDLEY'S RESTAURANT
380 S. Mill St., Lexington, KY 40508; (859) 252-1010 **Wine list** *California, France* **Wine prices** *Moderate* **Corkage** *$20* **Cuisine** *American* **Menu prices** *$14–$28*

EQUUS RESTAURANT
122 Sears Ave., Louisville, KY 40207; (502) 897-9721 **Wine list** *California* **Wine prices** *Moderate* **Corkage** *$10* **Cuisine** *Regional* **Menu prices** *$19–$28*

HOLLY HILL INN
426 N. Winter St., Midway, KY 40347; (859) 846-4732 **Wine list** *California, France* **Wine prices** *Moderate* **Cuisine** *French/continental* **Menu prices** *Prix fixe only; $30*

JICAMA GRILL
1538 Bardstown Road, Louisville, KY 40205; (502) 454-4383 **Wine list** *California* **Wine prices** *Moderate* **Corkage** *$15* **Cuisine** *Contemporary Latin* **Menu prices** *$10–$26*

JUDGE ROY BEAN'S
1801 Bardstown Road, Louisville, KY 40205; (502) 451-4982 **Wine list** *California* **Wine prices** Inexpensive **Cuisine** *Southwestern* **Menu prices** *$9–$17*

Grand Award · Best of Award of Excellence · Award of Excellence

KENTUCKY COVE 🍷
501 W. Main St., Louisville, KY 40202; (502) 589-5060
Wine list *California* **Wine prices** *Moderate* **Cuisine** *Regional* **Menu prices** *$14–$28*

LE RELAIS RESTAURANT 🍷
2817 Taylorsville Road, Louisville, KY 40205; (502) 451-9020 **Wine list** *California, France* **Wine prices** *Moderate* **Cuisine** *Provençal* **Menu prices** *$17–$28*

LILLY'S 🍷
1147 Bardstown Road, Louisville, KY 40204; (502) 451-0447 **Wine list** *California* **Wine prices** *Moderate* **Cuisine** *Regional* **Menu prices** *$10–$32*

MALONE'S 🍷
3347 Tates Creek Road, Lexington, KY 40502; (859) 335-6500 **Wine list** *California* **Wine prices** *Moderate* **Cuisine** *Steak house* **Menu prices** *$18–$34*

MORTON'S OF CHICAGO 🍷
626 W. Main St., Louisville, KY 40202; (502) 584-0421
Wine list *California* **Wine prices** *Expensive* **Cuisine** *Steak house* **Menu prices** *$20–$35*

NAPA RIVER GRILL 🍷
3938 Dupont Circle, Louisville, KY 40207; (502) 893-0141
Wine list *California* **Wine prices** *Moderate* **Cuisine** *Californian* **Menu prices** *$11–$25*

THE OAKROOM 🍷🍷
The Seelbach Hilton, 500 Fourth Ave., Louisville, KY 40202; (502) 807-3463 **Wine list** *France, California* **Wine prices** *Moderate* **Corkage** *$20* **Cuisine** *American* **Menu prices** *$20–$38*

PORTOFINO 🍷
249 E. Main St., Lexington, KY 40507; (859) 253-9300
Wine list *California, Bordeaux, Italy* **Wine prices** *Moderate* **Cuisine** *Italian* **Menu prices** *$17–$29*

RUTH'S CHRIS STEAK HOUSE 🍷
Kaden Tower, 6100 Dutchman's Lane, Louisville, KY 40205; (502) 479-0026 **Wine list** *California* **Wine prices** *Expensive* **Cuisine** *Steak house* **Menu prices** *$25–$55*

SONOMA 🍷
313 Greenup St., Covington, KY 41011; (859) 261-7626
Wine list *California* **Wine prices** *Moderate* **Corkage** *$10* **Cuisine** *Californian/Mediterranean* **Menu prices** *$13–$25*

211 CLOVER LANE RESTAURANT 🍷
211 Clover Lane, Louisville, KY 40207; (502) 896-9570
Wine list *California* **Wine prices** Inexpensive **Corkage** *$15*
Cuisine *Continental/French* **Menu prices** *$15–$24*

VINCENZO'S 🍷
150 S. Fifth St., Louisville, KY 40202; (502) 580-1350
Wine list *California, France* **Wine prices** *Moderate* **Cuisine** *Northern Italian* **Menu prices** *$20–$34*

WELLINGHURST'S STEAKHOUSE 🍷
401 E. Main St., Louisville, KY 40202; (502) 515-0172
Wine list *California, Australia* **Wine prices** *Moderate* **Cuisine** *Steak house* **Menu prices** *$17–$38*

WINSTON'S RESTAURANT 🍷
3101 Bardstown Road, Louisville, KY 40205; (502) 456-0980 **Wine list** *California* **Wine prices** *Moderate* **Cuisine** *International* **Menu prices** *$22–$32*

Z'S OYSTER BAR & STEAKHOUSE 🍷
101 Whittington Parkway, Louisville, KY 40222; (502) 429-8000 **Wine list** *California* **Wine prices** *Moderate* **Cuisine** *Steak house/seafood* **Menu prices** *$13–$44*

LOUISIANA

NEW ORLEANS

ALEX PATOUT'S LOUISIANA RESTAURANT 🍷
720 Saint Louis St., New Orleans, LA 70130; (504) 525-7788 **Wine list** *California* **Wine prices** Inexpensive **Cuisine** *Creole/Cajun* **Menu prices** *$17–$29*

THE BISTRO AT MAISON DE VILLE 🍷
Hotel Maison de Ville, 727 Rue Toulouse, New Orleans, LA 70130; (504) 528-9206 **Wine list** *California, France* **Wine prices** *Expensive* **Corkage** *$10* **Cuisine** *French/creole* **Menu prices** *$21–$28*

BRENNAN'S RESTAURANT 🍷🍷🍷
417 Royal St., New Orleans, LA 70130; (504) 525-9711
Wine list *California, Bordeaux, Burgundy, Champagne* **Wine selections** *3,000* **Number of bottles** *35,000* **Wine prices** *Moderate* **Cuisine** *French/creole/Cajun* **Menu prices** *$30–$35*
Credit cards *AX, MC, VS, DV*
Grand Award since 1983

BROUSSARD'S 🍷
819 Rue Conti, New Orleans, LA 70112; (504) 581-3866 **Wine list** *California, France* **Wine prices** *Moderate* **Cuisine** *French/creole* **Menu prices** *$24–$36*

CAFÉ GIOVANNI 🍷
117 Decatur St., New Orleans, LA 70130; (504) 529-2154 **Wine list** *California, Italy* **Wine prices** *Moderate* **Cuisine** *Italian/American* **Menu prices** *$16–$26*

CAFÉ INDO 🍷
216 N. Carrollton Ave., New Orleans, LA 70119; (504) 488-0444 **Wine list** *California, France* **Wine prices** *Moderate* **Corkage** *$10* **Cuisine** *Contemporary French/international* **Menu prices** *$15–$23*

CHATEAUBRIAND 🍷
310 N. Carrollton Ave., New Orleans, LA 70119; (504) 207-0016 **Wine list** *California* **Wine prices** *Moderate* **Corkage** *$15* **Cuisine** *Steak house* **Menu prices** *$20–$33*

COBALT 🍷
Hotel Monaco, 333 Saint Charles Ave., New Orleans, LA 70130; (504) 565-5595 **Wine list** *California* **Wine prices** *Moderate* **Corkage** *$15* **Cuisine** *American* **Menu prices** *$16–$25*

COMMANDER'S PALACE 🍷
1403 Washington Ave., New Orleans, LA 70130; (504) 899-8221 **Wine list** *California, France* **Wine prices** *Expensive* **Cuisine** *Creole* **Menu prices** *$24–$37*

THE COURT OF TWO SISTERS 🍷
613 Rue Royale, New Orleans, LA 70130; (504) 522-7261 **Wine list** *France, California* **Wine prices** *Moderate* **Cuisine** *Creole* **Menu prices** *$17–$39*

DICKIE BRENNAN'S STEAKHOUSE 🍷
716 Iberville St., New Orleans, LA 70130; (504) 522-2467 **Wine list** *California* **Wine prices** *Moderate* **Cuisine** *Steak house* **Menu prices** *$22–$35*

DOMINIQUE'S 🍷🍷
Maison Depuy Hotel, 1001 Rue Toulouse, New Orleans, LA 70112; (504) 522-8800 **Wine list** *California, France* **Wine prices** *Moderate* **Corkage** *$30* **Cuisine** *French* **Menu prices** *$20–$28*

EMERIL'S 🍷🍷🍷
800 Tchoupitoulas St., New Orleans, LA 70130; (504) 528-9393 **Wine list** *California, Burgundy, Rhône, Bordeaux, Austria, Germany* **Wine selections** *1,560* **Number of bottles** *15,000* **Wine prices** *Expensive* **Cuisine** *Contemporary New Orleans* **Menu prices** *$22–$36* **Credit cards** *AX, MC, VS, DV*
Grand Award since 1999

EMERIL'S DELMONICO RESTAURANT & BAR 🍷🍷
1300 Saint Charles Ave., New Orleans, LA 70130; (504) 525-4937 **Wine list** *California, France, Australia, Germany, Austria* **Wine prices** *Expensive* **Corkage** *$25* **Cuisine** *Creole* **Menu prices** *$19–$34*

GABRIELLE RESTAURANT 🍷
3201 Esplanade Ave., New Orleans, LA 70119; (504) 948-6233 **Wine list** *California* **Wine prices** *Moderate* **Cuisine** *Contemporary Creole* **Menu prices** *$14–$28*

THE GRILL ROOM 🍷🍷
Windsor Court Hotel, 300 Gravier St., New Orleans, LA 70130; (504) 522-1992 **Wine list** *California, France, Germany* **Wine prices** *Moderate* **Corkage** *$35* **Cuisine** *Contemporary American* **Menu prices** *$27–$39*

GW FINS 🍷
808 Bienville St., New Orleans, LA 70112; (504) 581-3467 **Wine list** *California* **Wine prices** *Moderate* **Corkage** *$10* **Cuisine** *Seafood* **Menu prices** *$20–$31*

HERBSAINT BAR & RESTAURANT 🍷
701 Saint Charles Ave., New Orleans, LA 70130; (504) 524-4114 **Wine list** *France* **Wine prices** *Moderate* **Corkage** *$20* **Cuisine** *French/American* **Menu prices** *$14–$24*

KELSEY'S RESTAURANT 🍷
3923 Magazine St., New Orleans, LA 70115; (504) 897-6722 **Wine list** *California* **Wine prices** *Moderate* **Corkage** *$10* **Cuisine** *Louisianan* **Menu prices** *$14–$26*

MARISOL 🍷
437 Esplanade Ave., New Orleans, LA 70116; (504) 943-1912 **Wine list** *France* **Wine prices** *Moderate* **Corkage** *$15* **Cuisine** *French/Asian/Mediterranean* **Menu prices** *$18–$29*

MAT & NADDIE'S RESTAURANT 🍷
937 Leonidas St., New Orleans, LA 70118; (504) 861-9600
Wine list *California, France* **Wine prices** Inexpensive
Corkage *$8* **Cuisine** *Contemporary Louisianan* **Menu prices** *$15–$25*

MAXIMO'S ITALIAN GRILL 🍷
1117 Decatur St., New Orleans, LA 70116; (504) 586-8883
Wine list *Italy, California* **Wine prices** *Moderate* **Cuisine** *Northern Italian* **Menu prices** *$11–$30*

MORTON'S OF CHICAGO 🍷
365 Canal St., New Orleans, LA 70130; (504) 566-0221
Wine list *California* **Wine prices** *Expensive* **Cuisine** *Steak house* **Menu prices** *$30–$70*

MR. B'S BISTRO 🍷
201 Royal St., New Orleans, LA 70130; (504) 523-2078
Wine list *California* **Wine prices** *Moderate* **Corkage** *$12*
Cuisine *Contemporary/creole* **Menu prices** *$16–$28*

MURIEL'S JACKSON SQUARE 🍷
801 Chartres St., New Orleans, LA 70116; (504) 568-1885
Wine list *California* **Wine prices** *Moderate* **Corkage** *$12*
Cuisine *Contemporary Louisianan* **Menu prices** *$15–$29*

NOLA 🍷🍷
534 Rue Saint Louis, New Orleans, LA 70130; (504) 522-NOLA **Wine list** *France, California, Italy* **Wine prices** *Moderate* **Corkage** *$20* **Cuisine** *Contemporary American/creole*
Menu prices *$20–$32*

PALACE CAFÉ 🍷
605 Canal St., New Orleans, LA 70130; (504) 523-1661
Wine list *California* **Wine prices** *Expensive* **Corkage** *$15*
Cuisine *Contemporary creole* **Menu prices** *$19–$25*

THE PELICAN CLUB RESTAURANT & BAR 🍷
312 Exchange Place, New Orleans, LA 70130; (504) 523-1504 **Wine list** *California, France* **Wine prices** *Moderate*
Corkage *$20* **Cuisine** *Contemporary Louisianan* **Menu prices** *$18–$42*

PERISTYLE 🍷
1041 Dumaine St., New Orleans, LA 70116; (504) 593-9535 **Wine list** *California* **Wine prices** *Moderate* **Corkage** *$20* **Cuisine** *French/Louisianian* **Menu prices** *$24–$27*

LOUISIANA

RENÉ BISTROT 🍷
Renaissance Pere Marquette, 817 Common St., New Orleans, LA 70112; (504) 412-2580 **Wine list** *France, California* **Wine prices** *Moderate* **Corkage** *$20* **Cuisine** *French* **Menu prices** *$15–$23*

RESTAURANT AUGUST 🍷
301 Tchoupitoulas St., New Orleans, LA 70130; (504) 299-9777 **Wine list** *California, France* **Wine prices** *Expensive* **Corkage** *$20* **Cuisine** *Contemporary French* **Menu prices** *$18–$32*

RESTAURANT CUVÉE 🍷
322 Rue Magazine, New Orleans, LA 70130; (504) 587-9001 **Wine list** *California, France* **Wine prices** *Moderate* **Corkage** *$25* **Cuisine** *Louisianan/French/Spanish* **Menu prices** *$18–$29*

RISTORANTE CARMELO 🍷
541 Decatur St., New Orleans, LA 70130; (504) 586-1414 **Wine list** *Tuscany* **Wine prices** *Moderate* **Cuisine** *Italian* **Menu prices** *$12–$28*

RUTH'S CHRIS STEAK HOUSE 🍷
711 N. Broad St., New Orleans, LA 70119; (504) 486-0810 **Wine list** *California* **Wine prices** *Moderate* **Corkage** *$15* **Cuisine** *Steak house* **Menu prices** *$18–$65*

SMITH & WOLLENSKY 🍷
1009 Poydras St., New Orleans, LA 70112; (504) 561-0770 **Wine list** *California* **Wine prices** *Moderate* **Cuisine** *Steak house* **Menu prices** *$18–$29*

UPPERLINE RESTAURANT 🍷
1413 Upperline St., New Orleans, LA 70115; (504) 891-9822 **Wine list** *California* **Wine prices** *Moderate* **Corkage** *$15* **Cuisine** *Contemporary creole* **Menu prices** *$18–$30*

WOLFE'S OF NEW ORLEANS 🍷
7224 Ponchartrain Blvd., New Orleans, LA 70124; (504) 284-6004 **Wine list** *California, France* **Wine prices** *Moderate* **Corkage** *$15* **Cuisine** *Contemporary New Orleans/creole* **Menu prices** *$18–$26*

🍷🍷🍷 Grand Award 🍷🍷 Best of Award of Excellence 🍷 Award of Excellence

LOUISIANA

OTHER CITIES

ANDREA'S

3100 19th St., Metairie, LA 70002; (504) 834-8583 **Wine list** *Italy, California* **Wine prices** *Moderate* **Cuisine** *Northern Italian* **Menu prices** *$15–$32*

ARTESIA

21516 Highway 36, Abita Springs, LA 70420; (504) 892-1662 **Wine list** *California* **Wine prices** *Moderate* **Corkage** *$10* **Cuisine** *Contemporary French* **Menu prices** *$18–$38*

CHIANTI RESTAURANT

6535 Line Ave., Shreveport, LA 71106; (318) 868-8866 **Wine list** *Italy, California* **Wine prices** *Moderate* **Corkage** *$7* **Cuisine** *Northern Italian* **Menu prices** *$14–$28*

THE DAKOTA RESTAURANT

629 N. Highway 190, Covington, LA 70433; (985) 892-3712 **Wine list** *California* **Wine prices** *Moderate* **Corkage** *$25* **Cuisine** *Contemporary Louisianan* **Menu prices** *$17–$30*

ÉTOILE RESTAURANT & WINE BAR

407 N. Columbia St., Covington, LA 70433; (985) 892-4578 **Wine list** *California, France* **Wine prices** *Moderate* **Cuisine** *French* **Menu prices** *$8–$20*

FERTITTA'S 6301 RESTAURANT

6301 Line Ave., Shreveport, LA 71106; (318) 865-6301 **Wine list** *California, France* **Wine prices** *Moderate* **Corkage** *$15* **Cuisine** *American* **Menu prices** *$15–$30*

FIORE

Harrah's Casino, 315 Clyde Fant Parkway, Shreveport, LA 71101; (318) 424-7777 **Wine list** *California* **Wine prices** *Moderate* **Corkage** *$10* **Cuisine** *Continental* **Menu prices** *$25–$40*

THE FRENCH TABLE

3216 W. Esplanade Ave. N., Metairie, LA 70002; (504) 833-8108 **Wine list** *France* **Wine prices** *Moderate* **Cuisine** *French* **Menu prices** *$18–$32*

GINO'S RESTAURANT

4542 Bennington Ave., Baton Rouge, LA 70808; (225) 927-7156 **Wine list** *California, Italy* **Wine prices** *Moderate* **Corkage** *$15* **Cuisine** *Italian* **Menu prices** *$15–$35*

JUBAN'S RESTAURANT 🍷
3739 Perkins Road, Baton Rouge, LA 70808; (225) 346-8422 **Wine list** *California* **Wine prices** *Moderate* **Corkage** *$15* **Cuisine** *Creole/French* **Menu prices** *$16–$34*

LUCKY PALACE 🍷
750 Isle of Capri Blvd., Bossier City, LA 71111; (318) 752-1888 **Wine list** *California* **Wine prices** Inexpensive **Cuisine** *Chinese* **Menu prices** *$7–$37*

MAGGIO'S RISTORANTE 🍷
4710 O'Neal Lane, Baton Rouge, LA 70817; (225) 752-3354 **Wine list** *Italy, California* **Wine prices** Inexpensive **Corkage** *$10* **Cuisine** *Italian* **Menu prices** *$12–$34*

MANSUR'S 🍷
3044 College Drive, Baton Rouge, LA 70808; (225) 923-3366 **Wine list** *California* **Wine prices** *Moderate* **Cuisine** *Contemporary Louisianan* **Menu prices** *$18–$27*

RUTH'S CHRIS STEAK HOUSE 🍷
620 W. Pinhook Road, Lafayette, LA 70503; (337) 237-6123 **Wine list** *California* **Wine prices** *Moderate* **Corkage** *$15* **Cuisine** *Steak house* **Menu prices** *$22–$38*

RUTH'S CHRIS STEAK HOUSE 🍷
3633 Veterans Blvd., Metairie, LA 70002; (504) 888-3600 **Wine list** *California* **Wine prices** *Moderate* **Cuisine** *Steak house* **Menu prices** *$18–$32*

SULLIVAN'S STEAKHOUSE 🍷
5252 Corporate Blvd., Baton Rouge, LA 70808; (225) 925-1161 **Wine list** *California* **Wine prices** *Moderate* **Corkage** *$10* **Cuisine** *Steak house* **Menu prices** *$18–$30*

SUPERIOR'S STEAKHOUSE 🍷
855 Pierremont Road, Shreveport, LA 71106; (318) 219-7692 **Wine list** *California* **Wine prices** *Moderate* **Corkage** *$20* **Cuisine** *Steak house* **Menu prices** *$19–$35*

MAINE

ARROWS RESTAURANT 🍷
Berwick Road, Ogunquit, ME 03907; (207) 361-1100 **Wine list** *France, California* **Wine prices** *Moderate* **Cuisine** *American* **Menu prices** *$39–$45*

THE BACK BAY GRILL
65 Portland St., Portland, ME 04101; (207) 772-8833 **Wine list** *California, Bordeaux* **Wine prices** *Moderate* **Cuisine** *American* **Menu prices** *$19–$33*

THE BRADLEY INN
3063 Bristol Road, New Harbor, ME 04554; (207) 677-2105 **Wine list** *California* **Wine prices** *Moderate* **Cuisine** *Contemporary American* **Menu prices** *$22–$33*

THE BROOKLIN INN
Main St., Route 175, Brooklin, ME 04616; (207) 359-2777 **Wine list** *California* **Wine prices** *Moderate* **Cuisine** *Contemporary American* **Menu prices** *$15–$28*

CAPE NEDDICK INN
1233 Route 1, York, ME 03902; (207) 363-2899 **Wine list** *California, France* **Wine prices** *Moderate* **Cuisine** *French/American* **Menu prices** *$18–$28*

THE CASTINE INN
The Castine Inn, Main St., Castine, ME 04421; (207) 326-4365 **Wine list** *France* **Wine prices** *Moderate* **Cuisine** *Contemporary* **Menu prices** *Prix fixe only; $65*

CINQUE TERRE
36 Wharf St., Portland, ME 04101; (207) 347-6154 **Wine list** *Italy* **Wine prices** *Moderate* **Cuisine** *Northern Italian* **Menu prices** *$12–$25*

CONUNDRUM WINE & MARTINI BISTRO
117 U.S. Route 1, Freeport, ME 04032; (207) 865-0303 **Wine list** *California* **Wine prices** Inexpensive **Cuisine** *International* **Menu prices** *$8–$14*

GEORGE'S
7 Stephens Lane, Bar Harbor, ME 04609; (207) 288-4505 **Wine list** *California* **Wine prices** *Expensive* **Cuisine** *Mediterranean* **Menu prices** *$10–$25*

GYPSY SWEETHEARTS
31 Shore Road, Ogunquit, ME 03907; (207) 646-7021 **Wine list** *California* **Wine prices** Inexpensive **Cuisine** *International* **Menu prices** *$15–$25*

HURRICANE RESTAURANT
29 Dock Square, Kennebunkport, ME 04046; (207) 967-9111 **Wine list** *California* **Wine prices** *Moderate* **Cuisine** *Seafood* **Menu prices** *$14–$39*

HURRICANE RESTAURANT 🍷
111 Perkins Cove Road, Ogunquit, ME 03907; (207) 646-6348 **Wine list** *California* **Wine prices** Inexpensive **Cuisine** *Seafood* **Menu prices** *$16–$39*

LAKE HOUSE 🍷
686 Waterford Road, Waterford, ME 04088; (800) 223-4182 **Wine list** *California, France* **Wine prices** *Moderate* **Corkage** *$15* **Cuisine** *Continental* **Menu prices** *$17–$28*

LE DOMAINE RESTAURANT FRANÇAIS 🍷
Le Domaine Inn, Rural Route 1, Hancock, ME 04640; (800) 554-8498 **Wine list** *France* **Wine prices** *Moderate* **Cuisine** *French* **Menu prices** *$26–$32*

MAINE DINING ROOM 🍷
Harraseeket Inn, 162 Main St., Freeport, ME 04032; (800) 342-6423 **Wine list** *France, California* **Wine prices** Inexpensive **Cuisine** *Contemporary New England* **Menu prices** *$22–$40*

MARCEL'S 🍷
Samoset Resort, 220 Warrenton St., Rockport, ME 04856; (207) 594-2511 **Wine list** *California, France* **Wine prices** *Moderate* **Cuisine** *French/American* **Menu prices** *$16–$30*

ON THE MARSH 🍷
46 Western Ave., Kennebunkport, ME 04046; (207) 967-2299 **Wine list** *California* **Wine prices** *Moderate* **Cuisine** *European* **Menu prices** *$18–$38*

THE PORTER HOUSE RESTAURANT 🍷
Route 27, Eustis, ME 04936; (207) 246-7932 **Wine list** *California* **Wine prices** Inexpensive **Cuisine** *American* **Menu prices** *$12–$21*

THE ROSE GARDEN 🍷
Bluenose Inn, 90 Eden St., Bar Harbor, ME 04609; (207) 288-3348 **Wine list** *California* **Wine prices** *Moderate* **Cuisine** *Contemporary American* **Menu prices** *Prix fixe only; $56*

SEASCAPES 🍷
77 Pier Road, Cape Porpoise, Kennebunkport, ME 04014; (207) 967-8500 **Wine list** *France* **Wine prices** Inexpensive **Cuisine** *New England/Californian* **Menu prices** *$19–$35*

THRUMCAP 🍷
123 Cottage St., Bar Harbor, ME 04609; (207) 288-3884 **Wine list** *California, France, Italy* **Wine prices** *Moderate* **Cuisine** *Contemporary American* **Menu prices** *$16–$25*

VARANO'S ITALIAN RESTAURANT
60 Mile Road, Wells, ME 04090; (207) 641-8550 **Wine list** *Italy* **Wine prices** *Moderate* **Cuisine** *Italian* **Menu prices** *$11–$25*

THE WHITE BARN INN
37 Beach Ave., Kennebunkport, ME 04046; (207) 967-2321 **Wine list** *California, France, Italy* **Wine prices** *Moderate* **Cuisine** *New England* **Menu prices** *Prix fixe only; $83*

WINDOWS ON THE WATER
12 Chase Hill Road, Kennebunk, ME 04043; (207) 967-3313 **Wine list** *California* **Wine prices** *Moderate* **Cuisine** *Contemporary American* **Menu prices** *$18–$38*

MARYLAND

AGRODOLCE
21030-J Frederick Road, Germantown, MD 20876; (301) 528-6150 **Wine list** *California, Italy* **Wine prices** *Moderate* **Cuisine** *Italian* **Menu prices** *$14–$28*

ALDO'S RISTORANTE ITALIANO
306 S. High St., Baltimore, MD 21202; (410) 727-0700 **Wine list** *Italy* **Wine prices** *Moderate* **Cuisine** *Southern Italian* **Menu prices** *$16–$48*

ANTRIM 1844 COUNTRY INN
30 Trevanion Road, Taneytown, MD 21787; (800) 858-1844 **Wine list** *California, France* **Wine prices** *Moderate* **Cuisine** *Regional/French* **Menu prices** *Prix fixe only; $63*

THE BRASS ELEPHANT
924 N. Charles St., Baltimore, MD 21201; (410) 547-8480 **Wine list** *California* **Wine prices** *Moderate* **Cuisine** *Continental/Northern Italian* **Menu prices** *$18–$29*

CHARLESTON
1000 Lancaster St., Baltimore, MD 21202; (410) 332-7373 **Wine list** *California, Rhône, Bordeaux* **Wine prices** *Moderate* **Cuisine** *Regional* **Menu prices** *$26–$34*

CLYDE'S OF COLUMBIA
10221 Wincopin Circle, Columbia, MD 21044; (410) 730-2829 **Wine list** *California* **Wine prices** *Moderate* **Cuisine** *American* **Menu prices** *$12–$23*

CORKS 🍷
1026 S. Charles St., Baltimore, MD 21230; (410) 752-3810
Wine list *California, Oregon* **Wine prices** *Moderate* **Cuisine** *Contemporary American* **Menu prices** *$20–$32*

THE CROSSING AT CASEY JONES 🍷
417 E. Charles St., La Plata, MD 20646; (301) 932-6226
Wine list *California, Australia, Italy* **Wine prices** Inexpensive **Cuisine** *Contemporary American* **Menu prices** *$14–$29*

DELLA NOTTE RISTORANTE 🍷🍷
801 Eastern Ave., Baltimore, MD 21202; (410) 837-5500
Wine list *Piedmont, Tuscany, California* **Wine prices** *Moderate* **Cuisine** *Italian* **Menu prices** *$12–$45*

THE ELKRIDGE FURNACE INN 🍷
5745 Furnace Ave., Elkridge, MD 21075; (410) 379-9336
Wine list *California* **Wine prices** *Moderate* **Cuisine** *French* **Menu prices** *$17–$30*

FAGER'S ISLAND 🍷
Lighthouse Club & The Edge Hotel, 201 60th St., Ocean City, MD 21842; (410) 524-5500 **Wine list** *California, France* **Wine prices** *Moderate* **Cuisine** *International* **Menu prices** *$14–$25*

FLEMING'S PRIME STEAKHOUSE & WINE BAR 🍷
720 Aliceanna St., Baltimore, MD 21202; (410) 332-1666
Wine list *California* **Wine prices** *Moderate* **Cuisine** *Steak house* **Menu prices** *$19–$32*

GALAXY BAR & GRILLE 🍷
6601 Coastal Highway, Ocean City, MD 21842; (410) 723-6762 **Wine list** *California* **Wine prices** *Moderate* **Cuisine** *Contemporary American* **Menu prices** *$18–$40*

GRAPESEED 🍷
4865-C Cordell Ave., Bethesda, MD 20814; (301) 986-9592
Wine list *California* **Wine prices** *Moderate* **Cuisine** *Contemporary American* **Menu prices** *$20–$26*

HAMPTON'S 🍷
Harbor Court Hotel, 550 Light St., Baltimore, MD 21202; (410) 234-0550 **Wine list** *France, California* **Wine prices** *Expensive* **Cuisine** *American* **Menu prices** *$31–$41*

🍷🍷🍷 Grand Award 🍷🍷 Best of Award of Excellence 🍷 Award of Excellence

HARRYMAN HOUSE 🍷
340 Main St., Reisterstown, MD 21136; (410) 833-8850 **Wine list** *California* **Wine prices** Inexpensive **Corkage** *$10* **Cuisine** *American* **Menu prices** *$15–$28*

THE HOBBIT RESTAURANT 🍷
101 81st St., Ocean City, MD 21842; (410) 524-8100 **Wine list** *California* **Wine prices** *Moderate* **Cuisine** *Continental* **Menu prices** *$19–$35*

HORIZONS RESTAURANT & NIGHTCLUB 🍷
Clarion Resort Fontainebleu, 10100 Coastal Highway, Ocean City, MD 21842; (410) 524-3535 **Wine list** *California* **Wine prices** *Moderate* **Cuisine** *American/continental* **Menu prices** *$16–$34*

KALI'S COURT 🍷
1606 Thames St., Baltimore, MD 21231; (410) 276-4700 **Wine list** *California, France* **Wine prices** *Moderate* **Corkage** *$15* **Cuisine** *Seafood* **Menu prices** *$18–$28*

THE KINGS CONTRIVANCE 🍷🍷
10150 Shaker Drive, Columbia, MD 21046; (410) 995-0500 **Wine list** *California, France* **Wine prices** *Moderate* **Cuisine** *American/continental* **Menu prices** *$20–$28*

LEGAL SEA FOODS 🍷
100 E. Pratt St., Baltimore, MD 21202; (410) 332-7360 **Wine list** *California* **Wine prices** Inexpensive **Cuisine** *Seafood* **Menu prices** *$11–$47*

LEGAL SEA FOODS 🍷
Montgomery Mall, 7101 Democracy Blvd., Bethesda, MD 20814; (301) 469-5900 **Wine list** *California* **Wine prices** Inexpensive **Cuisine** *Seafood* **Menu prices** *$11–$48*

LEWNES' STEAKHOUSE 🍷
401 Fourth St., Annapolis, MD 21403; (410) 263-1617 **Wine list** *California* **Wine prices** *Moderate* **Cuisine** *Steak house* **Menu prices** *$19–$52*

MASON'S 🍷
22 S. Harrison St., Easton, MD 21601; (410) 822-3204 **Wine list** *California* **Wine prices** Inexpensive **Cuisine** *French/Mediterranean* **Menu prices** *$20–$31*

MATHILDA'S 🍷
103 Mill St., Oxford, MD 21654; (410) 226-0056 **Wine list** *California* **Wine prices** *Moderate* **Corkage** *$10* **Cuisine** *Mediterranean* **Menu prices** *$20–$26*

MEALEY'S RESTAURANT
8 Main St., New Market, MD 21774; (301) 865-5488 **Wine list** *California, Spain* **Wine prices** *Moderate* **Cuisine** *American* **Menu prices** *$16–$26*

MIKE'S RESTAURANT & CRAB HOUSE
3030 Old Riva Road, Riva, MD 21140; (410) 956-2784 **Wine list** *California* **Wine prices** *Moderate* **Cuisine** *Seafood* **Menu prices** *$14–$33*

THE MILTON INN
14833 York Road, Sparks, MD 21152; (410) 771-4366 **Wine list** *California, France* **Wine prices** *Moderate* **Cuisine** *Regional* **Menu prices** *$22–$36*

MORTON'S OF CHICAGO
300 S. Charles St., Baltimore, MD 21201; (410) 547-8255 **Wine list** *California* **Wine prices** *Expensive* **Cuisine** *Steak house* **Menu prices** *$23–$33*

NORTHWOODS
609 Melvin Ave., Annapolis, MD 21401; (410) 269-6775 **Wine list** *California* **Wine prices** *Moderate* **Cuisine** *Continental* **Menu prices** *$20–$26*

OLD ANGLER'S INN
10801 MacArthur Blvd., Potomac, MD 20854; (301) 299-9097 **Wine list** *California, France* **Wine prices** *Moderate* **Cuisine** *Contemporary American* **Menu prices** *$28–$40*

THE OREGON GRILLE
1201 Shawan Road, Hunt Valley, MD 21030; (410) 771-0505 **Wine list** *California* **Wine prices** *Moderate* **Cuisine** *American/continental* **Menu prices** *$19–$32*

PERSIMMON
7003 Wisconsin Ave., Bethesda, MD 20815; (301) 654-9860 **Wine list** *California* **Wine prices** *Moderate* **Cuisine** *Contemporary American* **Menu prices** *$18–$26*

PETIT LOUIS BISTRO
4800 Roland Ave., Baltimore, MD 21210; (410) 366-9393 **Wine list** *France* **Wine prices** *Moderate* **Cuisine** *French* **Menu prices** *$12–$20*

REFLECTIONS
Holiday Inn Oceanfront, 67th Street, Coastal Highway, Ocean City, MD 21842; (410) 524-5252 **Wine list** *California* **Wine prices** *Inexpensive* **Cuisine** *Continental/American* **Menu prices** *$21–$32*

Grand Award · Best of Award of Excellence · Award of Excellence

RESTAURANT COLUMBIA
28 South Washington St., Easton, MD 21601; (410) 770-5172 **Wine list** *California* **Wine prices** *Moderate* **Corkage** *$15* **Cuisine** *Contemporary American* **Menu prices** *$22–$30*

RICCIUTI'S
3308 Olney-Sandy Spring Road, Olney, MD 20832; (301) 570-3388 **Wine list** *Italy, California* **Wine prices** Inexpensive **Corkage** *$10* **Cuisine** *Italian/American* **Menu prices** *$11–$22*

RICO Y RICO RESTAURANT
9811 Washingtonian Blvd., Gaithersburg, MD 20878; (301) 330-6611 **Wine list** *California, Italy* **Wine prices** *Moderate* **Cuisine** *Contemporary* **Menu prices** *$28–$25*

ROCCOCO
20 W. Washington St., Hagerstown, MD 21740; (301) 790-3331 **Wine list** *California, France* **Wine prices** *Moderate* **Cuisine** *American/Asian/Mediterranean* **Menu prices** *$12–$30*

RUTH'S CHRIS STEAK HOUSE
301 Severn Ave., Annapolis, MD 21403; (410) 990-0033 **Wine list** *California* **Wine prices** *Moderate* **Cuisine** *Steak house* **Menu prices** *$18–$63*

RUTH'S CHRIS STEAK HOUSE
600 Water St., Baltimore, MD 21202; (410) 783-0033 **Wine list** *California* **Wine prices** *Moderate* **Cuisine** *Steak house* **Menu prices** *$18–$34*

RUTH'S CHRIS STEAK HOUSE
1777 Reisterstown Road, Pikesville, MD 21208; (410) 837-0033 **Wine list** *California* **Wine prices** *Moderate* **Cuisine** *Steak house* **Menu prices** *$18–$34*

SAM'S WATERFRONT CAFÉ
2020 Chesapeake Harbour Drive E., Annapolis, MD 21403; (410) 263-3600 **Wine list** *California* **Wine prices** *Moderate* **Cuisine** *Contemporary American* **Menu prices** *$18–$30*

SAVAGE RIVER LODGE
1600 Mount Aetna Road, Frostburg, MD 21532; (301) 689-3200 **Wine list** *California* **Wine prices** Inexpensive **Cuisine** *American* **Menu prices** *$17–$42*

SHERWOOD LANDING 🍷
The Inn at Perry Cabin, 308 Watkins Lane, St. Michaels, MD 21663; (410) 745-2200 **Wine list** *France, California* **Wine prices** *Moderate* **Cuisine** *Regional* **Menu prices** *$25–$35*

SOTTO SOPRA 🍷
405 N. Charles St., Baltimore, MD 21201; (410) 625-0534 **Wine list** *Italy, California* **Wine prices** Inexpensive **Corkage** *$20* **Cuisine** *Northern Italian* **Menu prices** *$17–$30*

STONE MANOR 🍷
5820 Carroll Boyer Road, Middletown, MD 21769; (301) 473-5454 **Wine list** *California, France* **Wine prices** *Moderate* **Cuisine** *Contemporary American* **Menu prices** *Prix fixe only; $69*

TAURASO'S RISTORANTE & TRATTORIA 🍷
6 N. East St., Frederick, MD 21701; (301) 663-6600 **Wine list** *California* **Wine prices** *Moderate* **Cuisine** *Italian* **Menu prices** *$11–$26*

THE TILGHMAN ISLAND INN 🍷
21384 Coopertown Road, Tilghman Island, MD 21671; (410) 886-2141 **Wine list** *California, France* **Wine prices** Inexpensive **Corkage** *$15* **Cuisine** *American* **Menu prices** *$20–$32*

TRAGARA 🍷
4935 Cordell Ave., Bethesda, MD 20814; (301) 951-4935 **Wine list** *California, Italy* **Wine prices** *Moderate* **Cuisine** *Northern Italian* **Menu prices** *$16–$27*

WILD ORCHID CAFÉ 🍷
909 Bay Ridge Ave., Annapolis, MD 21403; (410) 268-8009 **Wine list** *California* **Wine prices** Inexpensive **Corkage** *$10* **Cuisine** *Contemporary American* **Menu prices** *$24–$27*

MASSACHUSETTS

BOSTON

ABE & LOUIE'S 🍷
793 Boylston St., Boston, MA 02116; (617) 536-6300 **Wine list** *California* **Wine prices** *Moderate* **Cuisine** *Steak house* **Menu prices** *$19–$32*

ANTHONY'S PIER 4 🍷🍷
140 Northern Ave., Boston, MA 02210; (617) 482-6262 **Wine list** *California, France, Italy* **Wine prices** *Moderate* **Cuisine** *American* **Menu prices** *$17–$45*

AQUITAINE BAR À VIN BISTROT 🍷
569 Tremont St., Boston, MA 02118; (617) 424-8577 **Wine list** *France* **Wine prices** *Moderate* **Cuisine** *French* **Menu prices** *$18–$30*

AUJOURD'HUI 🍷
Four Seasons Hotel Boston, 200 Boylston St., Boston, MA 02116; (617) 351-2037 **Wine list** *California, Burgundy* **Wine prices** *Moderate* **Cuisine** *American* **Menu prices** *$35–$44*

AZURE 🍷
The Lenox Hotel, 61 Exeter St., Boston, MA 02116; (617) 933-4800 **Wine list** *California, France* **Wine prices** *Moderate* **Cuisine** *Contemporary American/French/Asian* **Menu prices** *$24–$36*

THE BAY TOWER 🍷
60 State St., Boston, MA 02109; (617) 723-1666 **Wine list** *California* **Wine prices** *Moderate* **Cuisine** *Contemporary regional* **Menu prices** *$26–$40*

BLU 🍷
4 Avery St., Boston, MA 02111; (617) 375-8550 **Wine list** *California, France* **Wine prices** *Moderate* **Cuisine** *American* **Menu prices** *$24–$36*

BONFIRE 🍷
50 Park Plaza, Boston, MA 02116; (617) 262-3473 **Wine list** *Argentina, Chile* **Wine prices** *Moderate* **Corkage** *$27* **Cuisine** *Steak house* **Menu prices** *$20–$43*

BRASSERIE JO 🍷
The Colonnade Hotel, 120 Huntington Ave., Boston, MA 02116; (617) 425-3240 **Wine list** *France* **Wine prices** *Moderate* **Cuisine** *French* **Menu prices** *$15–$32*

CAFÉ LOUIS 🍷
234 Berkeley St., Boston, MA 02116; (617) 266-4680 **Wine list** *Italy, California, France* **Wine prices** *Moderate* **Cuisine** *Italian* **Menu prices** *$18–$35*

THE CAPITAL GRILLE 🍷
359 Newbury St., Boston, MA 02115; (617) 262-8900
Wine list *California, Bordeaux* **Wine prices** *Moderate* **Cuisine** *Steak house* **Menu prices** *$17–$30*

DAVIDE RESTAURANT 🍷
326 Commercial St., Boston, MA 02109; (617) 227-5745
Wine list *California, Italy* **Wine prices** *Expensive* **Cuisine** *Northern Italian* **Menu prices** *$18–$36*

DAVIO'S 🍷
75 Arlington St., Boston, MA 02116; (617) 357-4810 **Wine list** *California* **Wine prices** *Moderate* **Cuisine** *Northern Italian* **Menu prices** *$19–$37*

THE FEDERALIST 🍷🍷🍷
Fifteen Beacon, 15 Beacon St., Boston, MA 02108; (617) 670-2515 **Wine list** *California, Bordeaux, Burgundy, Rhône* **Wine selections** *2,300* **Number of bottles** *24,275* **Wine prices** *Expensive* **Cuisine** *Contemporary American* **Menu prices** *$31–$45* **Credit cards** *AX, MC, VS, DV*
Grand Award since 2001

FLEMING'S PRIME STEAKHOUSE & WINE BAR 🍷
217 Stuart St., Boston, MA 02116; (617) 292-0808 **Wine list** *California* **Wine prices** *Moderate* **Cuisine** *Steak house* **Menu prices** *$18–$27*

GRILL 23 & BAR 🍷🍷
161 Berkeley St., Boston, MA 02116; (617) 542-2255 **Wine list** *California, Bordeaux* **Wine prices** *Expensive* **Cuisine** *American* **Menu prices** *$23–$40*

HAMERSLEY'S BISTRO 🍷
553 Tremont St., Boston, MA 02116; (617) 423-2700 **Wine list** *France* **Wine prices** Inexpensive **Cuisine** *French/American* **Menu prices** *$24–$39*

ICARUS 🍷
3 Appleton St., Boston, MA 02116; (617) 426-1790 **Wine list** *California, France* **Wine prices** *Expensive* **Corkage** *$20* **Cuisine** *Regional* **Menu prices** *$24–$34*

JIMMY'S HARBORSIDE RESTAURANT 🍷
242 Northern Ave., Boston, MA 02210; (617) 423-1000 **Wine list** *California* **Wine prices** *Moderate* **Cuisine** *Seafood* **Menu prices** *$9–$25*

JULIEN
Meridien Boston, 250 Franklin St., Boston, MA 02110; (617) 956-8752 **Wine list** *France, California* **Wine prices** *Expensive* **Cuisine** *French* **Menu prices** *$27–$40*

KASHMIR
279 Newbury St., Boston, MA 02116; (617) 536-1695 **Wine list** *California* **Wine prices** *Moderate* **Cuisine** *Indian* **Menu prices** *$12–$20*

KINGFISH HALL
188 South Market Building, Faneuil Hall Marketplace, Boston, MA 01209; (617) 523-8862 **Wine list** *California* **Wine prices** *Moderate* **Cuisine** *Seafood* **Menu prices** *$17–$38*

LEGAL SEA FOODS
800 Boylston St., Boston, MA 02199; (617) 266-6800 **Wine list** *California, France* **Wine prices** Inexpensive **Cuisine** *Seafood* **Menu prices** *$11–$46*

LEGAL SEA FOODS
100 Huntington Ave., Boston, MA 02116; (617) 266-7775 **Wine list** *California, France* **Wine prices** Inexpensive **Cuisine** *Seafood* **Menu prices** *$11–$46*

LEGAL SEA FOODS
26 Park Square, Boston, MA 02116; (617) 426-4444 **Wine list** *California, Burgundy* **Wine prices** Inexpensive **Cuisine** *Seafood* **Menu prices** *$11–$46*

LEGAL SEA FOODS
255 State St., Boston, MA 02109; (617) 227-3115 **Wine list** *California, France* **Wine prices** Inexpensive **Cuisine** *Seafood* **Menu prices** *$11–$46*

L'ESPALIER
30 Gloucester St., Boston, MA 02115; (617) 262-3023 **Wine list** *France, California* **Wine prices** *Expensive* **Cuisine** *Contemporary French* **Menu prices** *Prix fixe only; $68*

LES ZYGOMATES WINE BAR & BISTRO
129 South St., Boston, MA 02111; (617) 542-5108 **Wine list** *France, California* **Wine prices** *Moderate* **Cuisine** *French* **Menu prices** *$19–$28*

LUCCA RESTAURANT
226 Hanover St., Boston, MA 02113; (617) 742-9200 **Wine list** *California, Italy* **Wine prices** *Moderate* **Cuisine** *Italian* **Menu prices** *$18–$30*

MERITAGE
Boston Harbor Hotel, 70 Rowes Wharf, Boston, MA 02110; (617) 439-3995 **Wine list** *California, Bordeaux* **Wine prices** *Expensive* **Cuisine** *Contemporary* **Menu prices** *$14–$28*

MISTRAL
223 Columbus Ave., Boston, MA 02116; (617) 867-9300 **Wine list** *California, France, Italy* **Wine prices** *Expensive* **Cuisine** *French/Mediterranean* **Menu prices** *$18–$42*

MORTON'S OF CHICAGO
1 Exeter Place, Boston, MA 02116; (617) 266-5858 **Wine list** *California* **Wine prices** *Expensive* **Cuisine** *Steak house* **Menu prices** *$22–$36*

NO. 9 PARK
9 Park St., Boston, MA 02108; (617) 742-9991 **Wine list** *France, Italy, California* **Wine prices** *Moderate* **Cuisine** *French/Italian* **Menu prices** *$26–$40*

THE PALM
The Westin Copley Place, 200 Dartmouth St., Boston, MA 02116; (617) 867-9292 **Wine list** *California* **Wine prices** *Moderate* **Cuisine** *Steak house* **Menu prices** *$14–$35*

PLAZA III-THE KANSAS CITY STEAKHOUSE
101 South Market Building, Faneuil Hall Marketplace, Boston, MA 02109; (617) 720-5570 **Wine list** *California* **Wine prices** *Moderate* **Cuisine** *Steak house* **Menu prices** *$20–$36*

PREZZA
24 Fleet St., Boston, MA 02113; (617) 227-1577 **Wine list** *California, Italy, France* **Wine prices** *Moderate* **Cuisine** *European/Mediterranean* **Menu prices** *$20–$28*

RADIUS
8 High St., Boston, MA 02110; (617) 426-1234 **Wine list** *France, California* **Wine prices** *Moderate* **Cuisine** *Contemporary French* **Menu prices** *$23–$37*

SEASONS
Millennium Bostonian Hotel, 26 North St., Boston, MA 02109; (617) 523-4119 **Wine list** *California* **Wine prices** *Moderate* **Cuisine** *American* **Menu prices** *$27–$36*

SEL DE LA TERRE
255 State St., Boston, MA 02109; (617) 720-1300 **Wine list** *France* **Wine prices** *Moderate* **Cuisine** *Southern French* **Menu prices** *$21–$28*

Grand Award · Best of Award of Excellence · Award of Excellence

SKIPJACK'S SEAFOOD EMPORIUM
199 Clarendon St., Boston, MA 02116; (617) 536-3500
Wine list *California* **Wine prices** *Moderate* **Cuisine** *Seafood*
Menu prices *$16–$25*

33 RESTAURANT & LOUNGE
33 Stanhope St., Boston, MA 02116; (617) 572-3311 **Wine list** *France, Italy* **Wine prices** *Moderate* **Cuisine** *French/Italian* **Menu prices** *$22–$39*

TOP OF THE HUB RESTAURANT & SKYWALK
Prudential Tower, 800 Boylston St., Boston, MA 02199; (617) 536-1775 **Wine list** *California* **Wine prices** *Moderate* **Cuisine** *Contemporary New England* **Menu prices** *$22–$37*

TRATTORIA À SCALINATELLA
253 Hanover St., Boston, MA 02113; (617) 742-1276 **Wine list** *Italy* **Wine prices** *Expensive* **Cuisine** *Italian* **Menu prices** *$19–$34*

TREMONT 647
647 Tremont St., Boston, MA 02118; (617) 266-4600 **Wine list** *California* **Wine prices** Inexpensive **Cuisine** *American*
Menu prices *$16–$25*

MASSACHUSETTS

OTHER CITIES

ABBICCI
43 Main St., Yarmouth Port, MA 02675; (508) 362-3501
Wine list *Italy* **Wine prices** *Moderate* **Cuisine** *Mediterranean*
Menu prices *$19–$37*

AMELIA'S
5 Amelia Drive, Nantucket, MA 02554; (508) 325-5151
Wine list *France* **Wine prices** Inexpensive **Cuisine** *French/American* **Menu prices** *$21–$39*

AMERICAN SEASONS
80 Centre St., Nantucket, MA 02554; (508) 228-7111
Wine list *California* **Wine prices** *Moderate* **Cuisine** *American*
Menu prices *$25–$34*

ANGELO'S RISTORANTE
237 Main St., Stoneham, MA 02180; (781) 279-9035 **Wine list** *California, Italy, Champagne* **Wine prices** Inexpensive **Cuisine** *Italian* **Menu prices** *$19–$30*

ATRIA 🍷
137 Main St., Edgartown, MA 02539; (508) 627-5850
Wine list *France, Australia* **Wine prices** *Moderate* **Cuisine** *Contemporary American* **Menu prices** *$24–$36*

THE BARLEY NECK INN & LODGE 🍷
5 Beach Road, East Orleans, MA 02643; (508) 255-0212
Wine list *California, France* **Wine prices** *Moderate* **Cuisine** *International/regional* **Menu prices** *$16–$24*

BLANTYRE 🍷🍷
16 Blantyre Road, Lenox, MA 01240; (413) 637-3556 **Wine list** *California, Burgundy* **Wine prices** *Moderate* **Cuisine** *French* **Menu prices** *Prix fixe only; $80*

BLUE GINGER 🍷
583 Washington St., Wellesley, MA 02482; (781) 283-5790
Wine list *California, France* **Wine prices** *Moderate* **Cuisine** *International* **Menu prices** *$19–$32*

BOARDING HOUSE 🍷
12 Federal St., Nantucket, MA 02554; (508) 228-9622
Wine list *California* **Wine prices** *Moderate* **Cuisine** *Contemporary European/Asian* **Menu prices** *$16–$35*

THE BRANT POINT GRILL 🍷
The White Elephant, 50 Easton St., Nantucket, MA 02554; (508) 325-1320 **Wine list** *California, France, Italy* **Wine prices** *Moderate* **Cuisine** *Steak house/seafood* **Menu prices** *$23–$58*

CAESAR'S BISTRO 🍷
Regency Hotel, 70 Southbridge St., Worcester, MA 01608; (508) 791-1400 **Wine list** *California* **Wine prices** *Moderate* **Cuisine** *Continental* **Menu prices** *$13–$24*

CAFÉ LUCIA 🍷
80 Church St., Lenox, MA 01240; (413) 637-2640 **Wine list** *California, Italy* **Wine prices** *Moderate* **Cuisine** *Italian* **Menu prices** *$14–$32*

THE CAPITAL GRILLE 🍷
250 Boylston St., Chestnut Hill, MA 02467; (617) 928-1400
Wine list *California, Bordeaux* **Wine prices** *Moderate* **Cuisine** *Steak house* **Menu prices** *$17–$32*

CASTLE RESTAURANT 🍷
1230 Main St., Leicester, MA 01524; (508) 892-9090 **Wine list** *California* **Wine prices** *Moderate* **Cuisine** *Continental* **Menu prices** *$21–$34*

CASTLE STREET CAFÉ 🍷

10 Castle St., Great Barrington, MA 01230; (413) 528-5244 **Wine list** *Bordeaux* **Wine prices** *Moderate* **Cuisine** *Contemporary* **Menu prices** *$16–$24*

CHANDLER'S 🍷

Routes 5 and 10, S. Deerfield, MA 01373; (413) 665-1277 **Wine list** *California* **Wine prices** *Moderate* **Cuisine** *American* **Menu prices** *$20–$26*

THE CHANTICLEER INN 🍷🍷🍷

9 New St., Siasconset, Nantucket, MA 02564; (508) 257-6231 **Wine list** *Burgundy, Bordeaux, Rhône* **Wine selections** *1,000* **Number of bottles** *30,000* **Wine prices** *Moderate* **Cuisine** *French* **Menu prices** *$25–$45*
Credit cards *AX, MC, VS*
Grand Award since 1987

CHESTER 🍷

404 Commercial St., Provincetown, MA 02657; (508) 487-8200 **Wine list** *California* **Wine prices** *Moderate* **Cuisine** *American* **Menu prices** *$19–$34*

CHILLINGSWORTH 🍷

2449 Main St., Route 6A, Brewster, MA 02631; (508) 896-3640 **Wine list** *California, France* **Wine prices** *Moderate* **Cuisine** *French/seafood* **Menu prices** *Prix fixe only; $56–$68*

CHURCH STREET CAFÉ 🍷

65 Church St., Lenox, MA 01240; (413) 637-2745 **Wine list** *California* **Wine prices** *Moderate* **Cuisine** *Contemporary* **Menu prices** *$18–$27*

CIOPPINO'S RESTAURANT & BAR 🍷

20 Broad St., Nantucket, MA 02554; (508) 228-4622 **Wine list** *California, France* **Wine prices** *Moderate* **Cuisine** *Italian/seafood* **Menu prices** *$17–$30*

COONAMESSETT INN 🍷

311 Gifford St., Falmouth, MA 02540; (508) 548-2300 **Wine list** *California* **Wine prices** *Moderate* **Cuisine** *Regional* **Menu prices** *$17–$27*

CRANWELL MANSION 🍷

Cranwell Resort, Spa & Golf Club, 55 Lee Road, Lenox, MA 01240; (413) 637-1364 **Wine list** *California, France* **Wine prices** *Moderate* **Cuisine** *Contemporary/Asian* **Menu prices** *$20–$35*

THE DAN'L WEBSTER INN 🍷🍷
149 Main St., Sandwich, MA 02563; (508) 888-3622 **Wine list** *California, Burgundy* **Wine prices** Inexpensive **Cuisine** *Contemporary American* **Menu prices** *$15–$28*

DEL RAYE BAR & GRILL 🍷🍷
1 Bridge St., Northampton, MA 01061; (413) 586-2664 **Wine list** *California* **Wine prices** *Moderate* **Cuisine** *French/American* **Menu prices** *$26–$28*

THE EGREMONT INN 🍷
10 Old Sheffield Road, South Egremont, MA 01258; (413) 528-2111 **Wine list** *California, France* **Wine prices** *Moderate* **Cuisine** *American* **Menu prices** *$17–$27*

FRONT STREET 🍷
230 Commercial St., Provincetown, MA 02657; (508) 487-9715 **Wine list** *France, California* **Wine prices** *Moderate* **Cuisine** *Continental* **Menu prices** *$16–$26*

GATEWAYS INN 🍷
51 Walker St., Lenox, MA 01240; (413) 637-2532 **Wine list** *Italy, California* **Wine prices** *Moderate* **Cuisine** *American/Italian* **Menu prices** *$20–$28*

GAVENS 🍷
119 S. Main St., Middleton, MA 01949; (978) 774-0500 **Wine list** *California* **Wine prices** *Moderate* **Cuisine** *Steak house* **Menu prices** *$19–$35*

GOLDEN TEMPLE 🍷
1651 Beacon St., Brookline, MA 02445; (617) 277-9722 **Wine list** *California* **Wine prices** *Moderate* **Cuisine** *Asian* **Menu prices** *$10–$43*

THE HARBOR VIEW HOTEL 🍷
131 N. Water St., Edgartown, MA 02539; (508) 627-7000 **Wine list** *California* **Wine prices** *Moderate* **Cuisine** *Regional* **Menu prices** *$19–$38*

HARVEST 🍷
44 Brattle St., Cambridge, MA 02138; (617) 868-2255 **Wine list** *California, France* **Wine prices** *Moderate* **Cuisine** *American* **Menu prices** *$20–$30*

IL CAPRICCIO 🍷
888 Main St., Waltham, MA 02453; (781) 894-2234 **Wine list** *Italy* **Wine prices** *Moderate* **Cuisine** *Northern Italian* **Menu prices** *$17–$35*

L'UVA RESTAURANT
133 Bradford St., Provincetown, MA 02657; (508) 487-2010 **Wine list** *California, Italy, France, Spain* **Wine prices** *Moderate* **Cuisine** *Mediterranean* **Menu prices** *$16–$26*

LAFAYETTE HOUSE
109 Washington St., Foxboro, MA 02035; (508) 543-5344 **Wine list** *California* **Wine prices** *Moderate* **Cuisine** *American/continental* **Menu prices** *$17–$28*

LE LANGUEDOC INN & BISTRO
24 Broad St., Nantucket, MA 02554; (508) 228-2552 **Wine list** *California, France* **Wine prices** *Moderate* **Corkage** *$40* **Cuisine** *French/American* **Menu prices** *$19–$34*

LEGAL SEA FOODS
250 Granite St., Braintree, MA 02184; (781) 356-3070 **Wine list** *California, France* **Wine prices** Inexpensive **Cuisine** *Seafood* **Menu prices** *$11–$36*

LEGAL SEA FOODS
Burlington Mall, 1131 Middlesex Turnpike, Burlington, MA 01803; (781) 270-9700 **Wine list** *California, France* **Wine prices** Inexpensive **Cuisine** *Seafood* **Menu prices** *$11–$36*

LEGAL SEA FOODS
5 Cambridge Center, Kendall Square, Cambridge, MA 02139; (617) 864-3400 **Wine list** *California, France* **Wine prices** Inexpensive **Cuisine** *Seafood* **Menu prices** *$11–$46*

LEGAL SEA FOODS
43 Boylston St., Chestnut Hill, MA 02167; (617) 277-7300 **Wine list** *California, France* **Wine prices** Inexpensive **Cuisine** *Seafood* **Menu prices** *$11–$46*

LEGAL SEA FOODS
50-60 Worcester Road, Framingham, MA 01702; (508) 766-0600 **Wine list** *California, France* **Wine prices** Inexpensive **Cuisine** *Seafood* **Menu prices** *$11–$47*

LEGAL SEA FOODS
Northshore Mall, Routes 128 and 114, Peabody, MA 01960; (978) 532-4500 **Wine list** *California, France* **Wine prices** Inexpensive **Cuisine** *Seafood* **Menu prices** *$11–$47*

NAUSET BEACH CLUB RESTAURANT
222 Main St., East Orleans, MA 02643; (508) 255-8547 **Wine list** *California* **Wine prices** *Moderate* **Cuisine** *Northern Italian* **Menu prices** *$18–$29*

THE OLD INN ON THE GREEN
The Old Inn on the Green & Gedney Farm, Route 57, New Marlborough, MA 01230; (413) 229-3131 **Wine list** *France, California* **Wine prices** *Moderate* **Cuisine** *Regional* **Menu prices** *$22–$36*

OLD YARMOUTH INN
223 Route 6A, Yarmouth Port, MA 02675; (508) 362-9962 **Wine list** *California* **Wine prices** Inexpensive **Cuisine** *Regional* **Menu prices** *$16–$25*

OLIVES
10 City Square, Charlestown, MA 02129; (617) 242-1999 **Wine list** *California, Burgundy* **Wine prices** *Moderate* **Cuisine** *Mediterranean* **Menu prices** *$17–$32*

ONE ELEVEN CHOP HOUSE
111 Shrewsbury St., Worcester, MA 01604; (508) 799-4111 **Wine list** *California* **Wine prices** *Moderate* **Cuisine** *Steak house* **Menu prices** *$16–$26*

THE PADDOCK
West End Rotary Street, Hyannis, MA 02601; (508) 775-7677 **Wine list** *California, France* **Wine prices** Inexpensive **Corkage** *$12* **Cuisine** *Continental/seafood* **Menu prices** *$16–$27*

THE PEARL
12 Federal St., Nantucket, MA 02554; (508) 228-9701 **Wine list** *California* **Wine prices** *Moderate* **Cuisine** *Contemporary French/Asian* **Menu prices** *$28–$52*

PELLINO'S FINE ITALIAN DINING
261 Washington St., Marblehead, MA 01945; (781) 631-3344 **Wine list** *California* **Wine prices** *Moderate* **Cuisine** *Italian/Provençal* **Menu prices** *$16–$25*

THE RED LION INN
30 Main St., Stockbridge, MA 01262; (413) 298-5545 **Wine list** *California, France* **Wine prices** *Moderate* **Cuisine** *Contemporary New England* **Menu prices** *$21–$35*

RIALTO
The Charles Hotel, 1 Bennett St., Cambridge, MA 02138; (617) 661-5050 **Wine list** *California, France* **Wine prices** *Expensive* **Cuisine** *Mediterranean* **Menu prices** *$22–$36*

SANDRINE'S BISTRO
8 Holyoke St., Cambridge, MA 02138; (617) 497-5300
Wine list *France* **Wine prices** *Moderate* **Cuisine** *Alsatian*
Menu prices *$21–$36*

SEAGRILLE
45 Sparks Ave., Nantucket, MA 02554; (508) 325-5700
Wine list *California* **Wine prices** *Moderate* **Cuisine** *Seafood*
Menu prices *$20–$30*

SHIP'S INN
13 Fair St., Nantucket, MA 02554; (508) 228-0040 **Wine list** *California, France* **Wine prices** *Moderate* **Corkage** *$15*
Cuisine *American/French* **Menu prices** *$19–$34*

SILKS AT STONEHEDGE INN
160 Pawtucket Blvd., Tyngsboro, MA 01879; (800) 648-7070 **Wine list** *California, Bordeaux, Burgundy, Italy* **Wine selections** *2,000* **Number of bottles** *96,000* **Wine prices** *Moderate* **Cuisine** *Contemporary French* **Menu prices** *$23–$34* **Credit cards** *AX, MC, VS, DV*
Grand Award since 1996

SKIPJACK'S SEAFOOD EMPORIUM
1400 Worcester Road, Natick, MA 01764; (508) 628-9900
Wine list *California* **Wine prices** Inexpensive **Cuisine** *Seafood* **Menu prices** *$14–$25*

SKIPJACK'S SEAFOOD EMPORIUM
55 Needham St., Newton, MA 02459; (617) 964-4244
Wine list *California* **Wine prices** *Moderate* **Cuisine** *Seafood*
Menu prices *$14–$22*

THE SOLE PROPRIETOR
118 Highland St., Worcester, MA 01609; (508) 798-FISH
Wine list *California* **Wine prices** Inexpensive **Cuisine** *Seafood* **Menu prices** *$14–$22*

SPENCER'S RESTAURANT
Thornewood Inn, 453 Stockbridge Road, Great Barrington, MA 01230; (413) 528-3828 **Wine list** *California* **Wine prices** *Moderate* **Corkage** *$20* **Cuisine** *Continental* **Menu prices** *$13–$27*

STRAIGHT WHARF RESTAURANT
6 Harbor Square, Nantucket, MA 02554; (508) 228-4499
Wine list *France, California* **Wine prices** *Moderate* **Cuisine** *Mediterranean* **Menu prices** *$29–$42*

THE SUMMER HOUSE RESTAURANT 🍷
17 Ocean Ave., Nantucket, MA 02554; (508) 257-9976
Wine list *California, France* **Wine prices** *Moderate* **Cuisine** *Contemporary American* **Menu prices** *$25–$49*

TOPPER'S AT THE WAUWINET 🍷🍷🍷
The Wauwinet Inn, 120 Wauwinet Road, Nantucket, MA 02554; (508) 228-8768 **Wine list** *California, Bordeaux, Burgundy* **Wine selections** *1,400* **Number of bottles** *20,000* **Wine prices** *Moderate* **Cuisine** *American* **Menu prices** *$35–$50* **Credit cards** *AX, MC, VS*
Grand Award since 1996

TOSCA 🍷
14 North St., Hingham, MA 02043; (781) 740-0080 **Wine list** *California, Italy* **Wine prices** *Moderate* **Cuisine** *Italian* **Menu prices** *$19–$29*

TWENTY EIGHT ATLANTIC 🍷
Wequassett Inn Resort & Golf Club, Pleasant Bay, Chatham, MA 02633; (508) 430-3000 **Wine list** *California, France* **Wine prices** *Moderate* **Cuisine** *Contemporary American* **Menu prices** *$23–$35*

21 FEDERAL 🍷
21 Federal St., Nantucket, MA 02554; (508) 228-2121
Wine list *France, California* **Wine prices** *Moderate* **Cuisine** *Contemporary American* **Menu prices** *$19–$36*

VIN & EDDIE'S RISTORANTE 🍷
1400 Bedford St., North Abington, MA 02351; (781) 871-1469 **Wine list** *Italy, California* **Wine prices** *Expensive* **Cuisine** *Northern Italian* **Menu prices** *$16–$20*

V.J.'S GRILLE ROOM 🍷
Cape Codder Resort & Spa, 1225 Iyanough Road, Hyannis, MA 02601; (508) 771-3000 **Wine list** *France, California* **Wine prices** *Moderate* **Cuisine** *Steak house* **Menu prices** *$18–$30*

WHEATLEIGH 🍷🍷
Wheatleigh Hotel, Hawthorne Road, Lenox, MA 01240; (413) 637-0610 **Wine list** *California, France* **Wine prices** *Moderate* **Corkage** *$25* **Cuisine** *Contemporary French* **Menu prices** *Prix fixe only; $82–$105*

WHITE RAINBOW RESTAURANT & MARTINI BAR
65 Main St., Gloucester, MA 01930; (978) 281-0017 **Wine list** *California, France* **Wine prices** *Moderate* **Cuisine** *Continental* **Menu prices** *$18–$35*

THE WOODBOX INN
29 Fair St., Nantucket, MA 02554; (508) 228-0587 **Wine list** *California* **Wine prices** *Moderate* **Cuisine** *Continental* **Menu prices** *$19–$32*

MICHIGAN

BIG ROCK CHOP & BREW HOUSE
245 S. Eton St., Birmingham, MI 48009; (248) 647-7774 **Wine list** *California* **Wine prices** *Moderate* **Cuisine** *Steak house* **Menu prices** *$17–$32*

THE BLACK SWAN RESTAURANT
3501 Greenleaf Blvd., Kalamazoo, MI 49008; (269) 375-2105 **Wine list** *California* **Wine prices** *Moderate* **Cuisine** *Continental* **Menu prices** *$16–$25*

BOWERS HARBOR INN
13512 Peninsula Drive, Traverse City, MI 49686; (231) 223-4222 **Wine list** *California* **Wine prices** *Moderate* **Cuisine** *Regional* **Menu prices** *$16–$28*

BUTCH'S RESTAURANT
44 E. Eighth St., Holland, MI 49423; (616) 396-8227 **Wine list** *California* **Wine prices** *Expensive* **Cuisine** *American* **Menu prices** *$15–$25*

THE CAPITAL GRILLE
2800 W. Big Beaver Road, Troy, MI 48084; (248) 649-5300 **Wine list** *California, Bordeaux* **Wine prices** *Moderate* **Cuisine** *Steak house* **Menu prices** *$17–$30*

CHAPS
8 Center St., Douglas, MI 49406; (269) 857-2699 **Wine list** *California* **Wine prices** *Moderate* **Cuisine** *Contemporary American* **Menu prices** *$20–$42*

THE CHOP HOUSE
322 S. Main St., Ann Arbor, MI 48104; (888) 456-3463 **Wine list** *California, Italy* **Wine prices** *Moderate* **Cuisine** *Steak house* **Menu prices** *$25–$40*

MICHIGAN

CITY PARK GRILL 🍷
432 E. Lake St., Petoskey, MI 49770; (231) 347-0101 **Wine list** *California* **Wine prices** Inexpensive **Corkage** *$10* **Cuisine** *International* **Menu prices** *$9–$18*

DUET 🍷
3663 Woodward Ave., Detroit, MI 48201; (313) 831-3838 **Wine list** *California, France* **Wine prices** *Moderate* **Cuisine** *Contemporary American* **Menu prices** *$18–$32*

DUSTY'S WINE BAR 🍷
1839 Grand River Ave., Okemos, MI 48864; (517) 349-8680 **Wine list** *California* **Wine prices** *Moderate* **Cuisine** *Contemporary* **Menu prices** *$11–$26*

THE EARLE 🍷🍷
121 W. Washington St., Ann Arbor, MI 48104; (734) 994-0211 **Wine list** *California, France, Italy, Germany* **Wine prices** *Moderate* **Cuisine** *French/Italian* **Menu prices** *$16–$28*

THE ENGLISH INN 🍷
728 S. Michigan Road, Eaton Rapids, MI 48827; (517) 663-2500 **Wine list** *California* **Wine prices** *Moderate* **Cuisine** *Continental* **Menu prices** *$17–$29*

EPIC BISTRO 🍷
359 S. Kalamazoo Mall, Kalamazoo, MI 49007; (269) 342-1300 **Wine list** *California, France* **Wine prices** Inexpensive **Cuisine** *International* **Menu prices** *$14–$24*

FANDANGLES' 🍷
The Marketplace at Flushing, G-6429 W. Pierson Road, Flushing, MI 48433; (810) 659-2700 **Wine list** *California* **Wine prices** Inexpensive **Cuisine** *Contemporary* **Menu prices** *$16–$35*

FIVE LAKES GRILL 🍷
424 N. Main St., Milford, MI 48381; (248) 684-7455 **Wine list** *California, France* **Wine prices** *Moderate* **Cuisine** *Contemporary American* **Menu prices** *$19–$30*

GIOVANNI'S RISTORANTE 🍷
330 S. Oakwood Blvd., Detroit, MI 48217; (313) 841-0122 **Wine list** *Italy* **Wine prices** *Moderate* **Cuisine** *Italian* **Menu prices** *$18–$34*

🍷🍷🍷 Grand Award 🍷🍷 Best of Award of Excellence 🍷 Award of Excellence

GRATZI
326 S. Main St., Ann Arbor, MI 48104; (734) 663-5555
Wine list *Italy* **Wine prices** *Moderate* **Cuisine** *Northern Italian*
Menu prices *$10–$30*

HATTIE'S
111 Saint Joseph St., Suttons Bay, MI 49682; (231) 271-6222 **Wine list** *California* **Wine prices** *Moderate* **Cuisine** *Regional* **Menu prices** *$23–$45*

LA BISTECCA ITALIAN GRILLE
39405 Plymouth Road, Plymouth, MI 48170; (734) 254-0400 **Wine list** *California, Italy* **Wine prices** *Moderate*
Corkage *$10* **Cuisine** *Italian* **Menu prices** *$18–$40*

THE LANTERN
1019 N. Water St., Bay City, MI 48708; (517) 894-0772
Wine list *California, Chile, Michigan* **Wine prices** *Moderate*
Cuisine *Seafood* **Menu prices** *$10–$20*

THE LARK
6430 Farmington Road, West Bloomfield, MI 48322; (248) 661-4466 **Wine list** *California, Bordeaux* **Wine prices** *Expensive* **Cuisine** *French* **Menu prices** *$28–$40*

THE LORD FOX
5400 Plymouth Road, Ann Arbor, MI 48105; (734) 662-1647 **Wine list** *France, California* **Wine prices** Inexpensive
Cuisine *European/American* **Menu prices** *$15–$24*

MR. PAUL'S CHOPHOUSE
29850 Groesbeck Highway, Roseville, MI 48066; (586) 777-7770 **Wine list** *California* **Wine prices** *Moderate* **Cuisine** *Continental* **Menu prices** *$16–$40*

MON JIN LAU
1515 E. Maple Road, Troy, MI 48083; (248) 689-2332
Wine list *California* **Wine prices** *Moderate* **Cuisine** *Asian*
Menu prices *$10–$25*

MONTAGUE INN
1581 S. Washington Ave., Saginaw, MI 48601; (989) 752-3939 **Wine list** *California* **Wine prices** Inexpensive **Corkage** *$21* **Cuisine** *Continental/American* **Menu prices** *$17–$24*

MORELS
30100 Telegraph Road, Bingham Farms, MI 48025; (248) 642-1094 **Wine list** *California* **Wine prices** *Moderate* **Cuisine** *American* **Menu prices** *$14–$30*

MORTON'S OF CHICAGO 🍷
1 Towne Square, Southfield, MI 48076; (248) 354-6006
Wine list *California* **Wine prices** *Expensive* **Cuisine** *Steak house* **Menu prices** *$20–$35*

THE NEW YORK RESTAURANT 🍷
101 State St., Harbor Springs, MI 49740; (616) 526-1904
Wine list *California, France* **Wine prices** *Moderate* **Cuisine** *Contemporary American* **Menu prices** *$16–$32*

NORTHERN LAKES SEAFOOD COMPANY 🍷
Kingsley Hotel & Suites, 39495 N. Woodward Ave., Bloomfield Hills, MI 48304; (248) 646-7900 **Wine list** *France, California* **Wine prices** *Moderate* **Cuisine** *Seafood* **Menu prices** *$15–$55*

NOTO'S OLD WORLD ITALIAN DINING 🍷
6600 28th St. S.E., Grand Rapids, MI 49546; (616) 493-6686 **Wine list** *Italy* **Wine prices** *Moderate* **Cuisine** *Italian* **Menu prices** *$13–$39*

NOVI CHOPHOUSE & LOBSTER BAR 🍷
Hotel Baronette, 27790 Novi Road, Novi, MI 48377; (248) 305-5210 **Wine list** *California* **Wine prices** *Moderate* **Cuisine** *Steak house* **Menu prices** *$19–$39*

OPUS ONE 🍷
565 E. Larned St., Detroit, MI 48226; (313) 961-7766
Wine list *California, France* **Wine prices** *Expensive* **Cuisine** *American/continental* **Menu prices** *$22–$38*

PAESANO'S 🍷
3411 Washtenaw Ave., Ann Arbor, MI 48104; (734) 971-0484 **Wine list** *Italy* **Wine prices** *Moderate* **Cuisine** *Italian* **Menu prices** *$11–$25*

THE PALM 🍷
5600 Crooks Road, Troy, MI 48098; (248) 813-7256 **Wine list** *California* **Wine prices** *Moderate* **Cuisine** *Steak house* **Menu prices** *$15–$35*

PARKWAY GRILLE 🍷
Detroit Marriott Pontiac at Centerpoint, 3600 Centerpoint Parkway, Pontiac, MI 48341; (248) 648-6034 **Wine list** *California* **Wine prices** *Moderate* **Cuisine** *American* **Menu prices** *$9–$28*

PONTRESINA
Lodge at Otsego Club & Resort, 696 M-32 E., Gaylord, MI 49735; (989) 732-5181 **Wine list** *California* **Wine prices** Inexpensive **Corkage** *$15* **Cuisine** *Regional* **Menu prices** *Prix fixe only; $38*

THE RATTLESNAKE CLUB
300 River Place, Detroit, MI 48207; (313) 567-4400 **Wine list** *California, France* **Wine prices** *Moderate* **Corkage** *$15* **Cuisine** *Contemporary American* **Menu prices** *$22–$35*

RESTAURANT TOULOUSE
248 Culver St., Saugatuck, MI 49453; (269) 857-1561 **Wine list** *California* **Wine prices** *Moderate* **Cuisine** *French* **Menu prices** *$16–$30*

RESTAURANT VILLEGAS
1735 W. Grand River Ave., Okemos, MI 48864; (517) 347-2080 **Wine list** *California* **Wine prices** *Moderate* **Cuisine** *Contemporary Midwestern* **Menu prices** *$12–$33*

RISTORANTE CAFÉ CORTINA
30715 W. 10 Mile Road, Farmington Hills, MI 48836; (248) 474-3033 **Wine list** *Italy, California* **Wine prices** Inexpensive **Cuisine** *Italian* **Menu prices** *$17–$30*

THE RIVERSIDE INN
302 River St., Leland, MI 49654; (231) 256-9971 **Wine list** *California, France* **Wine prices** Inexpensive **Cuisine** *Regional* **Menu prices** *$18–$28*

THE RUGBY GRILLE
The Townsend Hotel, 100 Townsend St., Birmingham, MI 48009; (248) 642-5999 **Wine list** *California* **Wine prices** *Expensive* **Cuisine** *European* **Menu prices** *$22–$42*

SAGAMORE'S RESTAURANT
The Inn at Bay Harbor, 3600 Village Harbor Drive, Bay Harbor, MI 49770; (231) 439-4059 **Wine list** *California* **Wine prices** *Moderate* **Cuisine** *Contemporary* **Menu prices** *$16–$32*

SALLE À MANGER
Grand Hotel Mackinac Island, 1 Grand Ave., Mackinac Island, MI 49757; (906) 847-3331 **Wine list** *California, France* **Wine prices** *Expensive* **Cuisine** *American* **Menu prices** *Prix fixe only; $75*

SHARI
The Willard Hillton, 1506 W. Beaver Road, Auburn, MI 48611; (989) 662-6621 **Wine list** *California* **Wine prices** *Moderate* **Cuisine** *French/American* **Menu prices** *$19–$37*

SHIRAZ
30100 Telegraph Road, Bingham Farms, MI 48025; (248) 645-5289 **Wine list** *California, France, Australia* **Wine prices** *Moderate* **Cuisine** *Steak house* **Menu prices** *$18–$36*

THE SIERRA ROOM
25 Ionia Ave. S.W., Grand Rapids, MI 49503; (616) 459-1764 **Wine list** *California* **Wine prices** *Moderate* **Corkage** *$20* **Cuisine** *Contemporary American* **Menu prices** *$18–$35*

THE STATE ROOM
Kellogg Hotel & Conference Center, Michigan State University, 55 S. Harrison Road, East Lansing, MI 48824; (517) 432-4000 **Wine list** *California, France, Washington, Michigan* **Wine prices** Inexpensive **Cuisine** *Contemporary* **Menu prices** *$16–$24*

SWEET GEORGIA BROWN
1045 Brush St., Detroit, MI 48226; (313) 965-1245 **Wine list** *California* **Wine prices** *Moderate* **Cuisine** *American* **Menu prices** *$21–$37*

SWEET LORRAINE'S CAFÉ & BAR
29101 Greenfield Road, Southfield, MI 48076; (248) 559-5985 **Wine list** *California* **Wine prices** *Moderate* **Cuisine** *International* **Menu prices** *$13–$24*

TAPAWINGO
9502 Lake St., Ellsworth, MI 49729; (231) 588-7971 **Wine list** *California, Burgundy, Bordeaux* **Wine prices** *Moderate* **Cuisine** *Contemporary American* **Menu prices** *Prix fixe only; $48–$59*

TEDDY GRIFFIN'S ROADHOUSE
50 Highland Pike Road, Harbor Springs, MI 49740; (231) 526-7805 **Wine list** *California* **Wine prices** Inexpensive **Cuisine** *American* **Menu prices** *$14–$28*

TILL MIDNIGHT
208 College Ave., Holland, MI 49423; (616) 392-6883 **Wine list** *California* **Wine prices** *Moderate* **Cuisine** *Contemporary American* **Menu prices** *$19–$27*

TRIBUTE 🍷🍷
31425 W. 12 Mile Road, Farmington Hills, MI 48334; (248) 848-9393 **Wine list** *California, Burgundy, Italy* **Wine prices** *Expensive* **Cuisine** *Contemporary French/Asian* **Menu prices** *$24–$36*

VILLA RISTORANTE ITALIANO 🍷🍷
887 Spring St., Petoskey, MI 49770; (231) 347-1440 **Wine list** *Tuscany, Piedmont* **Wine prices** *Moderate* **Cuisine** *Italian* **Menu prices** *$18–$25*

WEBER'S RESTAURANT 🍷
3050 Jackson Road, Ann Arbor, MI 48103; (734) 665-3636 **Wine list** *California* **Wine prices** Inexpensive **Cuisine** *American* **Menu prices** *$13–$24*

WINDOWS 🍷
7677 W. Bay Shore Drive, Traverse City, MI 49684; (616) 941-0100 **Wine list** *California, France* **Wine prices** *Moderate* **Cuisine** *American/French/creole* **Menu prices** *$27–$39*

MINNESOTA

AREZZO RISTORANTE 🍷
5057 France Ave. S., Minneapolis, MN 55410; (612) 285-7444 **Wine list** *Italy* **Wine prices** *Moderate* **Corkage** *$15* **Cuisine** *Italian* **Menu prices** *$12–$24*

BELLISIO'S ITALIAN RESTAURANT & WINE BAR 🍷🍷
405 Lake Ave. S., Duluth, MN 55802; (218) 727-4921 **Wine list** *Italy, California* **Wine prices** Inexpensive **Cuisine** *Italian* **Menu prices** *$10–$25*

BLUE POINT RESTAURANT 🍷
739 E. Lake St., Wayzata, MN 55391; (952) 475-3636 **Wine list** *California* **Wine prices** *Moderate* **Corkage** *$15* **Cuisine** *Seafood* **Menu prices** *$17–$30*

BURNTSIDE LODGE 🍷
2755 Burntside Lodge Road, Ely, MN 55731; (218) 365-3894 **Wine list** *California* **Wine prices** Inexpensive **Corkage** *$15* **Cuisine** *American* **Menu prices** *$14–$34*

CAFÉ LURÇAT 🍷
1624 Harmon Place, Minneapolis, MN 55403; (612) 486-5500 **Wine list** *France, California* **Wine prices** *Moderate* **Corkage** *$18* **Cuisine** *Contemporary American* **Menu prices** *$20–$35*

CALIFORNIA CAFÉ BAR & GRILL 🍷
Mall of America, 368 South Blvd., Bloomington, MN 55425; (952) 854-2233 **Wine list** *California* **Wine prices** *Moderate* **Cuisine** *Californian* **Menu prices** *$11–$28*

CANYON GRILLE 🍷
3490 Northdale Blvd., Coon Rapids, MN 55448; (763) 323-9100 **Wine list** *California* **Wine prices** *Moderate* **Cuisine** *American* **Menu prices** *$14–$29*

THE CAPITAL GRILLE 🍷
LaSalle Plaza, 801 Hennepin Ave., Minneapolis, MN 55402; (612) 692-9000 **Wine list** *California, Bordeaux* **Wine prices** *Moderate* **Cuisine** *Steak house* **Menu prices** *$16–$32*

CESARE'S WINE BAR 🍷
102 S. Second St., Stillwater, MN 55082; (651) 439-1352 **Wine list** *Italy, California* **Wine prices** Inexpensive **Corkage** *$20* **Cuisine** *Mediterranean* **Menu prices** *$19–$22*

CHARDONNAY 🍷🍷
723 Second St. S.W., Rochester, MN 55902; (507) 252-1310 **Wine list** *California, France, Spain* **Wine prices** *Moderate* **Corkage** *$10* **Cuisine** *French* **Menu prices** *$18–$31*

CHIANG MAI THAI 🍷
Calhoun Square, 3001 Hennepin Ave. S., Minneapolis, MN 55408; (612) 827-1606 **Wine list** *California* **Wine prices** Inexpensive **Cuisine** *Thai* **Menu prices** *$9–$18*

D'AMICO CUCINA 🍷
100 N. Sixth St., Minneapolis, MN 55403; (612) 338-2401 **Wine list** *Italy* **Wine prices** *Expensive* **Cuisine** *Contemporary Italian* **Menu prices** *$25–$32*

THE DAKOTA 🍷
Bandana Square, St. Paul, MN 55108; (651) 642-1442 **Wine list** *California* **Wine prices** Inexpensive **Corkage** *$10* **Cuisine** *Contemporary American* **Menu prices** *$17–$25*

FHIMA'S 🍷
6 W. Sixth St., St. Paul, MN 55102; (651) 287-0784 **Wine list** *California, France, Italy* **Wine prices** *Expensive* **Corkage** *$12* **Cuisine** *French* **Menu prices** *$18–$35*

GOODFELLOWS 🍷
40 S. Seventh St., Minneapolis, MN 55402; (612) 332-4800 **Wine list** *California* **Wine prices** *Moderate* **Corkage** *$15* **Cuisine** *American* **Menu prices** *$30–$40*

🍷🍷🍷 Grand Award 🍷🍷 Best of Award of Excellence 🍷 Award of Excellence

HEARTLAND
1806 Saint Clair Ave., St. Paul, MN 55105; (651) 699-3536 **Wine list** *California, France* **Wine prices** *Moderate* **Corkage** *$20* **Cuisine** *Regional* **Menu prices** *$25–$35*

IVEN'S ON THE BAY
19090 State Highway 371, Brainerd, MN 56401; (218) 829-9872 **Wine list** *California* **Wine prices** *Moderate* **Corkage** *$10* **Cuisine** *Regional* **Menu prices** *$14–$34*

LA BELLE VIE
312 S. Main St., Stillwater, MN 55082; (651) 430-3545 **Wine list** *France, Spain* **Wine prices** *Moderate* **Cuisine** *French/Mediterranean* **Menu prices** *$19–$36*

LA TOSCANA
3220 W. Lake St., Minneapolis, MN 55416; (612) 926-6668 **Wine list** *California, Italy* **Wine prices** *Moderate* **Corkage** *$10* **Cuisine** *Tuscan* **Menu prices** *$18–$29*

LAKE ELMO INN
3442 Lake Elmo Ave. N., Lake Elmo, MN 55042; (651) 777-8495 **Wine list** *California* **Wine prices** *Moderate* **Cuisine** *Continental* **Menu prices** *$15–$30*

LORD FLETCHER'S OLD LAKE LODGE
3746 Sunset Drive, Spring Park, MN 55384; (952) 471-8513 **Wine list** *California, France* **Wine prices** *Expensive* **Corkage** *$25* **Cuisine** *Continental* **Menu prices** *$12–$29*

LUCI ANCORA
2060 Randolph Ave., St. Paul, MN 55105; (651) 698-6889 **Wine list** *Italy* **Wine prices** *Moderate* **Cuisine** *Northern Italian* **Menu prices** *$10–$20*

MANNY'S STEAK HOUSE
Hyatt Regency Hotel, 1300 Nicollet Mall, Minneapolis, MN 55403; (612) 339-9900 **Wine list** *California* **Wine prices** *Moderate* **Cuisine** *Steak house* **Menu prices** *$18–$68*

MORTON'S OF CHICAGO
555 Nicollet Mall, Minneapolis, MN 55402; (612) 673-9700 **Wine list** *California* **Wine prices** *Expensive* **Cuisine** *Steak house* **Menu prices** *$20–$34*

MPLS CAFÉ
1110 Hennepin Ave. S., Minneapolis, MN 55403; (612) 672-9100 **Wine list** *California, France, Italy* **Wine prices** *Moderate* **Cuisine** *French/Mediterranean* **Menu prices** *$15–$29*

MURRAY'S
24 S. Sixth St., Minneapolis, MN 55402; (612) 339-0909 **Wine list** *France, California* **Wine prices** *Expensive* **Corkage** *$10* **Cuisine** *American* **Menu prices** *$20–$45*

NAPA VALLEY GRILLE
Mall of America, 220 W. Market, Bloomington, MN 55425; (952) 858-9934 **Wine list** *California* **Wine prices** *Expensive* **Cuisine** *Californian* **Menu prices** *$11–$30*

NICOLLET ISLAND INN
95 Merriam St., Minneapolis, MN 55401; (612) 331-3035 **Wine list** *California* **Wine prices** *Moderate* **Corkage** *$20* **Cuisine** *American* **Menu prices** *$22–$40*

THE OCEANAIRE SEAFOOD ROOM
Hyatt Regency Hotel, 1300 Nicollet Mall, Minneapolis, MN 55403; (612) 333-2277 **Wine list** *California* **Wine prices** *Moderate* **Corkage** *$20* **Cuisine** *Seafood* **Menu prices** *$13–$58*

THE PORT RESTAURANT
St. James Hotel, 406 Main St., Red Wing, MN 55066; (651) 388-2846 **Wine list** *California* **Wine prices** *Moderate* **Cuisine** *Contemporary American* **Menu prices** *$18–$26*

RISTORANTE LUCI
470 Cleveland Ave. S., St. Paul, MN 55105; (612) 699-8258 **Wine list** *Italy* **Wine prices** *Moderate* **Cuisine** *Italian* **Menu prices** *$10–$20*

RUTH'S CHRIS STEAK HOUSE
920 Second Ave. S., Minneapolis, MN 55402; (612) 672-9000 **Wine list** *California* **Wine prices** *Moderate* **Corkage** *$12* **Cuisine** *Steak house* **Menu prices** *$18–$33*

SABASTIAN'S
Radisson Hotel, 150 S. Broadway, Rochester, MN 55904; (507) 281-8000 **Wine list** *California* **Wine prices** *Moderate* **Cuisine** *Contemporary American* **Menu prices** *$16–$30*

ST. PAUL GRILL
The St. Paul Hotel, 350 Market St., St. Paul, MN 55102; (651) 224-7455 **Wine list** *California* **Wine prices** *Moderate* **Corkage** *$15* **Cuisine** *American* **Menu prices** *$18–$32*

STAGHEAD
219 Bush St., Red Wing, MN 55066; (651) 388-6581 **Wine list** *California* **Wine prices** *Moderate* **Cuisine** *Contemporary American* **Menu prices** *$11–$26*

3 MUSES 🍷
2817 Lyndale Ave. S., Minneapolis, MN 55408; (612) 870-0339 **Wine list** *France* **Wine prices** *Moderate* **Corkage** *$20* **Cuisine** *International* **Menu prices** *$8–$20*

URSULA'S WINE BAR & CAFÉ 🍷
2125 Fourth St., White Bear Lake, MN 55110; (651) 429-9600 **Wine list** *California* **Wine prices** *Moderate* **Corkage** *$7* **Cuisine** *American/French* **Menu prices** *$17–$28*

VINCENT...A RESTAURANT 🍷
1100 Nicollet Mall, Minneapolis, MN 55403; (612) 630-1189 **Wine list** *France* **Wine prices** *Moderate* **Corkage** *$15* **Cuisine** *Contemporary French* **Menu prices** *$15–$32*

W.A. FROST & COMPANY 🍷🍷
374 Selby Ave., St. Paul, MN 55102; (651) 224-5715 **Wine list** *California, France, Italy* **Wine prices** *Moderate* **Corkage** *$20* **Cuisine** *Continental* **Menu prices** *$10–$30*

ZANDER CAFÉ 🍷
525 Selby Ave., St. Paul, MN 55102; (651) 222-5224 **Wine list** *France, Italy, Oreon* **Wine prices** *Moderate* **Cuisine** *American* **Menu prices** *$15–$20*

MISSISSIPPI

BRAVO! 🍷
244 Highland Village, Jackson, MS 39211; (601) 982-8111 **Wine list** *California* **Wine prices** *Moderate* **Cuisine** *Italian/Californian* **Menu prices** *$16–$28*

CAFÉ SONOMA 🍷
Horseshoe Casino Hotel, 1021 Casino Center Drive, Robinsonville, MS 38664; (662) 357-5500 **Wine list** *California* **Wine prices** *Moderate* **Cuisine** *Seafood* **Menu prices** *$15–$29*

CITY GROCERY 🍷
152 Courthouse Square, Oxford, MS 38655; (662) 232-8080 **Wine list** *California* **Wine prices** *Moderate* **Cuisine** *Contemporary American* **Menu prices** *$19–$25*

DUNLEITH PLANTATION 🍷
84 Homochitto St., Natchez, MS 39120; (601) 446-8500 **Wine list** *California* **Wine prices** *Moderate* **Cuisine** *Contemporary Southern* **Menu prices** *$13–$36*

FAIRBANKS STEAKHOUSE 🍷
Hollywood Casino & Hotel, 1150 Casino Strip Blvd., Robinsonville, MS 38664; (662) 357-7700 **Wine list** *California* **Wine prices** Inexpensive **Cuisine** *Steak house* **Menu prices** *Prix fixe only; $–$45*

JACK BINION'S STEAK HOUSE 🍷
Horseshoe Casino Hotel, 1021 Casino Center Drive, Robinsonville, MS 38664; (662) 357-5500 **Wine list** *California* **Wine prices** *Moderate* **Cuisine** *Steak house* **Menu prices** *$17–$38*

NICK'S 🍷
1501 Lakeland Drive, Jackson, MS 39216; (601) 981-8017 **Wine list** *California, France* **Wine prices** *Moderate* **Cuisine** *Contemporary American* **Menu prices** *$17–$24*

THE PARKER HOUSE RESTAURANT 🍷
104 S.E. Madison Drive, Ridgeland, MS 39157; (601) 856-0043 **Wine list** *California* **Wine prices** Inexpensive **Cuisine** *Contemporary American* **Menu prices** *$17–$37*

PHILLIP M'S RESTAURANT 🍷
SilverStar Hotel & Casino, Highway 16 W., Choctaw, MS 39350; (601) 650-1234 **Wine list** *France, California* **Wine prices** *Moderate* **Cuisine** *Contemporary French* **Menu prices** *$22–$84*

SHAPLEY'S RESTAURANT 🍷🍷
868 Centre St., Ridgeland, MS 39157; (601) 957-3753 **Wine list** *California, France* **Wine prices** *Moderate* **Cuisine** *Steak house* **Menu prices** *$17–$35*

YASMIN'S ASIAN RESTAURANT 🍷
Horseshoe Casino Hotel, 1021 Casino Center Drive, Robinsonville, MS 38664; (662) 357-5500 **Wine list** *California* **Wine prices** *Moderate* **Cuisine** *Chinese* **Menu prices** *$12–$30*

MISSOURI

ANNIE GUNN'S 🍷🍷
16806 Chesterfield Airport Road, Chesterfield, MO 63005; (636) 532-7684 **Wine list** *California, France* **Wine prices** Inexpensive **Corkage** *$15* **Cuisine** *American* **Menu prices** *$19–$35*

AQUA VIN
16125 Chesterfield Parkway, Chesterfield, MO 63017; (636) 532-9300 **Wine list** *California* **Wine prices** Inexpensive **Corkage** *$10* **Cuisine** *Contemporary* **Menu prices** *$17–$30*

BIG SKY CAFÉ
47 S. Old Orchard, Wesbter Groves, MO 63119; (314) 962-5757 **Wine list** *California* **Wine prices** Inexpensive **Corkage** *$9* **Cuisine** *American* **Menu prices** *$13–$19*

BIJAN'S SEA & GRILLE
209 E. Walnut St., Springfield, MO 65806; (417) 831-1480 **Wine list** *California* **Wine prices** *Moderate* **Cuisine** *Contemporary* **Menu prices** *$12–$26*

BLUE HERON RESTAURANT
State Highway HH, Lake Ozark, MO 65049; (573) 365-4646 **Wine list** *California, France* **Wine prices** *Moderate* **Cuisine** *Continental* **Menu prices** *$20–$55*

THE BOUNTY RESTAURANT
430 W. Front St., Washington, MO 63090; (636) 390-2150 **Wine list** *California* **Wine prices** *Moderate* **Corkage** *$8* **Cuisine** *Contemporary American* **Menu prices** *$12–$22*

THE CAPITAL GRILLE
Country Club Plaza, 4740 Jefferson St., Kansas City, MO 64112; (816) 531-8345 **Wine list** *California* **Wine prices** *Moderate* **Cuisine** *Steak house* **Menu prices** *$18–$29*

CARDWELL'S AT THE PLAZA
94 Frontenac Plaza, St. Louis, MO 63131; (314) 997-8885 **Wine list** *California* **Wine prices** *Moderate* **Corkage** *$15* **Cuisine** *American* **Menu prices** *$15–$22*

CELEBRATIONS RESTAURANT & BAR
615 Bellevue St., Cape Girardeau, MO 63701; (573) 334-8330 **Wine list** *California* **Wine prices** *Moderate* **Cuisine** *Contemporary American* **Menu prices** *$14–$25*

CRAZY FISH
6 W. County Center, Des Peres, MO 63131; (314) 856-2111 **Wine list** *California* **Wine prices** *Moderate* **Corkage** *$10* **Cuisine** *International* **Menu prices** *$15–$26*

THE CROSSING
7823 Forsyth Blvd., St. Louis, MO 63105; (314) 721-7375 **Wine list** *California, France* **Wine prices** *Moderate* **Corkage** *$15* **Cuisine** *Contemporary American* **Menu prices** *$20–$28*

DIERDORF & HART'S 🍷
701 Market St., St. Louis, MO 63101; (314) 421-1772
Wine list *California* **Wine prices** *Moderate* **Cuisine** *Steak house* **Menu prices** *$16–$38*

DIERDORF & HART'S 🍷
323 West Port Plaza, St. Louis, MO 63146; (314) 878-1801
Wine list *California* **Wine prices** *Expensive* **Corkage** *$17* **Cuisine** *Steak house* **Menu prices** *$16–$38*

DUFF'S RESTAURANT 🍷
392 N. Euclid Ave., St. Louis, MO 63108; (314) 361-0522
Wine list *California* **Wine prices** *Moderate* **Corkage** *$10* **Cuisine** *Contemporary* **Menu prices** *$11–$20*

EBT RESTAURANT 🍷
1310 Carondelet Drive, Kansas City, MO 64114; (816) 942-8870 **Wine list** *California* **Wine prices** *Moderate* **Cuisine** *American* **Menu prices** *$19–$30*

FAUST'S RESTAURANT 🍷
Adams Mark Hotel St. Louis, Fourth and Chestnut Streets, St. Louis, MO 63102; (314) 342-4690 **Wine list** *California, France* **Wine prices** *Expensive* **Corkage** *$15* **Cuisine** *French* **Menu prices** *$20–$35*

FRONDIZI'S RISTORANTE 🍷🍷
4558 Main St., Kansas City, MO 64111; (816) 931-3322
Wine list *Italy, California* **Wine prices** *Moderate* **Cuisine** *Italian* **Menu prices** *$14–$24*

GERARD'S RESTAURANT 🍷
1153 Colonnade Center, St. Louis, MO 63131; (314) 821-7977 **Wine list** *California, Bordeaux* **Wine prices** *Moderate* **Corkage** *$10* **Cuisine** *American/continental* **Menu prices** *$17–$27*

HK'S RESTAURANT 🍷
The Lodge of Four Seasons, Horseshoe Bend Parkway, Lake Ozark, MO 65049; (573) 365-3000 **Wine list** *California* **Wine prices** Inexpensive **Cuisine** *Steak house* **Menu prices** *$17–$35*

ILIKI CAFÉ 🍷
6431 N. Cosby Ave., Kansas City, MO 64151; (816) 587-0009 **Wine list** *California, Spain* **Wine prices** Inexpensive **Cuisine** *Mediterranean* **Menu prices** *$9–$20*

JJ'S

910 W. 48th St., Kansas City, MO 64112; (816) 561-7136 **Wine list** *Bordeaux, Burgundy, California, Champagne* **Wine selections** *1,750* **Number of bottles** *33,000* **Wine prices** *Moderate* **Cuisine** *American/continental* **Menu prices** *$14–$30* **Credit cards** *AX, MC, VS, DV*
Grand Award since 1996

JOE D'S WINEBAR, CAFÉ & PATIO

6227 Brookside Plaza, Kansas City, MO 64113; (816) 333-6116 **Wine list** *California* **Wine prices** Inexpensive **Cuisine** *International* **Menu prices** *$14–$24*

LIDIA'S KANSAS CITY

101 W. 22nd St., Kansas City, MO 64108; (816) 221-3722 **Wine list** *Italy* **Wine prices** *Moderate* **Cuisine** *Italian* **Menu prices** *$12–$24*

THE MAJESTIC STEAKHOUSE

931 Broadway, Kansas City, MO 64105; (816) 471-8484 **Wine list** *California, France* **Wine prices** *Moderate* **Corkage** *$10* **Cuisine** *Steak house* **Menu prices** *$14–$45*

MASSA'S RESTAURANT

210 N. Kirkwood Road, Kirkwood, MO 63122; (314) 965-8050 **Wine list** *California* **Wine prices** Inexpensive **Cuisine** *Italian/American* **Menu prices** *$13–$18*

MORTON'S OF CHICAGO

7822 Bonhomme Ave., Clayton, MO 63105; (314) 725-4008 **Wine list** *California* **Wine prices** *Expensive* **Corkage** *$20* **Cuisine** *Steak house* **Menu prices** *$28–$35*

MORTON'S OF CHICAGO

2475 Grand Ave., Kansas City, MO 64108; (816) 474-0555 **Wine list** *California* **Wine prices** *Expensive* **Cuisine** *Steak house* **Menu prices** *$30–$65*

OSTERIA IL CENTRO

5101 Main St., Kansas City, MO 64112; (816) 561-2369 **Wine list** *California, Italy* **Wine prices** *Moderate* **Cuisine** *Italian* **Menu prices** *$11–$19*

PLAZA III-THE STEAKHOUSE

4749 Pennsylvania Ave., Kansas City, MO 64112; (816) 753-0000 **Wine list** *California* **Wine prices** *Moderate* **Cuisine** *Steak house* **Menu prices** *$18–$38*

PORTABELLA 🍷
15 N. Central Ave., St. Louis, MO 63105; (314) 725-6593
Wine list *California, Italy* **Wine prices** *Moderate* **Corkage** *$15*
Cuisine *Mediterranean* **Menu prices** *$14–$26*

THE POTTED STEER RESTAURANT 🍷
Highway 54, Osage Beach, MO 65065; (573) 348-5053
Wine list *California, France* **Wine prices** *Expensive* **Cuisine** *Continental* **Menu prices** *$19–$45*

REMY'S KITCHEN & WINE BAR 🍷
222 S. Bemiston Ave., Clayton, MO 63105; (314) 726-5757 **Wine list** *California* **Wine prices** *Moderate* **Corkage** *$9*
Cuisine *Mediterranean* **Menu prices** *$11–$19*

RIDDLE'S PENULTIMATE CAFÉ & WINE BAR 🍷
6307 Delmar Blvd., St. Louis, MO 63130; (314) 725-6985
Wine list *California, France* **Wine prices** Inexpensive
Cuisine *Continental/American* **Menu prices** *$10–$27*

RUTH'S CHRIS STEAK HOUSE 🍷
700 W. 47th St., Kansas City, MO 64112; (816) 531-4800
Wine list *California* **Wine prices** *Moderate* **Cuisine** *Steak house* **Menu prices** *$18–$35*

ST. LOUIS FISH MARKET 🍷
901 N. First St., St. Louis, MO 63102; (314) 621-4612
Wine list *California* **Wine prices** *Moderate* **Corkage** *$10*
Cuisine *Seafood* **Menu prices** *$16–$38*

STARKER'S RESERVE 🍷🍷🍷
201 W. 47th St., Kansas City, MO 64112; (816) 753-3565
Wine list *California, France, Italy* **Wine selections** *1,780*
Number of bottles *9,600* **Wine prices** *Moderate* **Cuisine** *Contemporary American/French* **Menu prices** *$16–$32* **Credit cards** *AX, MC, VS, DV*
Grand Award since 1992

TOLEDO'S 🍷
The Lodge of Four Seasons, Horseshoe Bend Parkway, Lake Ozark, MO 65049; (573) 365-3000 **Wine list** *California*
Wine prices Inexpensive **Cuisine** *American/French/Italian*
Menu prices *$19–$26*

TONY'S 🍷
410 Market St., St. Louis, MO 63102; (314) 231-7007
Wine list *California, France, Italy* **Wine prices** *Moderate*
Cuisine *Italian* **Menu prices** *$20–$38*

🍷🍷🍷 Grand Award 🍷🍷 Best of Award of Excellence 🍷 Award of Excellence

TRATTORIA MARCELLA
3600 Watson Road, St. Louis, MO 63109; (314) 352-7706
Wine list *Italy, California* **Wine prices** *Moderate* **Corkage** *$13*
Cuisine *Italian* **Menu prices** *$9–$17*

TRUFFLES
9202 Clayton Road, St. Louis, MO 63124; (314) 567-9100
Wine list *California, France, Italy* **Wine prices** *Moderate*
Corkage *$15* **Cuisine** *American/continental* **Menu prices**
$13–$33

MONTANA

BOODLES
215 E. Main St., Bozeman, MT 59715; (406) 587-2901
Wine list *California* **Wine prices** *Moderate* **Corkage** *$10*
Cuisine *American* **Menu prices** *$13–$26*

BRIDGE CREEK BACKCOUNTRY KITCHEN & WINE BAR
116 S. Broadway, Red Lodge, MT 59068; (406) 446-9900
Wine list *California* **Wine prices** *Moderate* **Corkage** *$10*
Cuisine *American* **Menu prices** *$9–$19*

BUCK'S T-4 LODGE
U.S. Highway 191, Big Sky, MT 59716; (406) 995-4111
Wine list *California* **Wine prices** *Moderate* **Corkage** *$12*
Cuisine *Steak house* **Menu prices** *$18–$32*

BY WORD OF MOUTH
2815 Aspen Drive, Big Sky, MT 59716; (406) 995-2992
Wine list *California* **Wine prices** *Moderate* **Corkage** *$15*
Cuisine *Continental* **Menu prices** *$10–$30*

CAFÉ KANDAHAR
Kandahar Lodge, 3824 Big Mountain Road, Whitefish, MT 59937; (406) 862-6247 **Wine list** *California* **Wine prices** *Moderate* **Corkage** *$10* **Cuisine** *Contemporary American* **Menu prices** *$18–$29*

CAFÉ MAX
121 Main St., Kalispell, MT 59903; (406) 755-7687 **Wine list** *California, France* **Wine prices** *Moderate* **Cuisine** *Italian/French* **Menu prices** *$16–$25*

THE DEPOT
201 Railroad St. W., Missoula, MT 59802; (406) 728-7007
Wine list *California* **Wine prices** *Moderate* **Corkage** *$10*
Cuisine *Steak house/seafood* **Menu prices** *$10–$25*

MONTANA

THE DINING ROOM AT CHICO 🍷
Chico Hot Springs Lodge, 1 Chico Road, Pray, MT 59065; (406) 333-4933 **Wine list** *California* **Wine prices** *Moderate* **Corkage** *$9* **Cuisine** *Continental* **Menu prices** *$18–$25*

GALLATIN RIVER GRILL 🍷
Gallatin River Lodge, 9105 Thorpe Road, Bozeman, MT 59718; (888) 387-0148 **Wine list** *California* **Wine prices** *Moderate* **Corkage** *$10* **Cuisine** *Continental* **Menu prices** *$15–$32*

THE GRILL 🍷
Grouse Mountain Lodge, 2 Fairway Drive, Whitefish, MT 59937; (406) 863-4700 **Wine list** *California* **Wine prices** *Moderate* **Cuisine** *Continental* **Menu prices** *$16–$26*

LA PROVENCE 🍷
408 Bridge St., Bigfork, MT 59911; (406) 837-2923 **Wine list** *California, France* **Wine prices** *Moderate* **Corkage** *$10* **Cuisine** *Mediterranean* **Menu prices** *$13–$19*

MAMBO ITALIANO 🍷
234 E. Second St., Whitefish, MT 59937; (406) 863-9600 **Wine list** *Italy* **Wine prices** Inexpensive **Cuisine** *Italian* **Menu prices** *$10–$17*

POLLO GRILL 🍷
1705 Wisconsin Ave., Whitefish, MT 59937; (406) 863-9400 **Wine list** *California* **Wine prices** *Moderate* **Cuisine** *Regional* **Menu prices** *$12–$23*

RAINBOW RANCH LODGE 🍷🍷
42950 Gallatin Road, Big Sky, MT 59716; (406) 995-4132 **Wine list** *California, France* **Wine prices** *Moderate* **Corkage** *$20* **Cuisine** *American* **Menu prices** *$15–$36*

SEASONS 🍷
Double Arrow Resort, Highway 83 N., MM 12, Seeley Lake, MT 59868; (406) 677-2777 **Wine list** *California* **Wine prices** Inexpensive **Cuisine** *Contemporary* **Menu prices** *$17–$29*

SHOWTHYME 🍷
548 Electric Ave., Bigfork, MT 59911; (406) 837-0707 **Wine list** *California* **Wine prices** Inexpensive **Corkage** *$7* **Cuisine** *Contemporary American* **Menu prices** *$12–$25*

TUPELO GRILLE 🍷
17 Central Ave., Whitefish, MT 59937; (406) 862-6136 **Wine list** *California* **Wine prices** *Moderate* **Corkage** *$10* **Cuisine** *Continental/Cajun/regional* **Menu prices** *$12–$22*

🍷🍷🍷 Grand Award 🍷🍷 Best of Award of Excellence 🍷 Award of Excellence

NEBRASKA

M'S PUB 🍷
422 S. 11th St., Omaha, NE 68102; (402) 342-2550 **Wine list** *California* **Wine prices** *Moderate* **Corkage** *$10* **Cuisine** *Contemporary* **Menu prices** *$12–$30*

THE OVEN 🍷
201 N. Eighth St., Lincoln, NE 68508; (402) 475-6118 **Wine list** *California* **Wine prices** *Moderate* **Corkage** *$10* **Cuisine** *Indian* **Menu prices** *$15–$18*

UPSTREAM BREWING COMPANY 🍷
514 S. 11th St., Omaha, NE 68102; (402) 344-0200 **Wine list** *California* **Wine prices** Inexpensive **Corkage** *$10* **Cuisine** *Contemporary American* **Menu prices** *$10–$28*

V. MERTZ 🍷
1022 Howard St., Omaha, NE 68102; (402) 345-8980 **Wine list** *California, France* **Wine prices** *Expensive* **Cuisine** *Continental* **Menu prices** *$25–$38*

NEVADA

LAS VEGAS

ALIZÉ AT THE TOP OF THE PALMS 🍷🍷
Palms Casino Resort, 4321 W. Flamingo Road, Las Vegas, NV 89103; (702) 951-7000 **Wine list** *California, France* **Wine prices** *Expensive* **Cuisine** *French* **Menu prices** *$23–$48*

ANDRE'S AT THE MONTE CARLO 🍷🍷
Monte Carlo Resort & Casino, 3770 Las Vegas Blvd. S., Las Vegas, NV 89109; (702) 798-7151 **Wine list** *California, France* **Wine prices** *Expensive* **Cuisine** *French* **Menu prices** *$27–$57*

ANDRE'S FRENCH RESTAURANT 🍷🍷
401 S. Sixth St., Las Vegas, NV 89101; (702) 385-5016 **Wine list** *California, France* **Wine prices** *Expensive* **Cuisine** *French* **Menu prices** *$21–$48*

AQUA 🍷
Bellagio, 3600 Las Vegas Blvd. S., Las Vegas, NV 89109; (702) 693-8199 **Wine list** *California, France, Germany* **Wine prices** *Moderate* **Cuisine** *Seafood* **Menu prices** *$33–$90*

AUREOLE 🍷🍷🍷
Mandalay Bay Hotel & Casino, 3950 Las Vegas Blvd. S., Las Vegas, NV 89119; (702) 632-7401 **Wine list** *Bordeaux, Burgundy, California, Austria, Germany* **Wine selections** *3,750* **Number of bottles** *55,000* **Wine prices** *Moderate* **Corkage** *$35* **Cuisine** *Contemporary American* **Menu prices** *$22–$35* **Credit cards** *AX, MC, VS, DV*
Grand Award since 2000

CHARLIE PALMER STEAK 🍷🍷
Four Seasons Hotel Las Vegas, 3960 Las Vegas Blvd. S., Las Vegas, NV 89119; (702) 632-5120 **Wine list** *California, France, Spain, Australia* **Wine prices** *Expensive* **Cuisine** *Steak house* **Menu prices** *$17–$36*

CHINA GRILL 🍷
Mandalay Bay Hotel & Casino, 3950 Las Vegas Blvd. S., Las Vegas, NV 89119; (702) 632-7404 **Wine list** *California* **Wine prices** *Moderate* **Corkage** *$30* **Cuisine** *International/Asian* **Menu prices** *$25–$75*

CHINOIS LAS VEGAS 🍷
The Forum Shops at Caesars, 3500 Las Vegas Blvd. S., Las Vegas, NV 89109; (702) 737-9700 **Wine list** *California* **Wine prices** *Expensive* **Corkage** *$16* **Cuisine** *Asian* **Menu prices** *$14–$28*

COMMANDER'S PALACE 🍷
Desert Passage at Aladdin Resort & Casino, 3663 Las Vegas Blvd. S., Las Vegas, NV 89101; (702) 892-8272 **Wine list** *France, California* **Wine prices** *Expensive* **Corkage** *$50* **Cuisine** *Creole* **Menu prices** *$26–$45*

DEL FRISCO'S DOUBLE EAGLE STEAK HOUSE 🍷🍷
3925 Paradise Road, Las Vegas, NV 89109; (702) 796-0063 **Wine list** *California, France* **Wine prices** *Expensive* **Cuisine** *Steak house* **Menu prices** *$25–$50*

DELMONICO STEAKHOUSE 🍷🍷
The Venetian Resort, Hotel & Casino, 3355 Las Vegas Blvd. S., Las Vegas, NV 89109; (702) 414-3737 **Wine list** *California, France, Italy, Australia, Spain* **Wine prices** *Moderate* **Corkage** *$20* **Cuisine** *Steak house* **Menu prices** *$21–$38*

DRAGON NOODLE CO. & SUSHI BAR 🍷
Monte Carlo Resort & Casino, 3770 Las Vegas Blvd. S., Las Vegas, NV 89109; (702) 730-7965 **Wine list** *California* **Wine prices** *Moderate* **Cuisine** *Chinese* **Menu prices** *$6–$14*

EIFFEL TOWER RESTAURANT
Paris Hotel, 3655 Las Vegas Blvd. S., Las Vegas, NV 89109; (702) 948-6937 **Wine list** *France, California* **Wine prices** *Expensive* **Cuisine** *French* **Menu prices** *$26–$50*

ELEMENTS
Aladdin Resort & Casino, 3667 Las Vegas Blvd. S., Las Vegas, NV 89109; (702) 785-9003 **Wine list** *France, California* **Wine prices** *Moderate* **Corkage** *$25* **Cuisine** *Steak house/seafood* **Menu prices** *$22–$38*

EMERIL'S NEW ORLEANS FISH HOUSE
MGM Grand Hotel, 3799 Las Vegas Blvd. S., Las Vegas, NV 89109; (702) 891-7374 **Wine list** *France, California, Italy* **Wine prices** *Expensive* **Corkage** *$25* **Cuisine** *Contemporary New Orleans* **Menu prices** *$18–$49*

FERRARO'S RESTAURANT
5900 W. Flamingo Road, Las Vegas, NV 89103; (702) 364-5300 **Wine list** *Italy, California* **Wine prices** *Moderate* **Cuisine** *Italian* **Menu prices** *$17–$36*

FLEMING'S PRIME STEAKHOUSE & WINE BAR
8721 W. Charleston Blvd., Las Vegas, NV 89117; (702) 838-4774 **Wine list** *California* **Wine prices** *Moderate* **Cuisine** *Steak house* **Menu prices** *$20–$30*

HUGO'S CELLAR
Four Queens Hotel, 202 E. Fremont St., Las Vegas, NV 89101; (702) 385-4011 **Wine list** *California, France* **Wine prices** *Moderate* **Corkage** *$15* **Cuisine** *American/continental* **Menu prices** *$28–$55*

IL FORNAIO CUCINA ITALIANA
New York New York Hotel & Casino, 3790 Las Vegas Blvd. S., Las Vegas, NV 89109; (702) 650-6500 **Wine list** *Italy* **Wine prices** *Moderate* **Cuisine** *Italian* **Menu prices** *$15–$30*

LE CIRQUE
Bellagio, 3600 Las Vegas Blvd. S., Las Vegas, NV 89109; (702) 693-8100 **Wine list** *Italy, Bordeaux, California* **Wine prices** *Expensive* **Cuisine** *French* **Menu prices** *$38–$48*

MARKET CITY CAFFÉ
Monte Carlo Resort & Casino, 3770 Las Vegas Blvd. S., Las Vegas, NV 89109; (702) 730-7966 **Wine list** *California* **Wine prices** *Moderate* **Cuisine** *Italian* **Menu prices** *$9–$25*

MORTON'S OF CHICAGO
400 E. Flamingo Road, Las Vegas, NV 89109; (702) 893-0703 **Wine list** *California* **Wine prices** *Expensive* **Corkage** *$15* **Cuisine** *Steak house* **Menu prices** *$20–$36*

N9NE STEAKHOUSE
Palms Casino Resort, 4321 W. Flamingo Road, Las Vegas, NV 89103; (702) 938-9900 **Wine list** *California, Bordeaux* **Wine prices** *Expensive* **Corkage** *$25* **Cuisine** *Steak house* **Menu prices** *$24–$72*

OLIVES
Bellagio, 3600 Las Vegas Blvd. S., Las Vegas, NV 89109; (702) 693-8181 **Wine list** *California, France* **Wine prices** *Expensive* **Cuisine** *Mediterranean* **Menu prices** *$20–$45*

OSTERIA DEL CIRCO
Bellagio, 3600 Las Vegas Blvd. S., Las Vegas, NV 89109; (702) 693-8150 **Wine list** *California, France, Italy* **Wine prices** *Expensive* **Cuisine** *Tuscan* **Menu prices** *$15–$38*

THE PALM
Caesars Palace, The Forum Shops at Caesars, 3500 Las Vegas Blvd. S., Las Vegas, NV 89109; (702) 732-7256 **Wine list** *California* **Wine prices** *Moderate* **Corkage** *$20* **Cuisine** *Steak house* **Menu prices** *$20–$66*

PICASSO
Bellagio, 3600 Las Vegas Blvd. S., Las Vegas, NV 89109; (702) 693-8105 **Wine list** *California, Burgundy, Bordeaux, Spain, Australia, Germany* **Wine selections** *1,300* **Number of bottles** *11,000* **Wine prices** *Expensive* **Corkage** *$35* **Cuisine** *French/Mediterranean* **Menu prices** *Prix fixe only; $79–$89* **Credit cards** *AX, MC, VS, DV*
Grand Award since 2003

PIERO SELVAGGIO VALENTINO
The Venetian Resort, Hotel & Casino, 3355 Las Vegas Blvd. S., Las Vegas, NV 89109; (702) 414-3000 **Wine list** *Bordeaux, Piedmont, California, Tuscany* **Wine selections** *2,275* **Number of bottles** *32,950* **Wine prices** *Expensive* **Corkage** *$35* **Cuisine** *Italian* **Menu prices** *$32–$40* **Credit cards** *AX, MC, VS, DV*
Grand Award since 2002

PIERO'S ITALIAN CUISINE
355 Convention Center Drive, Las Vegas, NV 89109; (702) 369-2305 **Wine list** *California, France* **Wine prices** *Moderate* **Cuisine** *Italian* **Menu prices** *$29–$60*

Grand Award · Best of Award of Excellence · Award of Excellence

PINOT BRASSERIE
The Venetian Resort, Hotel & Casino, 3355 Las Vegas Blvd. S., Las Vegas, NV 89109; (702) 414-8888 **Wine list** *California, France* **Wine prices** *Expensive* **Corkage** *No charge* **Cuisine** *French/American* **Menu prices** *$25–$34*

POSTRIO LAS VEGAS
The Venetian Resort, Hotel & Casino, 3355 Las Vegas Blvd. S., Las Vegas, NV 89109; (702) 796-1110 **Wine list** *California, France* **Wine prices** *Expensive* **Corkage** *$16* **Cuisine** *American* **Menu prices** *$14–$38*

PRIME STEAKHOUSE
Bellagio, 3600 Las Vegas Blvd. S., Las Vegas, NV 89109; (702) 693-8484 **Wine list** *California, Burgundy, Bordeaux, Italy* **Wine prices** *Moderate* **Corkage** *$35* **Cuisine** *Steak house* **Menu prices** *$24–$60*

RED SQUARE
Mandalay Bay Hotel & Casino, 3950 Las Vegas Blvd. S., Las Vegas, NV 89119; (702) 632-7407 **Wine list** *California* **Wine prices** *Expensive* **Corkage** *$25* **Cuisine** *Regional/French/Italian* **Menu prices** *$19–$85*

RENOIR
Mirage Hotel, 3400 Las Vegas Blvd. S., Las Vegas, NV 89109; (702) 791-7223 **Wine list** *France, California, Italy* **Wine prices** *Expensive* **Corkage** *$25* **Cuisine** *Contemporary French* **Menu prices** *$35–$44*

ROSEMARY'S AT THE RIO
Rio Suite Hotel & Casino, 3700 W. Flamingo Road, Las Vegas, NV 89103; (702) 777-2300 **Wine list** *California, France* **Wine prices** *Moderate* **Corkage** *$30* **Cuisine** *American/French* **Menu prices** *$25–$50*

ROSEMARY'S RESTAURANT
8125 W. Sahara Ave., Las Vegas, NV 89107; (702) 869-2251 **Wine list** *California, France* **Wine prices** *Moderate* **Corkage** *$15* **Cuisine** *American/French* **Menu prices** *$18–$30*

ROSEWOOD GRILLE
3763 Las Vegas Blvd. S., Las Vegas, NV 89109; (702) 740-4430 **Wine list** *California* **Wine prices** *Expensive* **Cuisine** *Steak house* **Menu prices** *$19–$70*

RUMJUNGLE 🍷
Mandalay Bay Hotel & Casino, 3950 Las Vegas Blvd. S., Las Vegas, NV 89119; (702) 632-7408 **Wine list** *California* **Wine prices** *Expensive* **Corkage** *$25* **Cuisine** *Caribbean/Brazilian* **Menu prices** *$18–$40*

RUTH'S CHRIS STEAK HOUSE 🍷
3900 Paradise Road, Las Vegas, NV 89109; (702) 791-7011 **Wine list** *California* **Wine prices** *Moderate* **Cuisine** *Steak house* **Menu prices** *$21–$36*

RUTH'S CHRIS STEAK HOUSE 🍷
4561 W. Flamingo Road, Las Vegas, NV 89103; (702) 248-7011 **Wine list** *California* **Wine prices** *Moderate* **Cuisine** *Steak house* **Menu prices** *$21–$53*

SMITH & WOLLENSKY 🍷
3767 Las Vegas Blvd. S., Las Vegas, NV 89109; (702) 862-4100 **Wine list** *California, Bordeaux* **Wine prices** *Moderate* **Cuisine** *Steak house* **Menu prices** *$19–$38*

SPAGO LAS VEGAS 🍷
The Forum Shops at Caesars, 3500 Las Vegas Blvd. S., Las Vegas, NV 89109; (702) 369-6300 **Wine list** *France, Spain, California* **Wine prices** *Moderate* **Corkage** *$16* **Cuisine** *American* **Menu prices** *$19–$36*

TOP OF THE WORLD RESTAURANT 🍷
Stratosphere Hotel & Casino, 2000 Las Vegas Blvd. S., Las Vegas, NV 89104; (702) 380-7711 **Wine list** *California* **Wine prices** *Moderate* **Corkage** *$15* **Cuisine** *Contemporary American* **Menu prices** *$32–$48*

TRATTORIA DEL LUPO 🍷
Mandalay Bay Hotel & Casino, 3950 Las Vegas Blvd. S., Las Vegas, NV 89109; (702) 740-5522 **Wine list** *Italy, California* **Wine prices** *Moderate* **Corkage** *$16* **Cuisine** *Italian* **Menu prices** *$15–$28*

TREMEZZO 🍷
Aladdin Resort & Casino, 3667 Las Vegas Blvd. S., Las Vegas, NV 89109; (702) 785-9013 **Wine list** *Italy* **Wine prices** *Moderate* **Corkage** *$25* **Cuisine** *Northern Italian* **Menu prices** *$19–$36*

WILD SAGE CAFÉ 🍷
600 E. Warm Springs Road, Las Vegas, NV 89119; (702) 944-SAGE **Wine list** *California* **Wine prices** *Moderate* **Corkage** *$10* **Cuisine** *American* **Menu prices** *$15–$27*

NEVADA

OTHER CITIES

ADELE'S
1112 N. Carson St., Carson City, NV 89701; (775) 882-3353 **Wine list** *California* **Wine prices** *Moderate* **Corkage** *$8* **Cuisine** *Contemporary* **Menu prices** *$16–$70*

ATLANTIS SEAFOOD STEAKHOUSE
Atlantis Casino Resort, 3800 S. Virginia St., Reno, NV 89502; (800) 723-6500 **Wine list** *California* **Wine prices** *Moderate* **Cuisine** *Steak house/seafood* **Menu prices** *$19–$57*

AUSTINS STEAKHOUSE
Texas Station Gambling Hall & Hotel, 2101 Texas Star Lane, North Las Vegas, NV 89032; (702) 631-1033 **Wine list** *California* **Wine prices** *Moderate* **Cuisine** *Steak house* **Menu prices** *$17–$32*

CAFÉ 333
333 Village Blvd., Incline Village, NV 89451; (775) 832-7333 **Wine list** *California* **Wine prices** *Moderate* **Corkage** *$15* **Cuisine** *Contemporary American* **Menu prices** *$20–$26*

FRENCH QUARTER RESTAURANT & CABARET
270 Lake St., Reno, NV 89501; (775) 786-7800 **Wine list** *California, France* **Wine prices** *Expensive* **Cuisine** *Steak house* **Menu prices** *$12–$30*

FRIDAY'S STATION
Harrah's Resort Hotel & Casino Lake Tahoe, Highway 50, Stateline, NV 89449; (775) 588-6611 **Wine list** *California* **Wine prices** *Moderate* **Corkage** *$25* **Cuisine** *Continental* **Menu prices** *$22–$62*

GALENA FOREST RESTAURANT & BAR
17025 Mount Rose Highway, Reno, NV 89511; (775) 849-2100 **Wine list** *California* **Wine prices** *Moderate* **Corkage** *$15* **Cuisine** *American* **Menu prices** *$12–$36*

LE BISTRO
120 Country Club Drive, Incline Village, NV 89451; (775) 831-0800 **Wine list** *California, France* **Wine prices** *Moderate* **Cuisine** *Contemporary French* **Menu prices** *$20–$25*

LLEWELLYN'S
Harveys Resort Hotel & Casino Lake Tahoe, Highway 50, Stateline, NV 89449; (775) 588-6611 **Wine list** *California, France* **Wine prices** *Moderate* **Corkage** *$25* **Cuisine** *Continental* **Menu prices** *$26–$62*

MONTEVIGNA ITALIAN RISTORANTÉ
Atlantis Casino Resort, 3800 S. Virginia St., Reno, NV 89502; (800) 723-6500 **Wine list** *California, Italy* **Wine prices** *Moderate* **Cuisine** *Tuscan* **Menu prices** *$10–$27*

THE RED HAWK ROOM
The Resort at Red Hawk, 6295 Wingfield Springs Road, Sparks, NV 89436; (775) 626-1000 **Wine list** *California* **Wine prices** *Moderate* **Corkage** *$12* **Cuisine** *American* **Menu prices** *$17–$25*

ROMANZA RISTORANTE ITALIANO
Peppermill Hotel Casino, 2707 S. Virginia St., Reno, NV 89502; (775) 826-2121 **Wine list** *California, France, Italy* **Wine prices** Inexpensive **Corkage** *$15* **Cuisine** *Italian* **Menu prices** *$14–$29*

ROXY
Eldorado Hotel & Casino, Fourth and Virginia Streets, Reno, NV 89501; (775) 785-9066 **Wine list** *California, France* **Wine prices** *Moderate* **Corkage** *$15* **Cuisine** *Continental* **Menu prices** *$17–$45*

THE SAGE ROOM STEAK HOUSE
Harveys Resort Hotel & Casino Lake Tahoe, Highway 50, Stateline, NV 89449; (800) 553-1022 **Wine list** *California* **Wine prices** *Moderate* **Corkage** *$25* **Cuisine** *Continental* **Menu prices** *$27–$62*

THE STEAK HOUSE AT HARRAH'S
Harrah's Casino Hotel, 219 N. Center St., Reno, NV 89501; (775) 788-2929 **Wine list** *California* **Wine prices** *Expensive* **Corkage** *$15* **Cuisine** *Steak house* **Menu prices** *$21–$33*

STERLINGS SEAFOOD STEAKHOUSE
Silver Legacy Resort Casino, Fourth and Virginia Streets, Reno, NV 89505; (775) 325-7573 **Wine list** *California* **Wine prices** *Moderate* **Corkage** *$25* **Cuisine** *Steak house* **Menu prices** *$14–$52*

Grand Award   Best of Award of Excellence   Award of Excellence

THE SUMMIT 🍷
Harrah's Resort Hotel & Casino Lake Tahoe, Highway 50, Stateline, NV 89449; (775) 588-6611 **Wine list** *California* **Wine prices** *Moderate* **Corkage** *$25* **Cuisine** *Continental* **Menu prices** *$22–$52*

VIAGGIO ITALIAN CUISINE & WINE SHOP 🍷
11261 S. Eastern Ave., Henderson, NV 89052; (702) 492-6900 **Wine list** *California, Italy* **Wine prices** *Moderate* **Corkage** *$20* **Cuisine** *Italian* **Menu prices** *$12–$26*

VIAGGIO ITALIAN CUISINE & WINE SHOP 🍷
2309 Kietzke Lane, Reno, NV 89502; (775) 828-2708 **Wine list** *California, Italy* **Wine prices** *Moderate* **Corkage** *$20* **Cuisine** *Italian* **Menu prices** *$12–$26*

WASHOE GRILL 🍷
4201 W. Fourth St., Reno, NV 89503; (775) 786-1323 **Wine list** *California* **Wine prices** *Moderate* **Corkage** *$12* **Cuisine** *Steak house* **Menu prices** *$15–$34*

WHITE ORCHID 🍷🍷
Peppermill Hotel Casino, 2707 S. Virginia St., Reno, NV 89502; (775) 689-7300 **Wine list** *California, France, Italy* **Wine prices** Inexpensive **Corkage** *$15* **Cuisine** *Contemporary* **Menu prices** *$21–$65*

NEW HAMPSHIRE

BALDWIN'S ON ELM 🍷
1105 Elm St., Manchester, NH 03101; (603) 622-5975 **Wine list** *California* **Wine prices** *Moderate* **Cuisine** *Contemporary* **Menu prices** *$17–$26*

THE BALSAMS 🍷
The Balsams Grand Resort Hotel, Route 26, Dixville Notch, NH 03576; (800) 255-0600 **Wine list** *California, France* **Wine prices** *Moderate* **Cuisine** *American* **Menu prices** *Prix fixe only; $–$38*

BEDFORD VILLAGE INN & RESTAURANT 🍷
Village Inn Lane, Bedford, NH 03110; (603) 472-2001 **Wine list** *California, France, Italy* **Wine prices** *Moderate* **Cuisine** *New England* **Menu prices** *$17–$39*

BONTA 🍷
287 Exeter Road, Hampton, NH 03842; (603) 929-7972 **Wine list** *California, Italy* **Wine prices** *Moderate* **Cuisine** *Italian* **Menu prices** *$18–$29*

CAFÉ BUON GUSTAIO 🍷
72 S. Main St., Hanover, NH 03755; (603) 643-5711 **Wine list** *Italy* **Wine prices** *Moderate* **Cuisine** *Italian* **Menu prices** *$14–$30*

COLBY HILL INN 🍷
3 The Oaks, Henniker, NH 03242; (603) 428-3281 **Wine list** *California* **Wine prices** *Moderate* **Cuisine** *Contemporary regional* **Menu prices** *$19–$30*

THE DANIEL WEBSTER ROOM 🍷
The Hanover Inn, Main and Wheelock Streets, Hanover, NH 03755; (603) 643-4300 **Wine list** *France, California* **Wine prices** Inexpensive **Cuisine** *Contemporary American* **Menu prices** *$18–$28*

THE HANCOCK INN 🍷
33 Main St., Hancock, NH 03449; (603) 525-3318 **Wine list** *California, France* **Wine prices** Inexpensive **Cuisine** *Regional* **Menu prices** *$20–$29*

HOME HILL INN 🍷
703 River Road, Plainfield, NH 03781; (603) 675-6165 **Wine list** *France* **Wine prices** *Expensive* **Cuisine** *French* **Menu prices** *$28–$36*

THE INN AT THORN HILL 🍷🍷
Thorn Hill Road, Jackson, NH 03846; (603) 383-4242 **Wine list** *France, California, Germany* **Wine prices** *Moderate* **Cuisine** *Contemporary American* **Menu prices** *$23–$29*

L'ESPRIT 🍷
181 Silver St., Dover, NH 03820; (603) 750-1504 **Wine list** *France, California* **Wine prices** Inexpensive **Cuisine** *Mediterranean* **Menu prices** *Prix fixe only; $17*

LEDGES DINING ROOM 🍷
White Mountain Hotel & Resort, Hale's Location, North Conway, NH 03860; (603) 356-7100 **Wine list** *California* **Wine prices** *Moderate* **Cuisine** *American* **Menu prices** *$18–$25*

THE MANOR ON GOLDEN POND
Manor Drive, Holderness, NH 03245; (800) 545-2141 **Wine list** *France, California* **Wine prices** *Moderate* **Cuisine** *French/American* **Menu prices** *$25–$38*

THE METRO, AN AMERICAN BISTRO
20 High St., Portsmouth, NH 03801; (603) 436-0521 **Wine list** *California* **Wine prices** Inexpensive **Cuisine** *Contemporary American* **Menu prices** *$12–$28*

MICHAEL TIMOTHY'S BISTRO
212 Main St., Nashua, NH 03060; (603) 595-9334 **Wine list** *California* **Wine prices** *Moderate* **Corkage** *$20* **Cuisine** *International* **Menu prices** *$15–$25*

THE MOUNT WASHINGTON HOTEL & RESORT
Route 302, Bretton Woods, NH 03575; (603) 278-1000 **Wine list** *California, France* **Wine prices** *Expensive* **Cuisine** *Regional* **Menu prices** *$30–$38*

PESCE BLUE
103 Congress St., Portsmouth, NH 03801; (603) 430-7766 **Wine list** *Italy, California* **Wine prices** *Moderate* **Corkage** *$10* **Cuisine** *Italian/seafood* **Menu prices** *$15–$27*

THE 1785 INN RESTAURANT
Route 16 at the Scenic Vista, North Conway, NH 03860; (800) 421-1785 **Wine list** *France, California* **Wine prices** *Moderate* **Cuisine** *French/American* **Menu prices** *$15–$25*

THE WENTWORTH
Route 16A, Jackson Village, NH 03846; (603) 383-9700 **Wine list** *California* **Wine prices** *Moderate* **Cuisine** *Regional* **Menu prices** *$19–$26*

NEW JERSEY

ADAGIO TAVERNA E RISTORANTE
401 Springfield Ave., Summit, NJ 07901; (908) 277-1677 **Wine list** *Italy, California* **Wine prices** *Moderate* **Corkage** *$20* **Cuisine** *Contemporary Italian* **Menu prices** *$19–$30*

BACARI GRILL
800 Ridgewood Road, Washington Township, NJ 07675; (201) 358-6330 **Wine list** *California* **Wine prices** *Moderate* **Cuisine** *American* **Menu prices** *$18–$28*

BARELI'S RESTAURANT 🍷
219 E. Route 3, Seacaucus, NJ 07094; (201) 865-0473
Wine list *Italy, California, France* **Wine prices** *Moderate*
Cuisine *Italian* **Menu prices** *$20–$37*

BARONE'S RESTAURANT 🍷
77 Route 206, Byram Township, NJ 07874; (973) 347-1812
Wine list *California, Italy* **Wine prices** Inexpensive **Cuisine** *Italian/continental* **Menu prices** *$14–$29*

THE BERNARDS INN 🍷🍷
27 Mine Brook Road, Bernardsville, NJ 07924; (908) 766-0002 **Wine list** *California, Burgundy, Bordeaux* **Wine prices** *Moderate* **Cuisine** *American/French* **Menu prices** *$24–$38*

BERTA'S CHATEAU 🍷🍷
7 Grove St., Wanaque, NJ 07465; (973) 835-0992 **Wine list** *Piedmont, Tuscany, France* **Wine prices** *Moderate* **Corkage** *$16* **Cuisine** *Italian* **Menu prices** *$13–$36*

BLACK FOREST INN 🍷
249 Route 206, Stanhope, NJ 07874; (973) 347-3344 **Wine list** *Germany, California* **Wine prices** *Moderate* **Cuisine** *German/continental* **Menu prices** *$19–$27*

CAFFÉ ALDO LAMBERTI 🍷
2011 Route 70 W., Cherry Hill, NJ 08002; (856) 663-1747
Wine list *California, Italy* **Wine prices** *Moderate* **Corkage** *$10*
Cuisine *Italian* **Menu prices** *$17–$30*

CHARLEY'S OTHER BROTHER RESTAURANT 🍷🍷
1383 Monmouth Road, Route 537, Eastampton, NJ 08060; (609) 261-1555 **Wine list** *California, Italy, France* **Wine prices** Inexpensive **Cuisine** *American* **Menu prices** *$14–$23*

CHENGDU 46 🍷
1105 Route 46 E., Clifton, NJ 07013; (973) 777-8855 **Wine list** *California* **Wine prices** *Moderate* **Cuisine** *Chinese* **Menu prices** *$14–$39*

CK'S STEAKHOUSE 🍷
Renaissance Meadowlands, 801 Rutherford Ave., Rutherford, NJ 07070; (201) 231-3141 **Wine list** *California, Italy* **Wine prices** *Moderate* **Cuisine** *Steak house* **Menu prices** *$23–$48*

COURT STREET RESTAURANT & BAR 🍷
61 Sixth St., Hoboken, NJ 07030; (201) 795-4515 **Wine list** *California* **Wine prices** Inexpensive **Cuisine** *Continental*
Menu prices *$8–$25*

🍷🍷🍷 Grand Award 🍷🍷 Best of Award of Excellence 🍷 Award of Excellence

CRAB'S CLAW INN
601 Grand Central Ave., Lavallette, NJ 08735; (732) 793-4447 **Wine list** *California* **Wine prices** *Moderate* **Cuisine** *American* **Menu prices** *$10–$26*

DIAMOND'S
132 Kent St., Trenton, NJ 08611; (609) 393-1000 **Wine list** *California, Italy* **Wine prices** *Moderate* **Cuisine** *Italian/continental* **Menu prices** *$17–$25*

DOCK'S OYSTER HOUSE
2405 Atlantic Ave., Atlantic City, NJ 08401; (609) 345-0092 **Wine list** *California* **Wine prices** *Moderate* **Cuisine** *Seafood* **Menu prices** *$21–$35*

DORIS & ED'S SEAFOOD BY THE SEA
348 Shore Drive, Highlands, NJ 07732; (732) 872-1565 **Wine list** *California* **Wine prices** *Moderate* **Cuisine** *Seafood* **Menu prices** *$21–$33*

THE EBBITT ROOM
The Virginia Hotel, 25 Jackson St., Cape May, NJ 08204; (609) 884-5700 **Wine list** *California, France* **Wine prices** *Moderate* **Cuisine** *Contemporary American* **Menu prices** *$23–$34*

ENGLESIDE INN
30 Engleside Ave., Beach Haven, NJ 08008; (609) 492-1251 **Wine list** *California* **Wine prices** Inexpensive **Cuisine** *Contemporary American* **Menu prices** *$14–$31*

THE FROG AND THE PEACH
29 Dennis St., New Brunswick, NJ 08901; (732) 846-3216 **Wine list** *California, France* **Wine prices** *Moderate* **Cuisine** *Contemporary American* **Menu prices** *$20–$37*

THE GRAND CAFÉ
42 Washington St., Morristown, NJ 07960; (973) 540-9444 **Wine list** *California* **Wine prices** *Expensive* **Cuisine** *French/continental* **Menu prices** *$22–$36*

GRAPPA
Somerset Hills Hotel, 200 Liberty Corner Road, Warren, NJ 07059; (908) 647-6700 **Wine list** *California, France, Italy* **Wine prices** *Expensive* **Cuisine** *Italian* **Menu prices** *$16–$32*

THE HARVEST MOON INN
1039 Old York Road, Ringoes, NJ 08551; (908) 806-6020 **Wine list** *California, France* **Wine prices** *Moderate* **Corkage** *$25* **Cuisine** *American* **Menu prices** *$19–$33*

HUNTLEY TAVERNE 🍷
3 Morris Ave., Summit, NJ 07901; (908) 273-3166 **Wine list** *California* **Wine prices** *Moderate* **Corkage** *$20* **Cuisine** *American* **Menu prices** *$13–$32*

IL CAPRICCIO RISTORANTE 🍷🍷
633 Route 10 E., Whippany, NJ 07981; (973) 884-9175 **Wine list** *Italy, California, Bordeaux* **Wine prices** *Moderate* **Cuisine** *Italian* **Menu prices** *$18–$30*

IRONWOOD RESTAURANT 🍷
Basking Ridge Country Club, 185 Madisonville Road, Basking Ridge, NJ 07920; (908) 766-8200 **Wine list** *California* **Wine prices** Inexpensive **Cuisine** *American* **Menu prices** *$17–$25*

JEFFREY'S OF WESTFIELD 🍷
114 Central Ave., Westfield, NJ 07090; (908) 232-4517 **Wine list** *California, France* **Wine prices** *Moderate* **Cuisine** *Contemporary American* **Menu prices** *$16–$25*

L'ALLEGRIA RESTAURANT & CAFÉ 🍷
11 Prospect St., Madison, NJ 07940; (973) 377-6808 **Wine list** *Italy* **Wine prices** *Moderate* **Cuisine** *Italian* **Menu prices** *$20–$30*

LA GRIGLIA 🍷
740 Boulevard, Kenilworth, NJ 07033; (908) 241-0031 **Wine list** *Italy, California* **Wine prices** *Moderate* **Corkage** *$15* **Cuisine** *Contemporary Italian* **Menu prices** *$13–$25*

LE PETIT CHATEAU 🍷🍷
121 Claremont Road, Bernardsville, NJ 07924; (908) 766-4544 **Wine list** *California, France* **Wine prices** *Moderate* **Corkage** *$25* **Cuisine** *Contemporary French* **Menu prices** *$20–$31*

LEGAL SEA FOODS 🍷
1 Garden State Plaza, Paramus, NJ 07652; (201) 843-8483 **Wine list** *California* **Wine prices** Inexpensive **Cuisine** *Seafood* **Menu prices** *$11–$48*

THE LINCROFT INN 🍷
700 Newman Springs Road, Lincroft, NJ 07738; (732) 747-0890 **Wine list** *Italy, California* **Wine prices** *Moderate* **Cuisine** *Continental/Northern Italian* **Menu prices** *$15–$29*

🍷🍷🍷 Grand Award 🍷🍷 Best of Award of Excellence 🍷 Award of Excellence

THE MANOR

111 Prospect Ave., West Orange, NJ 07052; (973) 731-2360 **Wine list** *California, France* **Wine prices** *Moderate* **Corkage** *$26* **Cuisine** *Continental* **Menu prices** *$26–$35*

MEDITERRA

29 Hulfish St., Princeton, NJ 08542; (609) 252-9680 **Wine list** *California* **Wine prices** *Moderate* **Corkage** *$15* **Cuisine** *Mediterranean* **Menu prices** *$16–$29*

MERITAGE

1969 Highway 34, Wall, NJ 07719; (732) 974-5566 **Wine list** *California, Italy* **Wine prices** *Moderate* **Cuisine** *American/French/Asian* **Menu prices** *$17–$27*

MORTON'S OF CHICAGO

1 Riverside Square, Hackensack, NJ 07601; (201) 487-1303 **Wine list** *California* **Wine prices** *Expensive* **Corkage** *$15* **Cuisine** *Steak house* **Menu prices** *$23–$72*

NAPA VALLEY GRILLE

1146 Garden State Plaza, Routes 4 and 17, Paramus, NJ 07652; (201) 845-5555 **Wine list** *California* **Wine prices** *Moderate* **Cuisine** *American/Mediterranean* **Menu prices** *$13–$28*

PANICO'S

103 Church St., New Brunswick, NJ 08901; (732) 545-6100 **Wine list** *Italy, France* **Wine prices** *Moderate* **Cuisine** *Italian* **Menu prices** *$18–$32*

PARK & ORCHARD RESTAURANT

240 Hackensack St., East Rutherford, NJ 07073; (201) 939-9292 **Wine list** *France, California* **Wine selections** *2,125* **Number of bottles** *16,500* **Wine prices** *Moderate* **Cuisine** *International* **Menu prices** *$15–$30* **Credit cards** *AX, MC, VS, DV*

Grand Award since 1991

PEGASUS RESTAURANT

50 Route 120, East Rutherford, NJ 07073; (201) 843-2446 **Wine list** *California* **Wine prices** *Expensive* **Cuisine** *International* **Menu prices** *$21–$33*

PIERRE'S 

995 Mount Kemble Ave., Morristown, NJ 07960; (973) 425-1212 **Wine list** *France* **Wine prices** *Moderate* **Corkage** *$10* **Cuisine** *French* **Menu prices** *$16–$28*

RAM'S HEAD INN 🍷
9 W. White Horse Pike, Galloway, NJ 08205; (609) 652-1700 **Wine list** *California, France* **Wine prices** *Moderate* **Corkage** *$15* **Cuisine** *Continental* **Menu prices** *$19–$32*

RAVEN & THE PEACH 🍷
740 River Road, Fair Haven, NJ 07704; (732) 747-4666 **Wine list** *California, France* **Wine prices** *Moderate* **Corkage** *$20* **Cuisine** *Contemporary American* **Menu prices** *$19–$42*

RESTAURANT NICHOLAS 🍷
160 Highway 35, Red Bank, NJ 07701; (732) 345-9977 **Wine list** *France, California* **Wine prices** *Expensive* **Cuisine** *Contemporary American* **Menu prices** *$28–$35*

RESTAURANT SERENADE 🍷
6 Roosevelt Ave., Chatham, NJ 07928; (973) 701-0303 **Wine list** *France, California* **Wine prices** *Moderate* **Corkage** *$25* **Cuisine** *French* **Menu prices** *$25–$35*

ROD'S STEAK & SEAFOOD GRILLE 🍷
The Madison Hotel, Route 124, Convent Station, NJ 07961; (973) 539-6666 **Wine list** *California* **Wine prices** *Moderate* **Cuisine** *Steak house* **Menu prices** *$15–$33*

ROONEY'S OCEAN CRAB HOUSE 🍷
100 Ocean Ave., Long Branch, NJ 07740; (732) 870-1200 **Wine list** *California* **Wine prices** *Moderate* **Cuisine** *Seafood* **Menu prices** *$15–$30*

ROSEMARY & SAGE 🍷
26 Hamburg Turnpike, Riverdale, NJ 07457; (973) 616-0606 **Wine list** *California* **Wine prices** Inexpensive **Corkage** *$20* **Cuisine** *Contemporary American* **Menu prices** *$20–$31*

RUTH'S CHRIS STEAK HOUSE 🍷
1 Hilton Court, Parsippany, NJ 07054; (973) 889-1400 **Wine list** *California* **Wine prices** *Moderate* **Cuisine** *Steak house* **Menu prices** *$20–$33*

RUTH'S CHRIS STEAK HOUSE 🍷
1000 Harbor Blvd., Weehawken, NJ 07086; (201) 863-5100 **Wine list** *California* **Wine prices** *Moderate* **Corkage** *$15* **Cuisine** *Steak house* **Menu prices** *$19–$65*

THE RYLAND INN 🍷🍷
Route 22 W., Whitehouse, NJ 08888; (908) 534-4011 **Wine list** *France, California, Germany* **Wine prices** *Expensive* **Corkage** *$20* **Cuisine** *Contemporary French/American* **Menu prices** *$34–$40*

SALT CREEK GRILLE
4 Bingham Ave., Rumson, NJ 07760; (732) 933-9272 **Wine list** *California* **Wine prices** *Moderate* **Corkage** *$20* **Cuisine** *American* **Menu prices** *$18–$29*

SAMMY'S YE OLD CIDER MILL
353 Mendham Road W., Mendham, NJ 07945; (973) 543-7675 **Wine list** *California* **Wine prices** *Moderate* **Cuisine** *American/continental* **Menu prices** *$28–$41*

SCALINI FEDELI
63 Main St., Chatham, NJ 07928; (973) 701-9200 **Wine list** *Italy, California* **Wine prices** *Moderate* **Corkage** *$15* **Cuisine** *Italian* **Menu prices** *Prix fixe only; $52*

THE SEA GRILL
225 21st St., Avalon, NJ 08202; (609) 967-5511 **Wine list** *California* **Wine prices** Inexpensive **Cuisine** *American* **Menu prices** *$17–$35*

THE SERGEANTSVILLE INN
601 Rosemont-Ringoes Road, Sergeantsville, NJ 08557; (609) 397-3700 **Wine list** *California* **Wine prices** Inexpensive **Cuisine** *Contemporary American* **Menu prices** *$15–$25*

SESTRI CAFFÉ & RISTORANTE
342 Valley Road, Gillette, NJ 07933; (908) 647-0697 **Wine list** *Italy, California* **Wine prices** *Moderate* **Cuisine** *Italian* **Menu prices** *$15–$28*

SMOKE CHOPHOUSE
36 Engle St., Englewood, NJ 07631; (201) 541-8530 **Wine list** *California, Bordeaux* **Wine prices** *Moderate* **Cuisine** *Continental* **Menu prices** *$29–$69*

SOHO ON GEORGE
335 George St., New Brunswick, NJ 08901; (732) 296-0533 **Wine list** *California* **Wine prices** *Moderate* **Cuisine** *Contemporary American* **Menu prices** *$16–$32*

SONOMA GRILL
64 Hoboken Road, East Rutherford, NJ 07073; (201) 507-8989 **Wine list** *California* **Wine prices** *Moderate* **Cuisine** *American* **Menu prices** *$15–$28*

SOUTH CITY GRILL
55 Route 17 S., Rochelle Park, NJ 07662; (201) 845-3737 **Wine list** *California* **Wine prices** *Moderate* **Corkage** *$12* **Cuisine** *Seafood* **Menu prices** *$16–$30*

STAGE LEFT RESTAURANT 🍷🍷
5 Livingston Ave., New Brunswick, NJ 08901; (732) 828-4444 **Wine list** *California, Burgundy, Germany, Italy* **Wine prices** *Moderate* **Cuisine** *American* **Menu prices** *$25–$36*

TEMPLE BAR & GRILL 🍷
Caesars Hotel & Casino, 2100 Pacific Ave., Atlantic City, NJ 08401; (609) 441-2345 **Wine list** *France, California* **Wine prices** *Expensive* **Corkage** *$15* **Cuisine** *Contemporary American* **Menu prices** *$20–$65*

THE TEWKSBURY INN 🍷
Main Street and Route 517, Oldwick, NJ 08858; (908) 439-2641 **Wine list** *California, France* **Wine prices** *Moderate* **Cuisine** *Contemporary American* **Menu prices** *$15–$30*

TRE FIGLIO 🍷
500 W. White Horse Pike, Galloway Township, Egg Harbor City, NJ 08215; (609) 965-3303 **Wine list** *Italy* **Wine prices** *Moderate* **Cuisine** *Italian* **Menu prices** *$14–$38*

TRE PIANI 🍷
120 Rockingham Row, Princeton, NJ 08540; (609) 452-1515 **Wine list** *Italy* **Wine prices** *Moderate* **Cuisine** *Italian/Mediterranean* **Menu prices** *$18–$35*

TWO IF BY SEA 🍷
141 Shrewsbury Ave., Red Bank, NJ 07701; (732) 747-1586 **Wine list** *California* **Wine prices** *Moderate* **Cuisine** *Seafood* **Menu prices** *$15–$30*

WASHINGTON INN 🍷🍷
801 Washington St., Cape May, NJ 08204; (609) 884-5697 **Wine list** *California, France, Italy* **Wine prices** *Moderate* **Corkage** *$20* **Cuisine** *American* **Menu prices** *$18–$30*

WATCHUNG'S LAKESIDE VILLA 🍷
141 Stirling Road, Watchung, NJ 07069; (908) 755-9344 **Wine list** *Italy, California* **Wine prices** *Moderate* **Cuisine** *Italian* **Menu prices** *$14–$30*

NEW MEXICO

ANASAZI 🍷
The Inn of the Anasazi, 113 Washington Ave., Santa Fe, NM 87501; (505) 988-3236 **Wine list** *California, France* **Wine prices** *Moderate* **Cuisine** *Contemporary Southwestern* **Menu prices** *$18–$33*

ANDIAMO! 🍷
322 Garfield St., Santa Fe, NM 87501; (505) 995-9595 **Wine list** *Italy, California* **Wine prices** *Moderate* **Cuisine** *Italian* **Menu prices** *$13–$20*

APPLE TREE RESTAURANT 🍷
123 Bent St., Taos, NM 87571; (505) 758-1900 **Wine list** *California, France* **Wine prices** Inexpensive **Cuisine** *Regional* **Menu prices** *$11–$23*

BILLY CREWS DINING ROOM 🍷🍷🍷
1200 Country Club Road, Santa Teresa, NM 88008; (505) 589-2071 **Wine list** *California, Bordeaux* **Wine selections** *2,165* **Number of bottles** *17,900* **Wine prices** *Moderate* **Cuisine** *American* **Menu prices** *$12–$30* **Credit cards** *AX, MC, VS, DV*
Grand Award since 1986

COYOTE CAFÉ 🍷
132 W. Water St., Santa Fe, NM 87501; (505) 983-1615 **Wine list** *California, France* **Wine prices** *Moderate* **Cuisine** *Contemporary Southwestern* **Menu prices** *$18–$42*

DOC MARTIN'S 🍷🍷
The Taos Inn, 125 Paseo del Pueblo N., Taos, NM 87571; (800) TAOS-INN **Wine list** *California, France* **Wine prices** *Moderate* **Cuisine** *Continental* **Menu prices** *$12–$28*

HONDO RESTAURANT 🍷
The Inn at Snakedance, 110 Sutton Place, Taos Ski Valley, NM 87525; (800) 322-9815 **Wine list** *California, France* **Wine prices** *Moderate* **Cuisine** *Contemporary American* **Menu prices** *$15–$28*

LA CASA SENA 🍷🍷
125 E. Palace Ave., Santa Fe, NM 87501; (505) 988-9232 **Wine list** *California, France, Spain, Tuscany, Germany* **Wine prices** *Expensive* **Cuisine** *Southwestern* **Menu prices** *$23–$27*

LE CAFÉ MICHE 🍷
1431 Wyoming Blvd. N.E., Albuquerque, NM 87112; (505) 299-6088 **Wine list** *California, France* **Wine prices** *Moderate* **Cuisine** *French* **Menu prices** *$15–$26*

MONTE VISTA FIRE STATION 🍷
3201 Central Ave. N.E., Albuquerque, NM 87106; (505) 255-2424 **Wine list** *California* **Wine prices** *Expensive* **Cuisine** *Southwestern* **Menu prices** *$13–$20*

OLD HOUSE RESTAURANT 🍷
Eldorado Hotel, 309 W. San Francisco St., Santa Fe, NM 87501; (505) 988-4455 **Wine list** *California* **Wine prices** *Moderate* **Cuisine** *Contemporary* **Menu prices** *$23–$30*

ORE HOUSE ON THE PLAZA 🍷
50 Lincoln Ave., Santa Fe, NM 87501; (505) 983-8687 **Wine list** *California* **Wine prices** *Moderate* **Cuisine** *Southwestern* **Menu prices** *$15–$28*

PRAIRIE STAR 🍷
288 Prairie Star Road, Santa Ana Pueblo, NM 87004; (505) 867-3327 **Wine list** *France, California, Italy* **Wine prices** *Moderate* **Corkage** *$15* **Cuisine** *Contemporary* **Menu prices** *$15–$29*

RANCHER'S CLUB OF NEW MEXICO 🍷
Albuquerque Hilton, 1901 University Blvd. N.E., Albuquerque, NM 87102; (505) 889-8071 **Wine list** *California* **Wine prices** *Moderate* **Cuisine** *Steak house* **Menu prices** *$25–$70*

RANCHO DE SAN JUAN 🍷
Highway 285, MM 340, Espanola, NM 87553; (505) 753-6818 **Wine list** *France, California* **Wine prices** *Moderate* **Cuisine** *American/European* **Menu prices** *Prix fixe only; $50–$55*

THE RESTAURANT AT THE INN AT LORETTO 🍷
211 Old Santa Fe Trail, Santa Fe, NM 87501; (505) 988-5531 **Wine list** *California* **Wine prices** *Moderate* **Corkage** *$10* **Cuisine** *Regional* **Menu prices** *$20–$33*

RESTAURANT JEZEBEL 🍷
2117 Sudderth Drive, Ruidoso, NM 88345; (505) 257-5883 **Wine list** *California* **Wine prices** *Moderate* **Cuisine** *Contemporary American* **Menu prices** *$17–$28*

RIO CHAMA STEAKHOUSE 🍷
414 Old Santa Fe Trail, Santa Fe, NM 87501; (505) 955-0765 **Wine list** *California* **Wine prices** *Moderate* **Cuisine** *Steak house* **Menu prices** *$20–$38*

ROCIADA 🍷
304 Johnson St., Santa Fe, NM 87501; (505) 983-3800 **Wine list** *France* **Wine prices** *Expensive* **Cuisine** *Mediterranean* **Menu prices** *$21–$34*

SEASONS ROTISSERIE & GRILL
2031 Mountain Road N.W., Albuquerque, NM 87104; (505) 766-5100 **Wine list** *California* **Wine prices** *Moderate* **Cuisine** *Contemporary American* **Menu prices** *$15–$25*

315 RESTAURANT & WINE BAR
315 Old Santa Fe Trail, Santa Fe, NM 87501; (505) 986-9190 **Wine list** *France, California* **Wine prices** *Moderate* **Cuisine** *French/American* **Menu prices** *$18–$25*

NEW YORK

MANHATTAN

AIX
2398 Broadway, New York, NY 10024; (212) 874-7400 **Wine list** *France* **Wine prices** *Moderate* **Corkage** *$25* **Cuisine** *Contemporary French* **Menu prices** *$24–$29*

ALAIN DUCASSE AT THE ESSEX HOUSE
The Essex House, 155 W. 58th St., New York, NY 10019; (212) 265-7300 **Wine list** *Burgundy, Bordeaux, California, Spain* **Wine selections** *1,350* **Number of bottles** *18,000* **Wine prices** *Expensive* **Cuisine** *Contemporary French* **Menu prices** *Prix fixe only; $150–$280* **Credit cards** *AX, MC, VS, DV*
Grand Award since 2003

ALFAMA, FINE PORTUGUESE CUISINE
551 Hudson St., New York, NY 10014; (212) 645-2500 **Wine list** *Portugal* **Wine prices** *Moderate* **Corkage** *$12* **Cuisine** *Portuguese* **Menu prices** *$17–$28*

ALFREDO OF ROME
4 W. 49th St., New York, NY 10020; (212) 397-0100 **Wine list** *Italy* **Wine prices** *Expensive* **Cuisine** *Italian* **Menu prices** *$19–$32*

ALOUETTE
2588 Broadway, New York, NY 10025; (212) 222-6808 **Wine list** *France* **Wine prices** *Moderate* **Cuisine** *Contemporary French* **Menu prices** *$15–$24*

AQUAGRILL
210 Spring St., New York, NY 10012; (212) 274-0505 **Wine list** *France* **Wine prices** *Moderate* **Cuisine** *Seafood* **Menu prices** *$19–$24*

AQUAVIT 🍷
13 W. 54th St., New York, NY 10019; (212) 307-7311
Wine list *Burgundy, California* **Wine prices** *Expensive* **Corkage** *$35* **Cuisine** *Scandanavian* **Menu prices** *$16–$30*

ARTISANAL 🍷
2 Park Ave., New York, NY 10016; (212) 725-8585 **Wine list** *France* **Wine prices** *Moderate* **Corkage** *$25* **Cuisine** *French* **Menu prices** *$17–$25*

ATELIER 🍷🍷
The Ritz-Carlton Central Park, 50 Central Park S., New York, NY 10019; (212) 521-6125 **Wine list** *Burgundy, Australia, California, Bordeaux, Austria* **Wine prices** *Expensive* **Corkage** *$50* **Cuisine** *French/American* **Menu prices** *Prix fixe only; $72*

ATLANTIC GRILL 🍷
1341 Third Ave., New York, NY 10021; (212) 988-9200
Wine list *California, France* **Wine prices** *Moderate* **Cuisine** *Seafood* **Menu prices** *$17–$25*

AUREOLE 🍷🍷
34 E. 61st St., New York, NY 10021; (212) 319-1660 **Wine list** *California, France* **Wine prices** *Expensive* **Cuisine** *American* **Menu prices** *Prix fixe only; $69–$85*

AZ 🍷🍷
21 W. 17th St., New York, NY 10011; (212) 691-8888
Wine list *California, France, Italy* **Wine prices** *Expensive* **Corkage** *$35* **Cuisine** *American/Asian* **Menu prices** *$25–$35*

BABBO 🍷🍷
110 Waverly Place, New York, NY 10011; (212) 777-0303
Wine list *Italy* **Wine prices** *Moderate* **Cuisine** *Italian* **Menu prices** *$18–$29*

BARAONDA 🍷
1439 Second Ave., New York, NY 10021; (212) 288-8555
Wine list *Italy* **Wine prices** *Moderate* **Cuisine** *Italian* **Menu prices** *$16–$35*

BARBETTA 🍷🍷
321 W. 46th St., New York, NY 10036; (212) 246-9171
Wine list *Piedmont, Tuscany* **Wine prices** *Expensive* **Corkage** *$15* **Cuisine** *Italian* **Menu prices** *$24–$32*

BAYARD'S
1 Hanover Square, New York, NY 10004; (212) 514-9454
Wine list *California, France, Italy, Port* **Wine prices** *Expensive* **Corkage** *$20* **Cuisine** *French/American* **Menu prices** *$25–$38*

BECCO
355 W. 46th St., New York, NY 10036; (212) 397-7597
Wine list *Italy* **Wine prices** *Moderate* **Cuisine** *Northern Italian* **Menu prices** *$18–$29*

BELLA BLU
967 Lexington Ave., New York, NY 10021; (212) 988-4624
Wine list *Italy* **Wine prices** *Moderate* **Cuisine** *Northern Italian* **Menu prices** *$18–$35*

BEN BENSON'S STEAK HOUSE
123 W. 52nd St., New York, NY 10019; (212) 581-8888
Wine list *California* **Wine prices** *Moderate* **Cuisine** *Steak house* **Menu prices** *$17–$34*

BEPPE
45 E. 22nd St., New York, NY 10010; (212) 982-8422
Wine list *Italy* **Wine prices** *Moderate* **Corkage** *$25* **Cuisine** *Tuscan* **Menu prices** *$24–$29*

BISTRO TEN 18
1018 Amsterdam Ave., New York, NY 10025; (212) 662-7600 **Wine list** *California, France* **Wine prices** *Moderate* **Cuisine** *French/American* **Menu prices** *$14–$27*

BLUE FIN
1567 Broadway, New York, NY 10023; (212) 918-1400
Wine list *California, France* **Wine prices** *Moderate* **Cuisine** *Seafood* **Menu prices** *$19–$29*

BLUE WATER GRILL
31 Union Square W., New York, NY 10003; (212) 675-9500
Wine list *France, California* **Wine prices** *Moderate* **Cuisine** *Seafood* **Menu prices** *$17–$28*

BOBBY VAN'S STEAKHOUSE
230 Park Ave., New York, NY 10169; (212) 867-5490
Wine list *California* **Wine prices** *Moderate* **Cuisine** *Steak house* **Menu prices** *$23–$37*

BOULEY
120 W. Broadway, New York, NY 10013; (212) 964-2525
Wine list *France, California* **Wine prices** *Expensive* **Cuisine** *Contemporary French* **Menu prices** *$30–$56*

BRASSERIE 🍷
100 E. 53rd St., New York, NY 10022; (212) 751-4840
Wine list *California, France* **Wine prices** *Moderate* **Corkage** *$15* **Cuisine** *French* **Menu prices** *$15–$29*

BRASSERIE 8 1/2 🍷
9 W. 57th St., New York, NY 10019; (212) 829-0812 **Wine list** *France, California* **Wine prices** *Moderate* **Corkage** *$25* **Cuisine** *French* **Menu prices** *$19–$32*

THE BUBBLE LOUNGE 🍷
228 W. Broadway, New York, NY 10013; (212) 431-3433
Wine list *Champagne* **Wine prices** *Expensive* **Cuisine** *American* **Menu prices** *$8–$15*

CAFÉ BOULUD 🍷🍷
20 E. 76th St., New York, NY 10021; (212) 772-2600 **Wine list** *California, Burgundy, Rhône* **Wine prices** *Expensive* **Cuisine** *French/American* **Menu prices** *$25–$35*

CAFÉ CENTRO 🍷
MetLife Building, 200 Park Ave., New York, NY 10166; (212) 818-1222 **Wine list** *France, California* **Wine prices** *Moderate* **Cuisine** *French* **Menu prices** *$16–$26*

CAFÉ DES ARTISTES 🍷
Hotel des Artistes, 1 W. 67th St., New York, NY 10023; (212) 877-3500 **Wine list** *France* **Wine prices** *Moderate* **Corkage** *$20* **Cuisine** *French* **Menu prices** *$24–$42*

CAFÉ FIORELLO'S 🍷
1900 Broadway, New York, NY 10023; (212) 595-5330
Wine list *Italy* **Wine prices** *Moderate* **Cuisine** *Italian* **Menu prices** *$18–$30*

CAPSOUTO FRÈRES 🍷
451 Washington St., New York, NY 10013; (212) 966-4900
Wine list *France* **Wine prices** *Expensive* **Cuisine** *Contemporary French* **Menu prices** *$14–$22*

THE CARLYLE RESTAURANT 🍷
The Carlyle Hotel, 35 E. 76th St., New York, NY 10021; (212) 744-1600 **Wine list** *France, California* **Wine prices** *Moderate* **Cuisine** *Contemporary* **Menu prices** *$32–$46*

CHIAM 🍷🍷
160 E. 48th St., New York, NY 10017; (212) 371-2323
Wine list *California* **Wine prices** *Moderate* **Cuisine** *Chinese* **Menu prices** *$20–$40*

🍷🍷🍷 Grand Award 🍷🍷 Best of Award of Excellence 🍷 Award of Excellence

CHURRASCARIA PLATAFORMA
316 W. 49th St., New York, NY 10019; (212) 245-0505
Wine list *Italy, California, Bordeaux* **Wine prices** *Expensive* **Cuisine** *Brazilian* **Menu prices** *Prix fixe only; $39*

CITÉ
120 W. 51st St., New York, NY 10020; (212) 956-7100
Wine list *California, France* **Wine prices** *Moderate* **Cuisine** *Steak house* **Menu prices** *$19–$29*

CITY HALL
131 Duane St., New York, NY 10013; (212) 227-7777
Wine list *California, France, Spain, Germany* **Wine prices** *Moderate* **Cuisine** *American* **Menu prices** *$19–$32*

COMPASS
208 W. 70th St., New York, NY 10023; (212) 875-8600
Wine list *California, France* **Wine prices** *Moderate* **Cuisine** *Contemporary American* **Menu prices** *$20–$30*

CUB ROOM
131 Sullivan St., New York, NY 10012; (212) 677-4100
Wine list *France, California, Italy* **Wine prices** *Moderate* **Corkage** *$15* **Cuisine** *Contemporary American* **Menu prices** *$20–$30*

DA FILIPPO RESTAURANT
1315 Second Ave., New York, NY 10021; (212) 472-6688
Wine list *Tuscany, California* **Wine prices** *Expensive* **Cuisine** *Italian* **Menu prices** *$19–$33*

DANIEL
60 E. 65th St., New York, NY 10021; (212) 288-0033 **Wine list** *Burgundy, Bordeaux* **Wine selections** *1,570* **Number of bottles** *24,000* **Wine prices** *Expensive* **Cuisine** *Contemporary French* **Menu prices** *Prix fixe only; $68–$140* **Credit cards** *AX, MC, VS, DV*
Grand Award since 2002

DB BISTRO MODERNE
55 W. 44th St., New York, NY 10036; (212) 391-2400
Wine list *France, California* **Wine prices** *Expensive* **Cuisine** *French* **Menu prices** *$27–$31*

DEL FRISCO'S DOUBLE EAGLE STEAK HOUSE
1221 Avenue of the Americas, New York, NY 10020; (212) 575-5129 **Wine list** *California, France* **Wine prices** *Expensive* **Cuisine** *Steak house* **Menu prices** *$28–$128*

DUE RESTAURANT 🍷
1396 Third Ave., New York, NY 10021; (212) 772-3331
Wine list *California, Italy* **Wine prices** *Moderate* **Cuisine** *Northern Italian* **Menu prices** *$13–$21*

ELEVEN MADISON PARK 🍷🍷
11 Madison Ave., New York, NY 10010; (212) 889-0905
Wine list *France, California* **Wine prices** *Moderate* **Corkage** *$20* **Cuisine** *American/French* **Menu prices** *$22–$31*

ESCA 🍷
402 W. 43rd St., New York, NY 10036; (212) 564-7272
Wine list *Italy* **Wine prices** *Moderate* **Cuisine** *Italian* **Menu prices** *$24–$28*

F.ILLI PONTE RISTORANTE 🍷
39 Desbrosses St., New York, NY 10013; (212) 226-4621
Wine list *Italy, California* **Wine prices** *Expensive* **Corkage** *$25* **Cuisine** *Italian* **Menu prices** *$22–$39*

FELIDIA RISTORANTE 🍷🍷🍷
243 E. 58th St., New York, NY 10022; (212) 758-1479
Wine list *Italy* **Wine selections** *1,200* **Number of bottles** *37,000* **Wine prices** *Expensive* **Cuisine** *Italian* **Menu prices** *$18–$32* **Credit cards** *AX, MC, VS, DV*
Grand Award since 1988

FIAMMA 🍷🍷
206 Spring St., New York, NY 10012; (212) 653-0100 **Wine list** *Italy, California* **Wine prices** *Expensive* **Cuisine** *Italian* **Menu prices** *$24–$36*

FLEUR DE SEL 🍷
5 E. 20th St., New York, NY 10003; (212) 460-9100 **Wine list** *Burgundy, Bordeaux, Loire* **Wine prices** *Moderate* **Corkage** *$25* **Cuisine** *Contemporary French* **Menu prices** *$25–$33*

FRANK RESTAURANT 🍷
88 Second Ave., New York, NY 10003; (212) 420-0202
Wine list *Italy* **Wine prices** *Moderate* **Cuisine** *Italian* **Menu prices** *$9–$22*

FRANKIE & JOHNNIE'S STEAKHOUSE 🍷
269 W. 45th St., New York, NY 10036; (212) 997-9494
Wine list *California* **Wine prices** *Moderate* **Cuisine** *Steak house* **Menu prices** *$16–$36*

FRANKIE & JOHNNIE'S STEAKHOUSE
32 W. 37th St., New York, NY 10018; (212) 947-8940
Wine list *California* **Wine prices** *Moderate* **Cuisine** *Steak house* **Menu prices** *$18–$38*

FRESH
105 Reade St., New York, NY 10013; (212) 406-1900 **Wine list** *France* **Wine prices** *Moderate* **Cuisine** *Seafood* **Menu prices** *$20–$34*

GABRIEL'S
11 W. 60th St., New York, NY 10023; (212) 956-4600
Wine list *Italy, California* **Wine prices** Inexpensive **Cuisine** *Italian* **Menu prices** *$18–$32*

GIOVANNI RISTORANTE
47 W. 55th St., New York, NY 10019; (212) 262-2828
Wine list *Italy, California, France* **Wine prices** *Moderate* **Cuisine** *Northern Italian* **Menu prices** *$15–$33*

GRAMERCY TAVERN
42 E. 20th St., New York, NY 10003; (212) GR7-0777
Wine list *California, France* **Wine prices** *Moderate* **Corkage** *$20* **Cuisine** *American* **Menu prices** *Prix fixe only; $68*

THE HARRISON
355 Greenwich St., New York, NY 10013; (212) 274-9310
Wine list *Italy* **Wine prices** *Moderate* **Cuisine** *American/Mediterranean* **Menu prices** *$18–$28*

HEARTBEAT RESTAURANT
W New York, 149 E. 49th St., New York, NY 10017; (212) 407-2900 **Wine list** *California, France* **Wine prices** *Moderate* **Cuisine** *Contemporary American* **Menu prices** *$21–$34*

HENRY'S EVERGREEN
1288 First Ave., New York, NY 10021; (212) 744-3266
Wine list *California, France* **Wine prices** *Moderate* **Corkage** *$10* **Cuisine** *Cantonese* **Menu prices** *$14–$35*

ICON RESTAURANT
W Court Hotel, 130 E. 39th St., New York, NY 10016; (212) 592-8888 **Wine list** *California* **Wine prices** *Moderate* **Cuisine** *Contemporary American* **Menu prices** *$17–$27*

I COPPI
432 E. 9th St., New York, NY 10009; (212) 254-2263 **Wine list** *Tuscany* **Wine prices** *Moderate* **Corkage** *$15* **Cuisine** *Tuscan* **Menu prices** *$17–$25*

I TRULLI
122 E. 27th St., New York, NY 10016; (212) 481-7372
Wine list *Italy* **Wine prices** *Moderate* **Cuisine** *Southern Italian*
Menu prices *$19–$34*

JEAN GEORGES
Trump International Hotel & Tower, 1 Central Park W., New York, NY 10023; (212) 299-3900 **Wine list** *France, California* **Wine prices** *Expensive* **Cuisine** *French* **Menu prices** *Prix fixe only; $87–$118*

JEAN-LUC
507 Columbus Ave., New York, NY 10024; (212) 712-1700
Wine list *France, California* **Wine prices** *Moderate* **Corkage** *$25* **Cuisine** *Contemporary French* **Menu prices** *$17–$32*

JOSEPHINA
1900 Broadway, New York, NY 10023; (212) 799-1000
Wine list *California* **Wine prices** *Moderate* **Cuisine** *Contemporary American* **Menu prices** *$16–$24*

JUDSON GRILL
152 W. 52nd St., New York, NY 10019; (212) 582-5252
Wine list *California, France, Italy* **Wine prices** *Moderate*
Corkage *$20* **Cuisine** *Contemporary American* **Menu prices** *$21–$34*

JW'S STEAKHOUSE
Marriott Marquis, 1535 Broadway, New York, NY 10036; (212) 704-8900 **Wine list** *California* **Wine prices** *Moderate*
Cuisine *Steak house* **Menu prices** *$22–$42*

KEENS STEAKHOUSE
72 W. 36th St., New York, NY 10018; (212) 947-3636
Wine list *California, France* **Wine prices** *Moderate* **Corkage** *$20* **Cuisine** *Steak house* **Menu prices** *$22–$40*

L'ABSINTHE
227 E. 67th St., New York, NY 10021; (212) 794-4950
Wine list *France, California* **Wine prices** *Expensive* **Cuisine** *Contemporary French* **Menu prices** *$20–$35*

L'ACAJOU
53 W. 19th St., New York, NY 10011; (212) 645-1706
Wine list *France* **Wine prices** *Moderate* **Cuisine** *French* **Menu prices** *$16–$27*

LA CANTINA TOSCANA
1109 First Ave., New York, NY 10021; (212) 754-5454
Wine list *Tuscany, Piedmont* **Wine prices** *Moderate* **Corkage** *$15* **Cuisine** *Tuscan* **Menu prices** *$15–$26*

LA CARAVELLE
33 W. 55th St., New York, NY 10019; (212) 586-4252
Wine list *Bordeaux, Burgundy* **Wine prices** *Expensive* **Corkage** *$30* **Cuisine** *Contemporary French* **Menu prices** *Prix fixe only; $72*

LA GOULUE
746 Madison Ave., New York, NY 10021; (212) 988-8169
Wine list *France, California* **Wine prices** *Moderate* **Corkage** *$30* **Cuisine** *French* **Menu prices** *$20–$37*

LA LANTERNA DI VITTORIO
129 MacDougal St., New York, NY 10012; (212) 529-5945
Wine list *Italy, California* **Wine prices** *Moderate* **Cuisine** *Italian* **Menu prices** *$10–$12*

LA LOCANDA DE VINI
737 Ninth Ave., New York, NY 10019; (212) 258-2900
Wine list *Italy, California* **Wine prices** *Moderate* **Cuisine** *Italian* **Menu prices** *$39–$45*

LA MANGEOIRE
1008 Second Ave., New York, NY 10022; (212) 759-7086
Wine list *France* **Wine prices** Inexpensive **Cuisine** *Provençal* **Menu prices** *$15–$30*

LA PIZZA FRESCA RISTORANTE
31 E. 20th St., New York, NY 10003; (212) 598-0141 **Wine list** *Italy* **Wine prices** *Moderate* **Corkage** *$25* **Cuisine** *Italian* **Menu prices** *$15–$25*

LAVAGNA
545 E. 5th St., New York, NY 10009; (212) 979-1005 **Wine list** *California, Italy* **Wine prices** *Moderate* **Corkage** *$15* **Cuisine** *Italian/Mediterranean* **Menu prices** *$15–$23*

LAWRENCE SCOTT RESTAURANT
1363 First Ave., New York, NY 10021; (212) 396-4555
Wine list *California, France, Italy* **Wine prices** *Moderate* **Cuisine** *Contemporary American* **Menu prices** *$18–$27*

LA VINERIA
19 W. 55th St., New York, NY 10019; (212) 247-3400
Wine list *Italy, California* **Wine prices** *Expensive* **Corkage** *$15* **Cuisine** *Southern Italian* **Menu prices** *$12–$23*

LE BERNARDIN 🍷🍷
155 W. 51st St., New York, NY 10019; (212) 554-1515
Wine list *France, California* **Wine prices** *Expensive* **Cuisine** *French/seafood* **Menu prices** *Prix fixe only; $84*

LE CIRQUE 2000 🍷🍷🍷
455 Madison Ave., New York, NY 10022; (212) 303-7788
Wine list *France, Italy, California* **Wine selections** *750*
Number of bottles *45,000* **Wine prices** *Expensive* **Cuisine** *French/Italian* **Menu prices** *$28–$39*
Credit cards *AX, MC, VS*
Grand Award since 1986

L'ECOLE, THE RESTAURANT OF THE FRENCH CULINARY INSTITUTE 🍷
462 Broadway, New York, NY 10013; (212) 219-3300 **Wine list** *France* **Wine prices** *Moderate* **Cuisine** *Contemporary French* **Menu prices** *Prix fixe only; $30*

L'EXPRESS 🍷
249 Park Ave. S., New York, NY 10003; (212) 254-5858
Wine list *France* **Wine prices** *Moderate* **Cuisine** *French* **Menu prices** *$8–$18*

L'IMPERO 🍷
45 Tudor City Place, New York, NY 10017; (212) 599-5045
Wine list *Italy, France* **Wine prices** *Moderate* **Corkage** *$25*
Cuisine *Italian* **Menu prices** *$15–$29*

LE MADELEINE 🍷
403 W. 43rd St., New York, NY 10036; (212) 246-2993
Wine list *France* **Wine prices** *Moderate* **Corkage** *$15* **Cuisine** *Contemporary French* **Menu prices** *$17–$25*

LE MONDE 🍷
2885 Broadway, New York, NY 10025; (212) 531-3939
Wine list *France, California* **Wine prices** Inexpensive
Cuisine *French* **Menu prices** *$10–$18*

LENOX ROOM 🍷
1278 Third Ave., New York, NY 10021; (212) 772-0404
Wine list *California, France* **Wine prices** *Moderate* **Corkage** *$20* **Cuisine** *Contemporary American* **Menu prices** *$19–$28*

LE PÉRIGORD 🍷
405 E. 52nd St., New York, NY 10022; (212) 755-6244
Wine list *France* **Wine prices** *Expensive* **Cuisine** *Contemporary French* **Menu prices** *$18–$24*

LES ROUTIERS
568 Amsterdam Ave., New York, NY 10024; (212) 874-2742 **Wine list** *France, California* **Wine prices** *Moderate* **Corkage** *$15* **Cuisine** *Contemporary French* **Menu prices** *$15–$28*

LUPA OSTERIA ROMANA
170 Thompson St., New York, NY 10012; (212) 982-5089 **Wine list** *Italy* **Wine prices** *Moderate* **Cuisine** *Italian* **Menu prices** *$21–$40*

LUSARDI'S RESTAURANT
1494 Second Ave., New York, NY 10021; (212) 249-2020 **Wine list** *Italy, California* **Wine prices** *Moderate* **Cuisine** *Northern Italian* **Menu prices** *$16–$29*

LUTÈCE
249 E. 50th St., New York, NY 10022; (212) 752-2225 **Wine list** *Burgundy, California* **Wine prices** *Expensive* **Corkage** *$25* **Cuisine** *Contemporary French* **Menu prices** *Prix fixe only; $59*

MADISON BISTRO
238 Madison Ave., New York, NY 10016; (212) 447-1919 **Wine list** *France* **Wine prices** *Moderate* **Cuisine** *French* **Menu prices** *$14–$30*

MALONEY & PORCELLI
37 E. 50th St., New York, NY 10022; (212) 750-2233 **Wine list** *Bordeaux, California* **Wine prices** *Expensive* **Cuisine** *American* **Menu prices** *$20–$30*

THE MANHATTAN OCEAN CLUB
57 W. 58th St., New York, NY 10019; (212) 371-7777 **Wine list** *California, France* **Wine prices** *Expensive* **Cuisine** *Seafood* **Menu prices** *$26–$35*

MARCH
405 E. 58th St., New York, NY 10022; (212) 754-6272 **Wine list** *California* **Wine prices** *Expensive* **Cuisine** *Contemporary American* **Menu prices** *Prix fixe only; $68–$108*

MARK'S RESTAURANT
The Mark, 25 E. 77th St., New York, NY 10021; (212) 879-1864 **Wine list** *California, France* **Wine prices** *Expensive* **Corkage** *$20* **Cuisine** *Contemporary American/French/Asian* **Menu prices** *$25–$35*

MARSEILLE 🍷
630 Ninth Ave., New York, NY 10036; (212) 333-2323
Wine list *France* **Wine prices** Inexpensive **Corkage** *$25*
Cuisine *French/Mediterranean* **Menu prices** *$17–$24*

MICHAEL JORDAN'S THE STEAK HOUSE NYC 🍷
Grand Central Terminal, 23 Vanderbilt Ave., New York, NY 10017; (212) 655-2300 **Wine list** *California, France* **Wine prices** *Expensive* **Cuisine** *Steak house* **Menu prices** *$18–$34*

MICHAEL'S NEW YORK 🍷🍷
24 W. 55th St., New York, NY 10019; (212) 767-0555
Wine list *California, Burgundy* **Wine prices** *Moderate* **Cuisine** *Contemporary American* **Menu prices** *$24–$36*

MONKEY BAR & GRILL 🍷
Hotel Elysée, 60 E. 54th St., New York, NY 10022; (212) 838-2600 **Wine list** *California, France* **Wine prices** *Expensive*
Cuisine *Contemporary American* **Menu prices** *$22–$35*

MONTPARNASSE 🍷
230 E. 51st St., New York, NY 10022; (212) 758-6633
Wine list *France, California* **Wine prices** *Moderate* **Corkage** *$20* **Cuisine** *French* **Menu prices** *$18–$25*

MONTRACHET 🍷🍷🍷
239 W. Broadway, New York, NY 10013; (212) 219-2777
Wine list *Burgundy, Rhône, Bordeaux, California, Champagne*
Wine selections *1,500* **Number of bottles** *25,000* **Wine prices** *Expensive* **Cuisine** *French* **Menu prices** *$25–$32*
Credit cards *AX, MC, VS, DV*
Grand Award since 1994

MORTON'S OF CHICAGO 🍷
551 Fifth Ave., New York, NY 10017; (212) 972-3315
Wine list *California* **Wine prices** *Expensive* **Corkage** *$15*
Cuisine *Steak house* **Menu prices** *$20–$35*

NICE MATIN 🍷
The Lucerne, 201 W. 79th St., New York, NY 10024; (212) 873-6423 **Wine list** *France* **Wine prices** *Moderate* **Corkage** *$10* **Cuisine** *French/Mediterranean* **Menu prices** *$12–$23*

NICK & STEF'S STEAKHOUSE 🍷
9 Penn Plaza, New York, NY 10001; (212) 563-4444 **Wine list** *California, France, Italy* **Wine prices** *Moderate* **Corkage** *$20* **Cuisine** *Steak house* **Menu prices** *$22–$36*

🍷🍷🍷 Grand Award 🍷🍷 Best of Award of Excellence 🍷 Award of Excellence

NORTH SQUARE
Washington Square Hotel, 103 Waverly Place, New York, NY 10011; (212) 254-1200 **Wine list** *California, France* **Wine prices** Inexpensive **Corkage** *$10* **Cuisine** *American* **Menu prices** *$14–$25*

THE OAK ROOM
The Plaza, 768 Fifth Ave., New York, NY 10019; (212) 546-5200 **Wine list** *France, California* **Wine prices** *Expensive* **Cuisine** *Steak house* **Menu prices** *$24–$40*

OCEAN GRILL
384 Columbus Ave., New York, NY 10024; (212) 579-2300 **Wine list** *California* **Wine prices** *Moderate* **Cuisine** *Seafood* **Menu prices** *$17–$23*

OCEANA RESTAURANT
55 E. 54th St., New York, NY 10022; (212) 759-5941 **Wine list** *California, Burgundy, Bordeaux, Loire* **Wine prices** *Moderate* **Cuisine** *Seafood* **Menu prices** *Prix fixe only; $68*

OLD HOMESTEAD
56 Ninth Ave., New York, NY 10011; (212) 242-9040 **Wine list** *California* **Wine prices** *Moderate* **Cuisine** *Steak house* **Menu prices** *$18–$41*

OLICA RESTAURANT MODERNE
The Kimberly Hotel, 145 E. 50th St., New York, NY 10022; (212) 583-0001 **Wine list** *California, France* **Wine prices** *Expensive* **Cuisine** *Contemporary French* **Menu prices** *$30–$50*

OLIVES NEW YORK
W New York Union Square, 201 Park Ave. S., New York, NY 10003; (212) 353-8345 **Wine list** *California, France, Italy* **Wine prices** *Moderate* **Cuisine** *Mediterranean* **Menu prices** *$18–$30*

ONE IF BY LAND, TWO IF BY SEA
17 Barrow St., New York, NY 10014; (212) 228-0822 **Wine list** *California, France* **Wine prices** *Expensive* **Corkage** *$25* **Cuisine** *American* **Menu prices** *Prix fixe only; $59*

ONE CPS
The Plaza, 1 Central Park S., New York, NY 10019; (212) 583-1111 **Wine list** *California, France* **Wine prices** *Moderate* **Cuisine** *Regional* **Menu prices** *$20–$38*

ORSAY
1057 Lexington Ave., New York, NY 10021; (212) 517-6400 **Wine list** *France* **Wine prices** *Moderate* **Corkage** *$25* **Cuisine** *French* **Menu prices** *$19–$33*

OSTERIA DEL CIRCO
120 W. 55th St., New York, NY 10019; (212) 265-3636 **Wine list** *Tuscany, Piedmont, California* **Wine prices** *Expensive* **Cuisine** *Northern Italian* **Menu prices** *$19–$37*

OSTERIA DEL GALLO NERO
192 Bleecker St., New York, NY 10012; (212) 475-2355 **Wine list** *Italy* **Wine prices** *Moderate* **Corkage** *$15* **Cuisine** *Tuscan* **Menu prices** *$16–$26*

OTTO
1 Fifth Ave., New York, NY 10003; (212) 995-9559 **Wine list** *Italy* **Wine prices** *Moderate* **Cuisine** *Italian* **Menu prices** *$7–$14*

OUEST
2315 Broadway, New York, NY 10024; (212) 580-8700 **Wine list** *California, France* **Wine prices** *Moderate* **Cuisine** *Contemporary American* **Menu prices** *$16–$31*

THE PALM
837 Second Ave., New York, NY 10017; (212) 687-2953 **Wine list** *California* **Wine prices** *Moderate* **Corkage** *$30* **Cuisine** *Steak house* **Menu prices** *$17–$120*

PALM TOO
840 Second Ave., New York, NY 10017; (212) 697-5198 **Wine list** *California* **Wine prices** *Moderate* **Corkage** *$20* **Cuisine** *Steak house* **Menu prices** *$16–$60*

THE PALM WEST
250 W. 50th St., New York, NY 10019; (212) 333-7256 **Wine list** *California* **Wine prices** *Moderate* **Cuisine** *Steak house* **Menu prices** *$25–$35*

PARK AVENUE CAFÉ
100 E. 63rd St., New York, NY 10021; (212) 644-1900 **Wine list** *California, France* **Wine prices** *Moderate* **Cuisine** *Contemporary American* **Menu prices** *$20–$34*

PATRIA
250 Park Ave. S., New York, NY 10003; (212) 777-6211 **Wine list** *Spain, Chile, Argentina, California* **Wine prices** *Moderate* **Cuisine** *Contemporary Latin* **Menu prices** *$23–$32*

Grand Award   Best of Award of Excellence   Award of Excellence

PATROON 🍷🍷
160 E. 46th St., New York, NY 10017; (212) 883-7373
Wine list *California, France* **Wine prices** *Expensive* **Cuisine** *American* **Menu prices** *$19–$33*

PAZO 🍷
106 E. 57th St., New York, NY 10022; (212) 752-7470
Wine list *France, Italy, California* **Wine prices** *Expensive* **Corkage** *$35* **Cuisine** *Mediterranean* **Menu prices** *$25–$35*

PICHOLINE 🍷
35 W. 64th St., New York, NY 10023; (212) 724-8585
Wine list *California, France* **Wine prices** *Moderate* **Corkage** *$50* **Cuisine** *French/Mediterranean* **Menu prices** *$28–$42*

PIGALLE 🍷
790 Eighth Ave., New York, NY 10019; (212) 489-2233
Wine list *France* **Wine prices** *Moderate* **Corkage** *$10* **Cuisine** *French* **Menu prices** *$14–$20*

THE POST HOUSE 🍷
28 E. 63rd St., New York, NY 10021; (212) 935-2888 **Wine list** *California, France* **Wine prices** *Expensive* **Cuisine** *Steak house* **Menu prices** *$22–$34*

Q56 RESTAURANT & COCKTAILS 🍷
Swissotel New York, 65 E. 56th St., New York, NY 10022; (212) 756-3800 **Wine list** *France* **Wine prices** *Expensive* **Cuisine** *Seafood* **Menu prices** *$18–$27*

THE RED CAT 🍷
227 10th Ave., New York, NY 10011; (212) 242-1122 **Wine list** *France* **Wine prices** *Moderate* **Cuisine** *American* **Menu prices** *$18–$28*

REDEYE GRILL 🍷
888 Seventh Ave., New York, NY 10009; (212) 541-9000
Wine list *California* **Wine prices** *Moderate* **Corkage** *$20* **Cuisine** *American* **Menu prices** *$18–$32*

REMI 🍷
145 W. 53rd St., New York, NY 10019; (212) 581-4242
Wine list *Italy, California* **Wine prices** *Moderate* **Cuisine** *Italian* **Menu prices** *$19–$29*

RENÉ PUJOL RESTAURANT 🍷
321 W. 51st St., New York, NY 10019; (212) 246-3023
Wine list *Bordeaux* **Wine prices** *Expensive* **Cuisine** *French* **Menu prices** *$22–$42*

RISTORANTE BAROLO 🍷🍷
398 W. Broadway, New York, NY 10012; (212) 226-1102 **Wine list** *Piedmont, Tuscany, California* **Wine prices** *Moderate* **Corkage** *$20* **Cuisine** *Northern Italian* **Menu prices** *$16–$29*

RISTORANTE DEGREZIA 🍷🍷
231 E. 50th St., New York, NY 10022; (212) 750-5353 **Wine list** *Tuscany, Piedmont, California* **Wine prices** *Moderate* **Cuisine** *Italian* **Menu prices** *$16–$30*

ROCK CENTER CAFÉ 🍷
20 W. 50th St., New York, NY 10020; (212) 332-7620 **Wine list** *California* **Wine prices** *Moderate* **Cuisine** *American* **Menu prices** *$19–$29*

ROTHMANN'S STEAKHOUSE 🍷
3 E. 54th St., New York, NY 10022; (212) 319-5500 **Wine list** *California, France* **Wine prices** *Expensive* **Corkage** *$15* **Cuisine** *Steak house* **Menu prices** *$20–$33*

ROUGE 🍷
135 E. 62nd St., New York, NY 10021; (212) 207-4601 **Wine list** *France, California* **Wine prices** *Moderate* **Corkage** *$15* **Cuisine** *French* **Menu prices** *$17–$22*

RUBY FOO'S TIMES SQUARE 🍷
1625 Broadway, New York, NY 10019; (212) 489-5600 **Wine list** *California* **Wine prices** *Moderate* **Cuisine** *Asian* **Menu prices** *$15–$23*

RUBY FOO'S UPTOWN 🍷
2182 Broadway, New York, NY 10024; (212) 724-6700 **Wine list** *California* **Wine prices** *Moderate* **Cuisine** *Asian* **Menu prices** *$12–$22*

RUTH'S CHRIS STEAK HOUSE 🍷
148 W. 51st St., New York, NY 10019; (212) 245-9600 **Wine list** *California* **Wine prices** *Moderate* **Corkage** *$25* **Cuisine** *Steak house* **Menu prices** *$19–$36*

SAN PIETRO 🍷🍷
18 E. 54th St., New York, NY 10022; (212) 753-9015 **Wine list** *Italy, California, France* **Wine prices** *Expensive* **Cuisine** *Southern Italian* **Menu prices** *$18–$32*

SCALINI FEDELI
165 Duane St., New York, NY 10013; (212) 528-0400
Wine list *Italy, California, France* **Wine prices** *Moderate* **Corkage** *$30* **Cuisine** *Italian/French* **Menu prices** *Prix fixe only; $60*

THE SEA GRILL
19 W. 49th St., New York, NY 10020; (212) 332-7610
Wine list *California* **Wine prices** *Expensive* **Cuisine** *Seafood* **Menu prices** *$22–$32*

SHAFFER CITY OYSTER BAR & GRILL
5 W. 21st St., New York, NY 10010; (212) 255-9827 **Wine list** *California* **Wine prices** *Moderate* **Cuisine** *Seafood* **Menu prices** *$20–$29*

SHELLY'S NEW YORK
104 W. 57th St., New York, NY 10019; (212) 245-2422
Wine list *California* **Wine prices** *Moderate* **Corkage** *$20* **Cuisine** *Steak house* **Menu prices** *$15–$65*

SHUN LEE PALACE
155 E. 55th St., New York, NY 10022; (212) 371-8844
Wine list *California, France* **Wine prices** *Expensive* **Cuisine** *Contemporary Chinese* **Menu prices** *$15–$30*

SMITH & WOLLENSKY
797 Third Ave., New York, NY 10022; (212) 753-1530
Wine list *California, France* **Wine prices** *Moderate* **Cuisine** *Steak house* **Menu prices** *$19–$45*

SPARKS STEAK HOUSE
210 E. 46th St., New York, NY 10017; (212) 687-4855
Wine list *Bordeaux, California* **Wine selections** *1,020* **Number of bottles** *255,000* **Wine prices** Inexpensive **Cuisine** *Steak house* **Menu prices** *$22–$35* **Credit cards** *AX, MC, VS, DV*
Grand Award since 1981

STRIP HOUSE
13 E. 12th St., New York, NY 10003; (212) 328-0000 **Wine list** *California, France* **Wine prices** *Moderate* **Cuisine** *Steak house* **Menu prices** *$18–$34*

SUPPER RESTAURANT
156 E. Second St., New York, NY 10009; (212) 477-7600
Wine list *Italy* **Wine prices** *Expensive* **Cuisine** *Northern Italian* **Menu prices** *$9–$20*

SUSHI SAMBA 🍷
87 Seventh Ave., New York, NY 10014; (212) 691-7885
Wine list *France, California* **Wine prices** *Expensive* **Corkage** *$20* **Cuisine** *Japanese/South American* **Menu prices** *$19–$39*

TABLA 🍷
11 Madison Ave., New York, NY 10010; (212) 889-0667
Wine list *California, France* **Wine prices** *Moderate* **Corkage** *$15* **Cuisine** *American/Indian* **Menu prices** *$24–$35*

TAVERN ON THE GREEN 🍷🍷
Central Park at W. 67th St., New York, NY 10023; (212) 873-3200 **Wine list** *Bordeaux, Burgundy, California* **Wine prices** *Moderate* **Cuisine** *Contemporary American* **Menu prices** *$21–$36*

TERRANCE BRENNAN'S SEAFOOD & CHOP HOUSE 🍷
Hotel Benjamin, 565 Lexington Ave., New York, NY 10022; (212) 715-2400 **Wine list** *California, France* **Wine prices** *Expensive* **Corkage** *$50* **Cuisine** *American* **Menu prices** *$26–$38*

THALASSA RESTAURANT 🍷
179 Franklin St., New York, NY 10013; (212) 941-7661
Wine list *Greece, California* **Wine prices** *Moderate* **Corkage** *$25* **Cuisine** *Mediterranean* **Menu prices** *$21–$29*

THALIA 🍷
828 Eighth Ave., New York, NY 10019; (212) 399-4444
Wine list *France, California* **Wine prices** *Moderate* **Cuisine** *American/European* **Menu prices** *$14–$26*

TRATTORIA DELL'ARTE 🍷
900 Seventh Ave., New York, NY 10019; (212) 245-9800
Wine list *Italy* **Wine prices** *Moderate* **Corkage** *$15* **Cuisine** *Italian* **Menu prices** *$18–$43*

TRIBECA GRILL 🍷🍷🍷
375 Greenwich St., New York, NY 10013; (212) 941-3900
Wine list *California, Rhône, Burgundy, Bordeaux* **Wine selections** *1,500* **Number of bottles** *20,000* **Wine prices** *Moderate* **Corkage** *$20* **Cuisine** *Contemporary American* **Menu prices** *$19–$29* **Credit cards** *AX, MC, VS, DV*
Grand Award since 2002

TRIOMPHE 🍷
Iroquois New York, 49 W. 44th St., New York, NY 10036; (212) 453-4233 **Wine list** *France, California* **Wine prices** *Moderate* **Cuisine** *French/American* **Menu prices** *$25–$32*

TROPICA BAR & SEAFOOD HOUSE 🍷
MetLife Building, 200 Park Ave., New York, NY 10166; (212) 867-6767 **Wine list** *France, California* **Wine prices** *Moderate* **Corkage** *$15* **Cuisine** *Seafood* **Menu prices** *$19–$32*

TSE YANG RESTAURANT 🍷
34 E. 51st St., New York, NY 10022; (212) 688-5447 **Wine list** *France, California* **Wine prices** *Expensive* **Corkage** *$30* **Cuisine** *Asian* **Menu prices** *$19–$52*

TUSCAN STEAK 🍷
622 Third Ave., New York, NY 10017; (212) 404-1700 **Wine list** *Italy, California* **Wine prices** *Expensive* **Cuisine** *Steak house* **Menu prices** *$26–$50*

21 CLUB 🍷🍷🍷
21 W. 52nd St., New York, NY 10019; (212) 582-7200 **Wine list** *Bordeaux, California, Burgundy, Port, Italy* **Wine selections** *1,060* **Number of bottles** *20,000* **Wine prices** *Expensive* **Cuisine** *Contemporary American* **Menu prices** *$27–$42* **Credit cards** *AX, MC, VS*
Grand Award since 2003

UNION PACIFIC 🍷
111 E. 22nd St., New York, NY 10010; (212) 995-8500 **Wine list** *Burgundy, Germany, Austria* **Wine prices** *Moderate* **Corkage** *$30* **Cuisine** *Contemporary American/Asian* **Menu prices** *Prix fixe only; $68*

UNION SQUARE CAFÉ 🍷🍷
21 E. 16th St., New York, NY 10003; (212) 243-4020 **Wine list** *France, Italy, California* **Wine prices** *Moderate* **Corkage** *$20* **Cuisine** *American/Italian* **Menu prices** *$22–$30*

VERITAS 🍷🍷🍷
43 E. 20th St., New York, NY 10003; (212) 353-3700 **Wine list** *Bordeaux, California, Burgundy, Rhône, Italy, Spain* **Wine selections** *3,000* **Number of bottles** *100,000* **Wine prices** *Moderate* **Cuisine** *Contemporary American* **Menu prices** *Prix fixe only; $68* **Credit cards** *AX, MC, VS, DV*
Grand Award since 2000

VINE 🍷
25 Broad St., New York, NY 10004; (212) 344-VINE **Wine list** *California* **Wine prices** *Moderate* **Cuisine** *Contemporary American* **Menu prices** *$22–$30*

VONG
200 E. 54th St., New York, NY 10022; (212) 486-9592
Wine list *France, California, Germany* **Wine prices** *Expensive* **Corkage** *$35* **Cuisine** *Thai/French* **Menu prices** *$16–$36*

WALLSÉ
344 W. 11th St., New York, NY 10014; (212) 352-2300
Wine list *Austria* **Wine prices** *Moderate* **Cuisine** *Austrian* **Menu prices** *$20–$30*

WASHINGTON PARK
24 Fifth Ave., New York, NY 10011; (212) 529-4400 **Wine list** *Burgundy, California, Bordeaux, Piedmont* **Wine prices** *Expensive* **Cuisine** *Contemporary American* **Menu prices** *$24–$31*

THE WATER CLUB
30 East River Drive, New York, NY 10016; (212) 683-3333
Wine list *California, France* **Wine prices** *Moderate* **Corkage** *$25* **Cuisine** *American* **Menu prices** *$25–$36*

WEST BANK CAFÉ
407 W. 42nd St., New York, NY 10036; (212) 695-6909
Wine list *California* **Wine prices** *Moderate* **Corkage** *$20* **Cuisine** *Contemporary American* **Menu prices** *$12–$23*

ZOË
90 Prince St., New York, NY 10012; (212) 966-6722 **Wine list** *California* **Wine prices** *Moderate* **Corkage** *$15* **Cuisine** *Contemporary American* **Menu prices** *$18–$28*

NEW YORK

OTHER CITIES

AIX EN-PROVENCE
134 New York Ave., Huntington, NY 11743; (631) 549-3338 **Wine list** *France, California* **Wine prices** *Moderate* **Corkage** *$20* **Cuisine** *American/French* **Menu prices** *$20–$28*

ALBERTO RESTAURANT
98-31 Metropolitan Ave., Forest Hills, NY 11375; (718) 268-7860 **Wine list** *Italy, California* **Wine prices** *Moderate* **Cuisine** *Northern Italian* **Menu prices** *$17–$27*

AL DI LA TRATTORIA 🍷
248 Fifth Ave., Brooklyn, NY 11215; (718) 783-4565 **Wine list** *Italy* **Wine prices** *Moderate* **Corkage** *$15* **Cuisine** *Venetian* **Menu prices** *$13–$22*

ALLYN'S RESTAURANT 🍷
4258 Route 44, Millbrook, NY 12545; (845) 677-5888 **Wine list** *California, France* **Wine prices** *Moderate* **Cuisine** *American/continental* **Menu prices** *$18–$26*

THE AMERICAN HOTEL 🍷🍷🍷
Main Street, Sag Harbor, NY 11963; (631) 725-3535 **Wine list** *France, California, Italy* **Wine selections** *2,500* **Number of bottles** *30,000* **Wine prices** *Moderate* **Cuisine** *Contemporary French* **Menu prices** *$20–$36* **Credit cards** *AX, MC, VS, DV*
Grand Award since 1981

ANTHONY'S RESTAURANT & BISTRO 🍷
Route 3 and Interstate 87, Plattsburgh, NY 12901; (518) 561-6420 **Wine list** *California, Italy, France* **Wine prices** *Moderate* **Cuisine** *Continental* **Menu prices** *$10–$24*

ARAD EVANS INN 🍷
7206 Genesee St., Fayetteville, NY 13066; (315) 637-2020 **Wine list** *California, France, Italy* **Wine prices** *Moderate* **Corkage** *$15* **Cuisine** *Contemporary American* **Menu prices** *$19–$23*

ARGYLE GRILL & TAVERN 🍷
90 Deer Park Ave., Babylon Village, NY 11702; (631) 321-4900 **Wine list** *California* **Wine prices** *Moderate* **Corkage** *$15* **Cuisine** *Contemporary American* **Menu prices** *$13–$29*

AVERIL CONWELL DINING ROOM 🍷
Mirror Lake Inn, 5 Mirror Lake Drive, Lake Placid, NY 12946; (518) 523-2544 **Wine list** *California, France* **Wine prices** *Moderate* **Corkage** *$25* **Cuisine** *American* **Menu prices** *$15–$30*

BACCHUS 🍷
56 W. Chippewa St., Buffalo, NY 14202; (716) 854-9463 **Wine list** *California, France* **Wine prices** Inexpensive **Cuisine** *International* **Menu prices** *$6–$18*

BARNEY'S 🍷
315 Buckram Road, Locust Valley, NY 11560; (516) 671-6300 **Wine list** *California, France* **Wine prices** *Moderate* **Corkage** *$25* **Cuisine** *American/French* **Menu prices** *$22–$32*

THE BEAR CAFÉ 🍷
295A Tinker St., Bearsville, NY 12409; (845) 679-5555 **Wine list** *California, France* **Wine prices** *Moderate* **Cuisine** *Contemporary American* **Menu prices** *$14–$26*

THE BELHURST CASTLE 🍷
The Belhurst Castle & White Springs Manor, Route 14 S., Geneva, NY 14456; (315) 781-0201 **Wine list** *New York* **Wine prices** Inexpensive **Cuisine** *American* **Menu prices** *$15–$30*

BELLA VITA CITY GRILL 🍷
430-16 N. Country Road, St. James, NY 11780; (631) 862-8060 **Wine list** *California* **Wine prices** *Moderate* **Corkage** *$20* **Cuisine** *Italian/American* **Menu prices** *$17–$32*

BLU - AN AMERICAN BISTRO 🍷
100 River St., Hastings-On-Hudson, NY 10706; (914) 478-4481 **Wine list** *California* **Wine prices** *Moderate* **Corkage** *$25* **Cuisine** *American* **Menu prices** *$18–$28*

BLUE MOUNTAIN BISTRO 🍷
1633 Glasco Turnpike, Woodstock, NY 12498; (845) 679-8519 **Wine list** *California* **Wine prices** Inexpensive **Corkage** *$15* **Cuisine** *French/Mediterranean* **Menu prices** *$16–$24*

THE BREWSTER INN 🍷
Route 20, Cazenovia, NY 13035; (315) 655-9232 **Wine list** *California* **Wine prices** *Moderate* **Corkage** *$20* **Cuisine** *Contemporary American* **Menu prices** *$20–$26*

CAFÉ LA STRADA 🍷
352 Wheeler Road, Hauppauge, NY 11788; (631) 234-5550 **Wine list** *Italy, California* **Wine prices** *Moderate* **Cuisine** *Italian* **Menu prices** *$12–$24*

CAFÉ MAX 🍷
85 Montauk Highway, East Hampton, NY 11937; (631) 324-2004 **Wine list** *California* **Wine prices** Inexpensive **Corkage** *$15* **Cuisine** *Contemporary American* **Menu prices** *$19–$26*

CAFÉ TAMAYO 🍷
89 Partition St., Saugerties, NY 12477-1512; (845) 246-9371 **Wine list** *New York, California* **Wine prices** *Moderate* **Corkage** *$10* **Cuisine** *American/French/Italian* **Menu prices** *$14–$22*

CAFFÈ ON THE GREEN 🍷
201-10 Cross Island Parkway, Bayside, NY 11360; (718) 423-7272 **Wine list** *California, Italy* **Wine prices** *Moderate* **Cuisine** *Northern Italian* **Menu prices** *$14–$27*

CALVANESO'S COSMOPOLITAN GRILLE 🍷
5185 Transit Road, Williamsville, NY 14221; (716) 633-6683 **Wine list** *California* **Wine prices** *Moderate* **Cuisine** *American* **Menu prices** *$14–$24*

CANAL SIDE INN 🍷
395 S. Ann St., Little Falls, NY 13365; (315) 823-1170 **Wine list** *California, France* **Wine prices** Inexpensive **Corkage** *$5* **Cuisine** *French* **Menu prices** *$16–$24*

THE CARLTUN 🍷🍷
Eisenhower Park, East Meadow, NY 11554; (516) 542-0700 **Wine list** *California, France, Italy, Australia* **Wine prices** *Moderate* **Corkage** *$15* **Cuisine** *Continental* **Menu prices** *$18–$30*

CASA DI COPANI 🍷
3414 Burnet Ave., Syracuse, NY 13206; (315) 463-1031 **Wine list** *California* **Wine prices** Inexpensive **Corkage** *$10* **Cuisine** *Italian/American* **Menu prices** *$10–$27*

CATHERINE'S 🍷
153 W. Main St., Goshen, NY 10924; (845) 294-8707 **Wine list** *California* **Wine prices** Inexpensive **Corkage** *$15* **Cuisine** *American* **Menu prices** *$14–$25*

CATHRYN'S TUSCAN GRILL 🍷
91 Main St., Cold Spring, NY 10516; (845) 265-5582 **Wine list** *Italy* **Wine prices** *Moderate* **Cuisine** *Tuscan* **Menu prices** *$12–$25*

CHEZ SOPHIE BISTRO 🍷
2853 Route 9, Malta Ridge, NY 12020; (518) 583-3538 **Wine list** *France* **Wine prices** *Moderate* **Corkage** *$20* **Cuisine** *French* **Menu prices** *$22–$32*

CHIANTI IL RISTORANTE 🍷
208 S. Broadway, Saratoga Springs, NY 12866; (518) 580-0025 **Wine list** *Italy, California* **Wine prices** *Moderate* **Cuisine** *Italian* **Menu prices** *$16–$24*

CITY GRILL 🍷
268 Main St., Buffalo, NY 14202; (716) 856-2651 **Wine list** *California* **Wine prices** *Moderate* **Corkage** *$15* **Cuisine** *Contemporary American* **Menu prices** *$14–$27*

COEUR DES VIGNES 🍷
L'Hotel Coeur des Vignes, 57225 Main Road, Southold, NY 11971; (631) 765-2656 **Wine list** *Long Island, California* **Wine prices** *Moderate* **Cuisine** *French* **Menu prices** *$18–$33*

COSIMO'S BRICK OVEN RESTAURANT & BAR 🍷
620 Route 211 E., Middletown, NY 10940; (845) 692-3242 **Wine list** *California, Italy* **Wine prices** Inexpensive **Cuisine** *Italian* **Menu prices** *$15–$29*

COSIMO'S ON UNION 🍷
1217 Route 300, Newburgh, NY 12550; (845) 567-1556 **Wine list** *California, Italy* **Wine prices** *Moderate* **Corkage** *$10* **Cuisine** *Italian/Californian* **Menu prices** *$15–$30*

CRABTREE'S KITTLE HOUSE INN 🍷🍷🍷
11 Kittle Road, Chappaqua, NY 10514; (914) 666-8044 **Wine list** *Burgundy, Rhône, California, Germany, Italy* **Wine selections** *5,200* **Number of bottles** *62,000* **Wine prices** *Moderate* **Cuisine** *Contemporary American* **Menu prices** *$17–$32* **Credit cards** *AX, MC, VS, DV*
Grand Award since 1994

THE CRAFTSMAN HOUSE 🍷
7300 E. Genesse St., Fayetteville, NY 13066; (315) 637-9999 **Wine list** *California* **Wine prices** Inexpensive **Corkage** *$12* **Cuisine** *Regional* **Menu prices** *$14–$26*

CRAZY DOG 🍷
123 Montauk Highway, Westhampton Beach, NY 11978; (516) 288-1444 **Wine list** *California, Italy, France* **Wine prices** *Moderate* **Cuisine** *American* **Menu prices** *$17–$32*

CRIPPLE CREEK RESTAURANT 🍷
22 Garden St., Rhinebeck, NY 12572; (845) 876-4355 **Wine list** *California, France* **Wine prices** *Moderate* **Cuisine** *American* **Menu prices** *$23–$36*

ECCO 🍷
2370 Jericho Turnpike, Garden City Park, NY 11040; (516) 739-0505 **Wine list** *Italy* **Wine prices** *Moderate* **Cuisine** *Northern Italian* **Menu prices** *$17–$32*

EMERSON INN & SPA 🍷🍷
146 Mount Pleasant Road, Mount Tremper, NY 12457; (845) 688-7900 **Wine list** *California, France* **Wine prices** *Moderate* **Corkage** *$35* **Cuisine** *Continental* **Menu prices** *Prix fixe only; $36*

ENOTECA OF LOCUST VALLEY 🍷
146 Birch Hill Road, Locust Valley, NY 11560; (516) 671-9486 **Wine list** *California, France, Italy* **Wine prices** *Expensive* **Corkage** *$20* **Cuisine** *French/Northern Italian* **Menu prices** *$21–$38*

FIDDLEHEADS AMERICAN FISH HOUSE & GRILL 🍷
62 South St., Oyster Bay, NY 11771; (516) 922-2999 **Wine list** *California* **Wine prices** *Moderate* **Cuisine** *Seafood* **Menu prices** *$18–$32*

FINCH TAVERN 🍷
592 Route 22, Croton Falls, NY 10519; (914) 277-4580 **Wine list** *California, France* **Wine prices** *Moderate* **Corkage** *$15* **Cuisine** *Contemporary American* **Menu prices** *$18–$29*

40 WEST 🍷
40 W. Market St., Rhinebeck, NY 12572; (845) 876-2214 **Wine list** *California* **Wine prices** Inexpensive **Corkage** *$15* **Cuisine** *Contemporary* **Menu prices** *$16–$24*

FRANKIE & JOHNNIE'S STEAKHOUSE 🍷
77 Purchase St., Rye, NY 10580; (914) 925-3900 **Wine list** *California* **Wine prices** *Moderate* **Cuisine** *Steak house* **Menu prices** *$19–$38*

FRIENDS LAKE INN 🍷🍷🍷
Friends Lake Inn, 963 Friends Lake Road, Chestertown, NY 12817; (518) 494-4751 **Wine list** *California, Bordeaux, Burgundy, Rhône, Germany* **Wine selections** *2,440* **Number of bottles** *21,600* **Wine prices** *Moderate* **Cuisine** *Contemporary American* **Menu prices** *$22–$38* **Credit cards** *AX, MC, VS*
Grand Award since 1997

GAGE & TOLLNER 🍷
372 Fulton St., Brooklyn, NY 11201; (718) 875-5181 **Wine list** *France, California, Italy* **Wine prices** *Moderate* **Cuisine** *American/continental* **Menu prices** *$35–$45*

THE GINGER MAN 🍷
234 Western Ave., Albany, NY 12203; (518) 427-5963 **Wine list** *California* **Wine prices** *Moderate* **Cuisine** *American* **Menu prices** *$11–$20*

THE GIRAFFE ROOM 🍷
The Inn at Great Neck, 30 Cutter Mill Road, Great Neck, NY 11021; (516) 773-2000 **Wine list** *California* **Wine prices** Inexpensive **Corkage** *$15* **Cuisine** *American/continental* **Menu prices** *$19–$30*

GLOBE BAR & GRILL 🍷
1879 Palmer Ave., Larchmont, NY 10538; (914) 833-8600 **Wine list** *France, California* **Wine prices** *Moderate* **Corkage** *$20* **Cuisine** *American* **Menu prices** *$19–$30*

THE GRILL AT STRATHALLAN 🍷🍷
550 East Ave., Rochester, NY 14607; (585) 454-1880 **Wine list** *Italy, California* **Wine prices** *Moderate* **Corkage** *$25* **Cuisine** *American* **Menu prices** *$19–$32*

HEATHER'S OPEN CUCINA 🍷
12 N. Broadway, Nyack, NY 10960; (845) 358-8686 **Wine list** *Italy, California* **Wine prices** *Moderate* **Corkage** *$25* **Cuisine** *Contemporary Italian* **Menu prices** *$18–$30*

THE HEIGHTS CAFÉ & GRILL 🍷
903 Hanshaw Road, Ithaca, NY 14850; (607) 257-4144 **Wine list** *California, Italy* **Wine prices** *Moderate* **Corkage** *$20* **Cuisine** *American* **Menu prices** *$23–$28*

HEMINGWAY'S 🍷
1885 Wantagh Ave., Wantagh, NY 11793; (516) 781-2700 **Wine list** *California* **Wine prices** *Moderate* **Corkage** *$15* **Cuisine** *Contemporary American* **Menu prices** *$12–$25*

HENRY'S END RESTAURANT 🍷
44 Henry St., Brooklyn, NY 11201; (718) 834-1776 **Wine list** *California* **Wine prices** *Moderate* **Cuisine** *Contemporary American* **Menu prices** *$15–$21*

HUDSON HOUSE RIVER INN 🍷
2 Main St., Cold Spring, NY 10516; (845) 265-9355 **Wine list** *California* **Wine prices** *Moderate* **Cuisine** *Contemporary American* **Menu prices** *$18–$24*

HUDSON'S RIBS & FISH 🍷
1099 Route 9, Fishkill, NY 12524; (845) 297-5002 **Wine list** *California* **Wine prices** Inexpensive **Cuisine** *Steak house/seafood* **Menu prices** *$14–$23*

INN AT STONE CREEK 🍷
31 Route 376, Hopewell Junction, NY 12533; (845) 227-6631 **Wine list** *California* **Wine prices** *Moderate* **Cuisine** *American* **Menu prices** *$17–$25*

IRISES CAFÉ & WINE BAR 🍷
20-22 City Hall Place, Plattsburgh, NY 12901; (518) 566-7000 **Wine list** *California* **Wine prices** Inexpensive **Cuisine** *Contemporary American* **Menu prices** *$10–$20*

JACQUES CARTIER DINING ROOM 🍷
Riveredge Resort Hotel, 17 Holland St., Alexandria Bay, NY 13607; (315) 482-9917 **Wine list** *California, New York* **Wine prices** *Moderate* **Cuisine** *French* **Menu prices** *$24–$32*

JAMES LANE CAFÉ 🍷
Hedges Inn, 74 James Lane, East Hampton, NY 11937; (631) 324-7100 **Wine list** *California* **Wine prices** *Moderate* **Cuisine** *American* **Menu prices** *$18–$60*

JIMBO'S CLUB AT THE POINT 🍷
7201 State Route 8, Brant Lake, NY 12815; (518) 494-4460 **Wine list** *California* **Wine prices** *Moderate* **Cuisine** *American* **Menu prices** *$18–$26*

JUST A TASTE WINE & TAPAS BAR 🍷
116 N. Aurora St., Ithaca, NY 14850; (607) 277-9463 **Wine list** *California, Italy, New York* **Wine prices** Inexpensive **Corkage** *$5* **Cuisine** *Contemporary* **Menu prices** *$10–$14*

KETTLE LAKES RESTAURANT 🍷
5785 Route 80, Tully, NY 13159; (315) 696-3663 **Wine list** *California* **Wine prices** *Moderate* **Cuisine** *American* **Menu prices** *$18–$29*

KING UMBERTO 🍷
1343 Hempstead Turnpike, Elmont, NY 11003; (516) 352-3232 **Wine list** *California, Italy* **Wine prices** *Moderate* **Cuisine** *Italian* **Menu prices** *$14–$28*

THE KNOTTY PINE RESTAURANT 🍷
2776 Route 28, Thendara, NY 13472; (315) 369-6859 **Wine list** *California* **Wine prices** Inexpensive **Corkage** *$15* **Cuisine** *American* **Menu prices** *$11–$39*

LA CRÉMAILLÈRE 🍷🍷
46 Bedford-Banksville Road, Banksville, NY 10506; (914) 234-9647 **Wine list** *France* **Wine prices** *Moderate* **Corkage** *$60* **Cuisine** *French* **Menu prices** *$21–$36*

LAKE PLACID LODGE 🍷🍷
Whiteface Inn Road, Lake Placid, NY 12946; (518) 523-2700 **Wine list** *California, Bordeaux* **Wine prices** *Moderate* **Cuisine** *Contemporary American* **Menu prices** *$28–$36*

LEGAL SEA FOODS 🍷
Walt Whitman Mall, Huntington Station, NY 11746; (631) 271-9777 **Wine list** *California* **Wine prices** Inexpensive **Cuisine** *Seafood* **Menu prices** *$11–$48*

LEGAL SEA FOODS 🍷
4304 Palisades Center Drive, West Nyack, NY 10994; (845) 353-5757 **Wine list** *California* **Wine prices** Inexpensive **Cuisine** *Seafood* **Menu prices** *$11–$47*

LEMON GRASS 🍷🍷
238 W. Jefferson St., Syracuse, NY 13202; (315) 475-1111 **Wine list** *California, France* **Wine prices** *Moderate* **Cuisine** *Thai/Pacific Rim* **Menu prices** *$15–$25*

LINCKLAEN HOUSE 🍷
79 Albany St., Cazenovia, NY 13035; (315) 655-3461 **Wine list** *California, France* **Wine prices** *Moderate* **Cuisine** *American* **Menu prices** *$13–$19*

THE LODGE RESTAURANT 🍷
1 Nelson Ave., Saratoga Springs, NY 12866; (518) 584-7988 **Wine list** *California, France* **Wine prices** *Moderate* **Cuisine** *American* **Menu prices** *$10–$46*

LONGFELLOWS RESTAURANT 🍷
Longfellows Inn, 500 Union Ave., Saratoga Springs, NY 12866; (518) 587-0108 **Wine list** *California* **Wine prices** *Moderate* **Corkage** *$15* **Cuisine** *American* **Menu prices** *$14–$30*

LOUIS XVI 🍷
600 S. Ocean Ave., Patchogue, NY 11772; (516) 654-8970 **Wine list** *France, California* **Wine prices** *Expensive* **Corkage** *$25* **Cuisine** *Contemporary French* **Menu prices** *Prix fixe only; $71–$160*

LUIGI'S RESTAURANT & BAR 🍷
265-21 Union Turnpike, New Hyde Park, NY 11040; (718) 347-7136 **Wine list** *California, Italy* **Wine prices** *Moderate* **Corkage** *$10* **Cuisine** *Italian/American* **Menu prices** *$10–$16*

LUSARDI'S RESTAURANT 🍷
1885 Palmer Ave., Larchmont, NY 10538; (914) 834-5555 **Wine list** *Italy, California* **Wine prices** *Moderate* **Cuisine** *Northern Italian* **Menu prices** *$15–$25*

LUSHANE'S 🍷
8 N. Broadway, Nyack, NY 10960; (845) 358-5556 **Wine list** *France, California* **Wine prices** *Moderate* **Corkage** *$25* **Cuisine** *Contemporary* **Menu prices** *$20–$30*

MACKENZIE-CHILDS
3260 State Route 90, Aurora, NY 13026; (315) 364-9688 **Wine list** *New York, California* **Wine prices** *Moderate* **Cuisine** *Contemporary* **Menu prices** *$17–$26*

THE MAIDSTONE ARMS
207 Main St., East Hampton, NY 11937; (631) 324-5494 **Wine list** *France, California* **Wine prices** *Moderate* **Cuisine** *Contemporary American* **Menu prices** *$20–$32*

MAMMA LOMBARDI'S
400 Furrows Road, Holbrook, NY 11741; (631) 737-0774 **Wine list** *Italy, California* **Wine prices** *Moderate* **Cuisine** *Italian* **Menu prices** *$13–$27*

MARCO POLO RISTORANTE
345 Court St., Brooklyn, NY 11231; (718) 852-5015 **Wine list** *Italy* **Wine prices** *Moderate* **Cuisine** *Italian* **Menu prices** *$18–$24*

MARIO'S VIA ABRUZZI
2740 Monroe Ave., Rochester, NY 14618; (585) 271-1111 **Wine list** *Italy, California* **Wine prices** *Moderate* **Corkage** *$10* **Cuisine** *Italian* **Menu prices** *$13–$28*

MAXIE'S SUPPER CLUB & OYSTER BAR
635 W. State St., Ithaca, NY 14850; (607) 272-4136 **Wine list** *France, New York* **Wine prices** *Moderate* **Corkage** *$10* **Cuisine** *Seafood* **Menu prices** *$12–$24*

MAZZI
493 E. Jericho Turnpike, Huntington, NY 11746; (631) 421-3390 **Wine list** *California, Italy* **Wine prices** *Moderate* **Cuisine** *Continental* **Menu prices** *$16–$30*

MCKINNEY & DOYLE FINE FOODS CAFÉ
10 Charles Colman Blvd., Pawling, NY 12564; (845) 855-3875 **Wine list** *California* **Wine prices** *Moderate* **Corkage** *$10* **Cuisine** *American* **Menu prices** *$16–$22*

MILANO RESTAURANT
594 New Loudon Road, Latham, NY 12210; (518) 783-3334 **Wine list** *California, Italy* **Wine prices** *Moderate* **Corkage** *$5* **Cuisine** *Northern Italian* **Menu prices** *$9–$25*

MIRBEAU INN & SPA
851 W. Genesee St., Skaneateles, NY 13152; (315) 685-5006 **Wine list** *California* **Wine prices** *Moderate* **Corkage** *$15* **Cuisine** *French* **Menu prices** *$27–$34*

MOHONK MOUNTAIN HOUSE 🍷
Lake Mohonk, New Paltz, NY 12561; (800) 772-6646 **Wine list** *France, California* **Wine prices** *Expensive* **Cuisine** *Continental* **Menu prices** *$45–$50*

MORTON'S OF CHICAGO 🍷
777 Northern Blvd., Great Neck, NY 11020; (516) 498-2950 **Wine list** *California* **Wine prices** *Expensive* **Corkage** *$25* **Cuisine** *Steak house* **Menu prices** *$22–$65*

MOSCATO RISTORANTE 🍷
874 Scarsdale Ave., Scarsdale, NY 10583; (914) 723-5700 **Wine list** *Italy, California* **Wine prices** *Moderate* **Cuisine** *Northern Italian* **Menu prices** *$16–$25*

NICOLE'S 🍷
Canandaigua Inn on The Lake, 770 S. Main St., Canandaigua, NY 14424; (585) 394-7800 **Wine list** *New York, California* **Wine prices** Inexpensive **Cuisine** *American/international* **Menu prices** *$14–$24*

THE 1906 RESTAURANT 🍷
41 Lower Main St., Callicoon, NY 12723; (845) 887-1906 **Wine list** *California* **Wine prices** *Moderate* **Cuisine** *American* **Menu prices** *$17–$25*

NUMBER 5 🍷
33 S. Washington St., Binghamton, NY 13903; (607) 723-0555 **Wine list** *California* **Wine prices** Inexpensive **Corkage** *$15* **Cuisine** *Steak house* **Menu prices** *$16–$29*

OLD DROVERS INN 🍷
196 E. Duncan Hill Road, Dover Plains, NY 12522; (845) 832-9311 **Wine list** *France, Italy* **Wine prices** *Moderate* **Cuisine** *Contemporary American* **Menu prices** *$17–$35*

OLIVER'S RESTAURANT 🍷
2095 Delaware Ave., Buffalo, NY 14216; (716) 877-9662 **Wine list** *California, France* **Wine prices** *Moderate* **Cuisine** *American* **Menu prices** *$18–$34*

OZNOT'S DISH 🍷
79 Berry St., Brooklyn, NY 11211; (718) 599-6596 **Wine list** *California, France, Germany* **Wine prices** *Moderate* **Cuisine** *Mediterranean* **Menu prices** *$11–$20*

THE PALM 🍷
Huntting Inn, 94 Main St., East Hampton, NY 11937; (631) 324-0410 **Wine list** *California* **Wine prices** *Moderate* **Cuisine** *Steak house* **Menu prices** *$20–$60*

PASCALE WINE BAR & RESTAURANT
204 W. Fayette St., Syracuse, NY 13202; (315) 471-3040 **Wine list** *France, California* **Wine prices** *Moderate* **Cuisine** *Contemporary American* **Menu prices** *$15–$25*

PAT RUSSO'S DUGOUT
43 Main St., South Glens Falls, NY 12803; (518) 793-9560 **Wine list** *California* **Wine prices** *Inexpensive* **Cuisine** *Italian/American* **Menu prices** *$11–$27*

THE PLAZA CAFÉ
61 Hill St., Southampton, NY 11968; (631) 283-9323 **Wine list** *California* **Wine prices** *Moderate* **Cuisine** *Contemporary American/seafood* **Menu prices** *$22–$40*

POLO RESTAURANT
Garden City Hotel, 45 Seventh St., Garden City, NY 11530; (516) 747-3000 **Wine list** *California, France* **Wine prices** *Moderate* **Cuisine** *American/European* **Menu prices** *$23–$35*

THE PROSPECT RESTAURANT
Scribner Hollow Lodge, Route 23A, Hunter, NY 12442; (518) 263-4211 **Wine list** *California, New York* **Wine prices** *Moderate* **Cuisine** *American* **Menu prices** *$16–$29*

PROVENCE
Stuyvesant Plaza, Albany, NY 12203; (518) 689-7777 **Wine list** *California, France* **Wine prices** *Inexpensive* **Corkage** *$12* **Cuisine** *Mediterranean* **Menu prices** *$12–$26*

P.S. RESTAURANT
Giant Plaza, 100 Rano Blvd., Vestal, NY 13850; (607) 770-0056 **Wine list** *California, France* **Wine prices** *Inexpensive* **Cuisine** *French/Thai* **Menu prices** *$14–$29*

RED/BAR BRASSERIE
210 Hampton Road, Southampton, NY 11968; (631) 283-0704 **Wine list** *California, France* **Wine prices** *Moderate* **Corkage** *$25* **Cuisine** *American* **Menu prices** *$19–$34*

RICHARD'S FREESTYLE CUISINE
51 Main St., Lake Placid, NY 12946; (518) 523-5900 **Wine list** *California, France* **Wine prices** *Moderate* **Cuisine** *American* **Menu prices** *$18–$26*

THE RIO BAMBA
282 Alexander St., Rochester, NY 14607; (585) 244-8680 **Wine list** *California, France, Italy* **Wine prices** *Moderate* **Cuisine** *French* **Menu prices** *$24–$29*

THE RIVER CAFÉ 🍷🍷
1 Water St., Brooklyn, NY 11201; (718) 522-5200 **Wine list** *France, California* **Wine prices** *Expensive* **Cuisine** *American/continental* **Menu prices** *Prix fixe only; $70*

RIVERSIDE INN 🍷🍷
115 S. Water St., Lewiston, NY 14092; (716) 754-8206 **Wine list** *California, France* **Wine prices** Inexpensive **Cuisine** *Continental* **Menu prices** *$10–$60*

RUTH'S CHRIS STEAK HOUSE 🍷
600 Old Country Road, Garden City, NY 11530; (516) 222-0220 **Wine list** *California, Italy* **Wine prices** *Moderate* **Corkage** *$10* **Cuisine** *Steak house* **Menu prices** *$18–$37*

RUTH'S CHRIS STEAK HOUSE 🍷
Marriott Hotel, 670 White Plains Road, Tarrytown, NY 10591; (914) 631-3311 **Wine list** *California* **Wine prices** *Moderate* **Corkage** *$15* **Cuisine** *Steak house* **Menu prices** *$19–$69*

SAMM'S RESTAURANT & LOUNGE 🍷
8901 Third Ave., Brooklyn, NY 11209; (718) 238-0606 **Wine list** *California* **Wine prices** *Moderate* **Cuisine** *Contemporary American* **Menu prices** *$15–$24*

SAN MARCO RISTORANTE 🍷
658 Motor Parkway, Hauppauge, NY 11788; (516) 273-0088 **Wine list** *France, California* **Wine prices** *Moderate* **Cuisine** *Northern Italian* **Menu prices** *$14–$30*

SARGO'S 🍷
458 Union Ave., Saratoga Springs, NY 12866; (518) 583-4653 **Wine list** *California* **Wine prices** *Moderate* **Cuisine** *American* **Menu prices** *$19–$52*

SCOTCH 'N SIRLOIN 🍷
3687 Erie Blvd. E., Dewitt, NY 13214; (315) 446-1771 **Wine list** *California* **Wine prices** *Moderate* **Corkage** *$10* **Cuisine** *Steak house* **Menu prices** *$14–$72*

SCRIMSHAW 🍷
The Desmond, 660 Albany-Shaker Road, Albany, NY 12211; (518) 452-5801 **Wine list** *California, France* **Wine prices** *Moderate* **Corkage** *$17* **Cuisine** *Continental/American* **Menu prices** *$26–$24*

THE SEAFOOD BARGE 🍷
62980 Route 25, Southold, NY 11971; (631) 765-3010
Wine list *New York* **Wine prices** *Moderate* **Corkage** *$12*
Cuisine *Contemporary American* **Menu prices** *$18–$32*

75 MAIN 🍷
75 Main St., Southampton, NY 11968; (631) 283-7575
Wine list *California, Italy, France* **Wine prices** *Expensive*
Cuisine *International* **Menu prices** *$16–$28*

TASTINGS 🍷
3195 Monroe Ave., Pittsford, NY 14618; (585) 381-1881
Wine list *California* **Wine prices** Inexpensive **Corkage** *$10*
Cuisine *Contemporary American* **Menu prices** *$11–$28*

TEQUILA SUNRISE 🍷
145 Larchmont Ave., Larchmont, NY 10538; (914) 834-6378 **Wine list** *Spain* **Wine prices** *Moderate* **Cuisine** *Mexican*
Menu prices *$12–$28*

THREE VILLAGE INN 🍷
150 Main St., Stony Brook, NY 11790; (631) 751-0555
Wine list *California* **Wine prices** *Moderate* **Cuisine** *American*
Menu prices *$28–$37*

TIERRA MAR RESTAURANT 🍷🍷
Westhampton Bath & Tennis Hotel, 231 Dune Road, Westhampton Beach, NY 11978; (631) 288-2700 **Wine list** *Bordeaux, California, Long Island, Italy, Germany* **Wine prices** *Moderate* **Corkage** *$25* **Cuisine** *Contemporary American* **Menu prices** *$18–$36*

TRILLIUM 🍷
The Sagamore, 110 Sagamore Road, Bolton Landing, NY 12814; (800) 358-3585 **Wine list** *California, France* **Wine prices** *Moderate* **Corkage** *$15* **Cuisine** *American* **Menu prices** *$27–$31*

TROUTBECK 🍷
Leedsville Road, Amenia, NY 12501; (845) 373-9681 **Wine list** *California, France* **Wine prices** *Moderate* **Cuisine** *Contemporary American* **Menu prices** *$19–$28*

UNION HOUSE 🍷
1108 Main St., Fishkill, NY 12524; (845) 896-6129 **Wine list** *California* **Wine prices** Inexpensive **Cuisine** *Steak house*
Menu prices *$18–$35*

VILLAGE TAVERN RESTAURANT & INN 🍷

30 Mechanic St., Hammondsport, NY 14840; (607) 569-2528 **Wine list** *New York* **Wine prices** Inexpensive **Cuisine** *Seafood* **Menu prices** *$10–$33*

WALK STREET 🍷

176 Seventh St., Garden City, NY 11530; (516) 746-2592 **Wine list** *California* **Wine prices** Inexpensive **Cuisine** *Contemporary American* **Menu prices** *$15–$27*

WATER'S EDGE RESTAURANT 🍷🍷

44th Drive at East River, Long Island City, NY 11101; (718) 482-0033 **Wine list** *California, France* **Wine prices** *Expensive* **Cuisine** *American* **Menu prices** *$20–$32*

THE WILLETT HOUSE 🍷🍷

20 Willett Ave., Port Chester, NY 10573; (914) 939-7500 **Wine list** *California, Italy* **Wine prices** *Moderate* **Cuisine** *Steak house* **Menu prices** *$20–$45*

THE WINE BAR 🍷

417 Broadway, Saratoga Springs, NY 12866; (518) 584-8777 **Wine list** *California* **Wine prices** *Moderate* **Cuisine** *Contemporary American* **Menu prices** *$12–$20*

THE WOULD RESTAURANT 🍷

The Inn at Applewood, 120 North Road, Highland, NY 12528; (845) 691-9883 **Wine list** *California, France* **Wine prices** Inexpensive **Corkage** *$10* **Cuisine** *Contemporary American* **Menu prices** *$17–$26*

YONO'S 🍷

64 Colvin Ave., Albany, NY 12206; (518) 436-7747 **Wine list** *California, France* **Wine prices** *Moderate* **Corkage** *$8* **Cuisine** *Continental/Indonesian* **Menu prices** *$17–$33*

NORTH CAROLINA

THE ANGUS BARN 🍷🍷🍷

9401 Glenwood Ave., Raleigh, NC 27617; (919) 781-2444 **Wine list** *California, Bordeaux* **Wine selections** *1,300* **Number of bottles** *26,000* **Wine prices** *Moderate* **Corkage** *$10* **Cuisine** *American* **Menu prices** *$25–$48* **Credit cards** *AX, MC, VS, DV*

Grand Award since 1989

BASIL'S TRATTORIA & WINE BAR
1720 Battleground Ave., Greensboro, NC 27408; (336) 333-9833 **Wine list** *California* **Wine prices** *Moderate* **Corkage** *$10* **Cuisine** *Tuscan* **Menu prices** *$12–$29*

B. CHRISTOPHER'S
2260 S. Church St., Burlington, NC 27215; (336) 222-1177 **Wine list** *California* **Wine prices** *Moderate* **Corkage** *$10* **Cuisine** *Contemporary regional* **Menu prices** *$13–$29*

BEEF BARN
400 St. Andrews Drive, Greenville, NC 27834; (252) 756-1161 **Wine list** *California* **Wine prices** *Moderate* **Cuisine** *Steak house* **Menu prices** *$10–$28*

BERT'S SEAFOOD GRILLE
2419 Spring Garden St., Greensboro, NC 27403; (336) 854-2314 **Wine list** *California* **Wine prices** Inexpensive **Corkage** *$7* **Cuisine** *American* **Menu prices** *$15–$25*

BIJOUX BRASSERIE & BAR
201 N. Tryon St., Charlotte, NC 28202; (704) 377-0900 **Wine list** *Bordeaux, Burgundy* **Wine prices** *Moderate* **Cuisine** *French/American* **Menu prices** *$12–$18*

BISTRO 100
100 N. Tryon St., Charlotte, NC 28202; (704) 344-0515 **Wine list** *California* **Wine prices** *Moderate* **Cuisine** *French/American* **Menu prices** *$17–$26*

BISTRO SOFIA
616 Dolley Madison Road, Greensboro, NC 27410; (336) 855-1313 **Wine list** *France, California* **Wine prices** *Moderate* **Corkage** *$10* **Cuisine** *Provençal* **Menu prices** *$14–$30*

THE BLUE POINT BAR & GRILL
1240 Duck Road, Duck, NC 27949; (252) 261-8090 **Wine list** *California* **Wine prices** *Moderate* **Corkage** *$15* **Cuisine** *Regional* **Menu prices** *$17–$27*

BONTERRA DINING & WINE ROOM
1829 Cleveland Ave., Charlotte, NC 28203; (704) 333-9463 **Wine list** *California* **Wine prices** *Moderate* **Corkage** *$12* **Cuisine** *Contemporary American* **Menu prices** *$20–$32*

BRIDGE TENDER RESTAURANT
1414 Airlie Road, Wrightsville Beach, NC 28480; (910) 256-4519 **Wine list** *California* **Wine prices** Inexpensive **Cuisine** *Regional* **Menu prices** *$16–$40*

CAFÉ ATLANTIQUE
1900 Eastwood Road, Wilmington, NC 28403; (910) 256-0995 **Wine list** *California, France* **Wine prices** *Moderate* **Corkage** *$25* **Cuisine** *French/American* **Menu prices** *$17–$30*

CAFFÈ PHOENIX
9 S. Front St., Wilmington, NC 28401; (910) 343-1395 **Wine list** *California, France* **Wine prices** *Moderate* **Cuisine** *Mediterranean/American* **Menu prices** *$12–$29*

CAMPANIA
6414 Rea Road, Charlotte, NC 28277; (704) 541-8505 **Wine list** *Italy* **Wine prices** *Moderate* **Corkage** *$15* **Cuisine** *Italian* **Menu prices** *$15–$27*

THE CAPITAL GRILLE
IJL Financial Center, 201 N. Tryon St., Charlotte, NC 28202; (704) 348-1400 **Wine list** *California, Bordeaux* **Wine prices** *Moderate* **Cuisine** *Steak house* **Menu prices** *$17–$32*

CAROLINA CROSSROADS
The Carolina Inn, 211 Pittsboro St., Chapel Hill, NC 27516; (919) 918-2777 **Wine list** *California* **Wine prices** *Moderate* **Cuisine** *Contemporary Southern* **Menu prices** *$18–$24*

CAROLINA DINING ROOM
Carolina Hotel at Pinehurst, Carolina Vista, Village of Pinehurst, NC 28374; (910) 235-8434 **Wine list** *California, France* **Wine prices** *Moderate* **Cuisine** *Continental/American* **Menu prices** *Prix fixe only; $45*

CHOPS AT SUNSET TERRACE
Grove Park Inn Resort & Spa, 290 Macon Ave., Asheville, NC 28804; (828) 252-2711 **Wine list** *California, France* **Wine prices** *Expensive* **Cuisine** *Steak house* **Menu prices** *$22–$45*

DAKOTAS
8140 Providence Road, Charlotte, NC 28277; (704) 541-9990 **Wine list** *California, France* **Wine prices** *Moderate* **Corkage** *$15* **Cuisine** *Southern American* **Menu prices** *$13–$24*

DANIEL'S PIZZA PASTA CAFÉ
1430 N.C. Highway 55, Apex, NC 27502; (919) 303-1006 **Wine list** *California, Italy* **Wine prices** *Moderate* **Cuisine** *Italian* **Menu prices** *$8–$19*

DELUXE
114 Market St., Wilmington, NC 28401; (910) 251-0333 **Wine list** *California* **Wine prices** *Moderate* **Corkage** *$10* **Cuisine** *Contemporary American* **Menu prices** *$15–$27*

1895
The Holly Inn, Carolina Vista, Village of Pinehurst, NC 28374; (910) 235-8434 **Wine list** *California* **Wine prices** *Moderate* **Cuisine** *American/continental* **Menu prices** *Prix fixe only; $65*

ELAINE'S ON FRANKLIN
454 W. Franklin St., Chapel Hill, NC 27516; (919) 960-2770 **Wine list** *California, France* **Wine prices** *Moderate* **Corkage** *$10* **Cuisine** *International* **Menu prices** *$16–$24*

ELIZABETH'S CAFÉ & WINERY
Scarborough Faire Shoppes, Duck, NC 27949; (252) 261-6145 **Wine list** *California, France* **Wine prices** *Moderate* **Cuisine** *French* **Menu prices** *$25–$32*

ENOTECA VIN
410 Glenwood Ave., Raleigh, NC 27603; (919) 834-3070 **Wine list** *Burgundy, Italy, Austria* **Wine prices** *Moderate* **Cuisine** *Contemporary American* **Menu prices** *$15–$25*

EXPRESSIONS
114 N. Main St., Hendersonville, NC 28792; (828) 693-8516 **Wine list** *California* **Wine prices** Inexpensive **Cuisine** *American* **Menu prices** *$17–$29*

FAIRVIEW
Washington Duke Inn & Golf Club, 3001 Cameron Blvd., Durham, NC 27706; (919) 490-0999 **Wine list** *California* **Wine prices** Inexpensive **Cuisine** *Contemporary* **Menu prices** *$19–$38*

FEARRINGTON HOUSE RESTAURANT
Fearrington House Inn, 2000 Fearrington Village Center, Pittsboro, NC 27312; (919) 542-2121 **Wine list** *France, California* **Wine prices** *Moderate* **Corkage** *$40* **Cuisine** *American* **Menu prices** *Prix fixe only; $79*

FOUR SQUARE
2701 Chapel Hill Road, Durham, NC 27707; (919) 401-9877 **Wine list** *California, France* **Wine prices** *Moderate* **Corkage** *$25* **Cuisine** *Contemporary American* **Menu prices** *$18–$29*

FRONT STREET GRILL AT STILLWATER
300 Front St., Beaufort, NC 28516; (252) 728-4956 **Wine list** *California* **Wine prices** *Moderate* **Corkage** *$20* **Cuisine** *International* **Menu prices** *$18–$26*

GABRIELLE'S
Richmond Hill Inn, 87 Richmond Hill Drive, Asheville, NC 28806; (828) 252-7313 **Wine list** *California, France* **Wine prices** *Moderate* **Corkage** *$20* **Cuisine** *Contemporary American* **Menu prices** *$30–$45*

GREEN VALLEY GRILL
The O. Henry Hotel, 622 Green Valley Road, Greensboro, NC 27408; (336) 854-2015 **Wine list** *California* **Wine prices** *Moderate* **Cuisine** *European* **Menu prices** *$13–$27*

THE GREENERY RESTAURANT & LOUNGE
148 Tunnel Road, Asheville, NC 28805; (828) 253-2809 **Wine list** *California* **Wine prices** *Moderate* **Corkage** *$10* **Cuisine** *American/French* **Menu prices** *$15–$25*

GROUPER'S GRILLE & WINE BAR
790 Ocean Trail, Corolla, NC 27927; (252) 453-4077 **Wine list** *California* **Wine prices** Inexpensive **Cuisine** *International* **Menu prices** *$20–$38*

HEIRLOOMS
The Inn at Ragged Gardens, 203 Sunset Drive, Blowing Rock, NC 28605; (828) 295-9703 **Wine list** *California* **Wine prices** Inexpensive **Corkage** *$10* **Cuisine** *Contemporary American* **Menu prices** *$17–$32*

HIGHLAND LAKE INN
Highland Lake Road, Flat Rock, NC 28731; (828) 696-9094 **Wine list** *California, France* **Wine prices** *Moderate* **Corkage** *$8* **Cuisine** *Contemporary American* **Menu prices** *$16–$24*

HORIZONS
Grove Park Inn Resort & Spa, 290 Macon Ave., Asheville, NC 28804; (828) 252-2711 **Wine list** *California, France* **Wine prices** *Moderate* **Corkage** *$10* **Cuisine** *American* **Menu prices** *$35–$50*

IL PALIO
The Siena, 1505 E. Franklin St., Chapel Hill, NC 27514; (800) 223-7379 **Wine list** *Italy* **Wine prices** *Moderate* **Corkage** *$20* **Cuisine** *Italian* **Menu prices** *$19–$25*

IL PARADISO STEAK & CHOP HOUSE 🍷
39 Elm St., Asheville, NC 28801; (828) 281-4310 **Wine list** *Italy, California* **Wine prices** *Moderate* **Cuisine** *Steak house* **Menu prices** *$16–$30*

INN ON CHURCH ST. 🍷
201 Third Ave. W., West Hendersonville, NC 28739; (800) 330-3836 **Wine list** *California* **Wine prices** *Moderate* **Corkage** *$10* **Cuisine** *Italian* **Menu prices** *$18–$26*

JACKALOPE'S VIEW 🍷
Archers Mountain Inn, 2489 Beach Mountain Parkway, Banner Elk, NC 28604; (828) 898-9004 **Wine list** *California* **Wine prices** Inexpensive **Cuisine** *Continental* **Menu prices** *$15–$27*

J. BASUL NOBLE'S RESTAURANT 🍷
101 S. Main St., High Point, NC 27260; (336) 889-3354 **Wine list** *California, France* **Wine prices** *Moderate* **Corkage** *$10* **Cuisine** *French/Italian* **Menu prices** *$12–$31*

LAKESIDE RESTAURANT 🍷
531 Smallwood Ave. on Harris Lake, Highlands, NC 28741; (828) 526-9419 **Wine list** *California* **Wine prices** *Moderate* **Corkage** *$25* **Cuisine** *American* **Menu prices** *$18–$32*

LARKIN'S ON THE LAKE 🍷
1020 Memorial Highway, Lake Lure, NC 28746; (828) 625-4075 **Wine list** *California* **Wine prices** Inexpensive **Cuisine** *Contemporary American* **Menu prices** *$12–$30*

THE LEFT BANK 🍷
The Sanderling, 1461 Duck Road, Duck, NC 27949; (252) 261-4111 **Wine list** *California* **Wine prices** *Moderate* **Corkage** *$25* **Cuisine** *American/French* **Menu prices** *$45–$70*

THE LIFESAVING STATION 🍷
The Sanderling, 1461 Duck Road, Duck, NC 27949; (252) 449-6654 **Wine list** *California* **Wine prices** *Moderate* **Corkage** *$25* **Cuisine** *Contemporary American* **Menu prices** *$18–$26*

LOUISIANA PURCHASE FOOD & SPIRITS 🍷🍷
397 Shawnechaw Ave., Banner Elk, NC 28604; (828) 963-5087 **Wine list** *California, France, Italy* **Wine prices** *Moderate* **Cuisine** *New Orleans/French/Northern Italian* **Menu prices** *$16–$32*

LUCKY 32 🍷
7307 Tryon Road, Carey, NC 27511; (919) 233-1632 **Wine list** *California* **Wine prices** Inexpensive **Cuisine** *Regional* **Menu prices** *$13–$22*

LUCKY 32 🍷
1421 Westover Terrace, Greensboro, NC 27408; (336) 370-0707 **Wine list** *California* **Wine prices** Inexpensive **Corkage** *No charge* **Cuisine** *Regional* **Menu prices** *$11–$23*

LUCKY 32 🍷
832 Spring Forest Road, Raleigh, NC 27609; (919) 876-9932 **Wine list** *California* **Wine prices** Inexpensive **Cuisine** *Regional* **Menu prices** *$11–$23*

LUCKY 32 🍷
109 S. Stratford Road, Winston-Salem, NC 27104; (336) 777-0032 **Wine list** *California* **Wine prices** Inexpensive **Corkage** *No charge* **Cuisine** *Regional* **Menu prices** *$11–$23*

LUIGI'S ITALIAN RESTAURANT & BAR 🍷
528 N. McPherson Church Road, Fayetteville, NC 28303; (910) 864-1810 **Wine list** *Italy, California* **Wine prices** Inexpensive **Corkage** *$10* **Cuisine** *Italian* **Menu prices** *$10–$24*

MARISOL 🍷
5834 E. High Point Road, Greensboro, NC 27407; (336) 852-3303 **Wine list** *California* **Wine prices** *Moderate* **Corkage** *$12* **Cuisine** *French/American* **Menu prices** *$28–$36*

MARK'S ON WESTOVER 🍷
1310 Westover Terrace, Greensboro, NC 27408; (336) 273-9090 **Wine list** *California* **Wine prices** *Moderate* **Corkage** *$8* **Cuisine** *Continental* **Menu prices** *$12–$27*

MCINTOSH'S STEAKS & SEAFOOD 🍷
1812 South Blvd., Charlotte, NC 28203; (704) 342-1088 **Wine list** *California, France* **Wine prices** *Moderate* **Corkage** *$15* **Cuisine** *Steak house* **Menu prices** *$20–$30*

MEETING HOUSE 🍷
801 Providence Road, Charlotte, NC 28207; (704) 334-6338 **Wine list** *California* **Wine prices** Inexpensive **Corkage** *$15* **Cuisine** *Contemporary American* **Menu prices** *$17–$29*

THE MELTING POT
230 E. WT Harris Blvd., Charlotte, NC 28262; (704) 548-2432 **Wine list** *California* **Wine prices** *Moderate* **Cuisine** *Fondue* **Menu prices** *$15–$36*

THE MELTING POT
Kings Court Plaza, 901 S. Kings Drive, Charlotte, NC 28204; (704) 334-4400 **Wine list** *California* **Wine prices** *Moderate* **Cuisine** *Fondue* **Menu prices** *$15–$36*

MICKEY & MOOCH
9723 Sam Furr Road, Huntersville, NC 28078; (704) 895-6654 **Wine list** *California* **Wine prices** *Moderate* **Cuisine** *Steak house* **Menu prices** *$10–$27*

MICKEY & MOOCH - THE OTHER JOINT
8128 Providence Road, Charlotte, NC 28277; (704) 752-8080 **Wine list** *California* **Wine prices** *Moderate* **Corkage** *$10* **Cuisine** *American* **Menu prices** *$10–$25*

MIMOSA GRILL
327 S. Tryon St., Charlotte, NC 28202; (704) 343-0700 **Wine list** *California, Italy* **Wine prices** *Moderate* **Corkage** *$15* **Cuisine** *American* **Menu prices** *$17–$25*

MORTON'S OF CHICAGO
227 W. Trade St., Charlotte, NC 28202; (704) 333-2602 **Wine list** *California* **Wine prices** *Expensive* **Cuisine** *Steak house* **Menu prices** *$20–$34*

MOSAIC RESTAURANT & WINE BAR
4608 W. Market St., Greensboro, NC 27407; (336) 297-4881 **Wine list** *California* **Wine prices** *Inexpensive* **Corkage** *$7* **Cuisine** *Contemporary American* **Menu prices** *$10–$32*

NANA'S
2514 University Drive, Durham, NC 27707; (919) 493-8545 **Wine list** *California, France* **Wine prices** *Moderate* **Corkage** *$15* **Cuisine** *American/French/Italian* **Menu prices** *$17–$25*

NICOLETTA'S ITALIAN CAFÉ
106 Ocean Trail, Corolla, NC 27927; (252) 453-4004 **Wine list** *Italy* **Wine prices** *Moderate* **Corkage** *$15* **Cuisine** *Italian* **Menu prices** *$16–$28*

NINA'S
Harvest Plaza, 8801 Leadmine Road, Raleigh, NC 27615; (919) 845-1122 **Wine list** *Italy* **Wine prices** *Moderate* **Corkage** *$15* **Cuisine** *Italian* **Menu prices** *$12–$24*

NOBLE'S GRILLE
380 Knollwood St., Winston-Salem, NC 27103; (336) 777-8477 **Wine list** *California, France* **Wine prices** Inexpensive **Cuisine** *French/Mediterranean* **Menu prices** *$13–$30*

NOBLE'S RESTAURANT
6801 Morrison Blvd., Charlotte, NC 28211; (704) 367-9463 **Wine list** *California* **Wine prices** *Moderate* **Corkage** *$15* **Cuisine** *French/Mediterranean/Tuscan* **Menu prices** *$14–$31*

ON THE VERANDAH
1536 Franklin Road, Highlands, NC 28741; (828) 526-2338 **Wine list** *California* **Wine prices** *Moderate* **Cuisine** *Contemporary American* **Menu prices** *$20–$30*

THE PAISLEY PINEAPPLE
345 S. Elm St., Greensboro, NC 27401; (336) 279-8488 **Wine list** *California, France* **Wine prices** Inexpensive **Corkage** *$10* **Cuisine** *American/French* **Menu prices** *$14–$25*

THE PALM
6705-B Phillips Place Court, Charlotte, NC 28210; (704) 552-7256 **Wine list** *California* **Wine prices** *Moderate* **Cuisine** *Steak house* **Menu prices** *$20–$40*

PALOMINO
525 N. Tryon St., Charlotte, NC 28202; (704) 373-9499 **Wine list** *California* **Wine prices** *Moderate* **Cuisine** *Mediterranean* **Menu prices** *$14–$29*

PENGUIN ISLE SOUNDSIDE GRILL & BAR
6708 S. Croaton Highway MP 16, Nags Head, NC 27959; (252) 441-2637 **Wine list** *California* **Wine prices** *Moderate* **Corkage** *$7* **Cuisine** *Californian* **Menu prices** *$14–$30*

THE PINE CREST INN
85 Pine Crest Lane, Tryon, NC 28782; (828) 859-9135 **Wine list** *California* **Wine prices** Inexpensive **Corkage** *$15* **Cuisine** *Contemporary Southern* **Menu prices** *$19–$29*

PORT LAND GRILLE
1908 Eastwood Road, Wilmington, NC 28403; (910) 256-6056 **Wine list** *California* **Wine prices** *Moderate* **Corkage** *$25* **Cuisine** *Contemporary American* **Menu prices** *$17–$35*

PRIME ONLY STEAK & SEAFOOD
9800 Leesville Road, Raleigh, NC 27613; (919) 844-1216 **Wine list** *California* **Wine prices** Inexpensive **Corkage** *$8* **Cuisine** *Steak house* **Menu prices** *$14–$39*

Grand Award | Best of Award of Excellence | Award of Excellence

PROVIDENCE BISTRO AT UNIVERSITY PLACE 🍷
8708 J.W. Clay Blvd., Charlotte, NC 28262; (704) 549-0050 **Wine list** *California* **Wine prices** *Moderate* **Corkage** *$15* **Cuisine** *Contemporary American* **Menu prices** *$10–$20*

PROVIDENCE CAFÉ 🍷
110 Perrin Place, Charlotte, NC 28207; (704) 376-2008 **Wine list** *California* **Wine prices** *Moderate* **Cuisine** *American* **Menu prices** *$6–$22*

REVIVAL GRILL 🍷
601 Milner Drive, Greensboro, NC 27410; (336) 297-0950 **Wine list** *California* **Wine prices** Inexpensive **Cuisine** *American* **Menu prices** *$6–$18*

RISTORANTE PAOLETTI 🍷🍷
440 Main St., Highlands, NC 28741; (828) 526-4906 **Wine list** *California, Piedmont, Bordeaux* **Wine prices** *Moderate* **Cuisine** *Italian* **Menu prices** *$17–$28*

ROY'S RIVERBOAT LANDING RESTAURANT 🍷
2 Market St., Wilmington, NC 28401; (910) 763-7227 **Wine list** *California* **Wine prices** *Moderate* **Cuisine** *Regional/Asian/French/Mediterranean* **Menu prices** *$17–$32*

RUTH'S CHRIS STEAK HOUSE 🍷
1130 Buck Jones Road, Raleigh, NC 27606; (919) 468-1133 **Wine list** *California* **Wine prices** *Moderate* **Cuisine** *Steak house* **Menu prices** *$18–$34*

THE SAVOY RESTAURANT 🍷
641 Merrimon Ave., Asheville, NC 28804; (828) 253-1077 **Wine list** *California* **Wine prices** *Moderate* **Corkage** *$15* **Cuisine** *Contemporary Italian* **Menu prices** *$14–$32*

SECOND EMPIRE RESTAURANT & TAVERN 🍷
330 Hillsborough St., Raleigh, NC 27603; (919) 829-3663 **Wine list** *France, California* **Wine prices** *Moderate* **Cuisine** *Contemporary American* **Menu prices** *$22–$32*

1703 🍷
1703 Robinhood Road, Winston-Salem, NC 27106; (336) 725-5767 **Wine list** *California* **Wine prices** Inexpensive **Cuisine** *Contemporary American* **Menu prices** *$20–$28*

SONOMA BISTRO & WINE BAR 🍷
129 W. Trade St., Charlotte, NC 28202; (704) 377-1333 **Wine list** *California* **Wine prices** *Moderate* **Cuisine** *Californian* **Menu prices** *$15–$24*

STARS WATERFRONT CAFÉ 🍷
14 Causeway Drive, Ocean Isle Beach, NC 28469; (910) 579-7838 **Wine list** *California* **Wine prices** *Inexpensive* **Corkage** *$15* **Cuisine** *Contemporary American* **Menu prices** *$13–$39*

SULLIVAN'S STEAKHOUSE 🍷
1928 South Blvd., Charlotte, NC 28203; (704) 335-8228 **Wine list** *California* **Wine prices** *Moderate* **Corkage** *$25* **Cuisine** *Steak house* **Menu prices** *$17–$29*

SULLIVAN'S STEAKHOUSE 🍷
414 Glenwood Ave., Raleigh, NC 27603; (919) 833-2888 **Wine list** *California* **Wine prices** *Moderate* **Cuisine** *Steak house* **Menu prices** *$17–$50*

TONY'S BOURBON STREET OYSTER BAR 🍷
107 Edinburgh Drive, Cary, NC 27511; (919) 462-6226 **Wine list** *California* **Wine prices** *Moderate* **Corkage** *$10* **Cuisine** *Cajun* **Menu prices** *$13–$45*

UNDERCURRENT 🍷
600 South Elm St., Greensboro, NC 27406; (336) 370-1266 **Wine list** *California* **Wine prices** *Moderate* **Corkage** *$10* **Cuisine** *Contemporary American* **Menu prices** *$14–$32*

UPSTREAM 🍷
6902 Phillips Place Court, Charlotte, NC 28210; (704) 556-7730 **Wine list** *California* **Wine prices** *Moderate* **Corkage** *$15* **Cuisine** *Seafood* **Menu prices** *$18–$30*

VILLAGE TAVERN 🍷
1903 Westridge Road, Greensboro, NC 27410; (336) 282-3063 **Wine list** *California* **Wine prices** *Moderate* **Cuisine** *American* **Menu prices** *$10–$24*

VILLAGE TAVERN 🍷
Hanes Mall Boulevard at Stratford Road, Winston-Salem, NC 27103; (336) 760-8686 **Wine list** *California* **Wine prices** *Moderate* **Cuisine** *American* **Menu prices** *$10–$23*

WOLFGANG'S ON MAIN 🍷🍷
474 Main St., Highlands, NC 28741; (828) 526-3807 **Wine list** *California, France* **Wine prices** *Moderate* **Cuisine** *American/Cajun/Bavarian* **Menu prices** *$17–$28*

YADKIN VALLEY STEAK HOUSE 🍷
140 Highway 740 Bypass E., Albemarle, NC 28001; (704) 983-2020 **Wine list** *California* **Wine prices** *Moderate* **Corkage** *$7* **Cuisine** *Steak house* **Menu prices** *$12–$34*

ZEBRA RESTAURANT 🍷🍷
4521 Sharon Road, Charlotte, NC 28211; (704) 442-9525
Wine list *California, France, Italy* **Wine prices** *Moderate* **Corkage** *$15* **Cuisine** *Contemporary French* **Menu prices** *$17–$29*

OHIO

ALANA'S FOOD & WINE 🍷
2333 N. High St., Columbus, OH 43202; (614) 294-6783
Wine list *California, France* **Wine prices** Inexpensive **Cuisine** *International* **Menu prices** *$16–$34*

THE BARICELLI INN 🍷
2203 Cornell Road, Cleveland, OH 44106; (216) 791-6500
Wine list *California, France, Italy* **Wine prices** *Moderate* **Cuisine** *Continental* **Menu prices** *$20–$35*

BATTUTO 🍷
12405 Mayfield Road, Cleveland, OH 44106; (216) 707-1055 **Wine list** *Italy, California* **Wine prices** *Moderate* **Cuisine** *Italian* **Menu prices** *$24–$30*

BEXLEY'S MONK 🍷
2232 E. Main St., Bexley, OH 43209; (614) 239-MONK
Wine list *California, France* **Wine prices** *Moderate* **Corkage** *$10* **Cuisine** *International* **Menu prices** *$15–$30*

BLACK & BLUE 🍷
Nationwide Arena, 200 W. Nationwide Blvd., Columbus, OH 43215; (614) 246-2800 **Wine list** *California* **Wine prices** *Moderate* **Cuisine** *Californian/French* **Menu prices** *$19–$29*

BLUE POINT GRILLE 🍷
700 W. St. Clair Ave., Cleveland, OH 44113; (216) 875-STAR **Wine list** *California* **Wine prices** *Moderate* **Corkage** *$20* **Cuisine** *Seafood* **Menu prices** *$17–$30*

THE CABIN CLUB 🍷
30651 Detroit Road, Westlake, OH 44145; (440) 899-1711
Wine list *California* **Wine prices** *Moderate* **Cuisine** *Steak house* **Menu prices** *$17–$39*

THE CELESTIAL RESTAURANT 🍷
1071 Celestial St., Cincinnati, OH 45202; (513) 241-4455
Wine list *California, France* **Wine prices** *Moderate* **Corkage** *$25* **Cuisine** *Contemporary* **Menu prices** *$32–$45*

CHANTRELLS RESTAURANT 🍷
20 Commerical Way, Springboro, OH 45066; (937) 743-6073 **Wine list** *California* **Wine prices** Inexpensive **Cuisine** *American/Italian* **Menu prices** *$18–$27*

CHEZ FRANÇOIS 🍷🍷
555 Main St., Vermilion, OH 44089; (440) 967-0630 **Wine list** *Bordeaux, California* **Wine prices** *Moderate* **Corkage** *$20* **Cuisine** *French* **Menu prices** *$22–$35*

CIAO! RISTORANTE 🍷
6064 Monroe St., Sylvania, OH 43560; (419) 882-2334 **Wine list** *Italy* **Wine prices** Inexpensive **Corkage** *No charge* **Cuisine** *Italian* **Menu prices** *$8–$23*

CORLEONE'S RISTORANTE & BAR 🍷
5669 Broadview Road, Parma, OH 44134; (216) 741-0220 **Wine list** *California, Italy* **Wine prices** *Moderate* **Corkage** *$20* **Cuisine** *Italian* **Menu prices** *$10–$29*

CREATIVE GOURMET/THE RESTAURANT 🍷
5629 N. Main St., Sylvania, OH 43560; (419) 885-0295 **Wine list** *California, Bordeaux* **Wine prices** *Moderate* **Cuisine** *Contemporary American* **Menu prices** *$20–$32*

DAVEED'S 🍷
934 Hatch St., Cincinnati, OH 45202; (513) 721-COOK **Wine list** *California* **Wine prices** Inexpensive **Corkage** *$10* **Cuisine** *Contemporary American* **Menu prices** *$20–$29*

EPIQ 🍷
9853 Johnnycake Ridge, Concord, OH 44060; (440) 357-0721 **Wine list** *California* **Wine prices** *Moderate* **Cuisine** *American* **Menu prices** *$17–$25*

GALAXY RESTAURANT 🍷
201 Park Centre Drive, Wadsworth, OH 44281; (330) 334-3663 **Wine list** *California* **Wine prices** *Moderate* **Corkage** *$5* **Cuisine** *American* **Menu prices** *$14–$35*

G. MICHAEL'S BISTRO 🍷
595 S. Third St., Columbus, OH 43215; (614) 464-0575 **Wine list** *California* **Wine prices** *Moderate* **Cuisine** *American* **Menu prices** *$11–$25*

THE INN AT TURNER'S MILL 🍷
36 E. Streetsboro St., Hudson, OH 44236; (330) 655-2949 **Wine list** *California* **Wine prices** *Moderate* **Cuisine** *Contemporary American* **Menu prices** *$19–$45*

🍷🍷🍷 Grand Award 🍷🍷 Best of Award of Excellence 🍷 Award of Excellence

OHIO

JAY'S RESTAURANT
225 E. Sixth St., Dayton, OH 45402; (937) 222-2892 **Wine list** *France, California* **Wine prices** *Moderate* **Cuisine** *Seafood* **Menu prices** *$15–$35*

JEAN-ROBERT AT PIGALL'S
127 W. Fourth St., Cincinnati, OH 45202; (513) 721-1345 **Wine list** *Burgundy, Bordeaux, Rhône, California* **Wine prices** *Expensive* **Cuisine** *French* **Menu prices** *Prix fixe only; $65*

JIMMY D'S STEAKHOUSE
7791 Cooper Road, Cincinnati, OH 45242; (513) 984-2914 **Wine list** *California* **Wine prices** *Moderate* **Corkage** *$10* **Cuisine** *Steak house* **Menu prices** *$18–$30*

JOHN PALMER'S
301 Center St., Chardon, OH 44024; (440) 286-6464 **Wine list** *California* **Wine prices** Inexpensive **Cuisine** *American/French/Italian* **Menu prices** *$18–$27*

JOHNNY'S BAR
3164 Fulton Road, Cleveland, OH 44109; (216) 281-0055 **Wine list** *California, France, Italy* **Wine prices** *Moderate* **Cuisine** *Northern Italian/continental* **Menu prices** *$15–$38*

JOHNNY'S DOWNTOWN
1406 W. Sixth St., Cleveland, OH 44113; (216) 623-0055 **Wine list** *France, California* **Wine prices** *Moderate* **Cuisine** *Northern Italian* **Menu prices** *$18–$34*

KEN STEWART'S GRILLE
1970 W. Market St., Akron, OH 44313; (330) 867-2555 **Wine list** *California, France* **Wine prices** *Moderate* **Cuisine** *Steak house* **Menu prices** *$13–$75*

KEN STEWART'S LODGE
1911 N. Cleveland-Massillon Road, Bath, OH 44210; (330) 666-8881 **Wine list** *California, France* **Wine prices** *Moderate* **Cuisine** *Continental* **Menu prices** *$13–$75*

LOCKKEEPERS
8001 Rockside Road, Valley View, OH 44125; (216) 524-9404 **Wine list** *France, California* **Wine prices** *Moderate* **Corkage** *$20* **Cuisine** *Contemporary American* **Menu prices** *$19–$37*

LOYAL OAK TAVERN
3044 Wadsworth Road, Norton, OH 44203; (330) 825-8280 **Wine list** *California* **Wine prices** *Moderate* **Cuisine** *American* **Menu prices** *$10–$23*

M 🍷
2 Miranova Drive, Columbus, OH 43215; (614) 629-0000 **Wine list** *California, France* **Wine prices** *Moderate* **Cuisine** *American/European/Pacific Rim* **Menu prices** *$17–$32*

MAISONETTE 🍷
114 E. Sixth St., Cincinnati, OH 45202; (513) 721-2260 **Wine list** *California, France* **Wine prices** *Moderate* **Corkage** *$25* **Cuisine** *Contemporary French* **Menu prices** *$34–$45*

MALLORCA 🍷
1390 W. Ninth St., Cleveland, OH 44113; (216) 687-9494 **Wine list** *California, Spain* **Wine prices** *Moderate* **Corkage** *$15* **Cuisine** *Spanish/Portuguese* **Menu prices** *$13–$30*

MARCONI'S RESTAURANT 🍷
424 Berlin Road, Huron, OH 44839; (419) 433-4341 **Wine list** *California, France, Italy* **Wine prices** *Moderate* **Corkage** *$10* **Cuisine** *Italian* **Menu prices** *$8–$29*

MORTON'S OF CHICAGO 🍷
28 W. Fourth St., Cincinnati, OH 45202; (513) 241-4104 **Wine list** *California* **Wine prices** *Expensive* **Cuisine** *Steak house* **Menu prices** *$22–$75*

MORTON'S OF CHICAGO 🍷
The Avenue at Tower City Center, 1600 W. Second St., Cleveland, OH 44113; (216) 621-6200 **Wine list** *California* **Wine prices** *Expensive* **Cuisine** *Steak house* **Menu prices** *$22–$36*

MORTON'S OF CHICAGO 🍷
2 Nationwide Plaza, Columbus, OH 43215; (614) 464-4442 **Wine list** *California* **Wine prices** *Expensive* **Cuisine** *Steak house* **Menu prices** *$22–$36*

MOXIE 🍷
3355 Richmond Road, Beachwood, OH 44122; (216) 831-5599 **Wine list** *California, Italy* **Wine prices** *Moderate* **Corkage** *$15* **Cuisine** *American* **Menu prices** *$20–$27*

PALACE RESTAURANT 🍷
Cincinnatian Hotel, 601 Vine St., Cincinnati, OH 45202; (513) 381-3000 **Wine list** *California* **Wine prices** *Expensive* **Corkage** *$15* **Cuisine** *Contemporary* **Menu prices** *$25–$40*

THE PALM COURT
Omni Netherlands Plaza, 35 W. Fifth St., Cincinnati, OH 45202; (513) 421-9100 **Wine list** *California* **Wine prices** *Moderate* **Cuisine** *Contemporary American* **Menu prices** *$16–$39*

PAPA JOE'S
1561 Akron-Peninsula Road, Akron, OH 44313; (330) 923-7999 **Wine list** *California, France, Italy* **Wine prices** *Moderate* **Cuisine** *Continental/Italian* **Menu prices** *$9–$24*

PRIMO VINO
12511 Mayfield Road, Cleveland, OH 44106; (216) 229-3334 **Wine list** *Italy* **Wine prices** *Moderate* **Cuisine** *Italian* **Menu prices** *$8–$14*

THE REFECTORY
1092 Bethel Road, Columbus, OH 43220; (614) 451-9774 **Wine list** *California, Bordeaux* **Wine prices** *Moderate* **Cuisine** *French* **Menu prices** *$26–$32*

THE RESTAURANT AT THE PHOENIX
812 Race St., Cincinnati, OH 45202; (513) 721-8901 **Wine list** *California* **Wine prices** Inexpensive **Cuisine** *American* **Menu prices** *$13–$25*

RISTORANTE GIOVANNI'S
25550 Chagrin Blvd., Beachwood, OH 44122; (216) 831-8625 **Wine list** *California, France, Italy* **Wine prices** *Moderate* **Cuisine** *Northern Italian* **Menu prices** *$20–$38*

RUTH'S CHRIS STEAK HOUSE
7550 High Cross Blvd., Columbus, OH 43235; (614) 885-2910 **Wine list** *California* **Wine prices** *Moderate* **Corkage** *$15* **Cuisine** *Steak house* **Menu prices** *$18–$65*

RUTH'S CHRIS STEAK HOUSE
28699 Chagrin Blvd., Woodmere Village, OH 44122; (216) 595-0809 **Wine list** *California* **Wine prices** *Moderate* **Corkage** *$15* **Cuisine** *Steak house* **Menu prices** *$19–$65*

SALMON DAVE'S
19015 Old Lake Road, Rocky River, OH 44116; (440) 331-2739 **Wine list** *California* **Wine prices** *Moderate* **Cuisine** *American/Pacific Rim* **Menu prices** *$15–$25*

OHIO

SAUCY BISTRO 🍷
20672 Center Ridge Road, Rocky River, OH 44116; (440) 331-2128 **Wine list** *California* **Wine prices** *Moderate* **Corkage** *$15* **Cuisine** *Continental/American* **Menu prices** *$15–$27*

SEVEN STARS 🍷
The Worthington Inn, 649 High St., Worthington, OH 43085; (614) 885-2600 **Wine list** *California* **Wine prices** Inexpensive **Cuisine** *Contemporary American* **Menu prices** *$18–$28*

SHAW'S RESTAURANT & INN 🍷
123 N. Broad St., Lancaster, OH 43130; (800) 654-2477 **Wine list** *California* **Wine prices** *Moderate* **Cuisine** *American/international* **Menu prices** *$15–$28*

SHOREBY CLUB 🍷
40 Shoreby Drive, Bratenahl, OH 44108; (216) 851-2582 **Wine list** *California* **Wine prices** *Moderate* **Cuisine** *Continental* **Menu prices** *$18–$29*

SMITH & WOLLENSKY 🍷
Easton Tower Center, 4145 The Strand W., Columbus, OH 43219; (614) 416-2400 **Wine list** *California, Bordeaux* **Wine prices** *Moderate* **Cuisine** *Steak house* **Menu prices** *$19–$35*

SWINGOS ON THE LAKE 🍷🍷
12900 Lake Road, Lakewood, OH 44107; (216) 221-6188 **Wine list** *California, Bordeaux* **Wine prices** *Moderate* **Corkage** *$15* **Cuisine** *Continental* **Menu prices** *$25–$75*

TELLER'S OF HYDE PARK 🍷
2710 Erie Ave., Cincinnati, OH 45208; (513) 321-4721 **Wine list** *California* **Wine prices** *Moderate* **Corkage** *$10* **Cuisine** *Contemporary American* **Menu prices** *$12–$25*

VERNON'S CAFÉ 🍷
720 Youngstown-Warren Road, Niles, OH 44446; (330) 652-1381 **Wine list** *California* **Wine prices** Inexpensive **Corkage** *$5* **Cuisine** *American* **Menu prices** *$9–$35*

VIVA BARCELONA 🍷
24600 Detroit Road, Westlake, OH 44145; (440) 892-8700 **Wine list** *California, Spain, Chile* **Wine prices** *Moderate* **Cuisine** *Spanish* **Menu prices** *$14–$30*

🍷🍷🍷 Grand Award 🍷🍷 Best of Award of Excellence 🍷 Award of Excellence

WATERMARK RESTAURANT
1250 Old River Road, Cleveland, OH 44113; (216) 241-1600 **Wine list** *California* **Wine prices** Inexpensive **Cuisine** *Contemporary American* **Menu prices** *$10–$25*

OKLAHOMA

ATLANTIC SEA GRILL
8321-A E. 61st St., Tulsa, OK 74133; (918) 252-7966 **Wine list** *California* **Wine prices** *Moderate* **Cuisine** *Seafood* **Menu prices** *$13–$50*

BODEAN SEAFOOD
3323 E. 51st St., Tulsa, OK 74135; (918) 743-3861 **Wine list** *California* **Wine prices** *Moderate* **Cuisine** *Seafood* **Menu prices** *$13–$26*

BOULEVARD STEAKHOUSE
505 S. Boulevard St., Edmond, OK 73034; (405) 715-BEEF **Wine list** *California* **Wine prices** *Moderate* **Cuisine** *Steak house* **Menu prices** *$19–$56*

CASCATA
801 Signal Ridge Road, Edmond, OK 73013; (405) 216-9880 **Wine list** *California, Italy* **Wine prices** *Expensive* **Cuisine** *Northern Italian* **Menu prices** *$16–$34*

THE COACH HOUSE RESTAURANT
6437 Avondale Drive, Nichols Hills, OK 73116; (405) 842-1000 **Wine list** *California* **Wine prices** *Moderate* **Cuisine** *American* **Menu prices** *$24–$49*

DANNY'S STEAKHOUSE
3750 W. Robinson St., Norman, OK 73072; (405) 364-4995 **Wine list** *California* **Wine prices** *Expensive* **Cuisine** *Steak house* **Menu prices** *$15–$30*

FLAVORS
6104 E. 71st St., Tulsa, OK 74136; (918) 492-7767 **Wine list** *California, Australia* **Wine prices** *Moderate* **Cuisine** *Contemporary American* **Menu prices** *$10–$35*

THE METRO WINE BAR & BISTRO
6418 N. Western Ave., Oklahoma City, OK 73116; (405) 840-9463 **Wine list** *California* **Wine prices** *Moderate* **Cuisine** *American* **Menu prices** *$12–$21*

NIKZ 🍷
United Founders Tower, 5900 Mosteller Drive, Oklahoma City, OK 73112; (405) 843-6450 **Wine list** *California, France* **Wine prices** *Moderate* **Cuisine** *American/continental* **Menu prices** *$16–$60*

THE POLO GRILL 🍷🍷
2038 Utica Square, Tulsa, OK 74114; (918) 744-4280 **Wine list** *California, Bordeaux* **Wine prices** *Moderate* **Cuisine** *Contemporary regional* **Menu prices** *$19–$29*

RANCH STEAKHOUSE 🍷
3000 W. Britton Road, Oklahoma City, OK 73120; (405) 755-3501 **Wine list** *California, France* **Wine prices** *Expensive* **Cuisine** *Steak house* **Menu prices** *$18–$50*

OREGON

ADAM'S PLACE 🍷
30 E. Broadway, Eugene, OR 97401; (541) 344-6948 **Wine list** *California, Oregon* **Wine prices** *Moderate* **Corkage** *$10* **Cuisine** *Asian/Pacific Northwest* **Menu prices** *$17–$27*

AMBROSIA RESTAURANT & BAR 🍷
174 E. Broadway, Eugene, OR 97401; (541) 342-4141 **Wine list** *Italy* **Wine prices** Inexpensive **Corkage** *$15* **Cuisine** *Italian* **Menu prices** *$12–$20*

ASSAGGIO 🍷
7742 S.E. 13th Ave., Portland, OR 97202; (503) 232-6151 **Wine list** *Italy* **Wine prices** *Moderate* **Corkage** *$10* **Cuisine** *Italian* **Menu prices** *$11–$19*

BASTAS TRATTORIA 🍷
410 N.W. 21st Ave., Portland, OR 97209; (503) 274-1572 **Wine list** *Italy* **Wine prices** *Moderate* **Cuisine** *Italian* **Menu prices** *$10–$20*

BAY HOUSE 🍷
5911 S.W. Highway 101, Lincoln City, OR 97367; (541) 996-3222 **Wine list** *California, Oregon* **Wine prices** Inexpensive **Corkage** *$15* **Cuisine** *Pacific Northwestern* **Menu prices** *$20–$32*

BRASSERIE MONTMARTRE 🍷
626 S.W. Park Ave., Portland, OR 97205; (503) 224-5552 **Wine list** *California, France* **Wine prices** Inexpensive **Cuisine** *French* **Menu prices** *$11–$20*

LAUTREC
Nemacolin Woodlands Resort & Spa, 1001 LaFayette Drive, Farmington, PA 15437; (800) 422-2736 **Wine list** *California, France, Italy* **Wine prices** *Expensive* **Corkage** *$15* **Cuisine** *French* **Menu prices** *$28–$36*

LE BEC-FIN
1523 Walnut St., Philadelphia, PA 19102; (215) 567-1000 **Wine list** *France, California* **Wine prices** *Expensive* **Cuisine** *French* **Menu prices** *Prix fixe only; $135*

LE JEUNE CHEF
Pennsylvania College of Technology, 1 College Ave., Williamsport, PA 17701; (570) 327-4776 **Wine list** *California, France* **Wine prices** *Moderate* **Cuisine** *American* **Menu prices** *$17–$30*

LE MONT RESTAURANT
1114 Grandview Ave., Pittsburgh, PA 15211; (412) 431-3100 **Wine list** *California, France* **Wine prices** *Expensive* **Cuisine** *Continental* **Menu prices** *$23–$48*

LIDIA'S PITTSBURGH
1400 Smallman St., Pittsburgh, PA 15222; (412) 552-0150 **Wine list** *Italy* **Wine prices** *Moderate* **Cuisine** *Northern Italian* **Menu prices** *$12–$23*

MALLORCA
2228 E. Carson St., Pittsburgh, PA 15203; (412) 488-1818 **Wine list** *California, Spain* **Wine prices** *Moderate* **Cuisine** *Spanish* **Menu prices** *$12–$27*

MICHAELANGELO'S
894 Old State Road, Clarks Summit, PA 18411; (570) 586-0755 **Wine list** *California, Australia, Italy* **Wine prices** *Moderate* **Cuisine** *Contemporary American* **Menu prices** *$20–$28*

MONTEREY BAY FISH GROTTO
1411 Grandview Ave., Pittsburgh, PA 15211; (412) 481-4414 **Wine list** *California* **Wine prices** *Moderate* **Corkage** *$10* **Cuisine** *Seafood* **Menu prices** *$16–$29*

MORTON'S OF CHICAGO
500 Mall Blvd., King of Prussia, PA 19406; (610) 491-1900 **Wine list** *California* **Wine prices** *Expensive* **Cuisine** *Steak house* **Menu prices** *$22–$70*

MORTON'S OF CHICAGO 🍷
1411 Walnut St., Philadelphia, PA 19102; (215) 557-0724 **Wine list** *California* **Wine prices** *Expensive* **Corkage** *$15* **Cuisine** *Steak house* **Menu prices** *$20–$77*

MORTON'S OF CHICAGO 🍷
CNG Tower, 625 Liberty Ave., Pittsburgh, PA 15222; (412) 261-7141 **Wine list** *California* **Wine prices** *Expensive* **Corkage** *$15* **Cuisine** *Steak house* **Menu prices** *$23–$75*

OFF CENTER GRILL 🍷
The Yorktowne Hotel, 48 E. Market St., York, PA 17403; (717) 815-2111 **Wine list** *California* **Wine prices** *Moderate* **Cuisine** *American* **Menu prices** *$18–$27*

THE OLD GUARD HOUSE INN 🍷
953 Youngsford Road, Gladwyne, PA 19035; (610) 649-9708 **Wine list** *California, France* **Wine prices** *Moderate* **Corkage** *$25* **Cuisine** *American/continental* **Menu prices** *$17–$34*

OLDE GREENFIELD INN 🍷
595 Greenfield Road, Lancaster, PA 17601; (717) 393-0668 **Wine list** *California* **Wine prices** *Moderate* **Cuisine** *American* **Menu prices** *$16–$30*

OPUS 🍷
Renaissance Pittsburgh, 107 Sixth St., Pittsburgh, PA 15222; (412) 992-2005 **Wine list** *California* **Wine prices** *Moderate* **Cuisine** *Mediterranean* **Menu prices** *$16–$29*

OPUS 251 🍷
251 S. 18th St., Philadelphia, PA 19103; (215) 735-6787 **Wine list** *California, France* **Wine prices** *Moderate* **Cuisine** *American/continental* **Menu prices** *$24–$38*

THE PALM 🍷
200 S. Broad St., Philadelphia, PA 19102; (215) 546-7256 **Wine list** *California* **Wine prices** *Expensive* **Cuisine** *Steak house* **Menu prices** *$35–$50*

PAREV 🍷
215 Pine St., Harrisburg, PA 17101; (717) 920-1800 **Wine list** *France, California* **Wine prices** *Moderate* **Cuisine** *Contemporary European* **Menu prices** *$20–$35*

PATSEL'S 🍷
1385 Lackawanna Trail, Clarks Summit, PA 18411; (570) 563-2000 **Wine list** *California* **Wine prices** Inexpensive **Corkage** *$10* **Cuisine** *Contemporary American* **Menu prices** *$23–$32*

PENNE RESTAURANT & WINE BAR 🍷
The Inn at Penn, 3611 Walnut St., Philadelphia, PA 19104; (215) 823-6222 **Wine list** *Italy* **Wine prices** Inexpensive **Cuisine** *Contemporary Italian* **Menu prices** *$16–$25*

THE RESTAURANT AT DONECKERS 🍷
333 N. State St., Ephrata, PA 17522; (717) 738-9501 **Wine list** *California, France, Italy* **Wine prices** *Expensive* **Cuisine** *French/American* **Menu prices** *$24–$30*

RESTAURANT PASSERELLE 🍷
175 King of Prussia Road, Radnor, PA 19807; (610) 293-9411 **Wine list** *California* **Wine prices** *Expensive* **Cuisine** *Contemporary American/French* **Menu prices** *$25–$37*

RISTORANTE PANORAMA 🍷🍷
Penn's View Inn Hotel, Front and Market Streets, Philadelphia, PA 19106; (215) 922-7800 **Wine list** *Italy, California* **Wine prices** *Expensive* **Cuisine** *Italian* **Menu prices** *$18–$26*

ROSE TREE INN 🍷
1243 Providence Road, Media, PA 19063; (610) 891-1205 **Wine list** *California, France* **Wine prices** *Moderate* **Cuisine** *Continental* **Menu prices** *$20–$28*

RUSSELL'S & CLANCY'S 🍷
117-125 W. Main St., Bloomsburg, PA 17815; (570) 387-1332 **Wine list** *California* **Wine prices** Inexpensive **Cuisine** *Continental* **Menu prices** *$14–$25*

RUTH'S CHRIS STEAK HOUSE 🍷
220 N. Gulph Road, King of Prussia, PA 19406; (610) 992-1818 **Wine list** *California* **Wine prices** *Moderate* **Cuisine** *Steak house* **Menu prices** *$35–$40*

RUTH'S CHRIS STEAK HOUSE 🍷
260 S. Broad St., Philadelphia, PA 19102; (215) 790-1515 **Wine list** *California* **Wine prices** *Moderate* **Cuisine** *Steak house* **Menu prices** *$17–$52*

RUTH'S CHRIS STEAK HOUSE 🍷
6 PPG Place, Pittsburgh, PA 15222; (412) 391-4800 **Wine list** *California* **Wine prices** *Moderate* **Corkage** *$15* **Cuisine** *Steak house* **Menu prices** *$30–$50*

THE RYAH HOUSE 🍷
The Inn at Nichols Village, 1101 Northern Blvd., Clarks Summit, PA 18411; (570) 587-4124 **Wine list** *California* **Wine prices** *Moderate* **Cuisine** *American* **Menu prices** *$22–$28*

SAVONA 🍷🍷
100 Old Gulph Road, Gulph Mills, PA 19428; (610) 520-1200 **Wine list** *Piedmont, Burgundy, California* **Wine prices** *Expensive* **Corkage** *$25* **Cuisine** *French/Italian* **Menu prices** *$25–$39*

THE SETTLERS INN 🍷
4 Main Ave., Hawley, PA 18428; (800) 833-8527 **Wine list** *California* **Wine prices** *Moderate* **Cuisine** *Regional* **Menu prices** *$15–$29*

SIMON PEARCE RESTAURANT 🍷
1333 Lenape Road, West Chester, PA 19382; (610) 793-0948 **Wine list** *California* **Wine prices** *Moderate* **Cuisine** *Contemporary American* **Menu prices** *$19–$30*

SKYTOP LODGE 🍷
1 Skytop, Skytop, PA 18357; (570) 595-7401 **Wine list** *California* **Wine prices** *Moderate* **Corkage** *$10* **Cuisine** *Contemporary American* **Menu prices** *$15–$23*

SMITH & WOLLENSKY 🍷
210 W. Rittenhouse Square, Philadelphia, PA 19103; (215) 545-1700 **Wine list** *California* **Wine prices** *Expensive* **Cuisine** *Steak house* **Menu prices** *$20–$35*

SOBA 🍷
5847 Ellsworth Ave., Pittsburgh, PA 15232; (412) 362-5656 **Wine list** *California, France* **Wine prices** *Moderate* **Corkage** *$15* **Cuisine** *Pan-Asian* **Menu prices** *$14–$31*

THE STEELHEAD GRILL 🍷
Pittsburgh Marriott City Center, 112 Washington Place, Pittsburgh, PA 15219; (412) 394-3474 **Wine list** *California, France* **Wine prices** *Moderate* **Corkage** *$15* **Cuisine** *American* **Menu prices** *$21–$32*

🍷🍷🍷 Grand Award 🍷🍷 Best of Award of Excellence 🍷 Award of Excellence

STOUDT'S BLACK ANGUS
Route 272, Adamstown, PA 19501; (717) 484-4385 **Wine list** *California* **Wine prices** *Moderate* **Cuisine** *Steak house* **Menu prices** *$15–$35*

STRAWBERRY HILL
128 W. Strawberry St., Lancaster, PA 17603; (717) 393-5544 **Wine list** *California, Bordeaux* **Wine prices** *Moderate* **Cuisine** *Contemporary American* **Menu prices** *$13–$32*

SULLIVAN'S STEAKHOUSE
700 W. Dekalb Pike, King of Prussia, PA 19406; (610) 878-9025 **Wine list** *California* **Wine prices** *Moderate* **Cuisine** *Steak house* **Menu prices** *$17–$35*

TAVERN ON THE HILL SEAFOOD & STEAK HOUSE
109 Howard St., Enola, PA 17025; (717) 732-2077 **Wine list** *California, France* **Wine prices** *Expensive* **Cuisine** *Steak house* **Menu prices** *$18–$45*

TOSCANA CUCINA RUSTICA
24 N. Merion Ave., Bryn Mawr, PA 19010; (610) 527-7700 **Wine list** *Italy, California* **Wine prices** *Moderate* **Cuisine** *Tuscan* **Menu prices** *$17–$30*

TRUST
121-127 S. 13th St., Philadelphia, PA 19107; (215) 629-1300 **Wine list** *California, France, Spain* **Wine prices** *Moderate* **Cuisine** *Mediterranean* **Menu prices** *$9–$18*

TWENTY21
2005 Market St., Philadelphia, PA 19103; (215) 851-6262 **Wine list** *California, France* **Wine prices** *Moderate* **Cuisine** *American* **Menu prices** *$20–$30*

VALLOZZI'S
Georges Station Road, Greensburg, PA 15601; (724) 836-7663 **Wine list** *Italy, California* **Wine prices** *Moderate* **Cuisine** *Italian/American* **Menu prices** *$13–$24*

VICKERS TAVERN
192 E. Welsh Pool Road, Exton, PA 19341; (610) 363-7998 **Wine list** *California, France* **Wine prices** *Expensive* **Cuisine** *Continental* **Menu prices** *$19–$30*

WOODEN ANGEL
308 Leopard Lane, Beaver, PA 15009; (724) 774-7880 **Wine list** *California* **Wine prices** *Moderate* **Cuisine** *American* **Menu prices** *$14–$27*

YANGMING 🍷
1051 Conestoga Road, Bryn Mawr, PA 19010; (610) 527-3200 **Wine list** *California* **Wine prices** *Moderate* **Cuisine** *Chinese/continental* **Menu prices** *$12–$27*

ZOLA NEW WORLD BISTRO 🍷
324 W. College Ave., State College, PA 16801; (814) 237-8474 **Wine list** *California* **Wine prices** *Moderate* **Cuisine** *Contemporary* **Menu prices** *$14–$26*

PUERTO RICO

ALLEGRO RISTORANTE 🍷
1350 Roosevelt Ave., San Juan, PR 00920; (787) 273-9055 **Wine list** *California, Italy, Spain* **Wine prices** *Moderate* **Corkage** *$25* **Cuisine** *Northern Italian* **Menu prices** *$13–$33*

DI VINO WINE BAR & GRILLE 🍷
Ave. Boulevard Bloque 12, 29 Santa Rosa, Bayamón, PR 00960; (787) 288-8087 **Wine list** *Spain, California* **Wine prices** *Moderate* **Corkage** *$15* **Cuisine** *Caribbean* **Menu prices** *$12–$16*

EL CASTILLO 🍷
The Mayagüez Resort & Casino, Carr. 104, KM 0.3, Algarrobo, Mayagüez, PR 00680; (787) 831-7575 **Wine list** *Spain, California* **Wine prices** *Moderate* **Cuisine** *International/Caribbean* **Menu prices** *$14–$32*

LA PICCOLA FONTANA 🍷
Wyndham El San Juan Hotel, 6063 Isla Verde Ave., Carolina, PR 00979; (787) 791-0966 **Wine list** *Italy, California, France* **Wine prices** *Moderate* **Corkage** *$15* **Cuisine** *Northern Italian* **Menu prices** *$17–$32*

MORTON'S OF CHICAGO 🍷
The Caribe Hilton Resort Hotel, Calle Rosales San Geranimo Grounds, San Juan, PR 00901; (787) 977-6262 **Wine list** *California* **Wine prices** *Expensive* **Corkage** *$15* **Cuisine** *Steak house* **Menu prices** *$20–$60*

THE PALM 🍷
El San Juan Hotel & Casino, 6063 Isla Verde Ave., Carolina, PR 00979; (787) 791-3300 **Wine list** *California* **Wine prices** *Moderate* **Corkage** *$25* **Cuisine** *Steak house* **Menu prices** *$17–$126*

RUTH'S CHRIS STEAK HOUSE
Intercontinental Resort & Casino, 5961 Isla Verde Ave., Carolina, PR 00979; (787) 253-1717 **Wine list** *California* **Wine prices** *Expensive* **Cuisine** *Steak house* **Menu prices** *$19–$40*

THE VINEYARD ROOM
The Ritz-Carlton San Juan, 6961 State Road 187, Isla Verde, Carolina, PR 00979; (787) 253-1700 **Wine list** *California, France* **Wine prices** *Expensive* **Cuisine** *Mediterranean/Californian* **Menu prices** *$33–$45*

RHODE ISLAND

ADESSO
161 Cushing St., Providence, RI 02906; (401) 521-0770 **Wine list** *California, Italy* **Wine prices** *Moderate* **Cuisine** *Californian* **Menu prices** *$12–$28*

AL FORNO
577 S. Main St., Providence, RI 02903; (401) 273-9760 **Wine list** *Italy* **Wine prices** *Moderate* **Cuisine** *Italian* **Menu prices** *$20–$38*

THE ATLANTIC INN
High Street, Block Island, RI 02807; (401) 466-5883 **Wine list** *California, France* **Wine prices** *Moderate* **Cuisine** *Contemporary American* **Menu prices** *Prix fixe only; $42*

BASIL'S RESTAURANT
22 Kingstown Road, Narragansett, RI 02882; (401) 789-3743 **Wine list** *California, France* **Wine prices** *Moderate* **Cuisine** *French* **Menu prices** *$16–$32*

BRICK ALLEY PUB
140 Thames St., Newport, RI 02840; (401) 849-6334 **Wine list** *California* **Wine prices** Inexpensive **Cuisine** *American* **Menu prices** *$12–$27*

CAFÉ NUOVO
1 Citizens Plaza, Providence, RI 02903; (401) 421-2525 **Wine list** *California* **Wine prices** *Expensive* **Cuisine** *Contemporary American* **Menu prices** *$17–$35*

CAFFÈ ITRI
1686 Cranston St., Cranston, RI 02920; (401) 942-1970 **Wine list** *Italy,* **Wine prices** Inexpensive **Cuisine** *Italian, California* **Menu prices** *$12–$24*

CAMILLE'S 🍷
71 Bradford St., Providence, RI 02903; (401) 751-4812
Wine list *California, Italy* **Wine prices** *Moderate* **Cuisine** *Italian/Mediterranean* **Menu prices** *$9–$32*

THE CAPITAL GRILLE 🍷
1 Union Station, Providence, RI 02903; (401) 521-5600
Wine list *California, Bordeaux* **Wine prices** *Moderate* **Cuisine** *Steak house* **Menu prices** *$16–$30*

CAPRICCIO 🍷
2 Pine St., Providence, RI 02903; (401) 421-1320 **Wine list** *California, Bordeaux* **Wine prices** Inexpensive **Cuisine** *Continental/Northern Italian* **Menu prices** *$17–$31*

CASTLE HILL INN & RESORT 🍷
590 Ocean Ave., Newport, RI 02840; (888) 466-1355 **Wine list** *California* **Wine prices** *Moderate* **Cuisine** *New England* **Menu prices** *$22–$38*

CLARKE COOKE HOUSE 🍷
Bannister's Wharf, Newport, RI 02840; (401) 849-2900
Wine list *California, France* **Wine prices** *Moderate* **Cuisine** *Mediterranean/New England* **Menu prices** *$19–$29*

COSTANTINO'S RISTORANTE-CAFFÉ 🍷
265 Atwells Ave., Providence, RI 02903; (401) 528-1100
Wine list *California, Italy* **Wine prices** *Moderate* **Cuisine** *Italian* **Menu prices** *$13–$30*

LEGAL SEA FOODS 🍷
2099 Post Road, Warwick, RI 02886; (401) 732-3663 **Wine list** *California* **Wine prices** Inexpensive **Cuisine** *Seafood* **Menu prices** *$13–$36*

MAMMA LUISA RESTAURANT 🍷
673 Thames St., Newport, RI 02840; (401) 848-5257 **Wine list** *Italy* **Wine prices** *Moderate* **Cuisine** *Italian* **Menu prices** *$12–$25*

THE MOORING 🍷🍷
Sayer's Wharf at The Newport Yachting Center, Newport, RI 02840; (401) 846-2260 **Wine list** *California, Italy* **Wine prices** *Moderate* **Cuisine** *New England/seafood* **Menu prices** *$10–$25*

NAISSANCE 🍷
242 Atwells Ave., Providence, RI 02903; (401) 272-9610
Wine list *California, Italy* **Wine prices** *Moderate* **Cuisine** *Contemporary* **Menu prices** *$16–$25*

🍷🍷🍷 Grand Award 🍷🍷 Best of Award of Excellence 🍷 Award of Excellence

NAPA VALLEY GRILLE
111 Providence Place, Providence, RI 02903; (401) 270-6272 **Wine list** *California* **Wine prices** *Moderate* **Cuisine** *Californian* **Menu prices** *$14–$23*

NEW RIVERS
7 Steeple St., Providence, RI 02903; (401) 751-0350 **Wine list** *California, France* **Wine prices** *Moderate* **Cuisine** *Contemporary American* **Menu prices** *$16–$26*

OLYMPIA TEA ROOM
74 Bay St., Watch Hill, RI 02891; (401) 348-8211 **Wine list** *California* **Wine prices** *Moderate* **Cuisine** *Contemporary American/international* **Menu prices** *$18–$35*

PARKSIDE ROTISSERIE & BAR
76 S. Main St., Providence, RI 02903; (401) 331-0003 **Wine list** *California, France* **Wine prices** *Moderate* **Cuisine** *Mediterranean* **Menu prices** *$16–$24*

POT AU FEU
44 Custom House St., Providence, RI 02903; (401) 273-8953 **Wine list** *California* **Wine prices** Inexpensive **Cuisine** *French* **Menu prices** *$13–$25*

RISTORANTE PIZZICO
762 Hope St., Providence, RI 02906; (401) 421-4114 **Wine list** *California, Italy, Bordeaux* **Wine prices** *Moderate* **Cuisine** *Italian* **Menu prices** *$16–$23*

SCALES & SHELLS RESTAURANT AND RAW BAR
527 Thames St., Newport, RI 02840; (401) 847-2000 **Wine list** *California, Italy* **Wine prices** Inexpensive **Cuisine** *Italian/seafood* **Menu prices** *$13–$21*

TEN PRIME STEAK & SUSHI
55 Pine St., Providence, RI 02903; (401) 453-2333 **Wine list** *California* **Wine prices** *Moderate* **Cuisine** *Steak house* **Menu prices** *$18–$29*

22 BOWEN'S
22 Bowen's Wharf, Newport, RI 02840; (401) 841-8884 **Wine list** *California* **Wine prices** *Moderate* **Corkage** *$20* **Cuisine** *Steak house* **Menu prices** *$24–$38*

THE UP RIVER CAFÉ
37 Main St., Westerly, RI 02891; (401) 348-9700 **Wine list** *California* **Wine prices** *Moderate* **Corkage** *$10* **Cuisine** *American* **Menu prices** *$15–$27*

THE WHITE HORSE TAVERN 🍷
26 Marlborough St., Newport, RI 02840; (401) 849-3600 **Wine list** *California, France* **Wine prices** *Expensive* **Cuisine** *Contemporary American/continental* **Menu prices** *$26–$35*

XO CAFÉ 🍷
125 N. Main St., Providence, RI 02903; (401) 273-9090 **Wine list** *California* **Wine prices** *Moderate* **Cuisine** *American* **Menu prices** *$18–$28*

SOUTH CAROLINA

ALEXANDER'S RESTAURANT 🍷
76 Queen's Folly Road, Hilton Head Island, SC 29938; (843) 785-4999 **Wine list** *California* **Wine prices** *Moderate* **Corkage** *$15* **Cuisine** *Contemporary* **Menu prices** *$19–$49*

ANSON RESTAURANT 🍷
12 Anson St., Charleston, SC 29401; (843) 577-0551 **Wine list** *California* **Wine prices** *Moderate* **Cuisine** *American* **Menu prices** *$16–$28*

ANTONIO'S 🍷
The Village at Wexford G-2, Hilton Head Island, SC 29928; (843) 842-5505 **Wine list** *California, Italy* **Wine prices** *Moderate* **Cuisine** *Italian* **Menu prices** *$16–$29*

THE ATLANTIC ROOM 🍷
Kiawah Island Inn, 12 Kiawah Beach Drive, Kiawah Island, SC 29455; (843) 768-2121 **Wine list** *California, France* **Wine prices** *Moderate* **Cuisine** *American* **Menu prices** *$21–$32*

BISTRO EUROPA 🍷
219 N. Main St., Greenville, SC 29601; (864) 467-9975 **Wine list** *California* **Wine prices** Inexpensive **Corkage** *$20* **Cuisine** *French* **Menu prices** *$12–$22*

BLOSSOM CAFÉ 🍷
171 E. Bay St., Charleston, SC 29401; (843) 722-9200 **Wine list** *California* **Wine prices** Inexpensive **Cuisine** *Italian/American* **Menu prices** *$9–$24*

THE BOATHOUSE AT BREACH INLET 🍷
101 Palm Blvd., Isle of Palms, SC 29451; (843) 886-8000 **Wine list** *California* **Wine prices** Inexpensive **Corkage** *$10* **Cuisine** *Seafood* **Menu prices** *$11–$25*

BOATHOUSE II RESTAURANT 🍷
397 Squire Pope Road, Hilton Head Island, SC 29926; (843) 681-3663 **Wine list** *California* **Wine prices** *Moderate* **Corkage** *$10* **Cuisine** *Regional* **Menu prices** *$16–$25*

THE BOATHOUSE ON EAST BAY 🍷
549 E. Bay St., Charleston, SC 29403; (843) 577-7171 **Wine list** *California* **Wine prices** Inexpensive **Corkage** *$10* **Cuisine** *Seafood* **Menu prices** *$10–$25*

BRETT'S RESTAURANT 🍷
1970 Maybank Highway, Charleston, SC 29412; (843) 795-9964 **Wine list** *California* **Wine prices** *Moderate* **Corkage** *$15* **Cuisine** *Italian/American* **Menu prices** *$14–$28*

CAFÉ EUROPA 🍷
160 Lighthouse Road, Harbour Town, Hilton Head Island, SC 29928; (843) 671-3399 **Wine list** *California* **Wine prices** Inexpensive **Corkage** *$15* **Cuisine** *Contemporary* **Menu prices** *$19–$28*

CHARLESTON GRILL 🍷🍷
Charleston Place Orient Express Hotel, 224 King St., Charleston, SC 29401; (843) 577-4522 **Wine list** *California, France* **Wine prices** *Moderate* **Cuisine** *Contemporary American* **Menu prices** *$18–$33*

CHARLEY'S CRAB 🍷
2 Hudson Road, Hilton Head Island, SC 29925; (843) 342-9066 **Wine list** *California* **Wine prices** *Moderate* **Corkage** *$15* **Cuisine** *Seafood* **Menu prices** *$15–$26*

CHARLIE'S L'ETOILE VERTE 🍷
1000 Plantation Center, Hilton Head Island, SC 29928; (843) 785-9277 **Wine list** *France, California* **Wine prices** *Moderate* **Corkage** *$15* **Cuisine** *Seafood* **Menu prices** *$21–$28*

CHIANTI SOUTH 🍷
2109 Highway 17 N., Little River, SC 29566; (843) 249-7888 **Wine list** *Italy, California* **Wine prices** Inexpensive **Cuisine** *Italian* **Menu prices** *$12–$25*

CHOPHOUSE '47 🍷
36 Beacon Drive, Greenville, SC 29615; (864) 286-8700 **Wine list** *California, Bordeaux* **Wine prices** *Moderate* **Cuisine** *Steak house* **Menu prices** *$30–$40*

CIRCA 1886 🍷
149 Wentworth St., Charleston, SC 29401; (843) 853-7828 **Wine list** *California* **Wine prices** *Moderate* **Cuisine** *Contemporary* **Menu prices** *$25–$35*

COLLECTORS CAFÉ 🍷
7726 N. Kings Highway, Myrtle Beach, SC 29572; (843) 449-9370 **Wine list** *California, France* **Wine prices** Inexpensive **Corkage** *$20* **Cuisine** *Mediterranean* **Menu prices** *$19–$27*

CQ'S RESTAURANT 🍷
140 Lighthouse Road, Hilton Head Island, SC 29928; (843) 671-2779 **Wine list** *California* **Wine prices** *Moderate* **Corkage** *$15* **Cuisine** *American/French* **Menu prices** *$19–$28*

CRANE'S TAVERN & STEAKHOUSE 🍷
26 New Orleans Road, Hilton Head Island, SC 29928; (843) 341-2333 **Wine list** *California* **Wine prices** *Moderate* **Cuisine** *Steak house/seafood* **Menu prices** *$15–$36*

CRIBB & GREENBAUM'S NEW YORK PRIME 🍷
405 28th Ave. N., Myrtle Beach, SC 29577; (843) 448-8081 **Wine list** *California* **Wine prices** *Moderate* **Cuisine** *Steak house* **Menu prices** *$34–$68*

CYPRESS LOWCOUNTRY GRILLE 🍷
167 E. Bay St., Charleston, SC 29401; (843) 727-0111 **Wine list** *California* **Wine prices** Inexpensive **Cuisine** *Regional* **Menu prices** *$17–$33*

THE DINING ROOM AT WOODLANDS 🍷🍷
Woodlands Resort & Inn, 125 Parsons Road, Summerville, SC 29483; (843) 875-2600 **Wine list** *California, Burgundy, Bordeaux, Italy* **Wine prices** *Moderate* **Cuisine** *Contemporary American* **Menu prices** *$22–$32*

DIVINE FISH HOUSE 🍷
3993 Highway 17 Business, Murrells Inlet, SC 29576; (843) 651-5800 **Wine list** *California* **Wine prices** *Moderate* **Cuisine** *American/Pacific rim* **Menu prices** *$18–$29*

GOATFEATHERS 🍷
2017 Devine St., Columbia, SC 29205; (803) 256-3325 **Wine list** *California, France* **Wine prices** *Moderate* **Cuisine** *American* **Menu prices** *$12–$20*

🍷🍷🍷 Grand Award 🍷🍷 Best of Award of Excellence 🍷 Award of Excellence

GREG NORMAN'S AUSTRALIAN GRILLE 🍷
4930 Highway 17 S., North Myrtle Beach, SC 29582; (843) 361-0000 **Wine list** *Australia, California* **Wine prices** *Moderate* **Cuisine** *Australian* **Menu prices** *$16–$42*

HAMPTON STREET VINEYARD 🍷🍷
1207 Hampton St., Columbia, SC 29201; (803) 252-0850 **Wine list** *California, France* **Wine prices** *Moderate* **Corkage** *$15* **Cuisine** *Continental* **Menu prices** *$15–$20*

HIGH COTTON 🍷
199 E. Bay St., Charleston, SC 29401; (843) 724-3815 **Wine list** *California* **Wine prices** *Moderate* **Corkage** *$15* **Cuisine** *Steak house* **Menu prices** *$18–$30*

THE IRON WOLF CHOP HOUSE 🍷
Village at Wexford, B-6, Hilton Head Island, SC 29928; (843) 341-CHOP **Wine list** *California* **Wine prices** *Moderate* **Corkage** *$10* **Cuisine** *American* **Menu prices** *$13–$29*

LOUIS'S AT PAWLEYS 🍷
10880 Ocean Highway, Pawley's Island, SC 29585; (843) 237-8757 **Wine list** *France, California* **Wine prices** *Moderate* **Corkage** *$15* **Cuisine** *Regional* **Menu prices** *$18–$29*

MAGNOLIAS 🍷
185 E. Bay St., Charleston, SC 29401; (843) 577-7771 **Wine list** *California* **Wine prices** Inexpensive **Cuisine** *American* **Menu prices** *$10–$23*

MCCRADY'S 🍷🍷
2 Unity Alley, Charleston, SC 29401; (843) 577-0025 **Wine list** *California, Rhône, Italy* **Wine prices** *Moderate* **Corkage** *$20* **Cuisine** *French/American* **Menu prices** *$18–$29*

THE MELTING POT 🍷
5001 N. Kings Highway, Myrtle Beach, SC 29577; (843) 692-9003 **Wine list** *California* **Wine prices** Inexpensive **Corkage** *$10* **Cuisine** *Fondue* **Menu prices** *$15–$35*

MERITÄGE 🍷
235 E. Bay St., Charleston, SC 29401; (843) 723-8181 **Wine list** *California* **Wine prices** Inexpensive **Corkage** *$15* **Cuisine** *Continental* **Menu prices** *$5–$10*

MERITÄGE 🍷
729 Lady St., Columbia, SC 29201; (803) 929-1110 **Wine list** *California* **Wine prices** *Moderate* **Corkage** *$10* **Cuisine** *Tapas* **Menu prices** *$3–$10*

SOUTH CAROLINA

MR. FRIENDLY'S NEW SOUTHERN CAFÉ
2001-A Greene St., Columbia, SC 29205; (803) 254-7828 **Wine list** *California* **Wine prices** Inexpensive **Corkage** *$10* **Cuisine** *Contemporary Southern* **Menu prices** *$10–$20*

OLD FORT PUB
65 Skull Creek Drive, Hilton Head Island, SC 29926; (843) 681-2386 **Wine list** *California* **Wine prices** *Moderate* **Cuisine** *American* **Menu prices** *$19–$30*

THE OLD OYSTER FACTORY
101 Marshland Road, Hilton Head Island, SC 29938; (843) 681-6040 **Wine list** *France, California* **Wine prices** *Moderate* **Cuisine** *Seafood* **Menu prices** *$10–$24*

THE OLD POST OFFICE RESTAURANT
1442 Highway 174, Edisto Island, SC 29438; (843) 869-2339 **Wine list** *California* **Wine prices** Inexpensive **Cuisine** *American* **Menu prices** *$18–$22*

THE PARSON'S TABLE
4305 McCorsley Ave., Little River, SC 29566; (843) 249-3702 **Wine list** *California* **Wine prices** *Moderate* **Cuisine** *Regional* **Menu prices** *$14–$47*

PENINSULA GRILL
Historic Planters Inn, 112 N. Market St., Charleston, SC 29401; (843) 723-0700 **Wine list** *California, France* **Wine prices** *Moderate* **Cuisine** *Regional* **Menu prices** *$19–$29*

QUEEN
82 Queen St., Charleston, SC 29401; (843) 723-7591 **Wine list** *California* **Wine prices** *Moderate* **Corkage** *$15* **Cuisine** *Regional* **Menu prices** *$18–$23*

RED FISH
8 Archer Road, Hilton Head Island, SC 29938; (843) 686-3388 **Wine list** *California, France* **Wine prices** Inexpensive **Corkage** *$20* **Cuisine** *Caribbean* **Menu prices** *$18–$26*

RESTAURANT 123
7001 Saint Andrews Road, Columbia, SC 29212; (803) 781-0118 **Wine list** *California* **Wine prices** *Moderate* **Corkage** *$10* **Cuisine** *Continental* **Menu prices** *$19–$33*

RISTORANTE DIVINO
803 Gervais St., Columbia, SC 29201; (803) 799-4550 **Wine list** *California, Italy* **Wine prices** *Moderate* **Corkage** *$10* **Cuisine** *Northern Italian* **Menu prices** *$15–$28*

Grand Award · Best of Award of Excellence · Award of Excellence

SOBY'S

207 S. Main St., Greenville, SC 29601; (864) 232-7007 **Wine list** *California, France* **Wine prices** Inexpensive **Corkage** *$15* **Cuisine** *Contemporary Southern* **Menu prices** *$16–$28*

STAX'S PEPPERMILL

30 Orchard Park Drive, Haywood Plaza Shopping Center, Greenville, SC 29615; (864) 288-9320 **Wine list** *California* **Wine prices** *Moderate* **Cuisine** *Continental* **Menu prices** *$18–$30*

STRIPES

The Courtyard Building, 32 Office Park Road, Hilton Head Island, SC 29228; (843) 686-4747 **Wine list** *California* **Wine prices** *Moderate* **Cuisine** *American* **Menu prices** *$18–$33*

SULLIVAN'S METROPOLITAN GRILL

208 S. Main St., Anderson, SC 29621; (864) 226-8945 **Wine list** *California* **Wine prices** *Moderate* **Corkage** *$10* **Cuisine** *American/Mediterranean* **Menu prices** *$12–$22*

39 RUE DE JEAN

39 John St., Charleston, SC 29403; (843) 722-8881 **Wine list** *France* **Wine prices** *Moderate* **Cuisine** *French* **Menu prices** *$14–$22*

THOROUGHBREDS

9706 N. King's Highway, Myrtle Beach, SC 29572; (843) 497-2636 **Wine list** *California* **Wine prices** *Moderate* **Corkage** *$15* **Cuisine** *Continental* **Menu prices** *$18–$29*

TRISTAN

French Quarter Inn, 55 S. Market St., Charleston, SC 29401; (843) 534-2155 **Wine list** *California, France* **Wine prices** *Moderate* **Corkage** *$25* **Cuisine** *Contemporary* **Menu prices** *$18–$32*

VINTAGE RESTAURANT & WINE BAR

14 N. Market St., Charleston, SC 29401; (843) 577-0090 **Wine list** *California, France, Italy* **Wine prices** *Moderate* **Corkage** *$15* **Cuisine** *Contemporary American* **Menu prices** *$18–$26*

WATER'S EDGE

1407 Shrimp Boat Lane, Mount Pleasant, SC 29464; (843) 884-4074 **Wine list** *California, France* **Wine prices** *Moderate* **Corkage** *$15* **Cuisine** *American* **Menu prices** *$8–$23*

SOUTH DAKOTA

JAKES FINE DINING 🍷

The Midnight Star Casino, 677 Main St., Deadwood, SD 57732; (605) 578-1555 **Wine list** *California* **Wine prices** *Moderate* **Corkage** *$8* **Cuisine** *American* **Menu prices** *$16–$32*

TENNESSEE

BAKER PETERS JAZZ CLUB 🍷

9000 Kingston Pike, Knoxville, TN 37923; (865) 690-8110 **Wine list** *California* **Wine prices** *Moderate* **Corkage** *$10* **Cuisine** *Contemporary American* **Menu prices** *$20–$45*

BEETHOVEN'S GRILLE 🍷

3061 Mallory Lane, Franklin, TN 37064; (615) 771-7459 **Wine list** *California* **Wine prices** Inexpensive **Corkage** *$25* **Cuisine** *American* **Menu prices** *$12–$20*

BELLE MEADE BRASSERIE 🍷

106 Harding Place, Nashville, TN 37205; (615) 356-5450 **Wine list** *California* **Wine prices** *Moderate* **Cuisine** *Contemporary American* **Menu prices** *$18–$30*

BLACKBERRY FARM 🍷🍷

1471 W. Millers Cove Road, Walland, TN 37886; (865) 984-8166 **Wine list** *California, France, Italy* **Wine prices** *Moderate* **Corkage** *$25* **Cuisine** *American* **Menu prices** *Prix fixe only; $87*

BOUND'RY 🍷

911 20th Ave. S., Nashville, TN 37212; (615) 321-3043 **Wine list** *California* **Wine prices** *Moderate* **Cuisine** *International* **Menu prices** *$14–$30*

BY THE TRACKS BISTRO 🍷

5200 Kingston Pike, Knoxville, TN 37919; (865) 558-9500 **Wine list** *California* **Wine prices** Inexpensive **Corkage** *$10* **Cuisine** *American* **Menu prices** *$16–$28*

CAFÉ PACIFIC 🍷

1033 Oakland Ave., Johnson City, TN 37604; (423) 610-0117 **Wine list** *California* **Wine prices** *Moderate* **Corkage** *$15* **Cuisine** *Contemporary American/Asian* **Menu prices** *$17–$39*

CHEZ PHILIPPE
The Peabody Memphis, 149 Union Ave., Memphis, TN 38103; (901) 529-4188 **Wine list** *California* **Wine prices** *Moderate* **Cuisine** *Southern French* **Menu prices** *$25–$35*

ERLING JENSEN, THE RESTAURANT
1044 S. Yates Road, Memphis, TN 38119; (901) 763-3700 **Wine list** *California* **Wine prices** *Moderate* **Corkage** *$10* **Cuisine** *International* **Menu prices** *$26–$40*

F. SCOTT'S
2210 Crestmoor Road, Nashville, TN 37215; (615) 269-5861 **Wine list** *California* **Wine prices** *Moderate* **Corkage** *$12* **Cuisine** *American* **Menu prices** *$16–$27*

FLEMING'S PRIME STEAKHOUSE & WINE BAR
2525 West End Ave., Nashville, TN 37203; (615) 342-0131 **Wine list** *California* **Wine prices** *Moderate* **Cuisine** *Steak house* **Menu prices** *$18–$31*

FOLK'S FOLLY PRIME STEAK HOUSE
551 S. Mendenhall Road, Memphis, TN 38117; (901) 762-8200 **Wine list** *California* **Wine prices** *Moderate* **Corkage** *$12* **Cuisine** *Steak house* **Menu prices** *$19–$42*

FRANK GRISANTI'S
Embassy Suites, 1022 Shady Grove Road, Memphis, TN 38120; (901) 761-9462 **Wine list** *California* **Wine prices** *Moderate* **Corkage** *$10* **Cuisine** *Northern Italian* **Menu prices** *$13–$32*

GALLOWAY'S RESTAURANT
The Carnegie Hotel, 1216 W. State of Franklin Road, Johnson City, TN 37604; (423) 979-6401 **Wine list** *California* **Wine prices** *Moderate* **Corkage** *$15* **Cuisine** *American/continental* **Menu prices** *$12–$24*

LA TOURELLE
2146 Monroe Ave., Memphis, TN 38104; (901) 726-5771 **Wine list** *California, France* **Wine prices** *Moderate* **Corkage** *$10* **Cuisine** *French* **Menu prices** *$20–$36*

THE MAD PLATTER
1239 Sixth Ave. N., Nashville, TN 37208; (615) 242-2563 **Wine list** *California* **Wine prices** *Moderate* **Cuisine** *International* **Menu prices** *$16–$29*

TENNESSEE

MARIO'S 🍷

2005 Broadway, Nashville, TN 37203; (615) 327-3232
Wine list *California, Italy* **Wine prices** *Expensive* **Cuisine** *Northern Italian* **Menu prices** *$18–$29*

MIDTOWN CAFÉ 🍷

102 19th Ave. S., Nashville, TN 37203; (615) 320-7176
Wine list *California* **Wine prices** *Moderate* **Corkage** *$15* **Cuisine** *Contemporary American* **Menu prices** *$14–$35*

MORTON'S OF CHICAGO 🍷

618 Church St., Nashville, TN 37219; (615) 259-4558
Wine list *California* **Wine prices** *Expensive* **Corkage** *$15* **Cuisine** *Steak house* **Menu prices** *$19–$63*

NAPLES ITALIAN RESTAURANT 🍷

5500 Kingston Pike, Knoxville, TN 37919; (865) 584-5033
Wine list *California, Italy* **Wine prices** *Moderate* **Corkage** *$8* **Cuisine** *Italian* **Menu prices** *$9–$19*

THE ORANGERY 🍷🍷

5412 Kingston Pike, Knoxville, TN 37919; (865) 588-2964
Wine list *Burgundy, California* **Wine prices** *Expensive* **Corkage** *$10* **Cuisine** *Continental/contemporary American* **Menu prices** *$15–$38*

THE PALM 🍷

140 Fifth Ave. S., Nashville, TN 37203; (615) 742-7256
Wine list *California* **Wine prices** *Moderate* **Cuisine** *Steak house* **Menu prices** *$15–$60*

RUTH'S CHRIS STEAK HOUSE 🍷

6120 Poplar Ave., Memphis, TN 38119; (901) 761-0055
Wine list *California* **Wine prices** *Moderate* **Corkage** *$20* **Cuisine** *Steak house* **Menu prices** *$16–$35*

SOUTHSIDE GRILL 🍷

1400 Cowart St., Chattanooga, TN 37408; (423) 266-9211
Wine list *California* **Wine prices** *Moderate* **Corkage** *$15* **Cuisine** *Contemporary American* **Menu prices** *$15–$29*

SPERRY'S RESTAURANT 🍷

5109 Harding Road, Nashville, TN 37205; (615) 353-0809
Wine list *California* **Wine prices** *Expensive* **Cuisine** *Steak house* **Menu prices** *$13–$35*

STOCK-YARD RESTAURANT 🍷

901 Second Ave. N., Nashville, TN 37201; (615) 255-6464
Wine list *California, France* **Wine prices** *Moderate* **Cuisine** *Steak house* **Menu prices** *$25–$120*

🍷🍷🍷 Grand Award 🍷🍷 Best of Award of Excellence 🍷 Award of Excellence

SUNSET GRILL
2001-A Belcourt Ave., Nashville, TN 37212; (615) 386-FOOD **Wine list** *California* **Wine prices** *Moderate* **Corkage** *$15* **Cuisine** *American* **Menu prices** *$13–$70*

212 MARKET RESTAURANT
212 Market St., Chattanooga, TN 37402; (423) 265-1212 **Wine list** *California, Italy, Australia* **Wine prices** *Moderate* **Cuisine** *American* **Menu prices** *$10–$30*

VALENTINO'S RISTORANTE
1907 West End Ave., Nashville, TN 37203; (615) 327-0148 **Wine list** *Italy, California* **Wine prices** *Moderate* **Cuisine** *Northern Italian* **Menu prices** *$15–$25*

THE WILD BOAR RESTAURANT
2014 Broadway, Nashville, TN 37203; (615) 329-1313 **Wine list** *Bordeaux, California* **Wine selections** *2,000* **Number of bottles** *15,000* **Wine prices** *Expensive* **Corkage** *$35* **Cuisine** *American/French* **Menu prices** *$23–$35* **Credit cards** *AX, MC, VS, DV*
Grand Award since 1993

TEXAS

DALLAS

ABACUS
4511 McKinney Ave., Dallas, TX 75205; (214) 559-3111 **Wine list** *California* **Wine prices** *Moderate* **Cuisine** *Contemporary* **Menu prices** *$25–$38*

ADELMO'S RISTORANTE
4537 Cole Ave., Dallas, TX 75205; (214) 559-0325 **Wine list** *Tuscany, California* **Wine prices** *Moderate* **Cuisine** *Mediterranean* **Menu prices** *$15–$33*

AL BIERNAT'S RESTAURANT
4217 Oaklawn Ave., Dallas, TX 75219; (214) 219-2201 **Wine list** *California, France* **Wine prices** *Expensive* **Cuisine** *Steak house* **Menu prices** *$18–$40*

ARCODORO & POMODORO RISTORANTE ITALIANI
2708 Routh St., Dallas, TX 75201; (214) 871-1924 **Wine list** *Italy* **Wine prices** *Moderate* **Cuisine** *Italian/Sardinian* **Menu prices** *$17–$32*

CAFÉ PACIFIC 🍷
24 Highland Park Village, Dallas, TX 75205; (214) 526-1170 **Wine list** *California* **Wine prices** *Moderate* **Cuisine** *Contemporary American/seafood* **Menu prices** *$15–$35*

THE CAPITAL GRILLE 🍷
500 Crescent Court, Dallas, TX 75201; (214) 303-0500 **Wine list** *California, Bordeaux* **Wine prices** *Moderate* **Cuisine** *Steak house* **Menu prices** *$17–$33*

CHAMBERLAIN'S STEAK & CHOP HOUSE 🍷
5330 Belt Line Road, Dallas, TX 75240; (972) 934-2467 **Wine list** *California* **Wine prices** *Moderate* **Cuisine** *Steak house* **Menu prices** *$15–$32*

CITY CAFÉ 🍷
5757 W. Lovers Lane, Dallas, TX 75209; (214) 351-2233 **Wine list** *California* **Wine prices** *Moderate* **Cuisine** *American* **Menu prices** *$14–$28*

DEL FRISCO'S DOUBLE EAGLE STEAK HOUSE 🍷🍷
5251 Spring Valley Road, Dallas, TX 75240; (972) 490-9000 **Wine list** *California, France* **Wine prices** *Expensive* **Cuisine** *Steak house* **Menu prices** *$20–$47*

FLEMING'S PRIME STEAKHOUSE & WINE BAR 🍷
18020 Dallas Parkway, Dallas, TX 75287; (972) 267-3050 **Wine list** *California* **Wine prices** *Moderate* **Cuisine** *Steak house* **Menu prices** *$18–$31*

THE GREEN ROOM 🍷
2715 Elm St., Dallas, TX 75226; (214) 748-7666 **Wine list** *California, France* **Wine prices** *Moderate* **Cuisine** *Contemporary American* **Menu prices** *$15–$32*

IL SOLE RESTAURANT & WINE BAR 🍷
4514 Travis St., Dallas, TX 75205; (214) 559-3888 **Wine list** *Italy, California* **Wine prices** *Moderate* **Cuisine** *Italian* **Menu prices** *$14–$28*

JEROBOAM 🍷
1501 Main St., Dallas, TX 75201; (214) 748-7226 **Wine list** *France* **Wine prices** *Moderate* **Cuisine** *French* **Menu prices** *$15–$25*

THE LANDMARK RESTAURANT 🍷
The Melrose Hotel, 3015 Oak Lawn Ave., Dallas, TX 75219; (214) 224-3152 **Wine list** *France, California* **Wine prices** *Moderate* **Cuisine** *Contemporary American* **Menu prices** *$26–$38*

LIBERTY NOODLES
5600 W. Lovers Lane, No. 136, Dallas, TX 75209; (214) 350-1133 **Wine list** *California* **Wine prices** *Inexpensive* **Cuisine** *Pan-Asian* **Menu prices** *$8–$22*

LOLA
2917 Fairmount St., Dallas, TX 75201; (214) 855-0700 **Wine list** *Bordeaux, Burgundy, California, Rhône, Italy* **Wine prices** *Moderate* **Corkage** *$5* **Cuisine** *Contemporary American* **Menu prices** *Prix fixe only; $34–$49*

THE MANSION ON TURTLE CREEK
2821 Turtle Creek Blvd., Dallas, TX 75219; (214) 559-2100 **Wine list** *California, Bordeaux* **Wine prices** *Expensive* **Cuisine** *Southwestern* **Menu prices** *$26–$55*

THE MELTING POT
4900 Beltline Road, Dallas, TX 75254; (972) 960-7027 **Wine list** *California* **Wine prices** *Inexpensive* **Cuisine** *Fondue* **Menu prices** *$13–$30*

MI PIACI
14854 Montfort Drive, Dallas, TX 75240; (972) 934-8424 **Wine list** *Italy* **Wine prices** *Moderate* **Cuisine** *Italian* **Menu prices** *$14–$36*

MODO MIO
18352 N. Dallas Parkway, Dallas, TX 75287; (972) 671-6636 **Wine list** *Italy, California* **Wine prices** *Moderate* **Cuisine** *Italian* **Menu prices** *$10–$28*

MORTON'S OF CHICAGO
501 Elm St., Dallas, TX 75202; (214) 741-2277 **Wine list** *California* **Wine prices** *Expensive* **Cuisine** *Steak house* **Menu prices** *$20–$35*

NANA
Wyndham Anatole Hotel, 2201 Stemmons Freeway, Dallas, TX 75207; (214) 761-7470 **Wine list** *California, France* **Wine prices** *Expensive* **Cuisine** *Contemporary American* **Menu prices** *$32–$65*

NEWPORT'S SEAFOOD & STEAK
703 McKinney Ave., Dallas, TX 75202; (214) 954-0220 **Wine list** *California* **Wine prices** *Expensive* **Cuisine** *Steak house* **Menu prices** *$20–$35*

NICK & SAM'S 🍷
3008 Maple Ave., Dallas, TX 75201; (214) 871-7444 **Wine list** *California, France* **Wine prices** *Moderate* **Cuisine** *Steak house* **Menu prices** *$16–$32*

THE OCEANAIRE SEAFOOD ROOM 🍷
The Westin Galleria, 13340 Dallas Parkway, Dallas, TX 75240; (972) 759-BASS **Wine list** *California* **Wine prices** *Moderate* **Cuisine** *Seafood* **Menu prices** *$18–$32*

THE PALM 🍷
701 Ross Ave., Dallas, TX 75202; (214) 698-0470 **Wine list** *California* **Wine prices** *Moderate* **Cuisine** *Steak house* **Menu prices** *$18–$60*

PAPPAS BROS. STEAKHOUSE DALLAS 🍷🍷
10477 Lombardy Lane, Dallas, TX 75220; (214) 366-2000 **Wine list** *California, France, Australia, Italy* **Wine prices** *Moderate* **Cuisine** *Steak house* **Menu prices** *$21–$36*

PAUL'S PORTERHOUSE STEAKHOUSE 🍷
10960 Composite Drive, Dallas, TX 75220; (214) 357-0279 **Wine list** *California* **Wine prices** *Expensive* **Cuisine** *Steak house* **Menu prices** *$24–$42*

ROOSTER 🍷
3521 Oak Grove Ave., Dallas, TX 75204; (214) 521-1234 **Wine list** *California* **Wine prices** *Moderate* **Cuisine** *Contemporary American Southern* **Menu prices** *$17–$28*

RUTH'S CHRIS STEAK HOUSE 🍷
5922 Cedar Springs Road, Dallas, TX 75235; (214) 902-8080 **Wine list** *California* **Wine prices** *Moderate* **Cuisine** *Steak house* **Menu prices** *$20–$35*

RUTH'S CHRIS STEAK HOUSE 🍷
17840 Dallas Parkway, Dallas, TX 75287; (972) 250-2244 **Wine list** *California* **Wine prices** *Moderate* **Cuisine** *Steak house* **Menu prices** *$20–$35*

STEEL RESTAURANT & LOUNGE 🍷🍷
3102 Oak Lawn Ave., Dallas, TX 75219; (214) 219-9908 **Wine list** *California, France* **Wine prices** *Expensive* **Cuisine** *Japanese/Vietnamese* **Menu prices** *$21–$39*

SULLIVAN'S STEAKHOUSE 🍷
17795 N. Dallas Parkway, Dallas, TX 75287; (972) 267-9393 **Wine list** *California* **Wine prices** *Expensive* **Cuisine** *Steak house* **Menu prices** *$20–$29*

🍷🍷🍷 Grand Award 🍷🍷 Best of Award of Excellence 🍷 Award of Excellence

III FORKS STEAKHOUSE 🍷🍷
17776 Dallas Parkway, Dallas, TX 75287; (972) 267-1776 **Wine list** *California, France* **Wine prices** *Moderate* **Cuisine** *Steak house* **Menu prices** *$20–$40*

ZIZIKI'S RESTAURANT & BAR 🍷
4514 Travis St., Dallas, TX 75205; (214) 521-2233 **Wine list** *California, Greece* **Wine prices** *Moderate* **Cuisine** *Mediterranean* **Menu prices** *$15–$25*

TEXAS

HOUSTON

ARCODORO RISTORANTE ITALIANO 🍷
5000 Westheimer Road, Houston, TX 77056; (713) 621-6888 **Wine list** *Italy* **Wine prices** *Expensive* **Cuisine** *Italian/Sardinian* **Menu prices** *$19–$33*

ARIES 🍷
4315 Montrose Blvd., Houston, TX 77006; (713) 526-4404 **Wine list** *California* **Wine prices** *Moderate* **Cuisine** *Contemporary American* **Menu prices** *$18–$32*

ASHIANA 🍷
12610 Briar Forest Drive, Houston, TX 77077; (281) 679-5555 **Wine list** *California* **Wine prices** *Moderate* **Cuisine** *Indian* **Menu prices** *$20–$75*

BACKSTREET CAFÉ 🍷
1103 S. Shepherd Drive, Houston, TX 77019; (713) 521-2239 **Wine list** *California, France* **Wine prices** *Moderate* **Cuisine** *Contemporary American* **Menu prices** *$13–$26*

BENJY'S 🍷
2424 Dunstan St., Houston, TX 77005; (713) 522-7602 **Wine list** *California* **Wine prices** *Moderate* **Cuisine** *Contemporary American* **Menu prices** *$12–$25*

BRENNAN'S OF HOUSTON 🍷
3300 Smith St., Houston, TX 77006; (713) 522-9711 **Wine list** *California, France* **Wine prices** *Moderate* **Cuisine** *Texan/creole* **Menu prices** *$20–$34*

CAFÉ RABELAIS 🍷
2462 Bolsover, Houston, TX 77005; (713) 526-6841 **Wine list** *France* **Wine prices** *Moderate* **Cuisine** *French* **Menu prices** *$13–$28*

THE CAPITAL GRILLE 🍷
5365 Westheimer Road, Houston, TX 77056; (713) 623-4600 **Wine list** *California, Bordeaux* **Wine prices** *Moderate* **Cuisine** *Steak house* **Menu prices** *$17–$30*

CARMELO'S RISTORANTE ITALIANO 🍷
14795 Memorial Drive, Houston, TX 77079; (281) 531-0696 **Wine list** *Italy, California* **Wine prices** *Moderate* **Cuisine** *Sicilian* **Menu prices** *$16–$36*

DA MARCO 🍷
1520 Westheimer Road, Houston, TX 77006; (713) 807-8857 **Wine list** *Italy* **Wine prices** *Moderate* **Cuisine** *Italian* **Menu prices** *$17–$32*

EL MESON 🍷
2425 University Blvd., Houston, TX 77005; (713) 522-9306 **Wine list** *Spain, California* **Wine prices** *Moderate* **Cuisine** *Cuban/Mexican/Spanish* **Menu prices** *$10–$18*

FLEMING'S PRIME STEAKHOUSE & WINE BAR 🍷
2405 W. Alabama St., Houston, TX 77098; (713) 520-5959 **Wine list** *California* **Wine prices** *Moderate* **Cuisine** *Steak house* **Menu prices** *$19–$32*

FOGO DE CHÃO 🍷
8250 Westheimer Road, Houston, TX 77063; (713) 978-6500 **Wine list** *California, Chile* **Wine prices** *Expensive* **Cuisine** *Brazilian* **Menu prices** *Prix fixe only; $39*

GUERIN'S CELLAR 🍷
11920 Westheimer Road, Houston, TX 77077; (281) 558-5095 **Wine list** *France* **Wine prices** *Moderate* **Cuisine** *Continental* **Menu prices** *$25–$36*

HUGO'S 🍷
1600 Westheimer Road, Houston, TX 77006; (713) 524-7744 **Wine list** *California* **Wine prices** Inexpensive **Cuisine** *Contemporary American* **Menu prices** *$12–$22*

LA STRADA 🍷
5161 San Felipe St., Houston, TX 77056; (713) 850-9999 **Wine list** *California, Italy* **Wine prices** *Moderate* **Cuisine** *Contemporary Italian* **Menu prices** *$11–$27*

LAURIER CAFÉ & WINE 🍷
3139 Richmond Ave., Houston, TX 77098; (713) 807-1632 **Wine list** *California* **Wine prices** *Moderate* **Cuisine** *Contemporary American* **Menu prices** *$12–$29*

🍷🍷🍷 Grand Award 🍷🍷 Best of Award of Excellence 🍷 Award of Excellence

LYNN'S STEAKHOUSE 🍷🍷
955 1/2 Dairy Ashford St., Houston, TX 77079; (281) 870-0807 **Wine list** *California, France* **Wine prices** *Moderate* **Cuisine** *Steak house* **Menu prices** *$29–$35*

MARK'S AMERICAN CUISINE 🍷
1658 Westheimer Road, Houston, TX 77006; (713) 523-3800 **Wine list** *California, France* **Wine prices** *Moderate* **Cuisine** *Contemporary American* **Menu prices** *$18–$40*

MORTON'S OF CHICAGO 🍷
5000 Westheimer Road, Houston, TX 77056; (713) 629-1946 **Wine list** *California* **Wine prices** *Expensive* **Cuisine** *Steak house* **Menu prices** *$28–$35*

THE PALM 🍷
6100 Westheimer Road, Houston, TX 77057; (713) 977-2544 **Wine list** *California* **Wine prices** *Moderate* **Corkage** *$15* **Cuisine** *Steak house* **Menu prices** *$20–$120*

PAPPAS BROS. STEAKHOUSE HOUSTON 🍷🍷
5839 Westheimer Road, Houston, TX 77057; (713) 780-7352 **Wine list** *California, France, Australia, Italy* **Wine prices** *Moderate* **Cuisine** *Steak house* **Menu prices** *$19–$35*

PERRY'S GRILLE & STEAKHOUSE 🍷
487 Bay Area Blvd., Clearlake, TX 77058; (281) 286-8800 **Wine list** *California* **Wine prices** *Moderate* **Cuisine** *Steak house* **Menu prices** *$11–$33*

PREGO 🍷
2520 Amherst St., Houston, TX 77005; (713) 529-2420 **Wine list** *California* **Wine prices** *Moderate* **Cuisine** *Mediterranean* **Menu prices** *$12–$24*

QUATTRO 🍷
Four Seasons Hotel Houston, 1300 Lamar St., Houston, TX 77010; (713) 276-4700 **Wine list** *California, France* **Wine prices** *Expensive* **Cuisine** *American/Italian* **Menu prices** *$15–$28*

RAINBOW LODGE 🍷
1 Birdsall St., Houston, TX 77007; (713) 861-8666 **Wine list** *California, France, Texas* **Wine prices** *Moderate* **Cuisine** *Regional* **Menu prices** *$16–$39*

RIVER OAKS GRILL 🍷
2630 Westheimer Road, Houston, TX 77098; (713) 520-1738 **Wine list** *California, France* **Wine prices** *Expensive* **Cuisine** *Continental* **Menu prices** *$20–$38*

ROTISSERIE FOR BEEF & BIRD 🍷🍷🍷
2200 Wilcrest St., Houston, TX 77042; (713) 977-9524
Wine list *Bordeaux, California* **Wine selections** *1,100* **Number of bottles** *19,000* **Wine prices** Inexpensive **Cuisine** *Steak house/seafood* **Menu prices** *$19–$33* **Credit cards** *AX, MC, VS, DV*
Grand Award since 1988

RUTH'S CHRIS STEAK HOUSE 🍷
6213 Richmond Ave., Houston, TX 77057; (713) 789-2333
Wine list *California* **Wine prices** *Moderate* **Cuisine** *Steak house* **Menu prices** *$18–$30*

SIERRA GRILL 🍷
4704 Montrose Blvd., Houston, TX 77006; (713) 942-7757
Wine list *California, France, Australia* **Wine prices** *Moderate* **Cuisine** *Contemporary American* **Menu prices** *$14–$39*

SULLIVAN'S STEAKHOUSE 🍷
4608 Westheimer Road, Houston, TX 77027; (713) 961-0333 **Wine list** *California* **Wine prices** *Expensive* **Cuisine** *Steak house* **Menu prices** *$19–$29*

TASTE OF TEXAS RESTAURANT 🍷
10505 Katy Freeway, Houston, TX 77024; (713) 932-6901
Wine list *California* **Wine prices** *Moderate* **Cuisine** *Steak house* **Menu prices** *$20–$40*

TWO CHEFS BISTRO 🍷
2300 Westheimer Road, Houston, TX 77098; (713) 523-2444 **Wine list** *California* **Wine prices** *Moderate* **Cuisine** *American* **Menu prices** *$13–$23*

TEXAS

OTHER CITIES

BASIL'S RESTAURANT 🍷
900 W. 10th St., Austin, TX 78703; (512) 477-5576 **Wine list** *California* **Wine prices** *Moderate* **Cuisine** *Italian* **Menu prices** *$14–$30*

BIGA ON THE BANKS 🍷
203 S. Saint Mary's St., San Antonio, TX 78205; (210) 225-0722 **Wine list** *California, France* **Wine prices** *Moderate* **Cuisine** *Contemporary American* **Menu prices** *$17–$36*

RUTH'S CHRIS STEAK HOUSE
14135 Southwest Freeway, Sugar Land, TX 77478; (281) 491-9300 **Wine list** *California* **Wine prices** *Moderate* **Cuisine** *Steak house* **Menu prices** *$23–$58*

SANTA FE STEAK HOUSE
1918 S. 10th St., McAllen, TX 78501; (956) 630-2331 **Wine list** *California* **Wine prices** *Moderate* **Corkage** *$15* **Cuisine** *Steak house* **Menu prices** *$15–$30*

SIENA RESTAURANT
6203 N. Capital of Texas Highway, Austin, TX 78731; (512) 349-7667 **Wine list** *Italy, California* **Wine prices** *Moderate* **Cuisine** *Tuscan* **Menu prices** *$11–$30*

SULLIVAN'S STEAKHOUSE
300 Colorado St., Austin, TX 78701; (512) 495-6504 **Wine list** *California* **Wine prices** *Moderate* **Cuisine** *Steak house* **Menu prices** *$17–$29*

THE TOWER RESTAURANT
701 E. Bowie St., San Antonio, TX 78205; (210) 223-3101 **Wine list** *California* **Wine prices** *Moderate* **Cuisine** *Continental* **Menu prices** *$17–$36*

TRULUCK'S
400 Colorado St., Austin, TX 78701; (512) 482-9000 **Wine list** *California* **Wine prices** *Moderate* **Cuisine** *Seafood* **Menu prices** *$15–$35*

ZINC CHAMPAGNE & WINE BAR
207 N. Presa St., San Antonio, TX 78205; (210) 224-2900 **Wine list** *California* **Wine prices** *Moderate* **Cuisine** *American* **Menu prices** *$11–$18*

UTAH

AERIE
Cliff Lodge, Snowbird Ski & Summer Resort, Little Cottonwood Canyon, Snowbird, UT 84092; (801) 933-2160 **Wine list** *California* **Wine prices** *Moderate* **Corkage** *$10* **Cuisine** *Contemporary American* **Menu prices** *$18–$34*

BACI TRATTORIA
140 W. Pierpont Ave., Salt Lake City, UT 84101; (801) 328-1500 **Wine list** *California* **Wine prices** Inexpensive **Corkage** *$8* **Cuisine** *Italian* **Menu prices** *$9–$33*

BANGKOK THAI 🍷
1400 Foothill Drive, Salt Lake City, UT 84108; (801) 582-8424 **Wine list** *California, France, Italy* **Wine prices** *Expensive* **Corkage** *$8* **Cuisine** *Thai/Pacific Rim* **Menu prices** *$9–$22*

BANGKOK THAI ON MAIN 🍷
Park Hotel, 605 Main St., Park City, UT 84060; (435) 649-THAI **Wine list** *California* **Wine prices** *Expensive* **Corkage** *$15* **Cuisine** *Thai* **Menu prices** *$13–$30*

BISTRO TOUJOURS 🍷
Chateaux at Silver Lake, 7815 Royal St. E., Park City, UT 84060; (435) 940-2200 **Wine list** *France, California* **Wine prices** *Expensive* **Corkage** *$20* **Cuisine** *French* **Menu prices** *$18–$38*

BLIND DOG GRILL 🍷
1781 Sidewinder Drive, Park City, UT 84060; (435) 655-0800 **Wine list** *California* **Wine prices** *Expensive* **Cuisine** *American* **Menu prices** *$19–$35*

BLUE BOAR INN & RESTAURANT 🍷
1235 Warm Springs Road, Midway, UT 84049; (435) 654-1400 **Wine list** *California, France* **Wine prices** *Moderate* **Corkage** *$10* **Cuisine** *Contemporary* **Menu prices** *$21–$32*

THE CABIN RESTAURANT 🍷
Grand Summit Resort Hotel, 4000 The Canyons Resort Drive, Park City, UT 84098; (435) 615-8060 **Wine list** *California* **Wine prices** *Expensive* **Corkage** *$12* **Cuisine** *Regional* **Menu prices** *$18–$38*

CHIMAYO 🍷
368 Main St., Park City, UT 84060; (435) 649-6222 **Wine list** *Spain, California* **Wine prices** *Expensive* **Corkage** *$12* **Cuisine** *French/Southwestern* **Menu prices** *$24–$36*

FLEMING'S PRIME STEAKHOUSE & WINE BAR 🍷
20 S. 400 West, Salt Lake City, UT 84101; (801) 355-3704 **Wine list** *California* **Wine prices** *Expensive* **Cuisine** *Steak house* **Menu prices** *$18–$31*

GLITRETIND RESTAURANT 🍷
Stein Eriksen Lodge, 7700 Stein Way, Park City, UT 84060; (435) 645-6455 **Wine list** *California, France* **Wine prices** *Moderate* **Corkage** *$18* **Cuisine** *Contemporary American* **Menu prices** *$22–$34*

GOLDENER HIRSCH
Goldener Hirsch Inn, 7570 Royal St. E., Park City, UT 84060; (435) 649-7770 **Wine list** *California, France* **Wine prices** *Expensive* **Cuisine** *Continental* **Menu prices** *$18–$36*

GRAPPA
151 Main St., Park City, UT 84060; (435) 645-0636 **Wine list** *Italy, California* **Wine prices** *Expensive* **Corkage** *$12* **Cuisine** *Italian* **Menu prices** *$24–$36*

INN ON THE CREEK
375 Rainbow Lane, Midway, UT 84049; (435) 654-0892 **Wine list** *California, France* **Wine prices** *Expensive* **Corkage** *$10* **Cuisine** *French/American* **Menu prices** *$15–$30*

LA CAILLE
The Cottage, 9565 Wasatch Blvd., Little Cottonwood Canyon, UT 84092; (801) 942-1751 **Wine list** *California* **Wine prices** *Expensive* **Cuisine** *French* **Menu prices** *$39–$70*

L'AVENUE BISTRO
1355 E. 2100 South, Salt Lake City, UT 84105; (801) 485-4494 **Wine list** *France, California* **Wine prices** *Moderate* **Corkage** *$8* **Cuisine** *French* **Menu prices** *$14–$24*

LOG HAVEN RESTAURANT
6451 E. Millcreek Canyon, Salt Lake City, UT 84109; (801) 272-8255 **Wine list** *France, California, Italy* **Wine prices** Inexpensive **Corkage** *$15* **Cuisine** *International* **Menu prices** *$14–$32*

LUGANO
3364 S. 2300 East, Salt Lake City, UT 84109; (801) 412-9994 **Wine list** *Italy, California* **Wine prices** *Moderate* **Corkage** *$8* **Cuisine** *Italian* **Menu prices** *$9–$19*

THE MARIPOSA
7600 Royal St., Park City, UT 84060; (435) 645-6715 **Wine list** *California* **Wine prices** *Expensive* **Corkage** *$15* **Cuisine** *Contemporary American* **Menu prices** *$27–$39*

MARKET STREET BROILER
260 S. 1300 East, Salt Lake City, UT 84102; (801) 583-8808 **Wine list** *California* **Wine prices** *Moderate* **Corkage** *$8* **Cuisine** *Seafood* **Menu prices** *$8–$16*

MARKET STREET GRILL
2985 E. 6580 South, Salt Lake City, UT 84121; (801) 942-8860 **Wine list** *California* **Wine prices** *Expensive* **Corkage** *$8* **Cuisine** *Seafood* **Menu prices** *$15–$30*

METROPOLITAN RESTAURANT 🍷
173 W. Broadway, Salt Lake City, UT 84101; (801) 364-3472 **Wine list** *California, France* **Wine prices** *Expensive* **Corkage** *$15* **Cuisine** *Contemporary American* **Menu prices** *$18–$30*

MONSOON THAI BISTRO 🍷
1615 S. Foothill Drive, Salt Lake City, UT 84108; (801) 583-5339 **Wine list** *California* **Wine prices** *Expensive* **Corkage** *$15* **Cuisine** *Thai* **Menu prices** *$10–$36*

THE PARIS BISTRO 🍷
1500 S. 1500 East, Salt Lake City, UT 84105; (801) 486-5585 **Wine list** *France* **Wine prices** *Moderate* **Corkage** *$10* **Cuisine** *Contemporary* **Menu prices** *$14–$28*

RIVERS RESTAURANT 🍷
6405 S. 3000 East, Salt Lake City, UT 84121; (801) 733-6600 **Wine list** *California* **Wine prices** *Expensive* **Corkage** *$8* **Cuisine** *Contemporary American* **Menu prices** *$13–$29*

SAI-SOMMET 🍷
Deer Valley Club, 7720 Royal St. East, Park City, UT 84068; (435) 645-9909 **Wine list** *California* **Wine prices** *Expensive* **Cuisine** *Swiss/American* **Menu prices** *$24–$31*

SHALLOW SHAFT 🍷
Utah Highway 210, Alta, UT 84092; (801) 742-2177 **Wine list** *California* **Wine prices** *Expensive* **Corkage** *$10* **Cuisine** *Southwestern* **Menu prices** *$18–$48*

SPENCER'S FOR STEAKS & CHOPS 🍷
Hilton Salt Lake City Center, 255 S. West Temple, Salt Lake City, UT 84101; (801) 238-4748 **Wine list** *California* **Wine prices** *Expensive* **Cuisine** *Steak house* **Menu prices** *$15–$30*

THIRD & MAIN 🍷
280 S. Main St., Salt Lake City, UT 84101; (801) 364-4600 **Wine list** *California* **Wine prices** *Moderate* **Corkage** *$8* **Cuisine** *American* **Menu prices** *$11–$23*

350 MAIN NEW AMERICAN BRASSERIE 🍷
350 Main St., Park City, UT 84060; (435) 649-3140 **Wine list** *California* **Wine prices** *Expensive* **Cuisine** *Contemporary American* **Menu prices** *$19–$26*

THE TREE ROOM 🍷
Sundance Resort, Sundance, UT 84604; (801) 223-4200 **Wine list** *California, France* **Wine prices** *Expensive* **Corkage** *$15* **Cuisine** *Regional* **Menu prices** *$22–$36*

TROFI RESTAURANT
Salt Lake City Hilton, 255 S. West Temple, Salt Lake City, UT 84101; (801) 238-4877 **Wine list** *California* **Wine prices** *Moderate* **Cuisine** *American* **Menu prices** *$11–$18*

TUSCANY
2832 E. 6200 South, Salt Lake City, UT 84121; (801) 277-9919 **Wine list** *California, France* **Wine prices** *Expensive* **Corkage** *$8* **Cuisine** *Northern Italian* **Menu prices** *$13–$29*

WAHSO
577 Main St., Park City, UT 84060; (435) 615-0300 **Wine list** *California* **Wine prices** *Expensive* **Corkage** *$12* **Cuisine** *Asian/French* **Menu prices** *$22–$36*

VERMONT

BARNARD INN RESTAURANT
5518 Route 12, Barnard, VT 05031; (802) 234-9961 **Wine list** *California, France* **Wine prices** *Moderate* **Cuisine** *American* **Menu prices** *$23–$31*

BASIN HARBOR CLUB
4800 Basin Harbor Road, Vergennes, VT 05491; (802) 475-2311 **Wine list** *California* **Wine prices** Inexpensive **Cuisine** *Continental/American* **Menu prices** *Prix fixe only; $35*

BISTRO HENRY
1778 Route 11/30, Manchester Center, VT 05255; (802) 362-4982 **Wine list** *California, France* **Wine prices** *Moderate* **Cuisine** *Mediterranean* **Menu prices** *$19–$35*

CHEF'S TABLE & MAIN STREET GRILL & BAR
118 Main St., Montpelier, VT 05602; (802) 229-9202 **Wine list** *California, France* **Wine prices** *Moderate* **Cuisine** *American* **Menu prices** *$15–$19*

COLONNADE ROOM
The Equinox, 3567 Main St., Manchester Village, VT 05254; (800) 362-4747 **Wine list** *California* **Wine prices** *Expensive* **Cuisine** *American* **Menu prices** *$20–$24*

DEERHILL INN & RESTAURANT
14 Valley View Road, West Dover, VT 05356; (802) 464-3100 **Wine list** *California* **Wine prices** *Moderate* **Cuisine** *Contemporary American* **Menu prices** *$23–$30*

EMILY'S 🍷

Stowehof Inn, 434 Edson Hill Road, Stowe, VT 05672; (802) 253-9722 **Wine list** *France, California* **Wine prices** *Moderate* **Cuisine** *American* **Menu prices** *$20–$28*

FOUR COLUMNS INN 🍷

21 West St., Newfane, VT 05345; (800) 787-6633 **Wine list** *California, France* **Wine prices** *Moderate* **Cuisine** *Contemporary American/French/Pacific Rim* **Menu prices** *$21–$36*

HEMINGWAY'S RESTAURANT 🍷

Route 4, Killington, VT 05751; (802) 422-3886 **Wine list** *California* **Wine prices** *Moderate* **Cuisine** *International* **Menu prices** *Prix fixe only; $55–$60*

HERMITAGE INN 🍷🍷🍷

Coldbrook Road, Wilmington, VT 05363; (802) 464-3511 **Wine list** *Burgundy, Bordeaux, California* **Wine selections** *2,000* **Number of bottles** *35,000* **Wine prices** *Moderate* **Cuisine** *Continental* **Menu prices** *$16–$30* **Credit cards** *AX, MC, VS, DV*

Grand Award since 1984

THE INN AT SAWMILL FARM 🍷🍷🍷

Route 100 and Crosstown Road, West Dover, VT 05356; (802) 464-8131 **Wine list** *Bordeaux, Burgundy, California* **Wine selections** *1,305* **Number of bottles** *28,000* **Wine prices** *Moderate* **Cuisine** *American/continental* **Menu prices** *$27–$38* **Credit cards** *AX, MC, VS*

Grand Award since 1992

THE INN AT SHELBURNE FARMS 🍷

1611 Harbor Road, Shelburne, VT 05482; (802) 985-8498 **Wine list** *California, France* **Wine prices** Inexpensive **Cuisine** *Regional* **Menu prices** *$18–$30*

INN AT WEST VIEW FARM 🍷

2928 Route 30, Dorset, VT 05251; (802) 867-5715 **Wine list** *California* **Wine prices** *Moderate* **Cuisine** *Contemporary American* **Menu prices** *$24–$32*

THE INN AT WESTON 🍷

Scenic Route 100, Weston, VT 05161; (802) 824-6789 **Wine list** *California* **Wine prices** *Moderate* **Cuisine** *Contemporary American* **Menu prices** *$27–$38*

THE INN ON THE COMMON
Main Street, Craftsbury Common, VT 05827; (800) 521-2233 **Wine list** *California, France* **Wine prices** *Moderate* **Cuisine** *Contemporary American/continental* **Menu prices** *Prix fixe only; $25–$45*

THE JACKSON HOUSE INN & RESTAURANT
114-3 Senior Lane, Woodstock, VT 05091; (802) 457-2065 **Wine list** *France* **Wine prices** *Moderate* **Cuisine** *Contemporary American/Mediterranean* **Menu prices** *Prix fixe only; $55–$65*

KEDRON VALLEY INN
Route 106, South Woodstock, VT 05071; (802) 457-1473 **Wine list** *California* **Wine prices** *Moderate* **Cuisine** *Contemporary American* **Menu prices** *$18–$27*

LA POULE À DENTS
Main Street, Norwich, VT 05055; (802) 649-2922 **Wine list** *France, California* **Wine prices** *Moderate* **Cuisine** *French* **Menu prices** *$14–$29*

MAXWELL'S
Topnotch Resort & Spa, 4000 Mountain Road, Stowe, VT 05672; (802) 253-8585 **Wine list** *California, France* **Wine prices** *Moderate* **Cuisine** *American* **Menu prices** *$17–$39*

MISTRAL'S AT TOLL GATE
10 Toll Gate Road, Manchester Center, VT 05255; (802) 362-1779 **Wine list** *California, France* **Wine prices** *Moderate* **Cuisine** *French* **Menu prices** *$26–$35*

THE MOONDANCE GRILLE
The Woods Resort, 53 Woods Road, Killington, VT 05751; (802) 422-2600 **Wine list** *California* **Wine prices** Inexpensive **Cuisine** *International* **Menu prices** *$14–$31*

THE MOUNTAIN TOP RESTAURANT
195 Mountain Top Road, Chittenden, VT 05737; (800) 445-2100 **Wine list** *California* **Wine prices** *Moderate* **Cuisine** *Contemporary American* **Menu prices** *$23–$35*

NECI COMMONS
25 Church St., Burlington, VT 05401; (802) 862-6324 **Wine list** *California* **Wine prices** *Moderate* **Cuisine** *Contemporary American* **Menu prices** *$13–$19*

NIKKI'S RESTAURANT 🍷
Route 103, Ludlow, VT 05149; (802) 228-7798 **Wine list** *California* **Wine prices** Inexpensive **Cuisine** *American* **Menu prices** *$12–$32*

PANGAEA 🍷
1 Prospect St., North Bennington, VT 05257; (802) 442-7171 **Wine list** *California* **Wine prices** *Moderate* **Cuisine** *Contemporary* **Menu prices** *$17–$31*

THE PITCHER INN 🍷
The Pitcher Inn, 275 Main St., Warren, VT 05674; (802) 496-6350 **Wine list** *California, France* **Wine prices** *Moderate* **Cuisine** *American* **Menu prices** *$20–$36*

RED CLOVER INN 🍷
Woodward Road, Mendon, VT 05701; (802) 775-2290 **Wine list** *California, France, Italy* **Wine prices** *Moderate* **Cuisine** *Contemporary American* **Menu prices** *$20–$32*

RIVER TAVERN 🍷
Hawk Inn and Mountain Resort, Route 100, Plymouth, VT 05056; (802) 672-3811 **Wine list** *California, France* **Wine prices** Inexpensive **Cuisine** *Contemporary American* **Menu prices** *$15–$32*

SIMON PEARCE RESTAURANT 🍷🍷
The Mill, Quechee, VT 05059; (802) 295-1470 **Wine list** *France, California, Italy* **Wine prices** *Expensive* **Cuisine** *American/Irish* **Menu prices** *$18–$32*

SMOKEJACKS 🍷
156 Church St., Burlington, VT 05401; (802) 658-1119 **Wine list** *California, France* **Wine prices** *Moderate* **Cuisine** *Contemporary American* **Menu prices** *$15–$24*

THREE MOUNTAIN INN 🍷
Route 30, Jamaica, VT 05343; (802) 874-4140 **Wine list** *California, France* **Wine prices** *Expensive* **Cuisine** *French* **Menu prices** *$28–$40*

TRAPP FAMILY LODGE 🍷
700 Trapp Hill Road, Stowe, VT 05672; (800) 826-7000 **Wine list** *California, France, Austria* **Wine prices** *Moderate* **Cuisine** *Continental* **Menu prices** *Prix fixe only; $36–$42*

TRATTORIA DELIA 🍷
152 Saint Paul St., Burlington, VT 05401; (802) 864-5253 **Wine list** *Italy* **Wine prices** Inexpensive **Cuisine** *Italian* **Menu prices** *$12–$28*

🍷🍷🍷 Grand Award 🍷🍷 Best of Award of Excellence 🍷 Award of Excellence

TRATTORIA LA FESTA
Toscana Country Inn, 4080 Mountain Road, Stowe, VT 05672; (802) 253-8480 **Wine list** *Italy* **Wine prices** *Moderate* **Cuisine** *Italian* **Menu prices** *$13–$21*

WINDHAM HILL INN
311 Lawrence Drive, West Townshend, VT 05359; (800) 944-4080 **Wine list** *California, France* **Wine prices** *Moderate* **Cuisine** *Contemporary American* **Menu prices** *$26–$31*

WINFIELD'S BISTRO
Stoweflake Mountain Resort & Spa, 1746 Mountain Road, Stowe, VT 05672; (802) 253-7355 **Wine list** *California* **Wine prices** *Moderate* **Cuisine** *Contemporary American* **Menu prices** *$18–$45*

YE OLDE TAVERN
5183 Main St., Manchester Center, VT 05255; (802) 362-0611 **Wine list** *California* **Wine prices** *Moderate* **Cuisine** *Regional* **Menu prices** *$16–$29*

VIRGINIA

ALDO'S RISTORANTE
La Promenade Shops, 1860 Laskin Road, Virginia Beach, VA 23454; (757) 491-1111 **Wine list** *California* **Wine prices** *Moderate* **Cuisine** *Italian* **Menu prices** *$9–$21*

BISTRO 309
309 William St., Fredericksburg, VA 22401; (540) 371-9999 **Wine list** *California* **Wine prices** *Moderate* **Cuisine** *Contemporary American* **Menu prices** *$18–$28*

THE BLUE HIPPO
147 Granby St., Norfolk, VA 23501; (757) 533-9664 **Wine list** *California* **Wine prices** Inexpensive **Corkage** *$10* **Cuisine** *International* **Menu prices** *$20–$29*

BRAY BISTRO
Kingsmill Resort, 1010 Kingsmill Road, Williamsburg, VA 23185; (757) 253-1703 **Wine list** *California* **Wine prices** *Moderate* **Corkage** *$10* **Cuisine** *Contemporary American* **Menu prices** *$24–$34*

BRUTTI'S 🍷

467 Court St., Old Towne Portsmouth, VA 23704; (757) 393-1923 **Wine list** *California, Italy* **Wine prices** Inexpensive **Corkage** *$18* **Cuisine** *American* **Menu prices** *$12–$29*

BUCKHEAD'S CHOP HOUSE 🍷🍷

8510 Patterson Ave., Richmond, VA 23229; (804) 750-2000 **Wine list** *California, France, Italy, Spain* **Wine prices** *Moderate* **Cuisine** *Steak house* **Menu prices** *$25–$40*

THE CAPITAL GRILLE 🍷

1861 International Drive, McLean, VA 22102; (703) 448-3900 **Wine list** *California* **Wine prices** *Expensive* **Cuisine** *Steak house* **Menu prices** *$18–$33*

CITIES GRILLE 🍷

605 Pilot House Drive, Newport News, VA 23606; (757) 595-6085 **Wine list** *California* **Wine prices** Inexpensive **Cuisine** *American* **Menu prices** *$9–$21*

CITIES GRILLE 🍷

4511-C John Tyler Highway, Williamsburg, VA 23185; (757) 564-3955 **Wine list** *California* **Wine prices** Inexpensive **Cuisine** *American* **Menu prices** *$10–$20*

THE CLIFTON INN 🍷

1296 Clifton Inn Drive, Charlottesville, VA 22911; (434) 971-1800 **Wine list** *France, California* **Wine prices** *Moderate* **Cuisine** *American* **Menu prices** *$22–$30*

CLUBSODA 🍷

111 Tazewell St., Norfolk, VA 23510; (757) 200-7632 **Wine list** *California, France* **Wine prices** *Moderate* **Cuisine** *Contemporary* **Menu prices** *$15–$25*

C & O RESTAURANT 🍷

515 E. Water St., Charlottesville, VA 22901; (804) 971-7044 **Wine list** *California, France* **Wine prices** *Moderate* **Cuisine** *French/Pacific Rim/regional* **Menu prices** *$14–$30*

THE DINING ROOM AT FORD'S COLONY 🍷🍷

240 Ford's Colony Drive, Williamsburg, VA 23188; (757) 258-4107 **Wine list** *California, Bordeaux, Germany* **Wine prices** *Expensive* **Cuisine** *American* **Menu prices** *Prix fixe only; $52–$86*

THE DOWNTOWN GRILLE
201 W. Main St., Charlottesville, VA 22902; (434) 817-7080 **Wine list** *California, France* **Wine prices** *Moderate* **Cuisine** *Steak house/seafood* **Menu prices** *$14–$28*

FLEMING'S PRIME STEAKHOUSE & WINE BAR
1960-A Chainbridge Road, McLean, VA 22102; (703) 442-8384 **Wine list** *California* **Wine prices** *Moderate* **Cuisine** *Steak house* **Menu prices** *$18–$27*

FRANKIE ROWLAND'S STEAKHOUSE
104 Jefferson St., Roanoke, VA 24011; (540) 527-2333 **Wine list** *California* **Wine prices** *Moderate* **Cuisine** *Steak house* **Menu prices** *$18–$31*

THE HOMESTEAD
U.S. Route 220, Hot Springs, VA 24445; (800) 838-1766 **Wine list** *California, Virginia* **Wine prices** *Expensive* **Cuisine** *Continental/European* **Menu prices** *Prix fixe only; $55–$85*

HONDOS
4204-C Cox Road, Glen Allen, VA 23060; (804) 968-4323 **Wine list** *California* **Wine prices** *Moderate* **Cuisine** *Steak house* **Menu prices** *$22–$45*

IL GIARDINO RISTORANTE
910 Atlantic Ave., Virginia Beach, VA 23451; (757) 422-6464 **Wine list** *California* **Wine prices** *Moderate* **Cuisine** *Italian* **Menu prices** *$11–$31*

THE INN AT LITTLE WASHINGTON
Middle and Main Streets, Washington, VA 22747; (540) 675-3800 **Wine list** *Bordeaux, Burgundy, California, Spain* **Wine selections** *1,600* **Number of bottles** *15,500* **Wine prices** *Expensive* **Cuisine** *American* **Menu prices** *Prix fixe only; $108–$148* **Credit cards** *MC, VS*
Grand Award since 1995

ISABELLA'S ITALIAN TRATTORIA
3225 Old Forest Road, Lynchburg, VA 24501; (804) 385-1660 **Wine list** *Italy* **Wine prices** *Moderate* **Cuisine** *Northern Italian* **Menu prices** *$9–$19*

THE JOSHUA WILTON HOUSE
412 S. Main St., Harrisonburg, VA 22801; (540) 434-4464 **Wine list** *California, Virginia* **Wine prices** *Moderate* **Cuisine** *Regional* **Menu prices** *$13–$26*

KENMORE INN 🍷
1200 Princess Anne St., Fredericksburg, VA 22401; (540) 371-7622 **Wine list** *California, France* **Wine prices** Inexpensive **Cuisine** *Continental* **Menu prices** *$16–$32*

KESWICK HALL 🍷
Monticello, 701 Club Drive, Keswick, VA 22947; (434) 979-3440 **Wine list** *France, California* **Wine prices** *Moderate* **Cuisine** *American* **Menu prices** *Prix fixe only; $58*

KINCAID'S FISH, CHOP & STEAK HOUSE 🍷
300 Monticello Ave., Norfolk, VA 23510; (757) 622-8000 **Wine list** *California* **Wine prices** *Moderate* **Corkage** *$10* **Cuisine** *Seafood* **Menu prices** *$15–$34*

L'AUBERGE CHEZ FRANÇOIS 🍷
332 Springvale Road, Great Falls, VA 22066; (703) 759-3800 **Wine list** *France, California* **Wine prices** *Moderate* **Cuisine** *Alsatian* **Menu prices** *Prix fixe only; $48–$56*

LA BERGERIE 🍷
218 N. Lee St., Alexandria, VA 22314; (703) 683-1007 **Wine list** *France, California* **Wine prices** *Moderate* **Cuisine** *French/Basque* **Menu prices** *$17–$29*

LA GALLERIA RISTORANTE 🍷
120 College Place, Norfolk, VA 23510; (757) 623-3939 **Wine list** *California, Italy* **Wine prices** *Moderate* **Cuisine** *Northern Italian* **Menu prices** *$13–$26*

LANSDOWNE GRILLE 🍷
Lansdowne Resort, 44050 Woodridge Parkway, Lansdowne, VA 22075; (703) 729-4073 **Wine list** *California* **Wine prices** *Moderate* **Cuisine** *Steak house* **Menu prices** *$25–$49*

L'AVVENTURA 🍷
220 W. Market St., Charlottesville, VA 22902; (434) 977-1912 **Wine list** *Italy* **Wine prices** *Moderate* **Cuisine** *Northern Italian* **Menu prices** *$13–$20*

LEGAL SEA FOODS 🍷
320 23rd St., Arlington, VA 22202; (703) 415-1200 **Wine list** *California* **Wine prices** Inexpensive **Cuisine** *Seafood* **Menu prices** *$11–$27*

LEGAL SEA FOODS 🍷
Tysons Galleria, 2001 International Drive, McLean, VA 22102; (703) 827-8900 **Wine list** *California* **Wine prices** Inexpensive **Cuisine** *Seafood* **Menu prices** *$11–$62*

LE RELAIS RESTAURANT & BAR À VIN
1025 Seneca Road, Great Falls, VA 22066; (703) 444-4060 **Wine list** *California, France* **Wine prices** *Expensive* **Corkage** *$15* **Cuisine** *French* **Menu prices** *$23–$34*

LIGHTFOOT RESTAURANT
11 N. King St., Leesburg, VA 20176; (703) 771-2233 **Wine list** *California* **Wine prices** *Moderate* **Cuisine** *Contemporary American* **Menu prices** *$18–$26*

MAESTRO
The Ritz-Carlton Tysons Corner, 1700 Tysons Blvd., McLean, VA 22102; (703) 821-1515 **Wine list** *Italy, France* **Wine prices** *Expensive* **Cuisine** *Contemporary Italian* **Menu prices** *Prix fixe only; $72–$112*

MAHI MAH'S SEAFOOD RESTAURANT
615 Atlantic Ave., Virginia Beach, VA 23451; (757) 437-8030 **Wine list** *California, Australia* **Wine prices** *Moderate* **Cuisine** *Seafood* **Menu prices** *$12–$21*

MANAKIN GRILL
12912 Plaza Drive, Richmond, VA 23233; (804) 784-0544 **Wine list** *California* **Wine prices** *Moderate* **Cuisine** *American* **Menu prices** *$15–$22*

THE MELTING POT
9704 Gayton Road, Richmond, VA 23233; (804) 741-3120 **Wine list** *California, France, Australia, Virginia* **Wine prices** *Moderate* **Cuisine** *Fondue* **Menu prices** *$15–$37*

THE MELTING POT
1564 Laskin Road, Virginia Beach, VA 23451; (757) 425-DINE **Wine list** *California* **Wine prices** *Moderate* **Cuisine** *Fondue* **Menu prices** *$13–$36*

MERIWETHER'S MARKET RESTAURANT
4925 Boonsboro Road, Lynchburg, VA 24503; (804) 384-3311 **Wine list** *California* **Wine prices** *Moderate* **Cuisine** *Contemporary American* **Menu prices** *$10–$20*

MONROE'S, AN AMERICAN TRATTORIA
1603 Commonwealth Ave., Alexandria, VA 22301; (703) 548-5792 **Wine list** *Italy* **Wine prices** *Moderate* **Cuisine** *Italian* **Menu prices** *$9–$17*

MORTON'S OF CHICAGO
1631 Crystal Drive, Arlington, VA 22202; (703) 418-1444 **Wine list** *California* **Wine prices** *Expensive* **Cuisine** *Steak house* **Menu prices** *$23–$75*

MORTON'S OF CHICAGO 🍷
11956 Market St., Reston, VA 20190; (703) 796-0128
Wine list *California* **Wine prices** *Expensive* **Cuisine** *Steak house* **Menu prices** *$22–$35*

MORTON'S OF CHICAGO 🍷
111 Virginia St., Richmond, VA 23219; (804) 648-1662
Wine list *California* **Wine prices** *Expensive* **Cuisine** *Steak house* **Menu prices** *$22–$35*

MORTON'S OF CHICAGO 🍷
8075 Leesburg Pike, Vienna, VA 22182; (703) 883-0800
Wine list *California* **Wine prices** *Expensive* **Cuisine** *Steak house* **Menu prices** *$22–$35*

THE OLD MILL ROOM 🍷
The Boar's Head Inn & Sports Club, 200 Ednam Drive, Charlottesville, VA 22903; (434) 972-2230 **Wine list** *California, France, Virginia* **Wine prices** *Expensive* **Cuisine** *French/American* **Menu prices** *$23–$30*

THE OLD ORIGINAL BOOKBINDER'S 🍷
2306 E. Cary St., Richmond, VA 23223; (804) 643-6900
Wine list *California* **Wine prices** *Moderate* **Cuisine** *American* **Menu prices** *$17–$40*

ONE FISH-TWO FISH 🍷
2109 W. Great Neck Road, Virginia Beach, VA 23451; (757) 496-4350 **Wine list** *California* **Wine prices** *Moderate* **Cuisine** *Contemporary American* **Menu prices** *$17–$25*

THE PALM 🍷
1750 Tysons Blvd., McLean, VA 22102; (703) 917-0200
Wine list *California* **Wine prices** *Moderate* **Corkage** *$20*
Cuisine *Steak house* **Menu prices** *$25–$35*

PAYA THAI 🍷
8417 Old Courthouse Road, Vienna, VA 22182; (703) 883-3881 **Wine list** *California, France* **Wine prices** Inexpensive
Cuisine *Thai* **Menu prices** *$10–$25*

REGENCY DINING ROOM 🍷
The Williamsburg Inn, 136 E. Francis St., Williamsburg, VA 23185; (757) 229-1000 **Wine list** *California, France* **Wine prices** *Expensive* **Cuisine** *American* **Menu prices** *$29–$38*

THE REGENCY ROOM

The Hotel Roanoke & Conference Center, 110 Shenandoah Ave., Roanoke, VA 24016; (540) 985-5900 **Wine list** *California* **Wine prices** Inexpensive **Cuisine** *Continental* **Menu prices** *$20–$28*

RELAIS & CHÂTEAUX MORRISON HOUSE

116 S. Alfred St., Alexandria, VA 22314; (703) 838-8000 **Wine list** *California, France* **Wine prices** *Moderate* **Cuisine** *Contemporary* **Menu prices** *$27–$40*

RESTAURANT SEVEN

8521 Leesburg Pike, Tysons Corner, VA 22182; (703) 847-0707 **Wine list** *California, France* **Wine prices** *Moderate* **Cuisine** *Contemporary American* **Menu prices** *$25–$28*

RISTORANTE GERANIO

722 King St., Alexandria, VA 22314; (703) 548-0088 **Wine list** *California, Italy* **Wine prices** *Moderate* **Cuisine** *Contemporary Italian* **Menu prices** *$15–$26*

RUTH'S CHRIS STEAK HOUSE

4100 Monument Corner Drive, Fairfax, VA 22030; (703) 266-1004 **Wine list** *California* **Wine prices** *Moderate* **Cuisine** *Steak house* **Menu prices** *$18–$33*

RUTH'S CHRIS STEAK HOUSE

11500 Huguenot Road, Midlothian, VA 23113; (804) 378-0600 **Wine list** *California* **Wine prices** *Moderate* **Cuisine** *Steak house* **Menu prices** *$20–$33*

SAM & HARRY'S

8240 Leesburg Pike, Tysons Corner, VA 22182; (703) 448-0088 **Wine list** *California, France* **Wine prices** *Moderate* **Cuisine** *Steak house* **Menu prices** *$24–$59*

SEAGAR'S

Hilton Alexandria Old Town, 1767 King St., Alexandria, VA 22314; (703) 836-1632 **Wine list** *California, France* **Wine prices** *Moderate* **Cuisine** *Steak house* **Menu prices** *$18–$36*

SILVER THATCH INN

3001 Hollymead Drive, Charlottesville, VA 22911; (434) 978-4686 **Wine list** *California* **Wine prices** Inexpensive **Cuisine** *Contemporary* **Menu prices** *$16–$30*

STARDUST RESTAURANT & LOUNGE

608 Montgomery St., Alexandria, VA 22314; (703) 548-9864 **Wine list** *California* **Wine prices** *Moderate* **Cuisine** *International* **Menu prices** *$15–$27*

TAUTOGS 🍷
205 23rd St., Virginia Beach, VA 23451; (757) 422-0081
Wine list *California* **Wine prices** Inexpensive **Cuisine** *Seafood* **Menu prices** *$11–$17*

THE TIDES INN 🍷
480 King Carter Drive, Irvington, VA 22480; (800) 843-3746 **Wine list** *California* **Wine prices** *Moderate* **Corkage** *$15* **Cuisine** *Regional* **Menu prices** *$21–$38*

TIVOLI RESTAURANT 🍷
1700 N. Moore St., Rosslyn, VA 22209; (703) 524-8900
Wine list *California, Italy* **Wine prices** *Moderate* **Cuisine** *Italian* **Menu prices** *$18–$28*

TODD JURICH'S BISTRO 🍷
150 W. Main St., Norfolk, VA 23510; (757) 622-3210
Wine list *California* **Wine prices** *Moderate* **Cuisine** *American* **Menu prices** *$19–$34*

THE TRELLIS 🍷
403 Duke of Gloucester St., Williamsburg, VA 23185; (757) 229-8610 **Wine list** *California, Virginia* **Wine prices** Inexpensive **Cuisine** *Contemporary American* **Menu prices** *$16–$28*

TUSCARORA MILL 🍷
203 Harrison St. S.E., Leesburg, VA 22075; (703) 771-9300 **Wine list** *California, France, Australia* **Wine prices** *Moderate* **Cuisine** *American* **Menu prices** *$15–$29*

WASHINGTON

SEATTLE

ANDALUCA 🍷
Mayflower Park Hotel, 407 Olive Way, Seattle, WA 98101; (206) 382-6999 **Wine list** *California, Spain* **Wine prices** *Moderate* **Corkage** *$20* **Cuisine** *Mediterranean* **Menu prices** *$18–$28*

ASSAGGIO RISTORANTE 🍷
2010 Fourth Ave., Seattle, WA 98121; (206) 441-1399
Wine list *Italy* **Wine prices** *Moderate* **Corkage** *$20* **Cuisine** *Italian* **Menu prices** *$9–$27*

BRAD'S SWINGSIDE CAFÉ 🍷
4212 Fremont Ave. N., Seattle, WA 98103; (206) 633-4057 **Wine list** *Italy* **Wine prices** Inexpensive **Corkage** *$15* **Cuisine** *Mediterranean* **Menu prices** *$14–$24*

BRASSERIE MARGAUX 🍷
The Warwick Seattle, 401 Lenora St., Seattle, WA 98121; (206) 777-1990 **Wine list** *Washington, Oregon* **Wine prices** *Moderate* **Corkage** *$10* **Cuisine** *Pacific Northwestern/French* **Menu prices** *$17–$25*

CAFÉ CAMPAGNE 🍷
1600 Post Alley, Seattle, WA 98101; (206) 728-2233 **Wine list** *France* **Wine prices** *Moderate* **Corkage** *$20* **Cuisine** *French* **Menu prices** *$15–$19*

CAMPAGNE 🍷
86 Pine St., Seattle, WA 98101; (206) 728-2800 **Wine list** *France* **Wine prices** *Moderate* **Corkage** *$20* **Cuisine** *French* **Menu prices** *$24–$38*

CANLIS 🍷🍷🍷
2576 Aurora Ave. N., Seattle, WA 98109; (206) 283-3313 **Wine list** *California, France, Washington, Italy* **Wine selections** *1,450* **Number of bottles** *15,000* **Wine prices** *Moderate* **Corkage** *$25* **Cuisine** *Pacific Northwestern* **Menu prices** *$21–$52* **Credit cards** *AX, MC, VS, DV*
Grand Award since 1997

CASCADIA RESTAURANT 🍷
2328 First Ave., Seattle, WA 98121; (206) 448-8884 **Wine list** *Washington, France* **Wine prices** *Moderate* **Corkage** *$25* **Cuisine** *Pacific Northwestern* **Menu prices** *$18–$42*

DANIEL'S BROILER 🍷
809 Fairview Place N., Seattle, WA 98109; (206) 621-8262 **Wine list** *California, Washington, France* **Wine prices** *Moderate* **Corkage** *$15* **Cuisine** *Steak house* **Menu prices** *$19–$80*

DULCES LATIN BISTRO 🍷🍷
1430 34th Ave., Seattle, WA 98122; (206) 322-5453 **Wine list** *California, Spain, Italy* **Wine prices** Inexpensive **Corkage** *$10* **Cuisine** *European* **Menu prices** *$17–$25*

EARTH & OCEAN 🍷🍷
W Seattle, 1112 Fourth Ave., Seattle, WA 98101; (206) 264-6060 **Wine list** *Washington, California* **Wine prices** *Moderate* **Corkage** *$20* **Cuisine** *Contemporary American* **Menu prices** *$16–$28*

EL GAUCHO 🍷
2505 First Ave., Seattle, WA 98121; (206) 728-1337 **Wine list** *California, Oregon, Washington, France* **Wine prices** *Expensive* **Corkage** *$20* **Cuisine** *Steak house* **Menu prices** *$19–$79*

FLEMING'S PRIME STEAKHOUSE & WINE BAR 🍷
1001 Third Ave., Seattle, WA 98104; (206) 587-5300 **Wine list** *California* **Wine prices** *Moderate* **Corkage** *$15* **Cuisine** *Steak house* **Menu prices** *$18–$31*

FLYING FISH 🍷
2234 First Ave., Seattle, WA 98121; (206) 728-8595 **Wine list** *Oregon, Washington* **Wine prices** *Moderate* **Corkage** *$20* **Cuisine** *Seafood* **Menu prices** *$14–$20*

THE GEORGIAN 🍷
Four Seasons Olympic Hotel, 411 University St., Seattle, WA 98101; (206) 621-1700 **Wine list** *Washington, France, California* **Wine prices** *Moderate* **Corkage** *$15* **Cuisine** *Regional* **Menu prices** *$20–$30*

ICON GRILL 🍷
1933 Fifth Ave., Seattle, WA 98101; (206) 441-6330 **Wine list** *California, Washington* **Wine prices** *Moderate* **Corkage** *$15* **Cuisine** *American* **Menu prices** *$14–$33*

IL FORNAIO CUCINA ITALIANA 🍷
600 Pine St., Seattle, WA 98101; (206) 264-0994 **Wine list** *California, Italy* **Wine prices** *Moderate* **Corkage** *$10* **Cuisine** *Italian* **Menu prices** *$10–$25*

METROPOLITAN GRILL 🍷🍷
820 Second Ave., Seattle, WA 98104; (206) 624-3287 **Wine list** *California, Washington, France, Italy* **Wine prices** *Moderate* **Corkage** *$20* **Cuisine** *Steak house* **Menu prices** *$18–$61*

MONSOON 🍷
615 19th Ave. E., Seattle, WA 98112; (206) 325-2111 **Wine list** *France, California* **Wine prices** Inexpensive **Corkage** *$20* **Cuisine** *Vietnamese* **Menu prices** *$10–$20*

MORTON'S OF CHICAGO 🍷
1511 Sixth Ave., Seattle, WA 98101; (206) 223-0550 **Wine list** *California* **Wine prices** *Expensive* **Corkage** *$15* **Cuisine** *Steak house* **Menu prices** *$20–$35*

🍷🍷🍷 Grand Award 🍷🍷 Best of Award of Excellence 🍷 Award of Excellence

NELL'S
6804 E. Green Lake Way N., Seattle, WA 98115; (206) 524-4044 **Wine list** *France, Washington* **Wine prices** Inexpensive **Corkage** *$20* **Cuisine** *Contemporary American* **Menu prices** *$18–$28*

THE OCEANAIRE SEAFOOD ROOM
1700 Seventh Ave., Seattle, WA 98101; (206) 627-BASS **Wine list** *California, Washington* **Wine prices** *Moderate* **Cuisine** *Seafood* **Menu prices** *$15–$58*

PLACE PIGALLE RESTAURANT & BAR
Pike Place Market, 81 Pike St., Seattle, WA 98101; (206) 624-1756 **Wine list** *California, France, Washington* **Wine prices** *Moderate* **Corkage** *$18* **Cuisine** *Pacific Northwestern* **Menu prices** *$15–$27*

PONTI SEAFOOD GRILL
3014 Third Ave. N., Seattle, WA 98109; (206) 284-3000 **Wine list** *California, France* **Wine prices** *Moderate* **Corkage** *$15* **Cuisine** *Pacific Northwestern/Pacific Rim* **Menu prices** *$13–$35*

QUEEN CITY GRILL
2201 First Ave., Seattle, WA 98121; (206) 443-0975 **Wine list** *Oregon, Washington, California* **Wine prices** Inexpensive **Corkage** *$15* **Cuisine** *American* **Menu prices** *$11–$30*

RAY'S BOATHOUSE
6049 Seaview Ave. N.W., Seattle, WA 98107; (206) 789-3770 **Wine list** *California, Washington, France, Australia* **Wine prices** *Moderate* **Corkage** *$15* **Cuisine** *Pacific Northwestern* **Menu prices** *$15–$35*

RESTAURANT ZOE
2137 Second Ave., Seattle, WA 98121; (206) 256-2060 **Wine list** *California* **Wine prices** *Moderate* **Corkage** *$15* **Cuisine** *American* **Menu prices** *$16–$23*

ROVER'S
2808 E. Madison St., Seattle, WA 98112; (206) 325-7442 **Wine list** *France, Washington, California* **Wine prices** *Expensive* **Cuisine** *Pacific Northwestern/French* **Menu prices** *Prix fixe only; $75–$110*

RUTH'S CHRIS STEAK HOUSE
800 Fifth Ave., Seattle, WA 98104; (206) 624-8524 **Wine list** *California* **Wine prices** *Moderate* **Cuisine** *Steak house* **Menu prices** *$17–$33*

SALTY'S ON ALKI BEACH 🍷
1936 Harbor Ave. S.W., Seattle, WA 98126; (206) 937-1600 **Wine list** *Washington* **Wine prices** *Moderate* **Corkage** *$20* **Cuisine** *Seafood* **Menu prices** *$19–$39*

727 PINE 🍷
Grand Hyatt Seattle, 727 Pine St., Seattle, WA 98101; (206) 774-6400 **Wine list** *France, California* **Wine prices** *Moderate* **Corkage** *$20* **Cuisine** *Pacific Northwestern* **Menu prices** *$24–$35*

TEN MERCER 🍷
10 Mercer St., Seattle, WA 98109; (206) 691-3723 **Wine list** *California, France* **Wine prices** Inexpensive **Corkage** *$15* **Cuisine** *Contemporary American* **Menu prices** *$9–$23*

TULIO 🍷
1100 Fifth Ave., Seattle, WA 98101; (206) 624-5500 **Wine list** *Italy* **Wine prices** *Moderate* **Corkage** *$15* **Cuisine** *Italian* **Menu prices** *$13–$27*

UNION SQUARE GRILL 🍷
621 Union St., Seattle, WA 98101; (206) 224-4321 **Wine list** *Washington, California* **Wine prices** *Moderate* **Corkage** *$20* **Cuisine** *Steak house* **Menu prices** *$20–$45*

WATERFRONT SEAFOOD GRILL 🍷
2801 Alaskan Way, Pier 70, Seattle, WA 98121; (206) 956-9171 **Wine list** *California, Oregon, Washington* **Wine prices** *Moderate* **Corkage** *$10* **Cuisine** *Seafood* **Menu prices** *$17–$78*

WILD GINGER 🍷
1401 Third Ave., Seattle, WA 98101; (206) 623-4450 **Wine list** *California, France, Germany* **Wine prices** *Moderate* **Cuisine** *Asian* **Menu prices** *$10–$30*

WASHINGTON

OTHER CITIES

BACCHUS RESTAURANT 🍷
3200 S.E. 164th Ave., Vancouver, WA 98683; (360) 882-9672 **Wine list** *California* **Wine prices** Inexpensive **Corkage** *$12* **Cuisine** *Pacific Northwestern/international* **Menu prices** *$18–$28*

BARKING FROG
Willows Lodge, 14580 N.E. 145th St., Woodinville, WA 98072; (425) 424-2999 **Wine list** *Washington* **Wine prices** *Moderate* **Corkage** *$20* **Cuisine** *Regional* **Menu prices** *$26–$36*

BELLA ITALIA
118 E. First St., Port Angeles, WA 98362; (360) 457-5442 **Wine list** *Italy, California* **Wine prices** *Moderate* **Corkage** *$10* **Cuisine** *Italian* **Menu prices** *$8–$24*

BIRCHFIELD MANOR
2018 Birchfield Road, Yakima, WA 98901; (509) 452-1960 **Wine list** *Washington* **Wine prices** *Moderate* **Cuisine** *European/Pacific Northwestern* **Menu prices** *$20–$25*

BIS ON MAIN
10213 Main St., Bellevue, WA 98004; (425) 455-2033 **Wine list** *California* **Wine prices** *Moderate* **Corkage** *$15* **Cuisine** *Continental* **Menu prices** *$15–$28*

CAFÉ JUANITA
9702 N.E. 120th Place, Kirkland, WA 98034; (425) 823-1505 **Wine list** *Italy, California* **Wine prices** Inexpensive **Corkage** *$15* **Cuisine** *Northern Italian* **Menu prices** *$17–$29*

CAMPBELL HOUSE CAFÉ
Campbell's Resort & Conference Center, 104 W. Woodin Ave., Chelan, WA 98816; (509) 682-2561 **Wine list** *Oregon, Washington* **Wine prices** Inexpensive **Corkage** *$15* **Cuisine** *Pacific Northwestern* **Menu prices** *$6–$18*

CIBO'S
1260 Commerce Ave., Longview, WA 98632; (360) 577-1746 **Wine list** *Washington, California* **Wine prices** *Moderate* **Corkage** *$10* **Cuisine** *Mediterranean/American* **Menu prices** *$17–$50*

THE FOGHORN RESTAURANT
6023 Lake Washington Blvd., Kirkland, WA 98033; (425) 827-0654 **Wine list** *Oregon, Washington* **Wine prices** Inexpensive **Corkage** *$13* **Cuisine** *Pacific Northwestern* **Menu prices** *$17–$29*

FRANKIE'S PIZZA & PASTA
16630 Redmond Way, Redmond, WA 98052; (425) 883-8407 **Wine list** *Italy* **Wine prices** Inexpensive **Corkage** *$5* **Cuisine** *Italian* **Menu prices** *$8–$15*

WASHINGTON

THE HERBFARM 🍷🍷
14590 N.E. 145th St., Woodinville, WA 98027; (425) 485-5300 **Wine list** *France, Washington, Oregon* **Wine prices** *Moderate* **Corkage** *$20* **Cuisine** *Contemporary American* **Menu prices** *Prix fixe only; $149–$179*

IL CAPRETTO D'ORO ITALIAN RESTAURANT 🍷
14471 Woodinville-Redmond Road, Woodinville, WA 98072; (425) 483-6791 **Wine list** *Italy* **Wine prices** *Moderate* **Corkage** *$25* **Cuisine** *Northern Italian* **Menu prices** *$8–$21*

LUNA 🍷
5620 S. Perry St., Spokane, WA 99223; (509) 448-2383 **Wine list** *Oregon, Washington, California* **Wine prices** Inexpensive **Corkage** *$15* **Cuisine** *American/Pacific Northwest* **Menu prices** *$10–$28*

THE OYSTER BAR ON CHUCKANUT DRIVE 🍷🍷
2578 Chuckanut Drive, Bow, WA 98232; (360) 766-6185 **Wine list** *California, Washington, France* **Wine prices** *Moderate* **Corkage** *$20* **Cuisine** *Contemporary Northwestern* **Menu prices** *$18–$50*

RIVERROCK GRILL 🍷
4050 Maple Valley Highway, Renton, WA 98058; (425) 430-0311 **Wine list** *California, Washington* **Wine prices** Inexpensive **Corkage** *$10* **Cuisine** *Pacific Northwestern* **Menu prices** *$8–$22*

RUTH'S CHRIS STEAK HOUSE 🍷
565 Bellevue Square, Bellevue, WA 98004; (425) 451-1550 **Wine list** *California, Washington* **Wine prices** *Moderate* **Cuisine** *Steak house* **Menu prices** *$11–$33*

THE SALISH LODGE DINING ROOM 🍷🍷
Salish Lodge & Spa, 6501 Rail Road Ave. S.E., Snoqualmie, WA 98065; (425) 888-2556 **Wine list** *California, Washington, Oregon, France* **Wine prices** *Moderate* **Corkage** *$25* **Cuisine** *Pacific Northwestern* **Menu prices** *$34–$76*

SEASTAR RESTAURANT & RAW BAR 🍷
205 108th Ave. N.E., Bellevue, WA 98004; (425) 456-0010 **Wine list** *California, France* **Wine prices** *Moderate* **Corkage** *$20* **Cuisine** *Pacific Northwestern* **Menu prices** *$18–$68*

🍷🍷🍷 Grand Award 🍷🍷 Best of Award of Excellence 🍷 Award of Excellence

SHOALWATER RESTAURANT
Shelburne Inn Hotel, 4415 Pacific Highway, Seaview, WA 98644; (360) 642-4142 **Wine list** *Washington, Oregon* **Wine prices** Inexpensive **Corkage** *$15* **Cuisine** *Pacific Northwestern* **Menu prices** *$12–$27*

SPENCER'S FOR STEAKS & CHOPS
Doubletree Hotel Spokane City Center, 322 N. Spokane Falls Court, Spokane, WA 99201; (509) 744-2372 **Wine list** *California, Washington* **Wine prices** *Moderate* **Corkage** *$10* **Cuisine** *Steak house* **Menu prices** *$17–$34*

VALLEY CAFÉ
105 W. Third Ave., Ellensburg, WA 98926; (509) 925-3050 **Wine list** *Washington* **Wine prices** Inexpensive **Corkage** *$10* **Cuisine** *Pacific Northwestern* **Menu prices** *$8–$25*

VISCONTI'S
1737 N. Wenatchee Ave., Wenatchee, WA 98801; (509) 662-5013 **Wine list** *Washington, Italy, California* **Wine prices** *Moderate* **Corkage** *$10* **Cuisine** *Italian* **Menu prices** *$12–$25*

VISONTI'S OF LEAVENWORTH
636 Front St., Leavenworth, WA 98826; (509) 548-1213 **Wine list** *Italy* **Wine prices** *Moderate* **Corkage** *$10* **Cuisine** *Italian* **Menu prices** *$10–$26*

YARROW BAY GRILL
1270 Carillon Point, Kirkland, WA 98033; (425) 889-9052 **Wine list** *Oregon, Washington, California* **Wine prices** *Moderate* **Cuisine** *Pacific Northwestern* **Menu prices** *$15–$39*

WEST VIRGINIA

BAVARIAN INN
Route 480, Shepherdstown, WV 25443; (304) 876-2551 **Wine list** *California, France* **Wine prices** *Moderate* **Cuisine** *German/continental* **Menu prices** *$16–$25*

THE CHOP HOUSE
1003 Charleston Town Center, Charleston, WV 25389; (304) 344-3954 **Wine list** *California* **Wine prices** *Moderate* **Cuisine** *Steak house* **Menu prices** *$20–$50*

THE GLASSHOUSE GRILLE 🍷
709 Beechurst Ave., Morgantown, WV 26505; (304) 296-8460 **Wine list** *California* **Wine prices** Inexpensive **Cuisine** *American* **Menu prices** *$10–$26*

THE GREENBRIER MAIN DINING ROOM 🍷
The Greenbrier Hotel, 300 W. Main St., White Sulphur Springs, WV 24986; (304) 536-1110 **Wine list** *California, France* **Wine prices** *Moderate* **Cuisine** *American/continental* **Menu prices** *Prix fixe only; $70*

THE RED FOX 🍷
Snowshoe Mountain Resort, 1 Whistlepunk Village, Snowshoe, WV 26209; (304) 572-1111 **Wine list** *France, California* **Wine prices** *Moderate* **Cuisine** *European* **Menu prices** *$18–$36*

ROBERT'S FINE DINING 🍷
Glade Springs Resort, 200 Lake Drive, Daniels, WV 25832; (304) 763-3033 **Wine list** *California* **Wine prices** Inexpensive **Corkage** *$15* **Cuisine** *Contemporary American* **Menu prices** *$24–$30*

SAVANNAH'S 🍷
1208 Sixth Ave., Huntington, WV 25701; (304) 529-0919 **Wine list** *California* **Wine prices** *Moderate* **Corkage** *$10* **Cuisine** *American* **Menu prices** *$12–$27*

TARRAGON RESTAURANT 🍷
Charleston Marriott Town Center, 200 Lee St. E., Charleston, WV 25301; (304) 353-3636 **Wine list** *California, France* **Wine prices** *Moderate* **Cuisine** *Contemporary American* **Menu prices** *$18–$32*

WISCONSIN

BARTOLOTTA'S LAKE PARK BISTRO 🍷
3133 E. Newberry Blvd., Milwaukee, WI 53211; (414) 962-6300 **Wine list** *France* **Wine prices** *Moderate* **Corkage** *$15* **Cuisine** *French* **Menu prices** *$16–$35*

BISTRO JOHN PAUL 🍷
1244 Main St., Green Bay, WI 54302; (920) 432-2897 **Wine list** *California, France* **Wine prices** *Moderate* **Cuisine** *French/American* **Menu prices** *$20–$24*

BLACKWOLF RUN RESTAURANT
The American Club, 1111 W. Riverside Drive, Kohler, WI 53044; (920) 457-4448 **Wine list** *California* **Wine prices** *Moderate* **Corkage** *$10* **Cuisine** *American* **Menu prices** *$20–$32*

CANOE BAY
W16065 Hogback Road, Chetek, WI 54728; (715) 924-4594 **Wine list** *California, France* **Wine prices** *Moderate* **Corkage** *$25* **Cuisine** *American* **Menu prices** *Prix fixe only; $55*

CAPTAIN BILL'S
2701 Century Harbor Road, Middleton, WI 53562; (608) 831-7327 **Wine list** *California* **Wine prices** *Moderate* **Cuisine** *Steak house/seafood* **Menu prices** *$9–$25*

CELIA
The Pfister Hotel, 424 E. Wisconsin Ave., Milwaukee, WI 53202; (414) 390-3832 **Wine list** *California, France* **Wine prices** *Moderate* **Corkage** *$20* **Cuisine** *Contemporary American* **Menu prices** *$15–$28*

COURTHOUSE PUB
1001 S. Eighth St., Manitowoc, WI 54221; (920) 686-1166 **Wine list** *France, Italy, California* **Wine prices** *Moderate* **Cuisine** *American* **Menu prices** *$12–$40*

THE DINING ROOM AT 209 MAIN
209 N. Main St., Monticello, WI 53570; (608) 938-2200 **Wine list** *California, France* **Wine prices** *Moderate* **Corkage** *$15* **Cuisine** *Contemporary American* **Menu prices** *$16–$25*

DREAM DANCE
1721 W. Canal St., Milwaukee, WI 53233; (414) 847-7883 **Wine list** *California* **Wine prices** *Moderate* **Cuisine** *Contemporary American* **Menu prices** *$24–$39*

EDDIE MARTINI'S
8612 Watertown Plank Road, Wauwatosa, WI 53226; (414) 771-6680 **Wine list** *California* **Wine prices** *Moderate* **Cuisine** *Steak house* **Menu prices** *$18–$42*

FANNY HILL RESTAURANT
Fanny Hill Victorian Inn, 3919 Crescent Ave., Eau Claire, WI 54703; (715) 836-8184 **Wine list** *California* **Wine prices** *Moderate* **Cuisine** *American* **Menu prices** *$18–$45*

FIELD'S AT THE WILDERNESS PREMIER STEAKHOUSE 🍷
Wilderness Hotel & Golf Resort, 511 E. Adams St., Wisconsin Dells, WI 53965; (608) 253-1400 **Wine list** *California* **Wine prices** *Moderate* **Cuisine** *Steak house* **Menu prices** *$19–$40*

FREIGHT HOUSE RESTAURANT 🍷
107 Vine St., La Crosse, WI 54601; (608) 784-6211 **Wine list** *California* **Wine prices** Inexpensive **Corkage** *$12* **Cuisine** *Steak house* **Menu prices** *$15–$35*

GILBERT'S 🍷
327 Wrigley Drive, Lake Geneva, WI 53147; (262) 248-6680 **Wine list** *California, France* **Wine prices** *Moderate* **Cuisine** *Contemporary American/European/Pacific Rim* **Menu prices** *$17–$36*

GRENADIER'S RESTAURANT 🍷
747 N. Broadway, Milwaukee, WI 53201; (414) 276-0747 **Wine list** *France, California* **Wine prices** *Moderate* **Corkage** *$15* **Cuisine** *Contemporary French* **Menu prices** *$24–$36*

GREY ROCK 🍷
Heidel House Resort, 643 Illinois Ave., Green Lake, WI 54941; (920) 294-3344 **Wine list** *California* **Wine prices** Inexpensive **Cuisine** *American* **Menu prices** *$16–$25*

HINTERLAND BREWERY & RESTAURANT 🍷
313 Dousman St., Green Bay, WI 54303; (920) 438-8050 **Wine list** *California* **Wine prices** *Moderate* **Corkage** *$15* **Cuisine** *Contemporary* **Menu prices** *$23–$60*

IMMIGRANT RESTAURANT 🍷
The American Club, Highland Drive, Kohler, WI 53044; (800) 344-2838 **Wine list** *France, California* **Wine prices** *Moderate* **Cuisine** *International* **Menu prices** *$27–$38*

KIRSCH'S RESTAURANT 🍷
French Country Inn, Highway 50 W., Lake Geneva, WI 53147; (262) 245-5756 **Wine list** *California, France* **Wine prices** *Moderate* **Cuisine** *French/American/Hawaiian* **Menu prices** *$19–$37*

LAKE STREET CAFÉ 🍷
21 S. Lake St., Elkhart Lake, WI 53020; (920) 876-2142 **Wine list** *California, France* **Wine prices** *Moderate* **Corkage** *$10* **Cuisine** *Californian* **Menu prices** *$16–$26*

L'ETOILE 🍷🍷
25 N. Pinckney St., Madison, WI 53703; (608) 251-0500 **Wine list** *Germany, France, California* **Wine prices** *Moderate* **Corkage** *$15* **Cuisine** *Regional/French* **Menu prices** *$25–$37*

LOGGING CAMP RESTAURANT & STILL 🍷
Pine-Aire Resort, 4443 Chain O' Lakes Road, Eagle River, WI 54521; (800) 597-6777 **Wine list** *California* **Wine prices** Inexpensive **Cuisine** *American* **Menu prices** *$12–$28*

THE MARINER'S INN 🍷
5339 Lighthouse Bay Drive, Madison, WI 53704; (608) 246-3120 **Wine list** *California* **Wine prices** *Moderate* **Cuisine** *Steak house* **Menu prices** *$15–$30*

MILWAUKEE CHOPHOUSE 🍷
Hilton Milwaukee City Center, 633 N. Fifth St., Milwaukee, WI 53203; (414) 226-2467 **Wine list** *California* **Wine prices** *Moderate* **Cuisine** *Steak house* **Menu prices** *$17–$67*

MISSION GRILLE 🍷
Highways 42 and 57, Sister Bay, WI 54234; (920) 854-9070 **Wine list** *California* **Wine prices** *Moderate* **Corkage** *$10* **Cuisine** *American* **Menu prices** *$12–$35*

MR. B'S 🍷
17700 W. Capital Drive, Brookfield, WI 53045; (262) 790-7005 **Wine list** *California* **Wine prices** *Moderate* **Corkage** *$15* **Cuisine** *Steak house* **Menu prices** *$17–$33*

MO'S, A PLACE FOR STEAKS 🍷
720 N. Plankinton Ave., Milwaukee, WI 53203; (414) 272-0720 **Wine list** *California* **Wine prices** *Expensive* **Corkage** *$25* **Cuisine** *Steak house* **Menu prices** *$19–$46*

NEWPORT GRILL 🍷
Grand Geneva Resort & Spa, 7036 Grand Geneva Way, Lake Geneva, WI 53147; (262) 249-4788 **Wine list** *California* **Wine prices** *Moderate* **Cuisine** *American* **Menu prices** *$18–$51*

PIGGY'S ON FRONT 🍷
328 S. Front St., La Crosse, WI 54601; (608) 784-4877 **Wine list** *California* **Wine prices** *Moderate* **Corkage** *$10* **Cuisine** *American* **Menu prices** *$17–$25*

PIZZA MAN 🍷
1800 E. North Ave., Milwaukee, WI 53201; (414) 272-1745 **Wine list** *California* **Wine prices** *Moderate* **Cuisine** *American* **Menu prices** *$11–$19*

RISTORANTE BARTOLOTTA 🍷
7616 W. State St., Wauwatosa, WI 53213; (414) 771-7910 **Wine list** *Italy* **Wine prices** *Moderate* **Corkage** *$15* **Cuisine** *Italian* **Menu prices** *$16–$29*

RISTORANTE BRISSAGO 🍷
Grand Geneva Resort & Spa, 7036 Grand Geneva Way, Lake Geneva, WI 53147; (262) 249-4788 **Wine list** *Italy, California* **Wine prices** Inexpensive **Cuisine** *Northern Italian* **Menu prices** *$10–$24*

SANFORD 🍷
1547 N. Jackson St., Milwaukee, WI 53202; (414) 276-9608 **Wine list** *California, France* **Wine prices** *Moderate* **Cuisine** *Contemporary* **Menu prices** *Prix fixe only; $45–$65*

STICKS & STONES 🍷
2300 N. Pilgrim Square Drive, Brookfield, WI 53005; (262) 786-5700 **Wine list** *California* **Wine prices** *Moderate* **Corkage** *$10* **Cuisine** *American* **Menu prices** *$18–$35*

T. ASHWELL'S FINE DINING 🍷
11976 Mink River Road, Ellison Bay, WI 54210; (920) 854-4306 **Wine list** *California, France* **Wine prices** *Moderate* **Cuisine** *American* **Menu prices** *$19–$32*

TWIN OAKS COUNTRY INN 🍷
30807 114th St., Wilmot, WI 53192; (262) 862-9377 **Wine list** *California* **Wine prices** *Moderate* **Cuisine** *American* **Menu prices** *$15–$30*

THE UNION HOUSE 🍷
S42 W31320 Highway 83, Genesee Depot, WI 53127; (262) 968-4281 **Wine list** *California* **Wine prices** Inexpensive **Cuisine** *American* **Menu prices** *$18–$33*

WAGON WHEEL SUPPER CLUB 🍷
3901 N. Sixth St., Wausau, WI 54403; (715) 675-2263 **Wine list** *California* **Wine prices** *Moderate* **Cuisine** *American* **Menu prices** *$13–$42*

WEISSGERBER'S SEVEN SEAS 🍷
1807 Nagawicka Road, Hartland, WI 53029; (262) 367-3903 **Wine list** *California, Germany, France* **Wine prices** Inexpensive **Corkage** *$10* **Cuisine** *Steak house/seafood* **Menu prices** *$15–$29*

🍷🍷🍷 Grand Award 🍷🍷 Best of Award of Excellence 🍷 Award of Excellence

WHISTLING STRAITS RESTAURANT 🍷
The American Club, N8501 County Highway LS, Sheboygan, WI 53083; (920) 565-6054 **Wine list** *California* **Wine prices** *Moderate* **Corkage** *$10* **Cuisine** *American* **Menu prices** *$22–$32*

THE WHITE HORSE INN 🍷
202 N. Henry St., Madison, WI 53703; (608) 255-9933 **Wine list** *California* **Wine prices** Inexpensive **Cuisine** *American* **Menu prices** *$16–$35*

WILD RICE RESTAURANT 🍷🍷
84860 Old San Road, Bayfield, WI 54814; (715) 779-9881 **Wine list** *California, France* **Wine prices** *Expensive* **Cuisine** *Contemporary American* **Menu prices** *$24–$34*

WYOMING

THE ALPENROSE 🍷
Alpenhof Lodge, Teton Village, Jackson Hole, WY 83025; (307) 733-3242 **Wine list** *California, France* **Wine prices** *Moderate* **Cuisine** *French/American* **Menu prices** *$20–$32*

DORNAN'S 🍷🍷
Spur Ranch Cabins, 105 Moose St., Moose, WY 83012; (307) 733-2415 **Wine list** *California, France* **Wine prices** Inexpensive **Cuisine** *Italian* **Menu prices** *$8–$25*

THE GRANARY AT SPRING CREEK RANCH 🍷
Spring Creek Ranch, 1800 Spirit Dance Road, Jackson, WY 83001; (307) 733-8833 **Wine list** *California* **Wine prices** *Moderate* **Corkage** *$10* **Cuisine** *Continental* **Menu prices** *$22–$32*

THE GRILL 🍷
Amangani Hotel, 1535 Northeast Butte, Jackson Hole, WY 83001; (307) 734-7333 **Wine list** *California* **Wine prices** *Moderate* **Corkage** *$20* **Cuisine** *Regional/Asian* **Menu prices** *$25–$33*

JENNY LAKE LODGE 🍷
Inner Loop Road, Grand Teton National Park, Moran, WY 83013; (307) 733-4647 **Wine list** *California* **Wine prices** *Moderate* **Corkage** *$10* **Cuisine** *American/French* **Menu prices** *Prix fixe only; $48*

OLD YELLOWSTONE GARAGE 🍷
175 Center St., Jackson, WY 83001; (307) 734-6161 **Wine list** *Piedmont* **Wine prices** *Moderate* **Corkage** *$15* **Cuisine** *Italian* **Menu prices** *$18–$32*

SWEETWATER RESTAURANT 🍷
85 King St., Jackson, WY 83001; (307) 733-3553 **Wine list** *California, France* **Wine prices** Inexpensive **Corkage** *$10* **Cuisine** *Mediterranean* **Menu prices** *$16–$28*

INTERNATIONAL

ARGENTINA

BISTRO M 🍷
Park Hyatt Mendoza, Chile 1124, Mendoza, M5500; (011) 54-26-1441-1234 **Wine list** *Argentina* **Wine prices** *Moderate* **Corkage** *$3* **Cuisine** *International* **Menu prices** *$7–$10*

LA BOURGOGNE 🍷
Alvear Palace Hotel, 1891 Ave. Alvear, Buenos Aires, 1129; (011) 54-11-4805-3857 **Wine list** *Argentina, France* **Wine prices** *Moderate* **Cuisine** *French* **Menu prices** *$16–$28*

VILLA HÍPICA 🍷
222 Diego Carman, San Isidro, Buenos Aires, 1642; (011) 54-11-4763-5533 **Wine list** *Argentina, France* **Wine prices** Inexpensive **Cuisine** *Argentinean/Mediterranean* **Menu prices** *$8–$14*

ARUBA

PASIÓN RESTAURANT - BODEGA 🍷
19-A Noord; (297) 86-47-52 **Wine list** *California, France* **Wine prices** *Moderate* **Corkage** *$15* **Cuisine** *International* **Menu prices** *$20–$40*

AUSTRALIA

ARIA RESTAURANT 🍷🍷
1 Macquarie St., Sydney, New South Wales 2000; (011) 61-2-9252-2555 **Wine list** *Australia, France, New Zealand* **Wine prices** *Moderate* **Cuisine** *Contemporary Australian* **Menu prices** *$20–$22*

CHARCOAL GRILL ON THE HILL
289 High St., Kew, Victoria 3101; (011) 61-3-9853-7535 **Wine list** *Australia, Burgundy* **Wine prices** *Moderate* **Cuisine** *Steak house* **Menu prices** *$15–$18*

CIRCA
The Prince, 2 Acland St., St. Kilda, Victoria 3182; (011) 61-3-9536-1122 **Wine list** *Australia, Burgundy, Italy* **Wine prices** *Moderate* **Cuisine** *Contemporary French* **Menu prices** *$16–$20*

GROSSI FLORENTINO
80 Bourke St., Melbourne, Victoria 3000; (011) 61-3-9662-1811 **Wine list** *Australia, Italy* **Wine prices** *Moderate* **Cuisine** *Italian* **Menu prices** *$25–$30*

LAKE HOUSE
King St., Daylesford, Victoria 3460; (011) 61-3-5348-3329 **Wine list** *Australia* **Wine prices** *Moderate* **Cuisine** *Contemporary Australian* **Menu prices** *$15–$18*

LANGTON'S RESTAURANT & WINE BAR
Sargood House, 61 Flinders Lane, Melbourne, Victoria 3000; (011) 61-3-9663-0222 **Wine list** *Australia, France* **Wine prices** *Moderate* **Cuisine** *Contemporary French* **Menu prices** *$17–$20*

MARYLANDS COUNTRY HOUSE
Falls Road, Marysville, Victoria 3779; (011) 61-3-5963-3204 **Wine list** *Australia* **Wine prices** *Moderate* **Cuisine** *Contemporary Australian* **Menu prices** *$14–$18*

MO MO
115 Collins St., Melbourne, Victoria; (011) 61-3-9650-0660 **Wine list** *California* **Wine prices** *Moderate* **Cuisine** *Contemporary Middle Eastern* **Menu prices** *$13–$17*

NUMBER 8
Crown Towers, 8 Whiteman St., Southbank, Melbourne, Victoria 3006; (011) 61-3-9292-7899 **Wine list** *Australia, France* **Wine prices** *Moderate* **Cuisine** *Contemporary Australian* **Menu prices** *$11–$17*

SAILS RESTAURANT
Park Road & Hastings Street, Noosa Heads, Queensland 4567; (011) 61-7-5447-4235 **Wine list** *Australia, New Zealand, France* **Wine prices** *Moderate* **Cuisine** *Contemporary Australian* **Menu prices** *$18–$35*

AUSTRIA

BERGHOTEL TULBINGERKOGEL 🍷🍷
Relais du Silence, 1 Tulbingerkogel, Mauerbach bei Wien 3001, Vienna; (011) 43-2273-73910 **Wine list** *Austria, Bordeaux, Burgundy* **Wine prices** *Moderate* **Cuisine** *Austrian* **Menu prices** *$15–$17*

GASTHAUS SCHWARZ 🍷🍷
3521 Nöhagen, 13 A-3521; (011) 43-2717-8209 **Wine list** *Austria, Bordeaux* **Wine prices** *Moderate* **Corkage** *$20* **Cuisine** *Austrian* **Menu prices** *$8–$20*

GASTWIRTSCHAFT FLOH 🍷🍷
1 Tullnerstrasse, Langenlebarn, 3425; (011) 43-2272-62809 **Wine list** *Austria, France, Italy* **Wine prices** *Moderate* **Corkage** *No charge* **Cuisine** *Austrian* **Menu prices** *$15–$20*

HANNER 🍷🍷
Hanner, 1 Mayerling, A-2534; (011) 43-2258-2378 **Wine list** *France, Austria* **Wine prices** *Moderate* **Cuisine** *Contemporary French/Austrian* **Menu prices** *$8–$28*

KIRCHENWIRT-GRAZ 🍷
Kirchenwirt, 9 Kirchplatz, Graz, 8044; (011) 43-3163-911120 **Wine list** *Austria, France, Italy* **Wine prices** *Moderate* **Corkage** *$9* **Cuisine** *Austrian/international* **Menu prices** *$8–$19*

RESTAURANT SCHAUER 🍷
Grand Hotel Wiesler, 4-8 Grieskal, Graz, A-8020; (011) 43-316-706683 **Wine list** *Austria* **Wine prices** Inexpensive **Cuisine** *International* **Menu prices** *$6–$33*

BARBADOS

LA TERRA RISTORANTE 🍷
The Club House, Royal Westmoreland Porters, Saint James; (246) 432-1099 **Wine list** *California, France* **Wine prices** *Moderate* **Corkage** *$12* **Cuisine** *Italian* **Menu prices** *$25–$40*

BELGIUM

HOF VAN CLEVE 🍷🍷

Riemegemstraat 1, Kruishoutem, 9770; (011) 32-9-383-5848 **Wine list** *France, Italy* **Wine prices** *Expensive* **Corkage** *$25* **Cuisine** *French* **Menu prices** *$35–$70*

RESTAURANT AU VIGNERON 🍷🍷

Hotel Oostendse Compagnie, Koningsstraat 79, Oostende, 8400; (011) 32-5-970-4816 **Wine list** *France, Italy* **Wine prices** *Expensive* **Cuisine** *French/Belgian* **Menu prices** *$30–$50*

BERMUDA

ASCOTS RESTAURANT 🍷

24 Rosemont Ave., Pembroke, HM 06; (441) 295-9644 **Wine list** *France, California* **Wine prices** *Moderate* **Cuisine** *Mediterranean/continental* **Menu prices** *$20–$32*

FOURWAYS INN 🍷🍷

Fourways Inn Cottage Colony, 1 Middle Road, Paget, PG BX; (441) 236-6517 **Wine list** *Bordeaux, Burgundy, Italy* **Wine prices** *Expensive* **Cuisine** *French/continental* **Menu prices** *$25–$40*

THE HARBOURFRONT 🍷

21 Front St. W., Hamilton, HM 11; (441) 295-4207 **Wine list** *California, France* **Wine prices** *Moderate* **Cuisine** *Steak house/sushi* **Menu prices** *$19–$31*

HORIZONS & COTTAGES 🍷

33 South Road, Paget, PG 04; (441) 236-0048 **Wine list** *California, France* **Wine prices** *Expensive* **Cuisine** *International* **Menu prices** *Prix fixe only; $55*

LA COQUILLE 🍷

B.U.E.I. Building, 40 Crow Lane, Pembroke; (441) 292-6122 **Wine list** *France* **Wine prices** *Moderate* **Cuisine** *French* **Menu prices** *$25–$35*

PORT O CALL RESTAURANT 🍷

87 Front St., Hamilton, HM 11; (441) 295-5373 **Wine list** *Italy, California* **Wine prices** *Moderate* **Cuisine** *Caribbean* **Menu prices** *$18–$25*

PRIMAVERA 🍷
69 Pitts Bay Road, Hamilton, HM 08; (441) 295-2167 **Wine list** *Italy* **Wine prices** *Moderate* **Corkage** *$10* **Cuisine** *Italian/sushi* **Menu prices** *$18–$37*

WATERLOT INN RESTAURANT 🍷
The Fairmont Southampton, 101 S. Shore Road, Southampton; (441) 238-2555 **Wine list** *California* **Wine prices** *Expensive* **Cuisine** *Caribbean* **Menu prices** *$28–$45*

THE WELLINGTON ROOM 🍷
The Waterloo House, 100 Pitts Bay Road, Pembroke, Hamilton; (441) 295-4480 **Wine list** *France, California, Italy* **Wine prices** *Moderate* **Corkage** *$25* **Cuisine** *European/continental* **Menu prices** *$28–$34*

BRAZIL

BOULEVARD 🍷
539 Rua Voluntarios da Patria, Curitiba, Parana, 80020-000; (011) 55-4122-4824-4 **Wine list** *France* **Wine prices** *Moderate* **Cuisine** *French* **Menu prices** *$20–$40*

CAFÉ LAGUIOLE 🍷
63 Rua Sete de Setembro, Centro, Rio de Janeiro, 20050-005; (011) 55-21-2509-7215 **Wine list** *Bordeaux, Italy, Spain* **Wine prices** *Moderate* **Cuisine** *French/Brazilian* **Menu prices** *$10–$20*

SOLAR FAZENDA DO CEDRO 🍷
BR 040 - KM 45, Petropolis, Rio-Juiz de Fora; (011) 55-24-2223-3618 **Wine list** *Chile, Argentina, Bordeaux* **Wine prices** *Moderate* **Corkage** *$8* **Cuisine** *European* **Menu prices** *$12–$25*

SPLENDIDO RISTORANTE 🍷
251 Rua Levindo Lopes, Savassi, Belo Horizonte, 30140-170; (011) 55-31-3227-6446 **Wine list** *Chile, Italy, Argentina, Portugal* **Wine prices** *Moderate* **Cuisine** *Italian* **Menu prices** *$7–$13*

TASTE-VIN 🍷
2105 Rua Curitiba, Belo Horizonte, 30170-122; (011) 55-31-3292-5423 **Wine list** *France, Italy, Chile, New Zealand* **Wine prices** *Moderate* **Cuisine** *French* **Menu prices** *$7–$16*

CAMBODIA

LE GRAND 🍷
Raffles Grand Hotel d'Angkor, 1 Vithei Charles de Gaulle, Khum Svay Dang Kum, Siem Reap; (011) 855-63-963-888 **Wine list** *France* **Wine prices** *Moderate* **Corkage** *$20* **Cuisine** *Cambodian* **Menu prices** *$15–$23*

CANADA

ALBERTA

THE BANFFSHIRE CLUB 🍷
The Fairmont Banff Springs, 405 Spray Ave., Banff, Alberta, T1L 1J4; (403) 762-2211 **Wine list** *France, Italy, California, Canada* **Wine prices** *Expensive* **Cuisine** *Contemporary* **Menu prices** *$25–$60*

THE BELVEDERE 🍷🍷
107 Eighth Ave. S.W., Calgary, Alberta, T2P 1B4; (403) 265-9595 **Wine list** *California, France* **Wine prices** *Moderate* **Cuisine** *Contemporary* **Menu prices** *$22–$48*

BLUE IGUANA GRILL 🍷
11304 104 Ave., Edmonton, Alberta, T5K 2W9; (780) 424-7222 **Wine list** *California* **Wine prices** Inexpensive **Cuisine** *Contemporary* **Menu prices** *$12–$30*

BONTERRA RESTAURANT 🍷
1016 Eighth St. S.W., Calgary, Alberta, T2R 1K2; (403) 262-8480 **Wine list** *Italy* **Wine prices** *Moderate* **Cuisine** *Contemporary Italian* **Menu prices** *$8–$36*

BUFFALO MOUNTAIN LODGE 🍷🍷
Tunnel Mountain Road, Banff, Alberta, T0L 0C0; (403) 760-4484 **Wine list** *California, France, Italy, Australia* **Wine prices** Inexpensive **Cuisine** *Regional* **Menu prices** *$17–$29*

CATCH 🍷
100 Stephen Ave. S.E., Calgary, Alberta, T2G 0K6; (403) 206-0000 **Wine list** *France, California* **Wine prices** *Moderate* **Cuisine** *Provençal* **Menu prices** *$14–$23*

CILANTRO RESTAURANT 🍷
338 17th Ave., Calgary, Alberta, T2S 0A8; (403) 229-1177 **Wine list** *California, France* **Wine prices** *Moderate* **Corkage** *$15* **Cuisine** *Californian/Southwestern* **Menu prices** *$17–$32*

EDEN 🍷🍷

Rimrock Resort Hotel, Mountain Avenue, Banff, Alberta, T1L 1J2; (403) 762-1865 **Wine list** *California, France, Italy* **Wine prices** *Moderate* **Cuisine** *French* **Menu prices** *Prix fixe only; $75–$115*

THE EDITH CAVELL 🍷

The Fairmont Jasper Park Lodge, Jasper Park Lodge Road, Jasper, Alberta, T0E 1E0; (780) 852-6052 **Wine list** *Canada, California, France* **Wine prices** *Moderate* **Corkage** *$12* **Cuisine** *Contemporary Canadian* **Menu prices** *Prix fixe only; $40–$60*

EVERGREEN FINE DINING 🍷

Royal Canadian Lodge, 459 Banff Ave., Banff, Alberta, T1L 1B4; (403) 762-3307 **Wine list** *Canada* **Wine prices** *Moderate* **Cuisine** *Canadian* **Menu prices** *$12–$20*

HARDWARE GRILL 🍷

9698 Jasper Ave., Edmonton, Alberta, T5H 3V5; (780) 423-0969 **Wine list** *California, France, Canada* **Wine prices** *Moderate* **Cuisine** *Canadian* **Menu prices** *$23–$30*

HY'S STEAK HOUSE 🍷

316 Fourth Ave. S.W., Calgary, Alberta, T2P 0H8; (403) 263-2222 **Wine list** *California, France* **Wine prices** *Moderate* **Cuisine** *Steak house* **Menu prices** *$17–$30*

HY'S STEAK LOFT 🍷

10013 101A Ave., Edmonton, Alberta, T5J 0C3; (780) 424-4444 **Wine list** *California, France* **Wine prices** *Moderate* **Cuisine** *Steak house* **Menu prices** *$17–$30*

IL PORTICO 🍷

10012 107th St., Edmonton, Alberta, T5J 1J2; (780) 424-0707 **Wine list** *Italy, California* **Wine prices** *Expensive* **Cuisine** *Italian* **Menu prices** *$10–$15*

LA CHAUMIÈRE RESTAURANT 🍷

139 17th Ave. S.W., Calgary, Alberta, T2S 0A1; (403) 228-5690 **Wine list** *Italy, France, California* **Wine prices** *Moderate* **Cuisine** *French* **Menu prices** *$15–$20*

MAPLE LEAF GRILLÉ & SPIRITS 🍷

137 Banff Ave., Banff, Alberta, T1L 1C8; (403) 760-7680 **Wine list** *California, Canada* **Wine prices** *Moderate* **Cuisine** *Contemporary* **Menu prices** *$11–$35*

MOUNT FAIRVIEW DINING ROOM
Deer Lodge, 109 Lake Louise Drive, Lake Louise, Alberta, T0L 1E0; (403) 522-3747 **Wine list** *California, Canada, France* **Wine prices** *Moderate* **Cuisine** *Regional* **Menu prices** *$14–$23*

THE OWL'S NEST
The Westin Calgary, 320 Fourth Ave. S.W., Calgary, Alberta, T2P 2S6; (403) 266-1611 **Wine list** *California, France* **Wine prices** *Expensive* **Cuisine** *French/international* **Menu prices** *$17–$38*

PARKALLEN RESTAURANT
7018 109th St., Edmonton, Alberta, T6H 3C1; (780) 436-8080 **Wine list** *France, California* **Wine prices** *Moderate* **Cuisine** *Lebanese/Mediterranean* **Menu prices** *$6–$20*

POST HOTEL DINING ROOM
Post Hotel, 200 Pipestone Road, Lake Louise, Alberta, T0L 1E0; (403) 522-3989 **Wine list** *California, Burgundy, Bordeaux* **Wine selections** *1,690* **Number of bottles** *28,500* **Wine prices** *Moderate* **Cuisine** *Contemporary* **Menu prices** *$20–$32* **Credit cards** *AX, MC, VS*
Grand Award since 2002

RESTAURANT LE BEAUJOLAIS
212 Buffalo St., Banff, Alberta, T0L 0C0; (403) 762-2712 **Wine list** *France, California* **Wine prices** *Moderate* **Cuisine** *French* **Menu prices** *$20–$32*

RIVER CAFÉ
Prince's Island Park, Calgary, Alberta; (403) 261-7670 **Wine list** *California, France, Italy* **Wine prices** *Moderate* **Cuisine** *Canadian* **Menu prices** *$14–$24*

TEATRO
200 Eighth Ave. S.E., Calgary, Alberta, T2G 0K7; (403) 290-1012 **Wine list** *California, France, Italy* **Wine prices** *Expensive* **Cuisine** *Italian* **Menu prices** *$15–$26*

WILDWOOD
2417 Fourth St. S.W., Calgary, Alberta, T2S 1X5; (403) 228-0100 **Wine list** *California, Canada* **Wine prices** *Moderate* **Cuisine** *Regional* **Menu prices** *$12–$20*

INTERNATIONAL

CANADA

BRITISH COLUMBIA

ALL SEASONS CAFÉ 🍷

620 Herridge Lane, Nelson, British Columbia, V1L 6A7; (250) 352-0101 **Wine list** *California, Canada* **Wine prices** *Moderate* **Cuisine** *Regional* **Menu prices** *$11–$23*

ARAXI RESTAURANT & BAR 🍷🍷

4222 Village Square, Whistler, British Columbia, V0N 1B4; (604) 932-4540 **Wine list** *California, Italy, France, Australia* **Wine prices** *Moderate* **Cuisine** *Pacific Northwestern* **Menu prices** *$13–$34*

THE AUBERGINE GRILLE 🍷

The Westin Resort & Spa, 4090 Whistler Way, Whistler, British Columbia, V0N 1B4; (604) 905-5000 **Wine list** *California, Canada* **Wine prices** *Moderate* **Cuisine** *Pacific Northwestern* **Menu prices** *$15–$45*

THE BEACH HOUSE AT DUNDARAVE PIER 🍷

150 25th St., West Vancouver, British Columbia, V7V 4H8; (604) 922-1414 **Wine list** *California, Canada* **Wine prices** *Moderate* **Cuisine** *Pacific Northwestern* **Menu prices** *$13–$24*

BEARFOOT BISTRO 🍷🍷

4121 Village Green, Whistler, British Columbia, V0N 1B4; (604) 932-3433 **Wine list** *California, Bordeaux, Italy, Germany* **Wine prices** *Expensive* **Cuisine** *French/international* **Menu prices** *Prix fixe only; $55–$105*

BLUE CRAB BAR & GRILL 🍷

146 Victoria St., Victoria, British Columbia, V8V 1V4; (250) 480-1999 **Wine list** *Canada, California* **Wine prices** *Moderate* **Cuisine** *Seafood* **Menu prices** *$21–$43*

BLUE WATER CAFÉ & RAW BAR 🍷🍷

1095 Hamilton St., Vancouver, British Columbia, V6B 5T4; (604) 688-8078 **Wine list** *California, France, Canada* **Wine prices** *Moderate* **Cuisine** *Seafood* **Menu prices** *$19–$40*

BRIDGES' RESTAURANT 🍷

1676 Duranleau St., No. 200, Vancouver, British Columbia, V6H 3S4; (604) 687-4400 **Wine list** *California, France* **Wine prices** *Moderate* **Cuisine** *Seafood* **Menu prices** *$12–$22*

🍷🍷🍷 Grand Award 🍷🍷 Best of Award of Excellence 🍷 Award of Excellence

C RESTAURANT
1600 Howe St., Vancouver, British Columbia, V6Z 2L9; (604) 681-1164 **Wine list** *California, France, Germany* **Wine prices** *Moderate* **Cuisine** *Seafood* **Menu prices** *$18–$25*

CAFÉ DE PARIS
751 Denman St., Vancouver, British Columbia, V6G 2L6; (604) 687-1418 **Wine list** *France* **Wine prices** *Moderate* **Cuisine** *French* **Menu prices** *$13–$19*

CAFFÉ DÉ MEDICI
1025 Robson St., Vancouver, British Columbia, V6E 1A9; (604) 669-9322 **Wine list** *Italy, California* **Wine prices** *Moderate* **Cuisine** *Italian* **Menu prices** *$18–$30*

THE CANNERY SEAFOOD RESTAURANT
2205 Commissioner St., Vancouver, British Columbia, V5L 1A4; (604) 254-9606 **Wine list** *California, France, Washington* **Wine prices** *Moderate* **Cuisine** *Seafood* **Menu prices** *$13–$20*

CHARTWELL
Four Seasons Hotel Vancouver, 791 W. Georgia St., Vancouver, British Columbia, V6C 2T4; (604) 689-9333 **Wine list** *California, France* **Wine prices** *Moderate* **Cuisine** *Contemporary European* **Menu prices** *$18–$35*

CINCIN RESTAURANT & BAR
1154 Robson St., Vancouver, British Columbia, V6E 1B5; (604) 688-7338 **Wine list** *Italy, California, France* **Wine prices** *Moderate* **Cuisine** *Italian/Mediterranean* **Menu prices** *$10–$20*

CIOPPINO'S MEDITERRANEAN GRILL
1133 Hamilton St., Vancouver, British Columbia, V6B 5P6; (604) 688-7466 **Wine list** *Italy, California, France* **Wine prices** *Moderate* **Cuisine** *Italian/Mediterranean* **Menu prices** *$15–$36*

CIRCOLO
1116 Mainland St., Vancouver, British Columbia, V6B 2T9; (604) 687-1116 **Wine list** *Italy, California, Canada* **Wine prices** *Moderate* **Cuisine** *Northern Italian* **Menu prices** *$12–$36*

DINING ROOM AT THE AERIE 🍷🍷
The Aerie Resort, 600 Ebedora Lane, Malahat, British Columbia, V0R 2L0; (800) 518-1933 **Wine list** *California, France, Canada* **Wine prices** *Expensive* **Cuisine** *French/Pacific Northwestern* **Menu prices** *$20–$30*

DIVA 🍷
Metropolitan Hotel, 645 Howe St., Vancouver, British Columbia, V6C 2Y9; (604) 602-7788 **Wine list** *California, Canada, France* **Wine prices** *Moderate* **Cuisine** *Regional/French* **Menu prices** *$18–$34*

EMERALD LAKE LODGE 🍷
1 Emerald Lake Road, Field, British Columbia, V0A 1G0; (250) 343-6321 **Wine list** *Canada, California, Italy* **Wine prices** *Moderate* **Cuisine** *Regional* **Menu prices** *$15–$22*

EMPRESS ROOM 🍷🍷
The Fairmont Victoria, 721 Government St., Victoria, British Columbia, V8W 1W5; (250) 389-2727 **Wine list** *France, California, Germany, Canada* **Wine prices** *Expensive* **Cuisine** *Continental* **Menu prices** *$20–$30*

THE FISH HOUSE 🍷
8901 Stanley Park Drive, Vancouver, British Columbia, V6G 3E2; (604) 681-7275 **Wine list** *California, Canada* **Wine prices** *Moderate* **Cuisine** *Pacific Northwestern* **Menu prices** *$15–$20*

THE FIVE SAILS RESTAURANT 🍷
The Pan-Pacific Hotel Vancouver, 300-999 Canada Place, Vancouver, British Columbia, V6C 3B5; (604) 662-8111 **Wine list** *California, France, Canada* **Wine prices** *Moderate* **Cuisine** *Pacific rim/French* **Menu prices** *$27–$42*

GLOWBAL GRILL & SATAY BAR 🍷
1079 Mainland St.-Yaletown, Vancouver, British Columbia, V6B 5P9; (604) 602-0835 **Wine list** *California* **Wine prices** *Moderate* **Cuisine** *Pacific Northwestern* **Menu prices** *$14–$28*

GOTHAM STEAKHOUSE & COCKTAIL BAR 🍷
615 Seymour St., Vancouver, British Columbia, V6B 3K3; (604) 605-8282 **Wine list** *California, Italy* **Wine prices** *Moderate* **Cuisine** *Steak house* **Menu prices** *$20–$40*

HASTINGS HOUSE 🍷
160 Upper Ganges Road, Salt Spring Island, British Columbia, V8K 2S2; (250) 537-2362 **Wine list** *California, Canada* **Wine prices** *Moderate* **Cuisine** *Regional* **Menu prices** *Prix fixe only; $65*

HOUSE PICCOLO 🍷
108 Hereford Ave., Salt Spring Island, British Columbia, V8K 2T4; (250) 537-1844 **Wine list** *Califorina, Canada, France* **Wine prices** *Moderate* **Cuisine** *European/Scandinavian* **Menu prices** *$16–$20*

IL GIARDINO 🍷
1382 Hornby St., Vancouver, British Columbia, V6Z 1W5; (604) 669-2422 **Wine list** *Italy, California, Canada* **Wine prices** *Moderate* **Cuisine** *Italian* **Menu prices** *$17–$24*

IL TERRAZZO RISTORANTE 🍷
555 Johnson St., Victoria, British Columbia, V8W 1M2; (250) 361-0028 **Wine list** *Italy, California, Canada* **Wine prices** *Moderate* **Cuisine** *Northern Italian* **Menu prices** *$12–$23*

JOE FORTES SEAFOOD & CHOP HOUSE 🍷
777 Thurlow St., Vancouver, British Columbia, V6E 3V5; (604) 669-1940 **Wine list** *California, France, Canada* **Wine prices** *Moderate* **Cuisine** *Steak house/seafood* **Menu prices** *$13–$28*

LA RÚA 🍷
4557 Blackcomb Way, Whistler, British Columbia, V0N 1B0; (604) 932-5011 **Wine list** *California, France, Italy* **Wine prices** *Expensive* **Cuisine** *Continental* **Menu prices** *$10–$19*

LA TERRAZZA 🍷🍷
1088 Cambie St., Vancouver, British Columbia, V6B 6J5; (604) 899-4449 **Wine list** *Italy, France, California, Canada* **Wine prices** *Moderate* **Corkage** *$35* **Cuisine** *Contemporary Italian* **Menu prices** *$20–$30*

LORENZO RISTORANTE 🍷
3605 W. Fourth Ave., Vancouver, British Columbia, V6R 1P2; (604) 731-2712 **Wine list** *Italy, Canada* **Wine prices** *Moderate* **Cuisine** *Italian* **Menu prices** *$15–$28*

LUMIÈRE 🍷
2551 W. Broadway, Vancouver, British Columbia, V6K 2E9; (604) 739-8185 **Wine list** *France* **Wine prices** *Moderate* **Cuisine** *Contemporary French* **Menu prices** *Prix fixe only; $40–$60*

THE MARINA RESTAURANT 🍷
1327 Beach Drive, Victoria, British Columbia, V8S 2N4; (250) 598-8555 **Wine list** *California, Canada* **Wine prices** *Moderate* **Cuisine** *Seafood* **Menu prices** *$12–$30*

MORTON'S OF CHICAGO 🍷
750 W. Cordova St., Vancouver, British Columbia, V6C 1A1; (604) 915-5105 **Wine list** *California* **Wine prices** *Expensive* **Cuisine** *Steak house* **Menu prices** *$25–$45*

O'DOUL'S RESTAURANT & BAR 🍷
Listel Vancouver Hotel, 1300 Robson St., Vancouver, British Columbia, V6E 1C5; (604) 661-1400 **Wine list** *California, Canada* **Wine prices** *Moderate* **Cuisine** *Pacific Northwestern* **Menu prices** *$15–$20*

THE OLD ELEVATOR 🍷
291 First Ave., Fernie, British Columbia, V0B 1M0; (250) 423-7115 **Wine list** *France, California, Canada* **Wine prices** *Moderate* **Cuisine** *Regional/European* **Menu prices** *$9–$22*

PICCOLO MONDO RESTAURANT 🍷
850 Thurlow St., Vancouver, British Columbia, V6E 1W2; (604) 688-1633 **Wine list** *Italy* **Wine prices** *Moderate* **Cuisine** *Italian* **Menu prices** *$11–$20*

THE POINTE RESTAURANT 🍷
The Wickaninnish Inn, Osprey Lane at Chesterman Beach, Tofino, British Columbia, V0R 2Z0; (250) 725-3106 **Wine list** *California, Canada, Bordeaux* **Wine prices** *Moderate* **Cuisine** *Canadian* **Menu prices** *$18–$34*

POWDER MAX DINING ROOM 🍷
Mike Wiegele Heli-Ski Resort on the Lake, Blue River, British Columbia, V0E 1J0; (250) 673-8381 **Wine list** *California, Canada* **Wine prices** *Moderate* **Corkage** *$15* **Cuisine** *Contemporary* **Menu prices** *$12–$26*

QUATTRO AT WHISTLER 🍷🍷
4319 Main St., Whistler, British Columbia, V0N 1B4; (604) 905-4844 **Wine list** *Italy, California* **Wine prices** *Moderate* **Cuisine** *Italian* **Menu prices** *$25–$30*

QUATTRO ON FOURTH 🍷

2611 W. Fourth Ave., Vancouver, British Columbia, V6K 1P8; (604) 734-4444 **Wine list** *Italy* **Wine prices** *Moderate* **Cuisine** *Italian/Mediterranean* **Menu prices** *$15–$30*

RAINCITY GRILL 🍷🍷

1193 Denman St., Vancouver, British Columbia, V6G 2N1; (604) 685-7337 **Wine list** *California, Oregon, Washington, Canada* **Wine prices** *Moderate* **Cuisine** *Pacific Northwestern* **Menu prices** *$12–$22*

SOOKE HARBOUR HOUSE 🍷🍷🍷

Sooke Harbour House Inn, 1528 Whiffen Spit Road, Sooke, British Columbia, V0S 1N0; (250) 642-3421 **Wine list** *California, Bordeaux, Burgundy, Oregon, Washington, Canada* **Wine selections** *2,720* **Number of bottles** *16,200* **Wine prices** *Moderate* **Cuisine** *Contemporary Canadian/seafood* **Menu prices** *$18–$30* **Credit cards** MC, VS
Grand Award since 2000

THE VICTORIAN RESTAURANT 🍷

Delta Victoria Ocean Pointe Resort, 45 Songhees Road, Victoria, British Columbia, V9A 6T3; (250) 360-5800 **Wine list** *California, France* **Wine prices** *Moderate* **Cuisine** *Pacific Northwestern* **Menu prices** *$15–$25*

THE VINEYARD 🍷

2296 W. 4th Ave., Vancouver, British Columbia, V6K 1N8; (604) 733-2420 **Wine list** *California, Italy* **Wine prices** *Moderate* **Cuisine** *Greek/Mediterranean* **Menu prices** *$10–$16*

WEST 🍷🍷

2881 Granville St., Vancouver, British Columbia, V6H 3J4; (604) 738-8938 **Wine list** *France, California, Canada, Australia* **Wine prices** *Moderate* **Cuisine** *Regional* **Menu prices** *$16–$25*

THE WILDFLOWER 🍷🍷

The Fairmont Château Whistler, 4599 Château Blvd., Whistler, British Columbia, V0N 1B4; (604) 938-2033 **Wine list** *California, Bordeaux, Canada* **Wine prices** *Moderate* **Cuisine** *Regional/French* **Menu prices** *$14–$37*

CANADA

ONTARIO

AIELLI 🍷

286 Lakeshore Road E., Mississauga, Ontario, L5G 1H2; (905) 278-2183 **Wine list** *Italy, California, Canada* **Wine prices** *Moderate* **Cuisine** *Italian* **Menu prices** *$15–$23*

BARBERIAN'S STEAK HOUSE 🍷🍷

7 Elm St., Toronto, Ontario, M5G 1H1; (416) 597-0335 **Wine list** *Bordeaux, Burgundy, California* **Wine prices** *Moderate* **Cuisine** *Steak house* **Menu prices** *$20–$35*

BARDI'S STEAK HOUSE 🍷

56 York St., Toronto, Ontario, M5J 1S8; (416) 366-9211 **Wine list** *California, Italy* **Wine prices** *Moderate* **Cuisine** *Steak house* **Menu prices** *$15–$30*

BIAGIO RISTORANTE 🍷

155 King St. E., Toronto, Ontario, M5C 1G9; (416) 366-4040 **Wine list** *Italy, California, France, Port* **Wine prices** *Moderate* **Cuisine** *Northern Italian* **Menu prices** *$14–$28*

BISTRO 1603 🍷

1603 Clarkson Road N., Mississauga, Ontario, L5J 2X1; (905) 822-5262 **Wine list** *California* **Wine prices** *Moderate* **Cuisine** *French* **Menu prices** *$15–$20*

BISTRO ONE 🍷

555 Dunlop St., Thunder Bay, Ontario, P7B 6S1; (807) 622-2478 **Wine list** *Italy, France, Chile* **Wine prices** *Moderate* **Cuisine** *Contemporary* **Menu prices** *$15–$30*

BLACKSHOP! RESTAURANT 🍷

20 Hobson St., Cambridge, Ontario, N1S 2M6; (519) 621-4180 **Wine list** *California, Canada* **Wine prices** *Moderate* **Cuisine** *International* **Menu prices** *$10–$20*

BREAKWATER FINE DINING RESTAURANT 🍷

The Waterside Inn, 15 Stavebank Road S., Mississauga, Ontario, L5G 2T2; (905) 891-7770 **Wine list** *California, France* **Wine prices** *Moderate* **Cuisine** *International* **Menu prices** *$15–$27*

BYMARK RESTAURANT 🍷

66 Wellington St. W., Toronto, Ontario, M5K 1J3; (416) 777-1144 **Wine list** *California, Australia, Italy* **Wine prices** *Expensive* **Cuisine** *Contemporary* **Menu prices** *$18–$30*

CAFÉ BRUSSEL 🍷🍷
124 Danforth Ave., Toronto, Ontario, M4K 1N1; (416) 465-7363 **Wine list** *California, Champange, Rhône, Bordeaux* **Wine prices** *Moderate* **Cuisine** *French/Belgian* **Menu prices** *$15–$25*

CARIBOU RESTAURANT & WINE BAR 🍷
727 Hewitson St., Thunder Bay, Ontario, P7B 6B5; (807) 628-8588 **Wine list** *California, Italy, Australia* **Wine prices** Inexpensive **Cuisine** *Contemporary* **Menu prices** *$12–$22*

CENTRO GRILL & WINE BAR 🍷🍷
2472 Yonge St., Toronto, Ontario, M4P 2H5; (416) 483-2211 **Wine list** *Bordeaux, Tuscany, California* **Wine prices** *Expensive* **Cuisine** *Italian/Californian* **Menu prices** *$20–$30*

ECLIPSE 🍷
Deerhurst Resort, 1235 Deerhurst Drive, Huntsville, Ontario, P1H 2E8; (705) 789-6411 **Wine list** *California, France* **Wine prices** *Moderate* **Cuisine** *Regional* **Menu prices** *$8–$25*

EMPIRE GRILL 🍷
47 Clarence St., Ottawa, Ontario, K1N 9K1; (613) 241-1343 **Wine list** *California, Canada* **Wine prices** *Moderate* **Cuisine** *Contemporary American* **Menu prices** *$10–$25*

FAR NIENTE 🍷
187 Bay St., Toronto, Ontario, M5L 1G5; (416) 214-9922 **Wine list** *California, Italy* **Wine prices** *Moderate* **Cuisine** *Californian* **Menu prices** *$12–$23*

FILET OF SOLE 🍷
11 Duncan St., Toronto, Ontario, M5H 3G6; (416) 598-3256 **Wine list** *Canada, California, France* **Wine prices** Inexpensive **Cuisine** *Seafood* **Menu prices** *$14–$25*

GRAPPA RISTORANTE 🍷
797 College St., Toronto, Ontario, M6G 1C7; (416) 535-3337 **Wine list** *Italy, California* **Wine prices** *Moderate* **Cuisine** *Italian* **Menu prices** *$10–$20*

HARBOUR SIXTY STEAKHOUSE 🍷
60 Harbour St., Toronto, Ontario, M5J 1B7; (416) 777-2111 **Wine list** *California, France, Italy* **Wine prices** *Moderate* **Cuisine** *Steak house* **Menu prices** *$20–$40*

HY'S STEAK HOUSE & COCKTAIL BAR 🍷
120 Adelaide Street W., Toronto, Ontario, M5H 1T1; (416) 364-6600 **Wine list** *California, France* **Wine prices** *Moderate* **Cuisine** *Steak house* **Menu prices** *$20–$30*

THE INN AT MANITOU 🍷
McKellar Center Road, Manitouwabing, Ontario, P0G 1C0; (800) 571-8818 **Wine list** *Bordeaux* **Wine prices** *Moderate* **Cuisine** *Contemporary French* **Menu prices** *$20–$40*

JUNIPER 🍷
1293 Wellington St., Ottawa, Ontario, K1Y 3B1; (613) 728-0220 **Wine list** *California, Canada* **Wine prices** *Moderate* **Cuisine** *Contemporary* **Menu prices** *$11–$18*

LA FENICE 🍷
319 King St. W., Toronto, Ontario, M5V 1J5; (416) 585-2377 **Wine list** *Italy, California* **Wine prices** *Moderate* **Cuisine** *Italian* **Menu prices** *$10–$22*

LA FORCHETTA RISTORANTE 🍷
613 College St., Toronto, Ontario, M6G 1B5; (416) 534-3100 **Wine list** *Italy* **Wine prices** *Moderate* **Cuisine** *Italian* **Menu prices** *$18–$29*

LANGDON HALL 🍷
Langdon Hall Country House Hotel & Spa, 1 Langdon Drive, Cambridge, Ontario, N3H 4R8; (800) 268-1898 **Wine list** *France, California* **Wine prices** *Moderate* **Cuisine** *French* **Menu prices** *$20–$25*

LE SÉLECT BISTRO 🍷🍷
328 Queen St. W., Toronto, Ontario, M5V 2A2; (416) 596-6405 **Wine list** *France, Italy, California, Australia* **Wine prices** *Moderate* **Cuisine** *French* **Menu prices** *$14–$22*

THE LITTLE INN OF BAYFIELD 🍷
26 Main St., Bayfield, Ontario, N0M 1G0; (519) 565-2611 **Wine list** *France, Canada* **Wine prices** *Moderate* **Cuisine** *Regional* **Menu prices** *$20–$30*

MASON-GIRARDOT ALAN MANOR 🍷
3203 Peter St., Windsor, Ontario, N9C 1H6; (519) 253-9212 **Wine list** *France* **Wine prices** *Moderate* **Cuisine** *Contemporary Canadian/Turkish/French* **Menu prices** *$8–$20*

MEDITHÉO RESTAURANT & WINE BAR 🍷
77 Clarence St., Ottawa, Ontario, K1N 5P5; (613) 562-2500 **Wine list** *Canada* **Wine prices** *Moderate* **Cuisine** *Mediterranean* **Menu prices** *$12–$30*

MONSOON RESTAURANT & LOUNGE 🍷
100 Simcoe St., Toronto, Ontario, M5H 3G2; (416) 979-7172 **Wine list** *France, California* **Wine prices** *Moderate* **Cuisine** *Contemporary Asian* **Menu prices** *$15–$25*

MORTON'S OF CHICAGO
Park Hyatt Toronto, 4 Avenue Road, Toronto, Ontario, M5R 2E8; (416) 925-0648 **Wine list** *California* **Wine prices** *Expensive* **Cuisine** *Steak house* **Menu prices** *$25–$45*

NOCE
875 Queen St. W., Toronto, Ontario, M6J 1G5; (416) 504-3463 **Wine list** *Italy, California* **Wine prices** *Moderate* **Cuisine** *Contemporary Italian* **Menu prices** *$20–$35*

NORTH 44°
2537 Yonge St., Toronto, Ontario, M4P 2H9; (416) 487-4897 **Wine list** *France, Italy, California* **Wine prices** *Expensive* **Cuisine** *Contemporary* **Menu prices** *$18–$30*

OLIVER'S OF OAKVILLE
141 Lakeshore Road E., Oakville, Ontario, L6J 1H3; (905) 845-9391 **Wine list** *California* **Wine prices** *Moderate* **Cuisine** *Continental/French* **Menu prices** *$15–$30*

OPUS RESTAURANT ON PRINCE ARTHUR
37 Prince Arthur Ave., Toronto, Ontario, M5R 1B2; (416) 921-3105 **Wine list** *France, Tuscany, California, Port* **Wine selections** *1,800* **Number of bottles** *26,000* **Wine prices** *Moderate* **Cuisine** *European/Canadian* **Menu prices** *$20–$26* **Credit cards** *AX, MC, VS*
Grand Award since 2002

ORO
45 Elm St., Toronto, Ontario, M5G 1H1; (416) 597-0155 **Wine list** *California, France, Italy, Canada* **Wine prices** *Moderate* **Cuisine** *Contemporary* **Menu prices** *$16–$26*

PAESE RESTAURANT
3827 Bathurst St., Downsview, Ontario, M3H 3N1; (416) 631-6585 **Wine list** *Italy, California* **Wine prices** *Moderate* **Cuisine** *Italian* **Menu prices** *$12–$22*

THE PLATINUM CLUB
40 Bay St., Toronto, Ontario, M5J 2X2; (416) 815-5648 **Wine list** *California, France* **Wine prices** *Moderate* **Cuisine** *Regional* **Menu prices** *$20–$40*

PROVENCE
12 Amelia St., Toronto, Ontario, M4X 1E1; (416) 924-9901 **Wine list** *Bordeaux* **Wine prices** *Expensive* **Cuisine** *French* **Menu prices** *$13–$22*

REDS BISTRO & BAR 🍷
77 Adelaide St. W., Toronto, Ontario, M5X 1B1; (416) 862-7337 **Wine list** *France, Italy, Canada* **Wine prices** *Moderate* **Cuisine** *Regional* **Menu prices** *$12–$24*

RESTAURANT EIGHTEEN 🍷
18 York St., Ottawa, Ontario, K1N 5T5; (613) 244-1188 **Wine list** *California, France, Canada* **Wine prices** *Moderate* **Cuisine** *International* **Menu prices** *$25–$32*

ROSEWATER SUPPER CLUB 🍷
19 Toronto St., Toronto, Ontario, M5C 2R1; (416) 214-5888 **Wine list** *Canada, France, California* **Wine prices** *Moderate* **Cuisine** *Contemporary French* **Menu prices** *$18–$27*

THE ROSSEAU ROOM AT WINDERMERE HOUSE 🍷
2508 Windermere Road, Windermere, Ontario, P0B 1P0; (705) 769-3611 **Wine list** *Canada, France* **Wine prices** *Moderate* **Cuisine** *Canadian* **Menu prices** *$15–$25*

RUTH'S CHRIS STEAK HOUSE 🍷
145 Richmond St. W., Toronto, Ontario, M5H 4B3; (416) 955-1455 **Wine list** *California* **Wine prices** *Moderate* **Cuisine** *Steak house* **Menu prices** *$25–$50*

SOLÉ RESTAURANT & WINE BAR 🍷
83 Erb St. W., Building No. 2, Waterloo, Ontario, N2L 6C2; (519) 747-5622 **Wine list** *California, Italy* **Wine prices** *Moderate* **Cuisine** *Continental/Mediterranean* **Menu prices** *$9–$18*

SPAGO 🍷
690 Erie St. E., Windsor, Ontario, N9A 3X9; (519) 252-2233 **Wine list** *Italy* **Wine prices** *Moderate* **Cuisine** *Italian* **Menu prices** *$7–$21*

SPLENDIDO BAR & GRILL 🍷
88 Harbord St., Toronto, Ontario, M5S 1G5; (416) 929-7788 **Wine list** *Italy, California, France* **Wine prices** *Moderate* **Cuisine** *International/French* **Menu prices** *$17–$30*

SPUNTINI 🍷
116 Avenue Road, Toronto, Ontario, M5R 2H4; (416) 962-1110 **Wine list** *Italy* **Wine prices** *Moderate* **Cuisine** *Italian/Mediterranean* **Menu prices** *$10–$14*

STEAMERS RESTAURANT 🍷
75 Highland Drive, Huntsville, Ontario, P1H 2E8; (705) 789-6411 **Wine list** *France, California, Italy* **Wine prices** *Moderate* **Cuisine** *Steak house* **Menu prices** *$10–$30*

SUPERIOR 🍷
253 Yonge St., Toronto, Ontario, M5B 1N8; (416) 214-0416 **Wine list** *France, Italy, California* **Wine prices** *Moderate* **Cuisine** *Contemporary* **Menu prices** *$9–$18*

TERRA RESTAURANT 🍷
8199 Yonge St., Thornhill, Ontario, L3T 2C6; (905) 731-6161 **Wine list** *California, France, Oregon, Washington, Canada* **Wine prices** *Moderate* **Cuisine** *International* **Menu prices** *$20–$40*

360 THE RESTAURANT AT THE CN TOWER 🍷🍷
301 Front St. W., Toronto, Ontario, M5V 2T6; (416) 362-5411 **Wine list** *California, France* **Wine prices** *Moderate* **Cuisine** *Canadian/international* **Menu prices** *$19–$32*

TOM JONES STEAK HOUSE 🍷🍷
17 Leader Lane, Toronto, Ontario, M5E 1L8; (416) 366-6583 **Wine list** *California, France, Italy* **Wine prices** *Expensive* **Cuisine** *Steak house* **Menu prices** *$18–$42*

TRATTORIA CAFFÈ ITALIA 🍷
254 Preston St., Ottawa, Ontario, K1R 7R4; (613) 236-1081 **Wine list** *Italy* **Wine prices** *Moderate* **Cuisine** *Italian* **Menu prices** *$10–$25*

TRATTORIA SOTTO SOTTO 🍷🍷
116A Avenue Road, Toronto, Ontario, M5R 2H4; (416) 962-0011 **Wine list** *Italy, California, Bordeaux, Canada* **Wine prices** *Expensive* **Cuisine** *Italian* **Menu prices** *$12–$37*

21 CLUB 🍷
5705 Falls Ave., Niagara Falls, Ontario, L2E 6T3; (905) 374-3598 **Wine list** *Canada, California* **Wine prices** *Inexpensive* **Cuisine** *Steak house* **Menu prices** *$15–$38*

VIA ALLEGRO RISTORANTE 🍷🍷🍷
3-1750 Queensway W., Etobicoke, Ontario, M9C 5H5; (416) 622-6677 **Wine list** *Tuscany, Piedmont, Bordeaux, California, Australia, Canada* **Wine selections** *3,725* **Number of bottles** *47,000* **Wine prices** *Expensive* **Cuisine** *Italian/French/Californian* **Menu prices** *$13–$39* **Credit cards** *AX, MC, VS*
Grand Award since 2003

VILLA CORNELIA 🍷
142 Kent St., London, Ontario, N6A 1L3; (519) 679-3444
Wine list *France, California* **Wine prices** *Moderate* **Cuisine** *Continental* **Menu prices** *$10–$22*

VINEYARDS WINE BAR BISTRO 🍷
54 York St., Ottawa, Ontario, K1N 5T1; (613) 241-4270
Wine list *Canada, California* **Wine prices** *Expensive* **Cuisine** *Regional* **Menu prices** *$7–$8*

VITTORIA TRATTORIA 🍷🍷
35 William St., Ottawa, Ontario, K1N 6Z9; (613) 789-8959
Wine list *Italy, France, California, Australia* **Wine prices** *Moderate* **Cuisine** *Italian* **Menu prices** *$10–$20*

VITTORIA TRATTORIA 🍷
8 Nelligan Lane, Ottowa, Ontario, K1V 2A4; (613) 731-8959 **Wine list** *Italy, France, Canada* **Wine prices** *Moderate* **Cuisine** *Italian* **Menu prices** *$10–$20*

WILDFIRE 🍷
Taboo Golf Resort, Muskoka Beach Road, R.R. No. 1, Gravenhurst, Ontario, P1P 1R1; (800) 461-0236 **Wine list** *California, France, Italy* **Wine prices** *Moderate* **Cuisine** *Contemporary Asian* **Menu prices** *$17–$27*

WILFRID'S RESTAURANT 🍷
Fairmont Château Laurier, 1 Rideau St., Ottawa, Ontario, K1N 8S7; (613) 562-7043 **Wine list** *Canada, California* **Wine prices** *Moderate* **Cuisine** *Regional* **Menu prices** *$11–$23*

YYZ RESTAURANT & WINE BAR 🍷
345 Adelaide St. W., Toronto, Ontario, M5V 1R5; (416) 599-3399 **Wine list** *California* **Wine prices** *Moderate* **Cuisine** *Contemporary* **Menu prices** *$18–$23*

CANADA

QUEBEC

AUBERGE GEORGEVILLE 🍷
71 Chemin Channel, Georgeville, Quebec, J0B 1T0; (888) 843-8686 **Wine list** *California* **Wine prices** *Moderate* **Cuisine** *Regional* **Menu prices** *Prix fixe only; $40*

AUBERGE HATLEY 🍷🍷
325 Virgin Hill Road N., Hatley, Quebec, J0B 2C0; (819) 842-2451 **Wine list** *Rhône, Loire, France* **Wine prices** *Expensive* **Cuisine** *Contemporary French* **Menu prices** *$24–$30*

AUBERGE LOUIS-HÉBERT 🍷
668 Grande-Allée E., Quebec City, Quebec, G1R 2K5; (418) 525-7812 **Wine list** *France* **Wine prices** *Moderate* **Cuisine** *French* **Menu prices** *$14–$20*

AUBERGE RIPPLECOVE 🍷
700 Rue Ripplecove, Ayer's Cliff, Quebec, J0B 1C0; (800) 668-4296 **Wine list** *France* **Wine prices** *Expensive* **Cuisine** *French/Pacific* **Menu prices** *Prix fixe only; $30–$60*

AUX TRUFFES 🍷
3035 Chemin de la Chapelle, Mont-Tremblant, Quebec, J0T 1Z0; (819) 681-4544 **Wine list** *France* **Wine prices** *Moderate* **Cuisine** *French* **Menu prices** *$20–$26*

THE BEAVER CLUB 🍷
The Fairmont Queen Elizabeth Hotel, 900 René Lévesque Blvd. W., Montreal, Quebec, H3B 4A5; (514) 861-3511 **Wine list** *France, Italy* **Wine prices** *Moderate* **Cuisine** *French* **Menu prices** *$30–$38*

BISTRO À CHAMPLAIN 🍷🍷🍷
75 Chemin Masson Ste.-Marguerite du Lac, Masson, Quebec, J0T 1L0; (450) 228-4988 **Wine list** *Bordeaux, Burgundy, California, Rhône* **Wine selections** *3,500* **Number of bottles** *36,000* **Wine prices** *Moderate* **Cuisine** *French* **Menu prices** *$8–$25* **Credit cards** *AX, MC, VS*
Grand Award since 1988

CAFÉ MASSAWIPPI 🍷
3050 Chemin Capelton, North Hatley, Quebec, J0B 2C0; (819) 842-4528 **Wine list** *California, France, Italy* **Wine prices** *Moderate* **Cuisine** *International* **Menu prices** *$20–$30*

CHARBON STEAKHOUSE 🍷
450 Gare du Palais, Vieux-Port, Quebec, G1K 3X2; (418) 522-0133 **Wine list** *France, California* **Wine prices** *Moderate* **Cuisine** *Steak house* **Menu prices** *$20–$35*

CHEZ LA MÈRE MICHEL 🍷
1209 Rue Guy, Montreal, Quebec, H3H 2K5; (514) 934-0473 **Wine list** *France* **Wine prices** *Moderate* **Cuisine** *French* **Menu prices** *$27–$35*

CHEZ QUEUX
158 E. Rue St.-Paul, Montreal, Quebec, H2Y 1G6; (514) 866-5194 **Wine list** *France* **Wine prices** *Moderate* **Cuisine** *French* **Menu prices** *$17–$25*

LA FENOUILLIÈRE
Best Western Hotel Aristocrate, 3100 Chemin St.-Louis, Ste.-Foy, Quebec, G1W 1R8; (418) 653-3886 **Wine list** *France, California* **Wine prices** *Moderate* **Cuisine** *French* **Menu prices** *$15–$19*

LA PINSONNIÈRE
Auberge La Pinsonnière, 124 St.-Raphaël, La Malbaie, Cap-à-l'Aigle, Quebec, G5A 1X9; (800) 387-4431 **Wine list** *Bordeaux, Burgundy* **Wine prices** *Expensive* **Cuisine** *French* **Menu prices** *$27–$35*

LA QUEUE DE CHEVAL
1221 René Lévesque Blvd., Montreal, Quebec, H3G 1T1; (514) 390-0090 **Wine list** *France, California* **Wine prices** *Expensive* **Cuisine** *Steak house* **Menu prices** *$19–$29*

L'EAU A LA BOUCHE
3003 Sainte-Adèle Blvd., St.-Adèle, Quebec, J8B 2L6; (450) 229-2991 **Wine list** *France* **Wine prices** *Moderate* **Cuisine** *French* **Menu prices** *$23–$30*

LE CHAMPLAIN RESTAURANT
The Fairmont Château Frontenac, 1 Rue des Carrières, Quebec City, Quebec, G1R 4P5; (418) 266-3905 **Wine list** *France* **Wine prices** *Moderate* **Cuisine** *French/Canadian* **Menu prices** *$25–$35*

LE CHARLEVOIX
The Fairmont Le Manoir Richelieu, 181 Rue Richelieu, La Malbaie, Quebec, G5A 1X7; (418) 665-3703 **Wine list** *France, California, Australia* **Wine prices** *Moderate* **Cuisine** *French* **Menu prices** *$30–$45*

LE PIMENT ROUGE
1170 Rue Peel, Montreal, Quebec, H3B 4P2; (514) 866-7816 **Wine list** *France, California* **Wine prices** *Expensive* **Cuisine** *Chinese* **Menu prices** *$20–$35*

LE PORTOFINO
54 Rue Couillard, Vieux-Quebec, Quebec, G1R 3T3; (418) 692-8888 **Wine list** *Italy* **Wine prices** *Moderate* **Cuisine** *Italian* **Menu prices** *$20–$30*

LE SAINT-AMOUR

48 Rue Sainte-Ursule, Quebec City, Quebec, G1R 4E2; (418) 694-0667 **Wine list** *Bordeaux, Burgundy, Italy, California* **Wine prices** *Moderate* **Cuisine** *French* **Menu prices** *$15–$25*

LES FOUGÈRES

783 Route 105, Chelsea, Quebec, J9B 1P1; (819) 827-8942 **Wine list** *France* **Wine prices** Inexpensive **Cuisine** *Canadian* **Menu prices** *$13–$20*

LOUP-GAROU

The Fairmont Tremblant, 3045 Chemin de la Chapelle, Mont-Tremblant, Quebec, J8E 2H6; (819) 681-7685 **Wine list** *France* **Wine prices** *Moderate* **Cuisine** *Regional* **Menu prices** *$40–$70*

MANOIR HOVEY

575 Chemin Hovey, North Hatley, Quebec, J0B 2C0; (819) 842-2421 **Wine list** *France, California, Italy* **Wine prices** *Moderate* **Cuisine** *Contemporary French* **Menu prices** *$20–$25*

MOISHE'S STEAK HOUSE

3961 Sainte-Laurent Blvd., Montreal, Quebec, H2W 1Y4; (514) 845-3509 **Wine list** *France* **Wine prices** *Moderate* **Cuisine** *Steak house* **Menu prices** *$25–$45*

NUANCES

Casino de Montreal, 1 Ave. du Casino, Montreal, Quebec, H3C 4W7; (514) 392-2708 **Wine list** *France, California* **Wine prices** *Moderate* **Cuisine** *French* **Menu prices** *$22–$32*

RESTAURANT LE GRAFFITI

1191 Cartier Ave., Quebec City, Quebec, G1R 2S9; (418) 529-4949 **Wine list** *France, Italy* **Wine prices** *Expensive* **Cuisine** *Continental/French/Italian* **Menu prices** *$8–$17*

RESTAURANT MESS HALL

4858 Sherbrooke St. W., Montreal, Quebec, H3Z 1H1; (514) 482-2167 **Wine list** *Italy, California, France* **Wine prices** *Moderate* **Cuisine** *Contemporary Italian* **Menu prices** *$7–$25*

RIB 'N REEF

8105 Décaire Blvd., Montreal, Quebec, H4P 2H5; (514) 735-1601 **Wine list** *California, France* **Wine prices** *Moderate* **Cuisine** *Steak house* **Menu prices** *$16–$45*

RISTORANTE BUONA NOTTE 🍷

3518 Sainte-Laurent, Montreal, Quebec, H2X 2V2; (514) 848-0644 **Wine list** *Italy* **Wine prices** *Expensive* **Cuisine** *Italian* **Menu prices** *$15–$25*

RISTORANTE MICHELANGELO 🍷🍷

3111 Chemin St.-Louis, Ste.-Foy, Quebec, G1W 1R6; (418) 651-6262 **Wine list** *Italy* **Wine prices** *Moderate* **Cuisine** *Italian* **Menu prices** *$17–$30*

CANADA

OTHER PROVINCES

AMICI 🍷

326 Broadway, Winnipeg, Manitoba, R3C 0S5; (204) 943-4997 **Wine list** *Italy, California* **Wine prices** *Moderate* **Cuisine** *Northern Italian* **Menu prices** *$12–$30*

BIANCA'S 🍷🍷

171 Water St., St. John's, Newfoundland, A1C 1A9; (709) 726-9016 **Wine list** *Bordeaux, California, Australia, Italy* **Wine prices** *Expensive* **Cuisine** *Contemporary Canadian* **Menu prices** *$12–$30*

BLOMIDON INN 🍷

195 Main St., Wolfville, Nova Scotia, B4P 1C3; (800) 565-2291 **Wine list** *California, France* **Wine prices** *Expensive* **Cuisine** *Canadian* **Menu prices** *$12–$26*

BREWBAKERS 🍷

546 King St., Fredericton, New Brunswick, E38 1E6; (506) 459-0067 **Wine list** *France, Italy* **Wine prices** Inexpensive **Cuisine** *Italian* **Menu prices** *$9–$20*

529 WELLINGTON 🍷🍷

529 Wellington Crescent, Winnipeg, Manitoba, R2M 5G8; (204) 487-8325 **Wine list** *California, Italy, France* **Wine prices** *Moderate* **Cuisine** *Steak house* **Menu prices** *$17–$32*

HY'S STEAK LOFT 🍷

216 Kennedy St., Winnipeg, Manitoba, R3C 1T1; (204) 942-1000 **Wine list** *California* **Wine prices** *Expensive* **Cuisine** *Steak house* **Menu prices** *$16–$32*

KINGSBRAE ARMS 🍷

219 King St., St. Andrews, New Brunswick, E5B 1Y1; (506) 529-1897 **Wine list** *France* **Wine prices** *Moderate* **Corkage** *$25* **Cuisine** *International* **Menu prices** *$20–$30*

L'HÉRITAGE RESTAURANT FRANÇAIS
5019 49th St., Yellowknife, Northwest Territories, X1A 2N6; (867) 873-9561 **Wine list** *France, California* **Wine prices** *Moderate* **Cuisine** *French* **Menu prices** *$35–$50*

PASTA LA VISTA
66-333 Saint Mary Ave., Winnipeg, Manitoba, R3C 4A5; (204) 956-2229 **Wine list** *California* **Wine prices** *Moderate* **Cuisine** *Californian/Italian* **Menu prices** *$7–$17*

PROVENCE BISTRO
620 Niakwa Road, Winnipeg, Manitoba, R2J 2X3; (204) 254-3000 **Wine list** *France* **Wine prices** *Moderate* **Cuisine** *French* **Menu prices** *$15–$20*

THE VELVET GLOVE
2 Lombard Place, Winnipeg, Manitoba, R3B 0Y3; (204) 957-1350 **Wine list** *Canada, Italy* **Wine prices** *Moderate* **Cuisine** *Continental* **Menu prices** *$14–$27*

CHINA

THE BOSTONIAN RESTAURANT
Great Eagle Hotel, 8 Peking Road, Tsimshatsui, Kowloon, Hong Kong; (011) 852-2375-1133 **Wine list** *California, France* **Wine prices** *Expensive* **Cuisine** *American* **Menu prices** *$30–$60*

COURTYARD
95 Donghaumen Ave., Beijing, 10006; (011) 86-10-6526-8883 **Wine list** *California, Australia, Bordeaux* **Wine prices** *Moderate* **Corkage** *$12* **Cuisine** *Contemporary* **Menu prices** *$14–$24*

THE GRILL ON FIFTY-SIX
Grand Hyatt Shanghai, 88 Century Blvd., Pudong, Shanghai, 200121; (011) 86-21-5049-1234 **Wine list** *France, Italy* **Wine prices** *Moderate* **Corkage** *$24* **Cuisine** *Steak house* **Menu prices** *$16–$58*

LOUISIANA RESTAURANT
Hilton Beijing, 1 Dong Fang Road, N. Dong Sanhuan Road, Chaoyang, Beijing, 100027; (011) 86-10-6466-2288 **Wine list** *California, Australia* **Wine prices** *Moderate* **Corkage** *$25* **Cuisine** *Cajun* **Menu prices** *$16–$36*

MARGAUX
Kowloon Shangri-La Hotel, 64 Mody Road, Tsimshatsui, Kowloon, Hong Kong; (011) 852-2721-2111 **Wine list** *Bordeaux, Australia* **Wine prices** *Moderate* **Cuisine** *French* **Menu prices** *$25–$45*

MORTON'S OF CHICAGO
3/F and 4/F Entertainment Building, 30 Queen's Road Central, Hong Kong; (011) 852-2804-6996 **Wine list** *California* **Wine prices** *Expensive* **Cuisine** *Steak house* **Menu prices** *$32–$72*

MORTON'S OF CHICAGO
Sheraton Hotel & Towers, 20 Nathan Road, Kowloon, Hong Kong; (011) 852-2732-2343 **Wine list** *Australia* **Wine prices** *Expensive* **Cuisine** *Steak house* **Menu prices** *$32–$143*

PALLADIO
The Ritz-Carlton Shanghai, Shanghai Centre 1376, Nanjing Xi Lu, Shanghai, 200040; (011) 86-21-6279-7188 **Wine list** *Italy, France* **Wine prices** *Expensive* **Cuisine** *Italian* **Menu prices** *$20–$50*

RESTAURANT PETRUS
Island Shangri-La, Pacific Place, Supreme Court Road Central, Hong Kong; (011) 852-2820-8590 **Wine list** *Bordeaux* **Wine prices** *Expensive* **Cuisine** *Contemporary French* **Menu prices** *$41–$58*

TAPAS BAR
Kowloon Shangri-La Hotel, 64 Mody Road, Tsimshatsui, Kowloon, Hong Kong; (011) 852-2721-2111 **Wine list** *Australia* **Wine prices** *Moderate* **Corkage** *$26* **Cuisine** *Tapas* **Menu prices** *$6–$7*

CYPRUS

BAROLO FOOD & WINE
248 Ayiou Andreou St., Limassol, 3036; (011) 357-25-760-767 **Wine list** *Greece, France* **Wine prices** *Moderate* **Corkage** *$10* **Cuisine** *Mediterranean* **Menu prices** *$10–$20*

DENMARK

BRØNDUMS HOTEL 🍷

3 Anchersvej, Skagen, 9990; (011) 45-9844-1555 **Wine list** *France* **Wine prices** *Moderate* **Cuisine** *Danish/French* **Menu prices** *$19–$32*

ERA ORA 🍷🍷

33B Overgaden Neden Vandet, Copenhagen, K 1414; (011) 45-3254-0693 **Wine list** *Italy* **Wine prices** *Moderate* **Corkage** *$50* **Cuisine** *Italian* **Menu prices** *Prix fixe only; $85–$110*

LE SOMMELIER 🍷🍷

63-65 Bredgade, Copenhagen, K 1260; (011) 45-3311-4515 **Wine list** *Bordeaux, Burgundy, Rhône, Italy, California* **Wine prices** *Moderate* **Cuisine** *French* **Menu prices** *$20–$25*

PIERRE ANDRÉ 🍷

21 Ny Ostergade, Copenhagen, K 1101; (011) 45-3316-1719 **Wine list** *France* **Wine prices** *Expensive* **Cuisine** *French* **Menu prices** *$25–$42*

RESTAURANT CASA D'ANTINO 🍷🍷

43 Dronningens Tvaergade, Copenhagen, 1303; (011) 45-3315-1505 **Wine list** *Piedmont, Tuscany, Veneto* **Wine prices** *Moderate* **Cuisine** *Italian* **Menu prices** *$18–$25*

RESTAURANT DE GAULLE 🍷

3 Kronborggade, Copenhagen, N 2200; (011) 45-3585-5866 **Wine list** *France* **Wine prices** *Moderate* **Cuisine** *French* **Menu prices** *$25–$35*

RESTAURANT LA COCOTTE 🍷🍷

Glostrup Park Hotel, 41 Hovedvejen, Glostrup, DK 2600; (011) 45-4396-0038 **Wine list** *Bordeaux, Burgundy, Italy* **Wine prices** *Moderate* **Cuisine** *French/Italian/Danish* **Menu prices** *$20–$25*

RISTORANTE LA BUCA DEGLI ARTISTI 🍷

209 Godthåbsvej, Vanløse, Copenhagen, 2720; (011) 45-3833-2022 **Wine list** *Piedmont, Tuscany* **Wine prices** Inexpensive **Cuisine** *Italian* **Menu prices** *$15–$24*

SØLLERØD KRO 🍷🍷

35 Søllerødvej, Holte, 2840; (011) 45-4580-2505 **Wine list** *Burgundy, Bordeaux, Piedmont* **Wine prices** *Moderate* **Corkage** *$30* **Cuisine** *Contemporary French* **Menu prices** *$25–$35*

TREE-TOP RESTAURANT 🍷🍷
Munkebjerg Hotel, Munkebjergvej, Vejle, 7100; (011) 45-7642-8500 **Wine list** *Burgundy, Bordeaux* **Wine prices** *Moderate* **Cuisine** *French* **Menu prices** *$34–$38*

ENGLAND

THE ANDERIDA RESTAURANT 🍷
Ashdown Park Hotel, Wych Cross, Forest Row, East Sussex, RH18 5JR; (011) 44-134-282-4988 **Wine list** *France* **Wine prices** *Moderate* **Cuisine** *Contemporary British* **Menu prices** *$45–$60*

BLEEDING HEART 🍷
Bleeding Heart Yard, Hatton Garden, London, EC1N 8SJ; (011) 44-207-242-2056 **Wine list** *France* **Wine prices** *Moderate* **Cuisine** *Contemporary French* **Menu prices** *$17–$25*

BUCKLAND MANOR 🍷🍷
Buckland Manor Country House Hotel, Buckland near Broadway, Worcestershire, WR12 7LY; (011) 44-138-685-2626 **Wine list** *Burgundy, Bordeaux* **Wine prices** *Expensive* **Cuisine** *English/French* **Menu prices** *$40–$48*

THE BURLINGTON RESTAURANT 🍷🍷
The Devonshire Arms, Bolton Abbey, Skipton, North Yorkshire, BD23 6AJ; (011) 44-175-671-8111 **Wine list** *Bordeaux, Burgundy, Italy, California* **Wine prices** *Moderate* **Cuisine** *Contemporary English/French* **Menu prices** *Prix fixe only; $82*

THE CAPITAL RESTAURANT 🍷🍷
The Capital Hotel, 22-24 Basil St., Knightsbridge, London, SW3 1AT; (011) 44-207-591-1202 **Wine list** *Bordeaux, Burgundy* **Wine prices** *Expensive* **Corkage** *$25* **Cuisine** *French* **Menu prices** *$25–$38*

THE DON 🍷
The Courtyard, 20 Saint Swithins Lane, London, EC4N 8AD; (011) 44-207-626-2606 **Wine list** *France, Port* **Wine prices** *Expensive* **Cuisine** *Contemporary European* **Menu prices** *$18–$25*

THE DORCHESTER 🍷
Park Lane, London, W1A 2HJ; (011) 44-207-629-8888 **Wine list** *France* **Wine prices** *Expensive* **Corkage** *$28* **Cuisine** *Asian/Italian/English* **Menu prices** *$30–$120*

FOLIAGE 🍷

Mandarin Oriental Hotel Hyde Park, 66 Knightsbridge, London, SW1X 7LA; (011) 44-207-201-3723 **Wine list** *Bordeaux, Burgundy* **Wine prices** *Moderate* **Cuisine** *Contemporary European* **Menu prices** *Prix fixe only; $30–$60*

GIDLEIGH PARK 🍷🍷

Gidleigh Park, Chagford, Devon, TQ13 8HH; (011) 44-164-743-2367 **Wine list** *California, France, Italy* **Wine prices** *Moderate* **Corkage** *$15* **Cuisine** *European* **Menu prices** *Prix fixe only; $100–$106*

L'ETRANGER 🍷

36 Gloucester Road, London, SW7 4QT; (011) 44-207-584-1118 **Wine list** *France, Italy, Australia* **Wine prices** *Moderate* **Cuisine** *French* **Menu prices** *$20–$30*

MAGGIORE'S 🍷

33 King St., London, WC2 8JD; (011) 44-207-379-9696 **Wine list** *France, Italy, Australia* **Wine prices** *Moderate* **Cuisine** *Contemporary European* **Menu prices** *$20–$27*

RANSOME'S DOCK 🍷

35-37 Parkgate Road, London, SW11 4NP; (011) 44-207-223-1611 **Wine list** *France, Australia, California* **Wine prices** *Moderate* **Corkage** *$15* **Cuisine** *Contemporary European* **Menu prices** *$17–$25*

SHARROW BAY COUNTRY HOUSE HOTEL 🍷🍷

Lake Ullswater, Penrith, Cumbria, CA10 2LZ; (011) 44-176-848-6301 **Wine list** *France, Australia, Spain* **Wine prices** *Moderate* **Cuisine** *English* **Menu prices** *Prix fixe only; $75*

THE SQUARE 🍷🍷

6-10 Bruton St., Mayfair, London, W1J 6PU; (011) 44-207-495-7100 **Wine list** *Burgundy, Bordeaux, California, Germany, Tuscany, Australia* **Wine prices** *Expensive* **Cuisine** *Contemporary French* **Menu prices** *Prix fixe only; $80*

THORNBURY CASTLE 🍷

Thornbury near Bristol, South Gloucestershire, BS351HH; (011) 44-145-428-1182 **Wine list** *France* **Wine prices** *Moderate* **Cuisine** *English/French* **Menu prices** *Prix fixe only; $35–$60*

THE VINEYARD 🍷🍷
Stock Cross near Newbury, Berkshire, RG20 8JU; (011) 44-163-552-8770 **Wine list** *California, France* **Wine prices** *Moderate* **Cuisine** *Contemporary British* **Menu prices** *$40–$50*

WHITE HORSE INN AT CHILGROVE 🍷
High Street, Chilgrove, West Sussex, PO18 9HX; (011) 44-124-353-5219 **Wine list** *France* **Wine prices** *Moderate* **Cuisine** *English/French* **Menu prices** *$15–$25*

ZAFFERANO 🍷🍷
15 Lowndes St., London, SW1X 9EY; (011) 44-207-235-5800 **Wine list** *Tuscany, Piedmont* **Wine prices** *Expensive* **Cuisine** *Contemporary Italian* **Menu prices** *$15–$20*

FINLAND

BACCHUS 🍷
4 Strandgatan, Vasa 10 65100; (011) 358-6-357-1326 **Wine list** *France* **Wine prices** *Moderate* **Cuisine** *French* **Menu prices** *Prix fixe only; $40*

RESTAURANT HULLU KUKKO 🍷
8 Simonkatu, Helsinki, 00100; (011) 358-9-685-9660 **Wine list** *France, Italy* **Wine prices** *Moderate* **Cuisine** *International* **Menu prices** *$15–$25*

FRANCE

ALAIN DUCASSE AU PLAZA ATHÉNÉE 🍷🍷🍷
Plaza Athénée, 25 Ave. Montaigne, Paris, 75008; (011) 33-1-53-67-65-00 **Wine list** *Bordeaux, Burgundy, Rhône* **Wine selections** *1,030* **Number of bottles** *45,000* **Wine prices** *Expensive* **Cuisine** *French* **Menu prices** *$80–$100* **Credit cards** *AX, MC, VS*
Grand Award since 1998

AU CROCODILE 🍷🍷🍷
10 Rue de l'Outre, Strasbourg, 67000; (011) 33-3-88-32-13-02 **Wine list** *Alsace, Bordeaux, Burgundy, Champagne* **Wine selections** *1,800* **Number of bottles** *58,000* **Wine prices** *Expensive* **Cuisine** *French* **Menu prices** *$37–$48* **Credit cards** *AX, MC, VS*
Grand Award since 1993

AUBERGE DE L'ILL
2 Rue de Collonges au M-d'Or, Illhaeusern, 68970; (011) 33-3-89-71-89-00 **Wine list** *Alsace, Bordeaux, Burgundy* **Wine prices** *Moderate* **Corkage** *$10* **Cuisine** *French* **Menu prices** *Prix fixe only; $120*

BISTROT DU SOMMELIER
97 Blvd. Haussmann, Paris, 75008; (011) 33-1-42-65-24-85 **Wine list** *France* **Wine prices** *Moderate* **Cuisine** *French* **Menu prices** *$15–$25*

GEORGES BLANC
Vonnas, 01540; (011) 33-4-74-50-90-90 **Wine list** *Burgundy, Bordeaux, Rhône* **Wine selections** *3,000* **Number of bottles** *120,000* **Wine prices** *Expensive* **Cuisine** *French* **Menu prices** *Prix fixe only; $95–$220* **Credit cards** *AX, MC, VS*
Grand Award since 1987

HOSTELLERIE BÉRARD
La Cadière d'Azur, 83740; (011) 33-4-94-90-11-43 **Wine list** *Provence, Bordeaux* **Wine prices** *Moderate* **Cuisine** *Provençal* **Menu prices** *$46–$114*

LA TOUR D'ARGENT
15 Quai de la Tournelle, Paris, 75005; (011) 33-1-43-54-23-31 **Wine list** *Bordeaux, Burgundy, Rhône* **Wine selections** *10,000* **Number of bottles** *500,000* **Wine prices** *Expensive* **Cuisine** *French* **Menu prices** *$62–$134* **Credit cards** *AX, MC, VS*
Grand Award since 1986

L'AUBERGE BRETONNE
2 Place Duguesclin, La Roche-Bernard, 56130; (011) 33-2-99-90-60-28 **Wine list** *Bordeaux, Rhône, Burgundy, Champagne, Alsace, Loire* **Wine prices** *Moderate* **Cuisine** *Contemporary* **Menu prices** *Prix fixe only; $42–$78*

LE CHAUDRON
7 Rue Sainte-Antoine, Tournon, 07300; (011) 33-4-75-08-17-90 **Wine list** *Rhône* **Wine prices** *Moderate* **Cuisine** *French* **Menu prices** *$22–$42*

LE CINQ
Four Seasons Hotel George V, 31 Ave. George V, Paris, 75008; (011) 33-1-49-52-71-54 **Wine list** *Bordeaux, Burgundy, Italy, Germany, Champagne* **Wine selections** *1,500* **Number of bottles** *40,000* **Wine prices** *Expensive* **Cuisine** *French* **Menu prices** *$35–$80* **Credit cards** *AX, MC, VS*
Grand Award since 2003

LES SOURCES DE CAUDALIE

Chemin de Smith-Haut-Lafitte, Bordeaux-Martillac, 33650; (011) 33-5-57-83-83-83 **Wine list** *Bordeaux* **Wine prices** *Moderate* **Cuisine** *Mediterranean* **Menu prices** *$25–$35*

MICHEL ROSTANG

20 Rue Rennequin, Paris, 75017; (011) 33-1-47-63-40-77 **Wine list** *Bordeaux, Rhône, Champagne* **Wine selections** *1,200* **Number of bottles** *39,000* **Wine prices** *Moderate* **Cuisine** *French* **Menu prices** *$55–$70* **Credit cards** *AX, MC, VS, DV*

Grand Award since 1993

RESTAURANT SCHAEFFER

Hôtel Schaeffer, Route Nationale 86, Serrières, 073-40; (011) 33-4-75-34-00-07 **Wine list** *Rhône* **Wine prices** *Moderate* **Corkage** *$30* **Cuisine** *French* **Menu prices** *Prix fixe only; $32–$80*

SEIZE AU SEIZE

16 Ave. Bugeaud, Paris, 75116; (011) 33-1-56-28-16-16 **Wine list** *France, California* **Wine prices** *Moderate* **Cuisine** *French* **Menu prices** *$23–$45*

TAILLEVENT

15 Rue Lamennais, Paris, 75008; (011) 33-1-44-95-15-01 **Wine list** *Bordeaux, Burgundy* **Wine selections** *325* **Number of bottles** *320,000* **Wine prices** *Moderate* **Cuisine** *French* **Menu prices** *$40–$50* **Credit cards** *AX, MC, VS, DV*

Grand Award since 1984

TAN DINH

60 Rue de Verneuil, Paris, 75007; (011) 33-1-45-44-04-84 **Wine list** *Burgundy, Bordeaux* **Wine prices** *Expensive* **Cuisine** *Vietnamese* **Menu prices** *$20–$24*

TROISGROS

Place Jean Troisgros, Roanne, 42300; (011) 33-4-77-71-66-97 **Wine list** *Burgundy, Bordeaux* **Wine selections** *1,200* **Number of bottles** *52,000* **Wine prices** *Expensive* **Cuisine** *French* **Menu prices** *$60–$75* **Credit cards** *AX, MC, VS*

Grand Award since 1996

GERMANY

BAREISS 🍷🍷

Hotel Bareiss, 14 Gärtenbühlweg, Baiersbronn-Mitteltal, 72261; (011) 49-74-42-47-0 **Wine list** *Burgundy, Bordeaux, Germany* **Wine prices** *Moderate* **Corkage** *$15* **Cuisine** *Contemporary French* **Menu prices** *$35–$50*

BURG SCHLITZ 🍷

Schlosshotel, Hohen Demzin, D-17166; (011) 49-39-96-12-70-0 **Wine list** *Germany, France* **Wine prices** *Moderate* **Cuisine** *French* **Menu prices** *$23–$30*

DIE QUADRIGA 🍷🍷

Hotel Brandenburger Hof, 14 Eislebener Str., Berlin, D-10789; (011) 49-30-21-40-50 **Wine list** *Germany* **Wine prices** *Moderate* **Corkage** *$25* **Cuisine** *French* **Menu prices** *$55–$90*

ENTE 🍷🍷🍷

Hotel Nassauer Hof, 3-4 Kaiser-Friedrich-Platz, Wiesbaden, 65183; (011) 49-611-13-36-66 **Wine list** *Germany, Bordeaux, Burgundy* **Wine selections** *1,490* **Number of bottles** *76,000* **Wine prices** *Moderate* **Cuisine** *European/Asian* **Menu prices** *$22–$36* **Credit cards** *AX, MC, VS*

Grand Award since 1985

FISCHERS WEINGENNUS & TAFELFREUDEN 🍷🍷

53 Hohenstaufenring, Köln, 50674; (011) 49-22-13-10-84-70 **Wine list** *Germany, France, Italy* **Wine prices** *Moderate* **Corkage** *$10* **Cuisine** *International* **Menu prices** *$18–$21*

FRIEDRICH VON SCHILLER 🍷🍷

Zum Schiller, Am historischen Marktplatz 5 Württemberg, Bietigheim, 74321; (011) 49-7142-90200 **Wine list** *Germany, France, Italy* **Wine prices** *Moderate* **Corkage** *$20* **Cuisine** *Contemporary German/French* **Menu prices** *$12–$27*

KULINARISCHES RESTAURANT ABTSTUBE 🍷🍷

Der Schafhof Amorbach, Amorbach, 63916; (011) 49-9373-97330 **Wine list** *Germany, France* **Wine prices** *Expensive* **Cuisine** *French/continental* **Menu prices** *$24–$41*

LA CAVE 🍷

30-32 Pütrichstrasse, Weilheim, 82362; (011) 49-88-19-23-63-33 **Wine list** *Bordeaux* **Wine prices** *Moderate* **Corkage** *$7* **Cuisine** *Regional/Mediterranean* **Menu prices** *$10–$25*

LANDHAUS DELLE 🍷🍷
16 Gutenfelsstrasse, Bacharach-Henschhausen, D-55422; (011) 49-67-43-17-65 **Wine list** *Germany, Austria, Italy, Burgundy, Spain* **Wine prices** *Moderate* **Cuisine** *European* **Menu prices** *$20–$24*

LANDHAUS STRICKER 🍷🍷
10 Boy-Nielsen-Strasse, Sylt-Tinnum, 25980; (011) 49-46-51-88-99-0 **Wine list** *Germany, France* **Wine prices** *Moderate* **Cuisine** *Mediterranean* **Menu prices** *$18–$25*

LOUIS C. JACOB 🍷🍷
Hotel Louis C. Jacob, 401-403 Elbchaussee, Hamburg, 22609; (011) 49-40-822-55-405 **Wine list** *Germany, Bordeaux* **Wine prices** *Moderate* **Corkage** *$23* **Cuisine** *French/regional* **Menu prices** *$25–$35*

MARK'S 🍷
Mandarin Oriental Hotel Munich, 1 Neuturmstrasse, Munich, 80331; (011) 49-89-29-09-88-62 **Wine list** *Germany, Bordeaux* **Wine prices** *Moderate* **Corkage** *$20* **Cuisine** *Mediterranean* **Menu prices** *$28–$31*

OBERLÄNDER WEINSTUBE 🍷🍷
7 Akademiestrasse, Karlsruhe, 76133; (011) 49-72-12-50-66 **Wine list** *Bordeaux, Burgundy, Germany* **Wine prices** *Moderate* **Cuisine** *French/German* **Menu prices** *$25–$30*

OSTERIA GALLO NERO 🍷
1 Grillparzerstrasse, Munich, 81675; (011) 49-8947-0547-2 **Wine list** *Italy* **Wine prices** *Moderate* **Cuisine** *Italian* **Menu prices** *$20–$26*

OTT'S LEOPOLDSHÖHE 🍷🍷
Ott's Hotel Leopoldshöhe, 4 Müllheimerstrasse, Weil am Rhein, 79576; (011) 49-7621-980-60 **Wine list** *Germany, France, Italy* **Wine prices** *Moderate* **Corkage** *$11* **Cuisine** *International* **Menu prices** *$14–$26*

RESTAURANT AT WALD & SCHLOSSHOTEL FRIEDRICHSRUHE 🍷
Wald & Schlosshotel Friedrichsruhe, Zweiflingen, Friedrichsruhe, 74639; (011) 49-7941-60-870 **Wine list** *Bordeaux* **Wine prices** *Expensive* **Cuisine** *German/French* **Menu prices** *$20–$35*

RESTAURANT DIETER MUELLER 🍷🍷
Schlosshotel Lerbach, Lerbacher Weg, Bergisch Gladbach, 51465; (011) 49-2202-2040 **Wine list** *France, Italy, Germany* **Wine prices** *Moderate* **Corkage** *$25* **Cuisine** *French/Mediterranean* **Menu prices** *$35–$46*

RESTAURANT HAERLIN 🍷🍷
Hotel Vier Jahreszeiten, 9-14 Neuer Jungfernstieg, Hamburg, D-20354; (011) 49-40-3494-3310 **Wine list** *Bordeaux, Burgundy, Germany, California, Italy, Spain* **Wine prices** *Expensive* **Corkage** *$15* **Cuisine** *French* **Menu prices** *$20–$32*

RESTAURANT JÖRG MÜLLER 🍷🍷🍷
8 Süderstrasse, Sylt-Westerland, 25980; (011) 49-4651-27-788 **Wine list** *Bordeaux, Burgundy, Germany, Italy* **Wine selections** *1,200* **Number of bottles** *30,000* **Wine prices** *Moderate* **Cuisine** *French/Italian/German* **Menu prices** *$30–$40* **Credit cards** *AX, MC, VS*
Grand Award since 1993

RESTAURANT KÖNIGSHOF 🍷🍷
Hotel Königshof, 25 Karlsplatz, Munich, 80335; (011) 49-89-55-136-142 **Wine list** *Bordeaux, Germany* **Wine prices** *Moderate* **Cuisine** *European* **Menu prices** *$25–$36*

RESTAURANT KRAUTKRÄMER 🍷🍷
Hotel Krautkrämer, 173 Zum Hiltruper See, Münster, 48165; (011) 49-2501-80-51-60 **Wine list** *Germany, Bordeaux* **Wine prices** *Moderate* **Cuisine** *Contemporary German/Mediterranean* **Menu prices** *$22–$29*

RESTAURANT SONNORA 🍷🍷
Waldhotel Sonnora, Auf dem Eichelfeld, Dreis, 54518; (011) 49-6578-406 **Wine list** *Germany, France, Italy* **Wine prices** *Moderate* **Cuisine** *Contemporary French* **Menu prices** *$31–$37*

RESTAURANT STERNECK 🍷
Badhotel Sternhagen, 86 Cuxhavener Strasse, Cuxhaven-Duhnen, 27476; (011) 49-4721-43-40 **Wine list** *Germany, France, Italy* **Wine prices** *Moderate* **Cuisine** *Contemporary/regional* **Menu prices** *$26–$28*

RESTAURANT ZIRBELSTUBE 🍷🍷
Hotel Victoria, 2-4 Poststrasse, Bad Mergentheim, 97980; (011) 49-79-31-59-30 **Wine list** *Italy, Burgundy, Germany* **Wine prices** *Moderate* **Corkage** *$15* **Cuisine** *Regional* **Menu prices** *$21–$28*

SCHWARZWALDSTUBE 🍷🍷

Hotel Traube Tonbach, 237 Tonbachstrasse, Baiersbronn, 72270; (011) 49-7442-49-26-65 **Wine list** *Bordeaux, Germany, Burgundy* **Wine prices** *Expensive* **Cuisine** *French* **Menu prices** *$30–$37*

VINTAGE 🍷🍷

31-35 Pfeilstrasse, Köln, D-50672; (011) 49-2-21-920-710 **Wine list** *France, Germany, Italy, California, Australia* **Wine prices** *Moderate* **Cuisine** *Mediterranean* **Menu prices** *$16–$23*

ZUR TRAUBE 🍷🍷

Zur Traube, 47 Bahnstrasse, Grevenbroich, 41515; (011) 49-21-81-68-767 **Wine list** *Germany, Champagne, Tuscany, Bordeaux, Spain* **Wine prices** Inexpensive **Cuisine** *French* **Menu prices** *$32–$48*

GREECE

BLUE LAGOON 🍷

Elounda Beach Hotel, 720 53 Elounda, Crete; (011) 30-28410-41412 **Wine list** *Greece, France* **Wine prices** *Expensive* **Cuisine** *Japanese/Polynesian* **Menu prices** *Prix fixe only; $26–$47*

BOSCHETTO 🍷

Entos Alsous Evangelismou, Athens, 10675; (011) 30-210-7210893 **Wine list** *Greece* **Wine prices** *Moderate* **Cuisine** *Italian/French* **Menu prices** *$40–$80*

CAPTAIN'S HOUSE RESTAURANT 🍷

Grand Resort Lagonissi, 19 Amerikis St., Athens, 106 72; (011) 30-22910-76000 **Wine list** *Greece, France* **Wine prices** *Moderate* **Cuisine** *Italian/Mediterranean* **Menu prices** *$80–$120*

DIONYSSOS 🍷

Elounda Beach Hotel, 720 53 Elounda, Crete; (011) 30-28410-41412 **Wine list** *Greece, France* **Wine prices** *Expensive* **Cuisine** *French* **Menu prices** *$35–$43*

KOHYLIA RESTAURANT 🍷

Grand Resort Lagonissi, 19 Amerikis St., Athens, 106 72; (011) 30-22910-76000 **Wine list** *Greece, France* **Wine prices** *Moderate* **Cuisine** *Polynesian/Japanese* **Menu prices** *$90–$120*

REMVIE RESTAURANT
The Belvedere Hotel, School of Fine Arts District, Mykonos, 84 600; (011) 30-22890-25122 **Wine list** *Greece, France* **Wine prices** *Moderate* **Cuisine** *Mediterranean/Japanese* **Menu prices** *$20–$28*

SALE & PEPE
34 Aristippoy, Athens, 10676; (011) 30-210-7234102 **Wine list** *Italy, Greece* **Wine prices** *Moderate* **Cuisine** *Northern Italian* **Menu prices** *$17–$24*

THALASSA
Elounda Bay Palace, 720 53 Elounda, Crete; (011) 30-28410-41412 **Wine list** *Greece* **Wine prices** *Expensive* **Cuisine** *Mediterranean* **Menu prices** *$34–$40*

INDIA

INDIGO
4 Mandlik Road, Colaba, Bombay, 400 001; (011) 91-22-5636-8999 **Wine list** *France, Italy* **Wine prices** *Moderate* **Cuisine** *European/Asian* **Menu prices** *$6–$20*

IRELAND

BEACHES
Kelly's Resort Hotel, Rosslare, County Wexford; (011) 353-53-32114 **Wine list** *France* **Wine prices** *Moderate* **Cuisine** *Irish/French* **Menu prices** *$20–$25*

THE GEORGE V ROOM
Ashford Castle, Cong, County Mayo; (011) 353-92-46003 **Wine list** *France, Italy, California* **Wine prices** *Moderate* **Cuisine** *European* **Menu prices** *$30–$70*

ITALY

AGATA E ROMEO
45 Via Carlo Alberto, Rome; (011) 39-0-64-466-115 **Wine list** *Piedmont, Tuscany* **Wine prices** *Moderate* **Cuisine** *Italian* **Menu prices** *$14–$26*

ANTICO PIGNOLO
Montecarlo Hotel, 451 Calle Specchieri, San Marco, Venice; (011) 39-0-41-522-8123 **Wine list** *Italy, Bordeaux* **Wine prices** *Expensive* **Cuisine** *Italian* **Menu prices** *$25–$50*

BOTTEGA DEL VINO 🍷🍷

3 Via Scudo di Francia, Verona, 37121; (011) 39-0-45-800-4535 **Wine list** *Tuscany, Piedmont, France* **Wine prices** *Moderate* **Cuisine** *Italian* **Menu prices** *$20–$35*

DUE CIGNI RISTORANTE 🍷🍷

19 Via S.S. Annunziata, Montecosaro Scalo, 62010; (011) 39-0-73-386-5182 **Wine list** *Italy* **Wine prices** *Moderate* **Cuisine** *Italian* **Menu prices** *$14–$40*

ENOTECA PINCHIORRI 🍷🍷🍷

87 Via Ghibellina, Florence, 50122; (011) 39-0-55-242-757 **Wine list** *Italy, France* **Wine selections** *2,700* **Number of bottles** *130,000* **Wine prices** *Expensive* **Cuisine** *Italian* **Menu prices** *$45–$85* **Credit cards** *AX, MC, VS*

Grand Award since 1984

ENOTRIA 🍷

50 Via delle Porte Nuove, Florence, 50144; (011) 39-0-55-354-350 **Wine list** *Italy* **Wine prices** *Moderate* **Corkage** *$6* **Cuisine** *Italian* **Menu prices** *$14–$18*

GUIDO RISTORANTE 🍷🍷🍷

Piazza della Chiesa Frazione Pollenzo, Bra-Cuneo, 12042; (011) 39-0-141-9660-12 **Wine list** *Piedmont* **Wine selections** *1,280* **Number of bottles** *34,700* **Wine prices** *Moderate* **Cuisine** *Italian* **Menu prices** *Prix fixe only; $25–$35* **Credit cards** *AX, MC, VS*

Grand Award since 1996

IL CONVIVIO TROIANI 🍷🍷

31 Vicolo dei Soldati, Rome, 00186; (011) 39-0-66-869-432 **Wine list** *Piedmont, Tuscany, Bordeaux* **Wine prices** *Moderate* **Cuisine** *Italian* **Menu prices** *$25–$30*

IL POETA CONTADINO 🍷🍷🍷

27 Via Indipendenza, Alberobello, 70011; (011) 39-0-80-432-1917 **Wine list** *Italy, Bordeaux* **Wine selections** *1,170* **Number of bottles** *12,000* **Wine prices** *Moderate* **Cuisine** *Italian* **Menu prices** *$15–$20* **Credit cards** *MC, VS*

Grand Award since 1997

IL SOLE DI RANCO 🍷🍷

5 Piazza Venezia, Ranco, 21020; (011) 39-0-33-197-6507 **Wine list** *Piedmont, Tuscany, Burgundy, Bordeaux* **Wine prices** *Moderate* **Corkage** *$65* **Cuisine** *Italian* **Menu prices** *$22–$38*

LA CASA DEGLI SPIRITI 🍷🍷
28 Via Monte Baldo, Costermano, Verona, 37010; (011) 39-0-45-620-0766 **Wine list** *Tuscany, Bordeaux* **Wine prices** *Moderate* **Cuisine** *Italian* **Menu prices** *$16–$25*

LA CIAU DEL TORNAVENTO 🍷
7 Piazza Baracco, Treiso, 12050; (011) 39-0-17-363-8333 **Wine list** *Piedmont, Tuscany, Bordeaux* **Wine prices** *Moderate* **Cuisine** *Contemporary* **Menu prices** *Prix fixe only; $40–$50*

LA FORTEZZA DEL BRUNELLO 🍷🍷
1-3 Sant'Angelo in Colle Costa Castellare, Montalcino, 53024; (011) 39-0-57-784-4175 **Wine list** *Italy* **Wine prices** *Moderate* **Cuisine** *Tuscan* **Menu prices** *$17–$22*

LA PERGOLA 🍷🍷
Rome Cavalieri Hilton, 101 Via Cadlolo, Rome, 00136; (011) 39-0-63-509-1 **Wine list** *Tuscany, Piedmont, Bordeaux* **Wine prices** *Moderate* **Cuisine** *Mediterranean* **Menu prices** *$30–$35*

LA STÜA DE MICHLI 🍷🍷
Romantik Hotel La Perla, 105 Strada Col Alt, Corvara Alta Badia, 39033; (011) 39-0-47-183-1000 **Wine list** *Italy, France* **Wine prices** *Expensive* **Corkage** $50 **Cuisine** *Contemporary* **Menu prices** *$25–$55*

PAPÀ GIOVANNI 🍷🍷
4 Via dei Sediari, Rome, 00186; (011) 39-0-66-880-4807 **Wine list** *Italy* **Wine prices** *Expensive* **Cuisine** *Italian/European* **Menu prices** *$18–$36*

RISTORANTE DON ALFONSO 1890 🍷🍷
11 Corso S. Agata, S. Agata sui due Golfi, 80064; (011) 39-0-81-878-0026 **Wine list** *Italy, France* **Wine prices** *Moderate* **Cuisine** *Mediterranean* **Menu prices** *$15–$32*

RISTORANTE LA SIRIOLA 🍷🍷
Hotel Ciasa Salares, 31 in Pre de Vi, San Cassiano, 39030; (011) 39-0-47-184-9445 **Wine list** *Tuscany, Northeast/Veneto, Burgundy* **Wine prices** *Moderate* **Cuisine** *Italian* **Menu prices** *$22–$31*

RISTORANTE LA TAVERNA 🍷🍷
2 Piazza Castello, Colloredo di Monte Albano, 33010; (011) 39-0-43-288-9045 **Wine list** *Tuscany, Piedmont, Veneto/Northeast* **Wine prices** *Moderate* **Cuisine** *Regional* **Menu prices** *$50–$63*

RISTORANTE LORENZO 🍷🍷
61 Via Carducci, Forte dei Marmi, 55042; (011) 39-0-58-487-4030 **Wine list** *Italy, Bordeaux* **Wine prices** *Moderate* **Cuisine** *Tuscan* **Menu prices** *$18–$40*

RISTORANTE ROMANO 🍷🍷
120 Via G. Mazzini, Viareggio, 55049; (011) 39-0-58-431-382 **Wine list** *Tuscany, Northeast, France* **Wine prices** Inexpensive **Cuisine** *Italian/Mediterranean* **Menu prices** *$16–$20*

SAPORI DEL LORD BYRON 🍷
Hotel Lord Byron, 5 Via Giuseppe De Notaris, Rome, 00197; (011) 39-0-63-220-404 **Wine list** *Italy* **Wine prices** *Expensive* **Cuisine** *Italian* **Menu prices** *$23–$35*

ST. HUBERTUS 🍷
Rosa Alpina, 20 Strada Micura de Ru, San Cassiano in Badia, I-39030; (011) 39-0-47-184-9500 **Wine list** *Piedmont, Northeast/Veneto, Tuscany* **Wine prices** *Moderate* **Cuisine** *Italian* **Menu prices** *$21–$28*

JAPAN

CHÂTEAU RESTAURANT TAILLEVENT ROBUCHON 🍷
1-13-1 Yebis Garden Place, Mita, Meguro-ku, Tokyo, 153-0062; (011) 81-3-5424-1338 **Wine list** *Bordeaux, Burgundy* **Wine prices** *Expensive* **Cuisine** *French* **Menu prices** *$143–$185*

ENOTECA PINCHIORRI-TOKYO 🍷🍷🍷
8-20 Ginza 5, Chome Chuo-Ku, Tokyo, 104-0061; (011) 81-3-3289-8081 **Wine list** *Tuscany, Bordeaux* **Wine selections** *1,750* **Number of bottles** *68,500* **Wine prices** *Expensive* **Cuisine** *Tuscan* **Menu prices** *$100–$150* **Credit cards** *AX, MC, VS*
Grand Award since 1994

NEW YORK GRILL 🍷
Park Hyatt Tokyo, 3-7-1-2, Nishi-Shinjuku Shinjuku-ku, Tokyo, 163-1055; (011) 81-3-5323-3458 **Wine list** *California* **Wine prices** *Expensive* **Cuisine** *American* **Menu prices** *$38–$75*

LEBANON

EAU DE VIE 🍷

Inter-Continental Phoenicia, Minet El Hosn, Beirut; (011) 961-369-100 **Wine list** *France* **Wine prices** *Moderate* **Cuisine** *French* **Menu prices** *$17–$40*

LUXEMBOURG

CHIGGERI RESTAURANT 🍷🍷

15 Rue du Nord, L-2229; (011) 352-22-99-36 **Wine list** *France* **Wine prices** *Moderate* **Cuisine** *French/international/vegetarian* **Menu prices** *$20–$25*

MACAU

ROBUCHON A GALERA 🍷🍷

Hotel Lisboa, 2-4 Avenida de Lisboa; (011) 853-377-666 **Wine list** *Bordeaux, Burgundy, Port* **Wine prices** *Expensive* **Cuisine** *French* **Menu prices** *$32–$126*

MALAYSIA

SHOOK! 🍷🍷

Starhill Centre, 181 Jalan Bukit Bintang, Kuala Lumpur, 55100; (011) 60-3-2716-8535 **Wine list** *France, California, Australia* **Wine prices** *Moderate* **Corkage** *$19* **Cuisine** *International* **Menu prices** *$10–$42*

VINTAGES 🍷

31 Jalan Telawi 3, Bangsar Baru, Kuala Lumpur, 59100; (011) 60-3-2287-3810 **Wine list** *Australia* **Wine prices** *Moderate* **Corkage** *$20* **Cuisine** *Pan-Asian* **Menu prices** *$31–$61*

MEXICO

ALFREDO DI ROMA 🍷🍷

Presidente InterContinental Mexico City, 218 Campos Eliseos, Mexico City, 11560; (011) 52-5-327-7776 **Wine list** *France, Italy, Spain* **Wine prices** *Expensive* **Cuisine** *Italian* **Menu prices** *$10–$25*

AU PIED DE COCHON 🍷🍷
Presidente InterContinental Mexico City, 218 Campos Eliseos, Mexico City, 11560; (011) 52-5-327-7700 **Wine list** *France, Italy, Spain* **Wine prices** *Expensive* **Cuisine** *French* **Menu prices** *$15–$25*

BISTRO DU VIN 🍷
400 Paseo de los Tamarindos, Local PB-13, Bosques de las Lomas, 05120; (011) 52-55-5258-0340 **Wine list** *France* **Wine prices** *Expensive* **Cuisine** *French* **Menu prices** *$9–$16*

LA HACIENDA DE LOS MORALES 🍷
525 Vasquez de Mella, Colonia del Bosque, Mexico City, 11510; (011) 52-5-096-3054 **Wine list** *Mexico* **Wine prices** *Expensive* **Cuisine** *International/Mexican* **Menu prices** *$13–$30*

THE PALM 🍷🍷
Presidente InterContinental Mexico City, 218 Campos Eliseos, Mexico City, 11560; (011) 52-5-327-7700 **Wine list** *California, Spain, Mexico* **Wine prices** *Expensive* **Cuisine** *Steak house* **Menu prices** *$12–$40*

PANGEA 🍷
110-20 Bosques del Valle, Colonia Bosques del Valle, Garza García, N.L., 66250; (011) 52-8-356-5612 **Wine list** *France, Mexico, Spain* **Wine prices** *Expensive* **Corkage** *$15* **Cuisine** *Mexican/Mediterranean* **Menu prices** *$10–$21*

THE RESTAURANT 🍷🍷
Las Ventanas al Paraiso, 19.5 km Careterra Transpeninsular, San José del Cabo, 23400; (011) 52-11-6241-4403-00 **Wine list** *California, France, Spain, Mexico* **Wine prices** *Expensive* **Cuisine** *Baja/Mediterranean* **Menu prices** *$26–$45*

RESTAURANT PUJOL 🍷
254 Francisco Petrarca, Chapultepec Morales, Polanco, 11570; (011) 52-5-545-4111 **Wine list** *Spain, Mexico* **Wine prices** *Expensive* **Corkage** *$20* **Cuisine** *Regional* **Menu prices** *$10–$25*

RESTAURANT VILLA DEL SOL 🍷
Hotel Villa del Sol, Playa La Ropa, Zihuatanejo, Gro., 40880; (011) 52-755-555-5500 **Wine list** *France, Mexico* **Wine prices** *Expensive* **Corkage** *$25* **Cuisine** *Regional/Mexican* **Menu prices** *$18–$40*

RESTAURANTE ALTAMIRA 🍷
22 Cerrada de Palomas, Colonia Reforma Social, 11650; (011) 52-5-520-2020 **Wine list** *Spain* **Wine prices** *Expensive* **Cuisine** *Spanish* **Menu prices** *$25–$40*

RESTAURANTE CENTRO ASTURIANO 🍷
4 Arquimedes, Polanco, 11550; (011) 52-5-280-6362 **Wine list** *Spain* **Wine prices** *Expensive* **Cuisine** *Spanish/continental* **Menu prices** *$8–$27*

SAINT-HONORÉ 🍷
341-A Avenida Presidente Mazarik, Polanco, 11560; (011) 52-5-280-9695 **Wine list** *Bordeaux, Spain* **Wine prices** *Expensive* **Cuisine** *French* **Menu prices** *$15–$40*

TUSCAN GRILL 🍷
275 Masaryk, Colonia Polanco, 11560; (011) 52-55-5282-3291 **Wine list** *Italy, Spain, Chile* **Wine prices** *Expensive* **Cuisine** *Italian* **Menu prices** *$30–$40*

MONACO

LE LOUIS XV - ALAIN DUCASSE 🍷🍷🍷
Hotel de Paris, Place du Casino, Monte-Carlo, 98000; (011) 377-92-16-29-76 **Wine list** *Bordeaux, Burgundy, Rhône, Italy, Spain* **Wine selections** *1,000* **Number of bottles** *400,000* **Wine prices** *Expensive* **Cuisine** *Mediterranean* **Menu prices** *$40–$235* **Credit cards** *AX, MC, VS*
Grand Award since 1995

NETHERLANDS

CAFÉ ROUX 🍷
The Grand Amsterdam, 197 Oudezijds Voorburgwal, Amsterdam, 1012 EX; (011) 31-20-555-3560 **Wine list** *Bordeaux, Burgundy* **Wine prices** *Moderate* **Corkage** *$23* **Cuisine** *French* **Menu prices** *$14–$29*

IMKO'S RESTAURANT 🍷
9C Halkade, IJmuiden, 1976 DC; (011) 31-255-517-526 **Wine list** *France* **Wine prices** *Moderate* **Cuisine** *French/international* **Menu prices** *$22–$34*

RESTAURANT VERMEER
Netherlands Barbizon Palace Hotel, 59-72 Prins Hendrikkade, Amsterdam, 1012 AD; (011) 31-20-556-4885 **Wine list** *France* **Wine prices** *Moderate* **Cuisine** *French* **Menu prices** *$32–$50*

NEW ZEALAND

GANTLEY'S
Arthurs Point Road, Queenstown; (011) 64-3-442-8999 **Wine list** *New Zealand, Australia* **Wine prices** *Moderate* **Corkage** *$7* **Cuisine** *International* **Menu prices** *$15–$20*

HERZOG WINERY & RESTAURANT
81 Jeffries Road/RD3, Blenheim, Marlborough; (011) 64-3-572-8770 **Wine list** *France, Italy, New Zealand* **Wine prices** *Moderate* **Cuisine** *Mediterranean* **Menu prices** *Prix fixe only; $39–$50*

O'CONNELL STREET BISTRO
3 O'Connell St., Auckland City; (011) 64-9-377-1884 **Wine list** *New Zealand, Australia* **Wine prices** *Moderate* **Cuisine** *Contemporary European* **Menu prices** *$10–$15*

PESCATORE RESTAURANT
The George, 50 Park Terrace, Christchurch, 8001; (011) 64-3-371-0257 **Wine list** *New Zealand* **Wine prices** *Moderate* **Cuisine** *Pacific rim* **Menu prices** *$15–$20*

SAGGIO DI VINO
185 Victoria St., Christchurch; (011) 64-3-379-4006 **Wine list** *New Zealand* **Wine prices** *Moderate* **Cuisine** *Mediterranean* **Menu prices** *$12–$15*

TE WHAU VINEYARD CAFÉ
218 Te Whau Drive, Waiheke Island; (011) 64-9-372-7191 **Wine list** *New Zealand, Burgundy, Bordeaux* **Wine prices** *Moderate* **Cuisine** *Pacific rim* **Menu prices** *$13–$15*

WHAREKAUHAU
Wharekauhau Country Estate, Western Lake Road, Palliser Bay, Featherston, RD3; (011) 64-6-307-7581 **Wine list** *New Zealand, Australia* **Wine prices** *Moderate* **Corkage** *$20* **Cuisine** *New Zealand/French/Italian* **Menu prices** *Prix fixe only; $80*

NORWAY

BAGATELLE 🍷🍷
3 Bygdoy Alle, Oslo, 0257; (011) 47-22-12-14-40 **Wine list** *France, Italy, Austria* **Wine prices** *Moderate* **Cuisine** *Contemporary European* **Menu prices** *$40–$50*

CAFÉ ITALIA 🍷
8 Skagen, Stavanger, 4006; (011) 47-51-85-92-90 **Wine list** *Italy* **Wine prices** *Moderate* **Cuisine** *Italian* **Menu prices** *$18–$26*

CRAIGS KJØKKEN 🍷🍷
Breitorget, Stavanger, 4006; (011) 47-51-93-95-90 **Wine list** *Rhône, Burgundy, Italy, California, Germany* **Wine prices** *Moderate* **Cuisine** *Mediterranean* **Menu prices** *$18–$28*

DR. KNEIPP'S WINE BAR 🍷🍷
12 Torvbakkgt., Inng Markvien, Oslo, 0550; (011) 47-22-37-22-97 **Wine list** *Italy* **Wine prices** *Moderate* **Cuisine** *International* **Menu prices** *$23–$27*

ELYSÉE 🍷🍷
Park Hotel Vossevangen, 1-3 Uttrågt, Voss, 5701; (011) 47-56-51-13-22 **Wine list** *Bordeaux, Burgundy, Tuscany, Germany, Alsace* **Wine prices** *Moderate* **Cuisine** *Norwegian/French* **Menu prices** *$22–$30*

MARKVEIEN MAT & VINHUS 🍷
12 Torvbakkgt., Inng Markvien, Oslo, 0550; (011) 47-22-37-22-97 **Wine list** *France, Italy* **Wine prices** *Expensive* **Cuisine** *International* **Menu prices** *$29–$37*

N.B. SØRENSENS 🍷
26 Skagen, Stavanger, N-4006; (011) 47-51-84-38-20 **Wine list** *Burgundy, Bordeaux, Italy* **Wine prices** *Moderate* **Cuisine** *European* **Menu prices** *$39–$42*

OSLO'S SPISEFORRETNING 🍷
15 Oslogate, Oslo, 0192; (011) 47-22-62-62-10 **Wine list** *France, Germany* **Wine prices** *Moderate* **Cuisine** *Norwegian* **Menu prices** *$26–$34*

RESTAURANT STATHOLDERGAARDEN 🍷
11 Radhusgaten, Oslo, 0151; (011) 47-22-41-88-00 **Wine list** *Burgundy, Bordeaux, Italy* **Wine prices** *Moderate* **Cuisine** *European/French* **Menu prices** *$30–$37*

SKYTTERKOLLEN 🍷
55 Daelimosen, Eiksmarka, 1359; (011) 47-67-14-29-25 **Wine list** *France, Austria* **Wine prices** *Moderate* **Cuisine** *Contemporary* **Menu prices** *$30–$40*

PANAMA

CHALET SUISSE 🍷🍷
Calle Eusebio A. Morales El Cangrejo, Panama 9A; (011) 507-263-8541 **Wine list** *France, California, Italy* **Wine prices** *Moderate* **Corkage** *$15* **Cuisine** *French/Swiss* **Menu prices** *$11–$32*

POLAND

RESTAURACJA BIBLIOTEKA 🍷
56/66 ul. Dobra, Warsaw; (011) 48-22-552-7195 **Wine list** *Italy, France* **Wine prices** *Moderate* **Cuisine** *International* **Menu prices** *$12–$20*

RESTAURACJA POD RÓZA 🍷
Hotel Pod Roza, 14 ul. Florianska, Krakow, 31-021; (011) 48-12-424-3381 **Wine list** *Italy* **Wine prices** *Moderate* **Cuisine** *International/Italian* **Menu prices** *$10–$20*

SCOTLAND

HALDANES RESTAURANT 🍷
39a Albany St., Edinburgh; (011) 44-131-556-8407 **Wine list** *France* **Wine prices** *Moderate* **Cuisine** *Contemporary Scottish* **Menu prices** *$22–$28*

TOWER RESTAURANT 🍷
Museum of Scotland, Chambers Street, Edinburgh, EH1 1JF; (011) 44-131-225-3003 **Wine list** *France* **Wine prices** *Moderate* **Cuisine** *Contemporary Scottish* **Menu prices** *$18–$25*

THE WITCHERY BY THE CASTLE 🍷
352 Castlehill, Royalmile, High Street, Edinburgh, EH1 2NF; (011) 44-131-225-5613 **Wine list** *France* **Wine prices** *Moderate* **Cuisine** *Contemporary Scottish* **Menu prices** *$24–$36*

SINGAPORE

AU JARDIN LES AMIS
EJH Corner House, Singapore Botanic Gardens, Cluny Road, 259569; (011) 65-6-466-8812 **Wine list** *Bordeaux, Burgundy* **Wine prices** *Expensive* **Cuisine** *French* **Menu prices** *Prix fixe only; $90*

8 ON THE BAY
50 Stadium Blvd., The Oasis, Oasis Complex, 397796; (011) 65-6-346-8089 **Wine list** *Australia* **Wine prices** *Moderate* **Cuisine** *European* **Menu prices** *$10–$20*

IL PRIMO TRATTORIA
2 Stadium Walk, No. 01-06, Stadium Waterfront, Singapore Indoor Stadium, 397691; (011) 65-6-346-5202 **Wine list** *Australia, California, Italy* **Wine prices** *Moderate* **Cuisine** *French/Italian* **Menu prices** *$15–$25*

JEREMY'S RESTAURANT & WINE BAR
76 Bras Basah Road, No. 01-02 Carlton Hotel Annexe, 189558; (011) 65-6-339-7398 **Wine list** *France, Australia* **Wine prices** *Moderate* **Corkage** *$12* **Cuisine** *Contemporary French* **Menu prices** *$20–$25*

LES AMIS
1 Scotts Road, No. 02-16, Shaw Centre, 228208; (011) 65-6-733-2225 **Wine list** *Bordeaux, Burgundy* **Wine selections** *1,500* **Number of bottles** *10,000* **Wine prices** *Expensive* **Cuisine** *French* **Menu prices** *$25–$35* **Credit cards** *AX, MC, VS*
Grand Award since 1996

MICHELANGELO'S
Blk. 44 Jalan Merah Saga, No. 02-60, Chip Bee Gardens, Holland Village, 278116; (011) 65-9-475-9069 **Wine list** *Australia, California, Italy* **Wine prices** *Moderate* **Cuisine** *Italian/Mediterranean* **Menu prices** *$13–$19*

ORIGINAL SIN
Blk. 43 Jalan Merah Saga, No. 01-62, Chip Bee Gardens, 278115; (011) 65-9-475-5605 **Wine list** *Australia, California* **Wine prices** *Moderate* **Cuisine** *Mediterranean* **Menu prices** *$14–$20*

RAFFLES GRILL
Raffles Hotel, 1 Beach Road, 189673; (011) 65-6-337-1886 **Wine list** *France, California* **Wine prices** *Moderate* **Corkage** *$50* **Cuisine** *French* **Menu prices** *$28–$35*

SISTINA GOURMET PIZZERIA 🍷🍷

Blk. 44 Jalan Merah Saga, No. 01-58, Chip Bee Gardens, 278116; (011) 65-6-476-7782 **Wine list** *Australia, California* **Wine prices** *Moderate* **Cuisine** *Italian/Mediterranean* **Menu prices** *$14–$21*

SPAIN

ATRIO 🍷🍷🍷

30 Avenida de España, Bloque 4, Cáceres, 10002; (011) 34-927-242-928 **Wine list** *Spain, Bordeaux, Burgundy* **Wine selections** *2,185* **Number of bottles** *25,000* **Wine prices** *Moderate* **Cuisine** *Spanish* **Menu prices** *$20–$25* **Credit cards** *MC, VS*

Grand Award since 2003

EL OLIVO RESTAURANTE 🍷

Hotel La Residencia, Finca Son Canals S/N, Deia, Mallorca, 07179; (011) 34-971-639-392 **Wine list** *Spain* **Wine prices** *Moderate* **Corkage** *$15* **Cuisine** *Mediterranean* **Menu prices** *$24–$32*

RESTAURANTE EL BOHIO 🍷🍷

81 Avenida Castilla-La Mancha, Illescas, 45200; (011) 34-925-511-126 **Wine list** *Spain* **Wine prices** Inexpensive **Cuisine** *Spanish* **Menu prices** *$50–$60*

SWEDEN

EDSBACKA KROG 🍷

220 Sollentunavagen, Sollentuna, 191 35; (011) 46-8-96-33-00 **Wine list** *France* **Wine prices** *Moderate* **Cuisine** *Swedish/French* **Menu prices** *$25–$40*

THE FRENCH DINING ROOM 🍷🍷

Grand Hôtel, 8 S. Blasieholmshamnen, Stockholm; (011) 46-8-679-3584 **Wine list** *Bordeaux, Burgundy* **Wine prices** *Moderate* **Cuisine** *French/Swedish* **Menu prices** *$24–$52*

GRAND HOTEL LUND 🍷🍷

1 Bantorget, Lund, 221 04; (011) 46-46-280-6130 **Wine list** *Bordeaux, Burgundy, Rhône* **Wine prices** *Moderate* **Cuisine** *International* **Menu prices** *$10–$34*

HASSLO WERDSHUS

73 Flottiljgatan, Vasteras, 72131; (011) 46-21-80-09-35 **Wine list** *France* **Wine prices** *Moderate* **Cuisine** *Swedish/ French* **Menu prices** *$16–$31*

RESTAURANT OPERAKÄLLAREN

Karl XII Torg, Stockholm, SE-111 86; (011) 46-8-676-5801 **Wine list** *Bordeaux, Burgundy, Rhône* **Wine prices** *Moderate* **Cuisine** *International* **Menu prices** *$29–$44*

SANKT MARKUS WINE CELLER

7 Malmborgsgatan, Malmö, 211 38; (011) 46-40-306-820 **Wine list** *France* **Wine prices** *Moderate* **Cuisine** *International* **Menu prices** *$18–$21*

SJÖMAGASINET

Klippans Kulturreservat, Göteborg, S-414 51; (011) 46-31-775-5920 **Wine list** *Burgundy, Bordeaux* **Wine prices** *Moderate* **Cuisine** *Seafood* **Menu prices** *$26–$35*

STUFVENAS GASTGIFVERI

Soderakra, S-38597; (011) 46-486-21900 **Wine list** *Bordeaux* **Wine prices** *Moderate* **Cuisine** *Swedish* **Menu prices** *$15–$23*

SWITZERLAND

AUBERGE DE ZAEHRINGEN

13 Rue de Zähringen, Case Postale 67, Fribourg, 1702; (011) 41-26-322-42-36 **Wine list** *France* **Wine prices** *Moderate* **Cuisine** *French* **Menu prices** *$34–$70*

BAD BUBENDORF

3 Kantonsstrasse, Bubendorf, CH-4416; (011) 41-61-935-55-55 **Wine list** *Italy, Switzerland* **Wine prices** *Moderate* **Corkage** *$15* **Cuisine** *Swiss/international* **Menu prices** *$30–$60*

CHRUEG

Hotel Restaurant Chrueg, 3 Bellevueweg, Wollerau, CH-8832; (011) 41-1-787-63-63 **Wine list** *Switzerland, Italy, France* **Wine prices** *Expensive* **Cuisine** *Contemporary* **Menu prices** *$20–$35*

HOTEL SEEROSE

Am Hallwilersee, Meisterschwanden, 5616; (011) 41-56-676-66-11 **Wine list** *Bordeaux* **Wine prices** *Moderate* **Corkage** *$22* **Cuisine** *French* **Menu prices** *$16–$38*

HOTEL WALDHAUS AM SEE 🍷🍷🍷
St. Moritz, CH-7500; (011) 41-81-836-60-00 **Wine list** *Bordeaux, Burgundy, Germany, Italy* **Wine selections** *970* **Number of bottles** *56,400* **Wine prices** Inexpensive **Cuisine** *Swiss/Italian/continental* **Menu prices** *$15–$20* **Credit cards** *AX, MC, VS*
Grand Award since 1998

JAEGERHOF 🍷
Jaegerhof Hotel, 11 Bruehlbleichestrasse, Saint Gallen, 9000; (011) 41-71-245-50-22 **Wine list** *Italy, Austria, France* **Wine prices** *Moderate* **Corkage** *$25* **Cuisine** *Contemporary* **Menu prices** *$25–$40*

KANTOREI 🍷
2 Neumarkt, Zürich, 8001; (011) 41-1-252-27-27 **Wine list** *France, Spain* **Wine prices** *Moderate* **Cuisine** *Regional* **Menu prices** *$20–$26*

LANDGASTHOF & VINOTHEK FARNSBURG 🍷🍷🍷
Farnsburg, Ormalingen, 4466; (011) 41-61-985-90-30 **Wine list** *California, Burgundy, Bordeaux* **Wine selections** *2,600* **Number of bottles** *34,500* **Wine prices** *Expensive* **Cuisine** *Swiss/Italian/French* **Menu prices** *$15–$25* **Credit cards** *None accepted*
Grand Award since 1992

LA PADELLA 🍷🍷
Hotel Donatz, 15 Plazzet Samedan, Saint Moritz, CH-7503; (011) 41-81-852-46-66 **Wine list** *Switzerland, Austria, Italy, France* **Wine prices** *Moderate* **Cuisine** *Swiss/Italian/French* **Menu prices** *$25–$45*

LE GRAND CHALET 🍷
Neueretstrasse, Gstaad, CH-3780; (011) 41-33-748-76-76 **Wine list** *Bordeaux* **Wine prices** *Moderate* **Cuisine** *French* **Menu prices** *$24–$40*

LE RESTAURANT 🍷🍷
Badrutt's Palace Hotel, Saint Moritz, CH-7500; (011) 41-81-837-10-00 **Wine list** *France, Italy* **Wine prices** *Expensive* **Cuisine** *French/Asian* **Menu prices** *$20–$40*

LE TRIANON AT LE MIRADOR 🍷🍷
Le Mirador Resort & Hotel, 1801 Mont Pelerin, Lake Geneva; (011) 41-21-925-11-11 **Wine list** *Bordeaux, Switzerland* **Wine prices** *Expensive* **Cuisine** *French* **Menu prices** *$25–$55*

PETERMANN'S KUNSTSTUBEN
160 Seestrasse, Küsnacht, 8700; (011) 41-1-910-07-15 **Wine list** *Bordeaux, Switzerland* **Wine prices** *Expensive* **Cuisine** *Contemporary* **Menu prices** *$90–$135*

RESTAURANT CONCA BELLA
Hotel Conca Bella, 2 Via Concabella, Vacallo-Chiasso, CH-6833; (011) 41-91-697-50-40 **Wine list** *Tuscany, Bordeaux* **Wine prices** *Moderate* **Cuisine** *Italian* **Menu prices** *$25–$35*

RESTAURANT HIRSCHEN
Landhotel Hirschen, 125 Hauptstrasse, Obererlinsbach bei Aarau, CH-5016; (011) 41-62-857-33-33 **Wine list** *France, Italy* **Wine prices** *Moderate* **Corkage** *$25* **Cuisine** *Contemporary* **Menu prices** *$18–$38*

RESTAURANT PIERROZ
Hotel Rosalp, Verbier, 1936; (011) 41-27-771-63-23 **Wine list** *Switzerland, Bordeaux* **Wine prices** *Expensive* **Cuisine** *Contemporary* **Menu prices** *$53–$55*

RESTAURANT RIESBÄCHLI
157 Zollikerstrasse, Zürich, 8008; (011) 41-1-422-23-24 **Wine list** *Bordeaux, Burgundy, Italy, Spain* **Wine selections** *3,200* **Number of bottles** *150,000* **Wine prices** *Moderate* **Cuisine** *French* **Menu prices** *$22–$43* **Credit cards** *AX, MC, VS*
Grand Award since 1990

RESTAURANT RÖSSLI
Büren zum Hof, 17 Limpachstrasse, CH-3313; (011) 41-317-67-82-96 **Wine list** *Bordeaux, Burgundy, Tuscany* **Wine prices** *Moderate* **Cuisine** *International* **Menu prices** *$15–$45*

RISTORANTE FORNI
Hotel Forni Airolo, Airolo, CH-6780; (011) 41-91-869-12-70 **Wine list** *Italy, France, Switzerland* **Wine prices** *Moderate* **Cuisine** *Contemporary* **Menu prices** *$14–$25*

WINE-BAR BARRIQUE
17 Beim Rathaus Marktgasse, Zürich, 8001; (011) 41-1-252-59-41 **Wine list** *Switzerland, Bordeaux, Italy* **Wine prices** *Moderate* **Cuisine** *International* **Menu prices** *$15–$30*

THAILAND

BAAN RIM PA
223 Prabaramee Road, T. Patong, A. Kathu, Phuket, 83150; (011) 66-76-340-789 **Wine list** *France* **Wine prices** *Moderate* **Corkage** *$10* **Cuisine** *Thai* **Menu prices** *$15–$36*

THE BOATHOUSE WINE & GRILL
Mom Tri's Boathouse & Villa Royale, 2/2 Moo 2 Patak Road, Tumbon Karon, Amphur Muang, Phuket, 83100; (011) 66-76-330-015 **Wine list** *France* **Wine prices** *Moderate* **Cuisine** *Thai/Mediterranean* **Menu prices** *$8–$20*

DA MAURIZIO
6/8-9 Moo 6, T. Kamala, A. Katu, Phuket, 83150; (011) 66-76-344-253 **Wine list** *Italy, France* **Wine prices** *Moderate* **Corkage** *$10* **Cuisine** *Italian* **Menu prices** *$10–$24*

THE ROYAL CLIFF GRILL ROOM & WINE CELLAR
Royal Cliff Beach Resort, 353 Phra Tamnuk Road, Pattaya, Cholburi, 20150; (011) 66-38-250-421 **Wine list** *France, California, Australia* **Wine prices** *Expensive* **Corkage** *$12* **Cuisine** *European* **Menu prices** *$9–$29*

UKRAINE

LIPSKY OSOBNIAK
15 Lipsky St., Kiev; (011) 38-044-254-0090 **Wine list** *France, Italy* **Wine prices** *Moderate* **Cuisine** *Ukranian* **Menu prices** *$12–$30*

VENEZUELA

DIVINUM
C.C. Torre Loreto II, piso 1 Avenida Las Américas, Pto. Ordaz Edo. Bolivar; (011) 58-286-923-1798 **Wine list** *Chile, Argentina, Spain* **Wine prices** *Moderate* **Cuisine** *Japanese/ Mediterranean* **Menu prices** *$10–$15*

VIETNAM

RESTAURANT BOBBY CHINN
1 Ba Trieu St., Hoan Kiem District, Hanoi; (011) 84-4-934-8577 **Wine list** *France, California* **Wine prices** *Moderate* **Corkage** *$12* **Cuisine** *Contemporary* **Menu prices** *$8–$12*

Grand Award   Best of Award of Excellence   Award of Excellence

THE RESTAURANT
Press Club, 59 A Ly Thai To, Hanoi; (011) 84-4-934-0888 **Wine list** *California, Italy, France* **Wine prices** Inexpensive **Corkage** *$15* **Cuisine** *International* **Menu prices** *$9–$40*

WEST INDIES

THE AGAVÉ TERRACE
Point Pleasant Resort, 4 Smith Bay, St. Thomas, U.S. Virgin Islands, 00802; (340) 775-4142 **Wine list** *California, France* **Wine prices** *Moderate* **Cuisine** *Caribbean* **Menu prices** *$18–$38*

BACCHUS
52 King St., Christiansted, St. Croix, U.S. Virgin Islands, 00822; (340) 692-9922 **Wine list** *California* **Wine prices** *Moderate* **Corkage** *$15* **Cuisine** *American* **Menu prices** *$14–$45*

BLANCHARD'S RESTAURANT
Meads Bay West End, Anguilla, British West Indies; (264) 497-6100 **Wine list** *California, France* **Wine prices** *Moderate* **Corkage** *$20* **Cuisine** *Caribbean/American/Asian* **Menu prices** *$32–$48*

BLUE MOON CAFÉ
Secret Harbour Beach Resort, 6501 Red Hook Plaza No. 201, St. Thomas, U.S. Virgin Islands; (340) 779-2262 **Wine list** *California* **Wine prices** *Moderate* **Corkage** *$15* **Cuisine** *Contemporary American* **Menu prices** *$14–$42*

CAPRICCIO RISTORANTE
1 Kralendijk, Kay Islariba, Bonaire, Netherlands Antilles; (011) 599-717-7230 **Wine list** *Italy* **Wine prices** *Moderate* **Cuisine** *Italian* **Menu prices** *$15–$25*

CASA HAVANA
The Westin Casuarina Resort, 30620 Seven Mile Beach, Grand Cayman Island, British West Indies; (345) 945-3800 **Wine list** *France, California* **Wine prices** *Moderate* **Cuisine** *Caribbean/continental* **Menu prices** *$28–$46*

CRAIG & SALLY'S
3525 Estate Honduras, St. Thomas, U.S. Virgin Islands, 00802-6487; (340) 777-9949 **Wine list** *California, France, Italy* **Wine prices** *Moderate* **Corkage** *$20* **Cuisine** *International* **Menu prices** *$15–$32*

DELI SWISS 🍷🍷
Calle Central No. 338, Guayacanes, Dominican Republic; (809) 526-1226 **Wine list** *Spain, France, Chile, Argentina* **Wine prices** *Moderate* **Cuisine** *French/Caribbean* **Menu prices** *$12–$20*

THE GATE HOUSE 🍷
Zion's Hill, Saba, Netherlands Antilles; (011) 599-416-2416 **Wine list** *France, California* **Wine prices** *Moderate* **Cuisine** *French/creole* **Menu prices** *$16–$27*

GRAND OLD HOUSE 🍷
South Church Street, Grand Cayman Island, British West Indies; (345) 949-9333 **Wine list** *France, Italy* **Wine prices** *Expensive* **Cuisine** *Continental/American/Caribbean* **Menu prices** *$22–$38*

GRAYCLIFF 🍷🍷🍷
Graycliff Hotel, West Hill Street, Nassau, Bahamas; (242) 322-2796 **Wine list** *Bordeaux, Burgundy, Italy, Port, California* **Wine selections** *2,270* **Number of bottles** *195,000* **Wine prices** *Expensive* **Cuisine** *French/Italian/Bahamian* **Menu prices** *$35–$45* **Credit cards** *AX, MC, VS, DV*
Grand Award since 1988

HERVÉ RESTAURANT & WINE BAR 🍷
Government Hill, St. Thomas, U.S. Virgin Islands, 00802; (340) 777-9703 **Wine list** *California* **Wine prices** *Moderate* **Corkage** *$25* **Cuisine** *American/French* **Menu prices** *$20–$36*

KOALKEEL RESTAURANT 🍷
Old Valley, Anguilla, British West Indies; (264) 497-2930 **Wine list** *France, Italy* **Wine prices** *Moderate* **Cuisine** *European/Carribean* **Menu prices** *$24–$30*

LA TARTARUGA RESTAURANT 🍷
Buccoo Bay Road, Buccoo, Tobago, British West Indies; (868) 639-0940 **Wine list** *Italy* **Wine prices** *Moderate* **Cuisine** *Italian* **Menu prices** *Prix fixe only; $35–$50*

LIGHTHOUSE AT BREAKERS 🍷
Breakers, Grand Cayman Island, British West Indies; (345) 947-2047 **Wine list** *Italy* **Wine prices** *Moderate* **Cuisine** *Italian/Caribbean* **Menu prices** *$25–$39*

MALLIOUHANA RESTAURANT

Hotel Malliouhana, Meads Bay, West End, Anguilla, British West Indies; (345) 497-6111 **Wine list** *Burgundy, Bordeaux, California, Champagne* **Wine selections** *1,400* **Number of bottles** *25,000* **Wine prices** *Moderate* **Cuisine** *French* **Menu prices** *$30–$52* **Credit cards** *AX, MC, VS*
Grand Award since 1999

THE OLD STONE FARMHOUSE

6501 Red Hook Plaza, St. Thomas, U.S. Virgin Islands, 00802; (340) 777-6277 **Wine list** *California* **Wine prices** *Moderate* **Corkage** *$25* **Cuisine** *Contemporary* **Menu prices** *$18–$31*

OLIVER'S SEASIDE GRILL

The Valley Longbay, Anguilla, British West Indies; (264) 497-8780 **Wine list** *France, California* **Wine prices** *Moderate* **Corkage** *$10* **Cuisine** *Contemporary* **Menu prices** *$20–$36*

RAGAZZI

Buckingham Square, West Bay Road, Grand Cayman Island, British West Indies; (345) 945-3484 **Wine list** *Italy, California* **Wine prices** *Moderate* **Corkage** *$15* **Cuisine** *Northern Italian* **Menu prices** *$22–$28*

RISTORANTE PAPPAGALLO

West Bay, Grand Cayman Island, British West Indies; (345) 949-1119 **Wine list** *Italy* **Wine prices** *Moderate* **Corkage** *$15* **Cuisine** *Northern Italian* **Menu prices** *$20–$40*

ROOM WITH A VIEW

Bluebeards Castle Hill, St. Thomas, U.S. Virgin Islands, 00801; (340) 774-2377 **Wine list** *California* **Wine prices** Inexpensive **Corkage** *$10* **Cuisine** *International* **Menu prices** *$18–$33*

STONE TERRACE

Cruz Bay, St. John, U.S. Virgin Islands, 00831; (340) 693-9370 **Wine list** *California* **Wine prices** *Moderate* **Corkage** *$20* **Cuisine** *International/Caribbean* **Menu prices** *$24–$44*

TURTLE BAY ESTATE HOUSE

Caneel Bay Resort, Northshore Road, St. John, U.S. Virgin Islands, 00830; (340) 776-6111 **Wine list** *California* **Wine prices** *Expensive* **Cuisine** *American* **Menu prices** *$29–$42*

NOTES

NOTES

NOTES

NOTES

NOTES

NOTES

NOTES

NOTES

NOTES